PRAISE FOR *THE PERSIAN PRINCE*

"In this gorgeously written tour de force, Hamid Dabashi spins the contrapuntal narrative of an archaic Iranian archetype as it weaves its way through political-poetical history. Building on his impressive body of work, *The Persian Prince* is a unique and formidable text that encapsulates the brilliance, vivacity, and political ferocity of Dabashi's mind."
—Jeanne Morefield, University of Oxford, author of *Unsettling the World*

"Hamid Dabashi's book takes the reader on a journey across time and place. 'More a persona than a person,' the Persian Prince reunites in one archetype such different images as the rebellious poet, the just monarch, and the charismatic prophet. Both a historical investigation and a philosophical-political proposal, the book will reward readers with many unusual intellectual encounters."
—Giovanni Giorgini, University of Bologna and Columbia University

"Disarmingly accessible, and laden with millennia of Persian cultural riches, *The Persian Prince* deftly and decisively shifts the axis of history and the conception of subjectivity itself. Colonizers and ayatollahs are mere blips in the long temporality of the Persian Prince, a figure of transformation that ultimately resides in the collective heart of rebellion."
—Laura U. Marks, Simon Fraser University, author of *Enfoldment and Infinity*

"Hamid Dabashi's illuminating study, while both provincializing and enriching the classic frameworks of Machiavelli and Gramsci, provides a provocative and compelling archetype for understanding political power and organization."
—Michael Hardt, Duke University, author of *The Subversive Seventies*

THE PERSIAN PRINCE

The Persian Prince

The Rise and Resurrection of an Imperial Archetype

HAMID DABASHI

STANFORD UNIVERSITY PRESS
Stanford, California

Stanford University Press
Stanford, California

© 2023 by Hamid Dabashi. All rights reserved.

No part of this book may be reproduced or transmitted in any form or by any means, electronic or mechanical, including photocopying and recording, or in any information storage or retrieval system, without the prior written permission of Stanford University Press.

Printed in the United States of America on acid-free, archival-quality paper

Library of Congress Cataloging-in-Publication Data
Names: Dabashi, Hamid, 1951– author.
Title: The Persian Prince : the rise and resurrection of an imperial archetype / Hamid Dabashi.
Description: Stanford, California : Stanford University Press, 2023. | Includes bibliographical references and index.
Identifiers: LCCN 2022039222 (print) | LCCN 2022039223 (ebook) | ISBN 9781503628823 (cloth) | ISBN 9781503636231 (paperback) | ISBN 9781503635753 (ebook)
Subjects: LCSH: Authority—Political aspects. | Archetype (Psychology) | Imperialism—Philosophy. | Political science—Philosophy. | Islamic countries—Politics and government.
Classification: LCC JC330 .D335 2023 (print) | LCC JC330 (ebook) | DDC 325/.3201—dc23/eng/20221115
LC record available at https://lccn.loc.gov/2022039222
LC ebook record available at https://lccn.loc.gov/2022039223

Cover design by George Kirkpatrick
Cover painting: Cristofano dell'Altissimo (1525–1605), *Portrait of Shah Ismail I of Persia* (1487–1524), The Uffizi Galleries, Florence, Italy
Typeset by Motto Publishing Services in 10.5/14.5 Arno Pro

For
Kaveh, Pardis, Chelgis, and Golchin
... all the very best of me

Khabar dari az khosrowan-e Ajam ...

Have you heard of the Persian princes
Who tyrannized those they ruled?
Neither that majesty and royalty remained—
Nor did that injustice upon the peasantry.

> Saʿdi, *Bustan*, "On Justice and Injustice
> and Their Consequences" (1257)

CONTENTS

PRELUDE — xiii
Who Is the Persian Prince—What Is the Persian Prince?

Map of the ancient Persian Empire — xvii

PART ONE
THE PROSPECTS OF AN ARCHETYPE

ONE The Idea and the Dominion of the Persian Prince — 3

TWO The Persian Prince Comes of Age — 26

PART TWO
THE RISE OF AN ARCHETYPE

THREE On the Histories, Geographies, and Iconographies of Muslim Empires — 59

FOUR The Persian Literary Provenance of Muslim Empires — 98

FIVE In the Light and Shadows of the Persian Prince — 137

PART THREE

THE RESURRECTION OF AN ARCHETYPE

SIX	The Resurrection of the Persian Prince Under Colonial Duress	169
SEVEN	Colonial Modernity and the Metamorphosis of the Persian Prince	205
EIGHT	The Nomadic Fate of the Persian Prince	229

CONCLUSION 229
The Sublimation of an Imperial Archetype   253

A Chronology   273

Acknowledgments   289

Notes   291

Index   319

PRELUDE

Who Is the Persian Prince—
What Is the Persian Prince?

We are here as trustworthy delegates
For all those Persians who have marched away.

Aeschylus, *The Persians* (472 BCE)

I AM SURE YOU REMEMBER HOW, early in Antoine de Saint-Exupéry's iconic book *The Little Prince* (1943), the eponymous narrator tells us how reasonable adults could not fathom the shape of a boa constrictor digesting an elephant and thought the picture he showed them represented a harmless hat. This book you are about to read is also the patient drawing of a picture that requires the child dwelling in your wise adulthood to imagine an idea dwelling inside an archetype that, instead of frightening you, will excite and invite you to a faraway landscape of our past and present humanity: why and wherefore we do as we are told, obey orders, seek the approval of the person sitting on the throne or inside the Oval Office, bend backward to accommodate their power, think better of ourselves if we do and worse if we do not—that even if we revolt, we rush to replace the prince we just overthrew with another prince to tell us what to do next.

This book is about the Persian Prince, an archaic Iranian archetype that, as I theorize it here, has gone through varied historic gestations, from ancient Persia to the Hebrew Bible to classical Greek antiquity to medieval European mirrors for princes to its Renaissance resurfacing in modern political thought down to its postcolonial resurrection as a rebel, a prophet, a poet, and a nomad—a white elephant inside the belly of a boa constrictor that is the political history of a significant part of our humanity habitually divided between East and West, which here I seek to reimagine as one expanded domain.

Who is the Persian Prince? What is the Persian Prince? Where is the Persian Prince? The Persian Prince is an idea, an ideal type, an archetype, a political proposition, a mode of contemplating politics, a manner of speaking history, culture, civilization, ethics, normative morality, moral philosophy. The Persian Prince is more a persona than a person, an idea than a reality, a character than a physiognomy. In this book I wish to introduce you to the idea of the Persian Prince—as a historical fact and a heuristic device, as a metonymic allegory of a mode of political thinking that has moved around and about history like a colorful chameleon, a floating signifier.

The Persian Prince was born and raised in Persia, from time immemorial, to Iranian, Indian, Greek, Arab, Armenian, Mongol, and Turkic parentage. The Persian Prince was Zoroastrian, Hindu, Manichean, Pagan, Mazdakite, Jewish, Christian, Muslim, agnostic. The Persian Prince spoke Avestan, Pahlavi, Persian, Sanskrit, Greek, Arabic, Mongolian, Armenian, Russian, Turkic... and now English, French, Spanish, German, Italian, and others. The Persian Prince appears in paintings, sings in songs and poetries, dwells in historical fact, hides in literary fictions, acts in dramas, dances in ballets, and resurfaces in operas. The Persian Prince is featured in Greek theater and revered in the Hebrew Bible; he hunts in Persian miniatures and waxes eloquent in Arabic prose, Turkish chronicles, Armenian memories, and European mirrors for princes and paintings.

The Persian Prince was first theorized by the Greek soldier and philosopher Xenophon in *Cyropaedia* (370 BCE) and first portrayed by Aeschylus, a Greek dramatist, in *The Persians* (472 BCE). This was all long after the Persian Prince was personified by Persians, sanctified by Zoroastrians, idealized by Indians, immortalized into holy scriptures—originally by Jews, then by Christians and Muslims. The words of Aeschylus first recited by the Chorus Leader in the play *The Persians* some 2,500 years ago have echoed throughout history:

> We are here as trustworthy delegates
> For all those Persians who have marched away.[1]

The Persian Prince is a poem, a prose, a politics, a philosophical treatise, a mystical tale on the purpose of being. The Persian Prince was a Poet, became a Prophet, and settled down on the royal throne, perpetually looking behind and beneath and beyond itself into a futurity that was always already somewhere else.

Prelude

The Persian Prince is a Shahryar, a Monarch, a Shah, a King, a Caliph, a Padeshah, a Sultan, an Amir, a Caesar—and yet the Persian Prince is a rebel, a revolutionary, a rabblerouser, an iconoclast. The Persian Prince is all of these at the very same time and without the slightest contradiction.

The Persian Prince is the alter ego of those who imagined it, an ideal prototype, a self-projection, a mirror image of those looking for the Persian Prince, the Perfect Person. The Persian Prince (as I theorize and stage it here) is the subject, the object, the subjection, the objection. The Persian Prince is the fusion of the thinker who thinks, the thinking, and the thought of the Persian Prince.

The Persian Prince was once normatively *monadic*, then it split and became narratively *dyadic* and ultimately unfolded upon its own formative forces and turned into a *nomadic* person, persona, character, condition, subjectivity. In the figure of the Persian Prince as I imagine it here, I have found the entire course of a vast spectrum of human civilization in a nutshell.

The Persian Prince is the Persian person in search of itself—a self-universalizing subject. It is degendered, androgynous, with the particularity of its own claims having a universal validity.

The Persian Prince has walked through the battlefields of history, climbed mountains of revolt, ruled with magnanimity, terrorized its subjects and tyrannized them with an iron fist—and then the Persian Prince has revolted against the Persian Prince. The Persian Prince is the Divine Gift of Grace, in specifically Zoroastrian terms. It glows if it has it—it dies if it loses it.

The Persian Prince has fallen, arisen, feared, fumbled, triumphed, and been soundly defeated, right before it has metamorphosed and been resurrected.

The Persian Prince has towered over all other poetic metaphors and stylized proses of our history, adorned the sacrosanct texts of Judaism, Christianity, Islam, and Vedic hymns.

The Persian Prince has defined and held together successive and mighty empires, worn regal robes and sung beautiful arias on theatrical stages as well as the silver screen, whispered into the ears of the most rebellious and iconoclastic dramatists, artists, and filmmakers—from Hollywood to Bollywood.

The Persian Prince has been lost to the heroic ages and has evaporated into the mythic air, the historical solidity of who and what and why we are—and why and wherefore we remember the Persian Prince. I plan to remember and remind you of the Persian Prince in this book, a rigorously detailed reflection on an ancient archetype, historicized, resurrected, remembered, forgotten, sublimated.

This book is (about) the Persian Prince. Once upon a time, a Persian Prince...

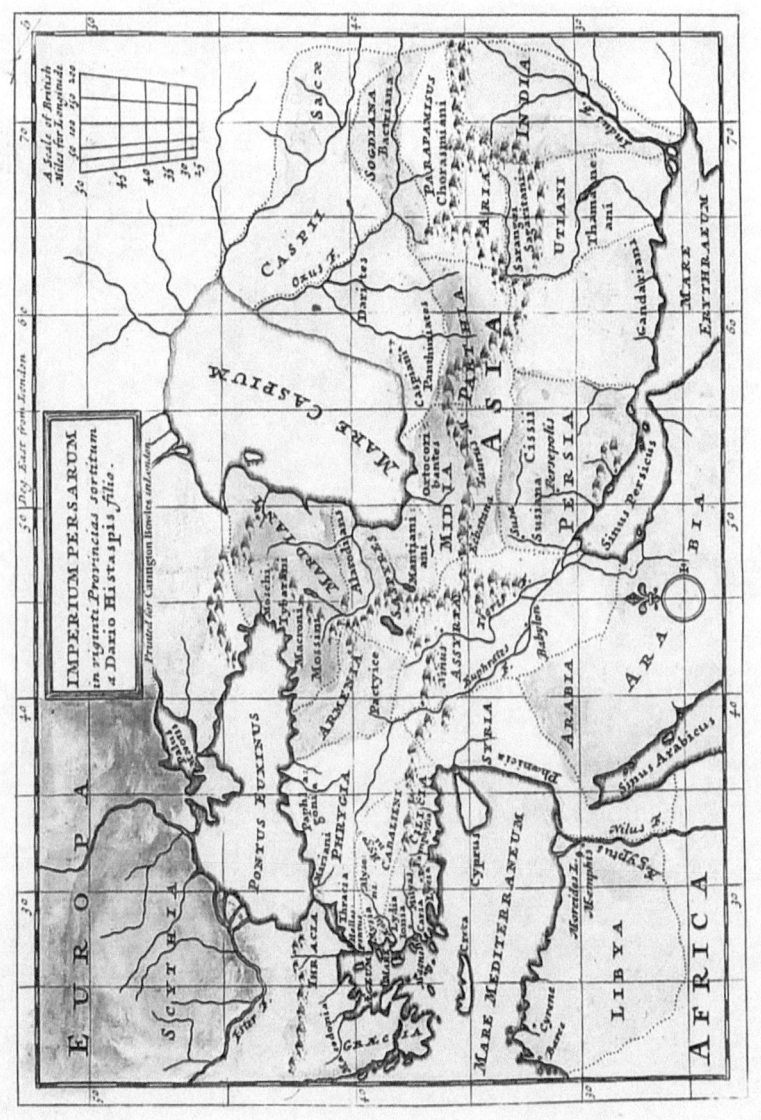

FIGURE 1 Map of the ancient Persian Empire (by Herman Moll, for *Encyclopedia Britannica*, 1764).

Part One

THE PROSPECTS OF AN ARCHETYPE

ONE

The Idea and the Dominion of the Persian Prince

Thus, as we meditated on this analogy, we were inclined to conclude that for man, as he is constituted, it is easier to rule over any and all other creatures than to rule over men. But when we reflected that there was one Cyrus, the Persian, who reduced to obedience a vast number of men and cities and nations, we were then compelled to change our opinion and decide that to rule men might be a task neither impossible nor even difficult, if one should only go about it in an intelligent manner. At all events, we know that people obeyed Cyrus willingly, although some of them were distant from him a journey of many days, and others of many months; others, although they had never seen him, and still others who knew well that they never should see him. Nevertheless, they were all willing to be his subjects.[1]

Xenophon, *Cyropaedia* (circa 370 BCE)

I have heard that on his deathbed
Thus spoke Anushirvan to [his son] Hormizd:
Protect the poor!
Don't indulge in your own luxuries!
No one will rest peacefully in thy realm
If you were after your own comfort and nothing else—
The wise would not see it right
For the shepherd asleep
While the wolf is loose among the sheep.[2]

Saʿdi, *Bustan* (1257 CE)

IN MIKE NEWELL'S FILM *Prince of Persia: The Sands of Time* (2010), Jake Gyllenhaal appears as Prince Dastan with Gemma Arterton as Princess Tamina. From the producer Jerry Bruckheimer and Walt Disney Studios, the film was an adaptation of the widely popular video game of the same name, with themes from other stories from the *Sands of Time* trilogy of the *Prince of Persia* also incorporated into the swashbuckler script. The adventures of the Prince and Princess of Persia made for a delightful summer spoof to be enjoyed with any teenagers in your family and an ample supply of popcorn and soda; inevitably, you would be interrupted halfway through the film by a rushed visit to the bathroom. The adventures of the Prince and Princess of Persia over, you walked out of the theater with the deafening score of Harry Gregson-Williams still resounding in your ears, wondering how in the world these old-fashioned Orientalist cream puffs (making the late Edward Said spin in his grave) still sell in North America, Western Europe, and beyond. They do sell. The global box office earnings of *Prince of Persia: The Sands of Time*, including Russia and China, according to Walt Disney officials, stood at US$133.3 million.[3]

Soon after the overthrow of the Pahlavi dynasty in Iran in the course of the 1977–1979 revolution, the crown prince of the dynasty, Reza Pahlavi (born 1960), emerged as the permanent Shahzadeh Reza Pahlavi, Prince Reza Pahlavi in exile. He was indeed the crown prince according to the Iranian constitution of 1906, which was of course annulled by the Constitution of the Islamic Republic of 1979—even disregarding the fact that his father, Mohammad Reza Pahlavi, fled Iran in 1953 following Mohammad Mosaddegh's nationalization of the Iranian oil industry and was brought back to power by the combined military coup of the CIA and MI6. In exile in the United States, "Prince" Reza Pahlavi cut quite a dismal character, far less handsome than Jake Gyllenhaal in the *Prince of Persia*, with a dubious if not altogether nonexistent claim to the nonexistent Iranian throne.[4] But the rambunctious Iranian monarchists in the United States and around the world were no less flamboyant than those in the movie in singing and dancing their claims to the Peacock Throne.

From the Italian Principe to the Persian Prince

Today the term "Persian Prince" has transfigured and atrophied into fertile grounds for Orientalist fantasies, ethnic nationalism, reactionary politics, misogynistic patriarchy, clichéd cinematic tropes, outdated fairy tales, or else as a marker of arrested modernity, fodder and forage for colonial conquests, nativist xenophobia, and even racist ressentiment. Persian cat, Persian carpet, Persian Prince: they all sound the same—the paraphernalia of a foregone Orientalist nostalgia that serves delusional fantasies of one sort or another. This degeneration and decline have to do in part with the history of the term "Persian" in English and other European languages. This also has to do with the epistemic chasm between scholarship performed in these languages and scholarship done in Persian, Arabic, Turkish, or other Islamic languages. But this very history of the word "Persian" and the term "Persian Prince" is among the issues that require closer examination. How did we get from there to here, from Persia as an empire to Persia as a Hollywood spoof—and, far more importantly, why does the historical trajectory of this journey matter?

In this book, I intend to revive the archetype of the Persian Prince for a radically different and diametrically opposed purpose from the one we see in our pop culture and reactionary politics alike by tracing it back to its classical antiquity, imperial and dynastic pedigrees, medieval and modern destinies, colonial and postcolonial gestations, literary and historical lexicography, poetic and philosophical renditions. I intend to do so by first going into a distant historical past and then cautiously and gently coming forward to our own time, when the Persian Prince archetype has survived in far subtler and far more enduring ways hidden behind these conceptual anxieties. I plan to map out in some detail the Persian theories and practices of rulership that survived the Arab conquest of the Sassanid Empire in the seventh century, linked the pre-Islamic and Islamic periods, and offered the vastest and most varied Muslim empires throughout history with one of the most effective models of imperial rule evident in the celebrated genre of "mirrors for princes" and other seminal literary and philosophical masterpieces. I wish to bring the poetics and the politics of the term "Persian Prince" together—and soon you will find out why this rapprochement is so necessary. I plan to do so not out of any antiquarian interest in bygone ages, or out of an academic exercise in futile curiosity, or in order to count how many Persian princes can dance on the head of that proverbial pin, as it were, but precisely to come forward in the opposite direction, to our own time, and to wonder how the figure of the Persian Prince metamorphosed into two other iconic figures of *the Prophet* and *the Poet* to redefine the nature and disposition of political authority in the wider Iranian and Islamic worlds. Three concurrent and coterminous figures and institutions—the Prince, the Prophet, and the Poet—will thus dwell at the core of this book, as I trace them in a *longue durée* (taken in a general sense) from pre-Islamic, through the Islamic, and down to the post-Islamist frames of references. So this will be a long journey, made of mud and mortars, hopes and fears, dreams and nightmares, of history itself, not of the old curiosity shop of the Hollywood apothecary or of even more outdated ethnic nationalism of one brand or another. I have quite a different story to share. You may not have heard or read anything like it before.

To anchor and locate my book on the Persian Prince in solid comparative and conceptual contexts, and furthest from such false anxieties, I borrow the title of this book intentionally from Niccolò Machiavelli's famous text *De Principatibus/Il Principe/The Prince* (1513/1532), an exceptionally important book I consider rather elementary in comparison to a text like Khwajah Nezam al-Molk al-Tusi's (1018–1092) *Siyasat-nameh* (Book of governance), which, composed centuries earlier, was one among countless other manuals of how to rule an empire—in real time and real terms, not in mere speculative theorization. But still, I think, in Machiavelli's little book we find a good starting point as to where we might go, furthest removed from his wildest imagination, as to how to rule the world, not just a small municipality in Florence or even a country in Europe.[5] To be sure, Machiavelli was fully aware of the imperial history of military conquest and population control, as evidenced in his discussions in the section he calls "Why the Kingdom of Darius Which Alexander Seized Did Not Rebel from His Successors after Alexander's Death."[6] Here he compares the Ottoman Empire (he calls them "the Turks") with France as two prime examples of his time, one ruled via imperial despotism and the other on the model of a royal oligarchy. While entirely tangential to Machiavelli's concerns in his *Prince*, in my Persian Prince that imperial pedigree from the Achaemenids to the Ottomans would be a far more immediate and much more detailed concern to me. Machiavelli was using those imperial cases as mere props to build his own case in his *Prince*. Here, I will reverse the gaze and use his Prince as prop to build the case for my Persian Prince. The case of Machiavelli's Prince will act like a European mirror, as it were, onto which I wish to project a richer and more powerful image of a different, a Persian, prince. Once we stand between Machiavelli's Prince and my "Persian Prince," a more detailed and sculpted view of world imperial histories will emerge that will be instrumental in understanding our own contemporary history better. I have other more urgently historical reasons to turn to Machiavelli's text, but all in good time.

As you begin to read me, you will realize how my initial move here is to detail a perspective on the multifaceted trajectories of Islamic and Persianate statecraft, in which I place the archaic idea of the Persian Prince and where my overriding question would be: How did Muslims and non-Muslims rule such vast empires? Of course, there is more than one answer to that question, and there are recognizable and well-documented factors and forces in the available historiography of early Islam that are the common staple of our reading of the rise of Muslim empires: wars of conquest from the Arabian Peninsula into the Sassanid and Byzantine territories, forced and voluntary conversions, the development of scholasticism and humanism as two competing imperial ideologies, and the eventual emergence of powerful mystical theories, practices, and orders. In this book, by no means do I intend to diminish the significance of such crucial factors. Quite to the contrary: I wish to add a new missing element to them—the archetype of the Persian Prince—that in and of itself requires a more detailed attention and understanding. To be sure, eminent Orientalists, like the late Ann Katharine Swynford Lambton (1912–2008) in her seminal book *Theory and Practice in Medieval Persian Government* (1980), have dealt extensively with such Persian elements. So have a whole host of other scholars within and outside Iran paid crucial attention to the Persian component of Islamic statecraft. I will certainly rely on and examine such earlier works. But the theoretical and historical trajectories of my book have a whole other point of origin and destination. My book seeks to use the heuristic and substantive example of Machiavelli's text to add a new, decidedly comparative frame of reference that will enrich, not supplant, our reading of all other factors. My contention is that the comparative perspective with Machiavelli's Prince offers a whole different angle of vision. The history and historiography of early Islam, from the establishment of the Umayyad dynasty to the rise of the gunpowder empires, offer us ample space to make such comparative assessments plausible and worthy of much wider consideration.

That crucial objective, however, is only a preparatory stage for an even more ambitious twist in my book. The temporal turning point would be in fact precisely the time of Machiavelli himself, when Europe starts to come into contestatory and eventually colonial contact with the larger Muslim world—from the Mughals in the East to the Safavids and the Ottomans in the West. Machiavelli's references in *The Prince* to "the Turks" speak to that European anxiety of his time. A good, and perhaps symbolic, indicator of this contact is the Italian artist Cristofano dell'Altissimo (1530–1605), who was in the service of Cosimo I de' Medici and the near contemporary of Machiavelli (1469–1527)—and actually painted a famous portrait of him, along with those of countless princes (world leaders), including one of the Safavid monarch Shah Ismail (1487–1524) and Tahmasp I (1514–1576). These portraits were housed in the corridors of the Uffizi and obviously represented the global awareness of the Medicis, who had employed him and Machiavelli almost at the same time.[7] We need to place this historical coincidence in the context of Machiavelli's *Prince*, in which he repeatedly refers back to Cyrus, Darius, and Alexander as archetypal princes—figures that I will now propose as examples of the idea and archetype of the Persian Prince at the heart of Machiavelli's *Prince* itself. We are therefore in the realm of an archetype—just as it is evident in the setting of Aeschylus's *The Persians* (performed in 472 BCE) and, after that, in Xenophon's *Cyropaedia* (composed circa 370 BCE)—that had long preceded Machiavelli's *Prince* and was, as the very titles of the works indicate, about a Persian monarch and his conquests. The link therefore between my idea of the Persian Prince and Machiavelli's theorization of his Prince, when he uses his contemporary Safavid or Ottoman monarchs as examples, becomes emblematic of a larger archetypal proposition, which Machiavelli and I share in our respective understanding of the (Persian) Prince. There is a Persian Prince, as it were, at the heart of Machiavelli's *Prince*.

It is quite crucial to keep in mind that Machiavelli's knowledge of Persian culture and Persian empires was not limited to his familiarity with classical antiquity. There is ample evidence of his own contemporary period of political interest in and knowledge about the Aq Qoyunlu, Safavid, and Ottoman empires. We have records of a number of Italian travelers going to Safavid Persia and its adjacent regions to pursue both diplomatic and commercial interests. For example, during Machiavelli's lifetime, in 1472, the Italian merchant, traveler, and diplomat Giosafat Barbaro (1413–1494) was officially sent as an ambassador to the Aq Qoyunlu court, a post he held for about five years, until 1478. His primary mission, in the company of an Iranian named Haci Muhammad, was to shore up a united front against the Ottomans. In 1487, Barbaro wrote his travelogue, *Viaggi fatti da Vinetia, alla Tana, in Persia* . . . His mission was "to solicit Aq Qoyunlu sovereign Uzun Hasan . . . to wage war upon the increasingly menacing power of the Ottoman Turks; but in the end he realized that Uzun Hasan had not the slightest intention of going against the Ottomans."[8] We know the historic significance of this travelogue and what it meant for the time—particularly exposure to Persian culture and history, geography and topography, trading routes and archeology, among them "the remains of 'Cilmynar' [Čehelmenar, i.e., Persepolis], the reliefs at Naqš-e Rostam, and the tomb of Cyrus; curious customs, manners of Sufis, qalandars, and dervishes."[9]

The last reference, to the tomb of Cyrus, is a clear indication that, however sporadically, the Italians of Machiavelli's time were fully aware of the contemporary lineage of the Safavid Empire and to the idea of Persian monarchy going back to classical antiquity. This textual fact is corroborated by two portraits dell'Altissimo did of two seminal monarchs of the Safavid dynasty. This is all to say that not only was Machiavelli aware of the contemporary geopolitics of the region in which the Safavids and the Ottomans were located, but the increasing European interest in Muslim lands brought the political provenance of Machiavelli's Prince into the immediate vicinity of my concern with the historical unfolding of the archetype of the Persian Prince. Thus, my attention to his seminal text is not merely for heuristic and comparative reasons. There are, in short, historical, textual, comparative, classical, contemporary, and theoretical links between Machiavelli's theorization of *The Prince* and my turn to the Persian Prince. But my turn to Machiavelli's classical text some five hundred years later is linked by yet another seminal text closer to Machiavelli's neighborhood.

From the Prince to the Modern Prince to the Persian Prince

There are solid historical and further theoretical reasons as to why I am drawing your attention to Machiavelli's seminal text by way of preparing you for my idea of the Persian Prince. Machiavelli's *Prince* is rightly considered a major turning point in European political theory, where abstract moral mandates yield to factual, pragmatic, and, according to some, even cynical reality.[10] Dedicated to Lorenzo de' Medici, Machiavelli's book is in the form of advice as to how a prince ought to run his realm with precision, brutality, and deceit if need be. This is presumably based on a deeply realistic understanding of human nature. Between being loved and feared, Machiavelli famously proposed, "one should wish to be both, but, because it is difficult to unite them in one person, it is much safer to be feared than loved, when, of the two, either must be dispensed with. Because this is to be asserted in general of men, that they are ungrateful, fickle, false, cowardly, covetous, and as long as you succeed they are yours entirely; they will offer you their blood, property, life, and children, as is said above, when the need is far distant; but when it approaches they turn against you."[11] The concern of Machiavelli here is therefore not with the nature of justice or the form of government as we have known it since Plato and Aristotle but in pure and undiluted power and how to sustain it. Absent from *The Prince* is even a pretense to

"Christian morality." Machiavelli seems to have invented a whole new way of thinking about politics.

From such premises the term "Machiavellianism" eventually emerged as a derogatory term for deceitful politics and unprincipled power-mongering. But this is not the way that, generations later, the eminent Italian Marxist philosopher Antonio Gramsci (1891–1937) would revisit and reread Machiavelli's *Prince*. Gramsci interpreted *The Prince* in a vastly different way. In his *Prison Notebooks*, Gramsci devoted a section to what he called the "Modern Prince."[12] Here Gramsci argued that Machiavelli's book ought to be read figuratively, for he was trying to form a national will to power in the figure of the prince. The mythic figure of "the prince," in other words, pivoted toward the formation of a national will to power. The same holds true now, Gramsci argued, that the vanguard political party of the labor class ought to do similarly toward the formation of a new national will. This modern "prince," for Gramsci, was no longer a real person but a progressive political party. This is how Gramsci formulated his argument:

> The modern prince, the myth-prince, cannot be a real person, a concrete individual. It can only be an organism, a complex element of society in which a collective will, which has already been recognized and has to some extent asserted itself in action, begins to take concrete form. History has already provided this organism, and it is the political party—the first cell in which there come together germs of a collective will tending to become universal and total.[13]

This Gramscian insight, particularly his allegorical and mythic reading of the figure of "the Prince" as a regulative agent of power and authority in politics, would become of immense importance to me once I began to trace the active transmutation of the ancient archetype of the Persian prince: under colonial duress, not into any weak and wobbly political party but into the far more potent formative forces of *the public and parapublic spheres* on which the heroic figure of the public intellectual as the prophetic voice of the time retrieves aspects of its historical memory and metamorphoses into the tragic figure of the rebel-poet.[14] In other words, here in this book I have a figurative conception of the archetype of the Persian Prince that remains constant in its authorial institution but metamorphic in its varied political manifestations in a long and winding history from the pre-Islamic to the post-Islamist periods.

At the very outset, we must note a strong Persian presence in the European historical imagination at the crucial and transformative moment of Machiavelli's

Prince.[15] However transformative and unique, Machiavelli's *Prince* was in the long tradition of European mirrors, which begins, quite poignantly for my purposes in this book, with Xenophon's *Cyropaedia* (circa 370 BCE), a significant mirror predicated on the author's imaginative construction of the life and leadership of the Persian emperor, of the "Persian Prince" par excellence.[16] Xenophon's positive conception of Cyrus is further complicated by the more critical assessment portrayed by Herodotus (circa 484–425 BCE) before him. Subsequently, such seminal texts as Cicero's *De Officiis* (44 BCE) and Seneca the Younger's *De Clementia* (55–56 CE) are among many other princely mirrors that appear throughout European history.

All of these texts, however, pale in comparison to such pivotal mirrors as Vishnu Sharma's *Panchatantra* (200 BCE) and Laozi's *Tao Te Ching* (sixth century BCE), both of which expand our knowledge of the genre of mirrors for princes to include the formidable body of Islamic sources in Arabic, Persian, Turkish, Urdu, and other languages, which have had a palpable influence on medieval Europe. From two sides, from the Greek side of *Cyropaedia* and the contemporary side of Muslim sources, the medieval European texts on mirrors of princes were framed within a Perso-Islamic context. As Xenophon's *Cyropaedia* went in one direction carrying the legacy of Persian imperial heritage into Greek, Roman, and thereafter European contexts, from the other side the Arabic and Persian renditions of a pre-Islamic Iranian heritage of imperial rule brought the selfsame legacy into Euro-Islamic contexts. The pre-Islamic Iranian pedigree of both the Greco-Roman-European sources on one side and the Islamic trajectories on the other locate my theorization of the figure of the Persian Prince at the epicenter of the manufactured binary between "Islam and the West"—and dismantles and overcomes them both.

This pedigree I just outlined makes Machiavelli's *Prince* a "Persianate" text if we were to use this term as an adjective for the Persophiliac proclivities of European political culture, as I have detailed extensively in *Persophilia*, and in the sense that it is in the direct line of Xenophon's *Cyropaedia* and is conversant with its contemporary resonances. With Gramsci, however, Machiavelli's Prince is liberated from its rootedness in ancient and medieval European contexts and brought to our contemporary and colonial world, though Gramsci himself was not too seriously engaged with that colonial world. Under the ruling fascist regime, Gramsci was imprisoned in 1926, and he wrote his *Prison Notebooks* between 1929 and 1935. This was the heyday of European colonial savagery around the world. This was the height of the Italian colonial consolidation of power in Libya in 1912 and, even before that, in Eritrea and Somalia in the 1880s. The French were in Algeria much earlier, in the 1830s, whereas Napoleon's campaign in Syria and Egypt dated even earlier (1798–1801). The British of course had beat them all by their presence in India, as had the Spanish and the Portuguese in the Americas, and the Belgians in Africa. None of these were of much interest to Gramsci or his Eurocentric Marxism, especially if he were to be compared with his contemporary Rosa Luxemburg (1875–1919), the utterly brilliant Marxist theorist, who was infinitely more aware of and politically and theoretically engaged with European colonialism.[17] To be sure, Gramsci's Italian contemporaries, older-generation anti-fascist thinkers like Gaetano Salvemini (1873–1957), were deeply against Italian colonial expansion into North Africa; indeed, Gramsci was critical of European imperialism in a generic and theoretical sense. But Asia, Africa, and Latin America were not really on his European radar. There are postcolonial thinkers and scholars who consider Gramsci crucial for their scholarship.[18] But Gramsci himself was too preoccupied with Europe to think much of the rest of the world. His reading of Machiavelli's *Prince* for his own contemporary Europe, however, gives me a solid bridge to trace the fate of the Persian Prince into the colonial contexts of its later resurrections.

Between Machiavelli's Prince and Gramsci's "Modern Prince," what does the Persian Prince, whose archetypal presence extends from the pre-Islamic to post-Islamist periods, look like and what could it teach us about the manner in which Muslims once ruled the world? By extension, how can it inform our contemporary thinking regarding the troubled formations of the postcolonial nation-state, public and parapublic spheres, and, perhaps most importantly, the postcolonial subject, or who and what and by what authority could claim political or public legitimacy? My initial project in this book is to provide a detailed panorama of the historical and textual contours of the Persian Prince and then to seek to explain how the idea consolidated the manner in which pre-Islamic Iranian ideals of just and legitimate governance metamorphosed into their Islamic gestations to provide the Muslim world with the longest running succession of world empires until the dawn of European colonial modernity.

But the story of the Persian Prince does not end in the course of that fateful encounter with European colonialism and will have a decisive resurrection very much in the spirit of, if not the precise, political parameters that Gramsci had theorized. Not in the shape of any political party, as Gramsci surmised, but in the prophetic voice of the rebel-poet, defining a new organicity to the postcolonial public intellectual, to continue to use Gramsci's own crucial conceptualizations, does the Persian Prince reemerge as the simulacrum of what Gramsci called the "myth-prince," here articulated not within any legitimate political organism but in the premise of a gendered and transnational public sphere that gives birth to the figure of the organic public intellectual—in the prophetic voice of the rebel-poet—as the "modern Persian prince." This sustained dialogue between my theorization of the Persian Prince with Gramsci's "Modern Prince" and Machiavelli's Prince—keeping in mind that all these dialogues are predicated on Xenophon's *Cyropaedia*, the Persian Prince par excellence—will sustain a comparative perspective that keeps the course of my investigations steady.

As you see in the very prose and politics that such comparative analytics occasion, we have long since passed our artificial limitations within one political culture or another. The figure of the Persian Prince as I outline it in this book is decidedly cross-cultural and transnational—as it maps out the configuration of a whole different way of thinking politics in multiple historical and cultural settings. This requires a certain degree of patience and perseverance from my readers to allow me to bring perhaps unfamiliar names and ideas and place them right next to those with which they might be more familiar. My emphatic turn to Gramsci, for example, and what he did with Machiavelli's Prince anticipates a similar twist to Gramsci himself as I reread his "Modern Prince" in a colonial and a postcolonial context far beyond his immediate (and perfectly legitimate) Eurocentric preoccupations. Gramsci was decidedly concerned with the party politics in Italy of his time.[19] The crucial link between my theorization of the Persian Prince in the colonial context is Gramsci's fascist Italy, which on the colonial edges of European modernity was a standard operation, whether we were ruled by colonial officers or their native tyrants. In the course of its affliction with fascism and Nazism, Europe tasted a bit of the poison it had been giving to the world at large. The link between Gramsci's and my readings of Machiavelli's *Prince* is his intuitive emphasis on the role of organic intellectuals and the literati. But while he was preoccupied with party politics, I am far more concerned with the disposition of the transnational public and parapublic spheres into which the figure of the Persian Prince dissolves, resurrects, and ultimately sublimates. In other words, under the epistemic shock of European colonialism the figure of the Persian Prince folds upon itself, leaves the Persianate court, enters and defines the public and parapublic spheres, and resurrects into the prophetic voice of the rebel-poet. Here we suddenly realize that the metamorphic figures of the grandest theorists of the power of the Persian Prince were the Persian poets, artists, and philosophers—as they spoke, painted, theorized, philosophized, and theologized the Persian Prince. There was a rebellious poet at the heart of the Persian Prince that he had to repress, hide, sublimate, and bypass in order to assert power and authority. The Persian Prince was always a paradoxical figure, a tragic hero, a political sublimation of a poetic instinct, a prophetic voice oscillating between the royal court and the revolutionary battlefields.

The Literary Abode of the Persian Prince

Let me expand on that latter point and turn to the literary habitat of the Persian Prince. Where does the Persian Prince reside and resonate, dwell and dominate, feel most at home—morally, ethically, imaginatively? The primary home and habitat of the Persian Prince are the Persian words and the worlds they project and implicate. This is not a "World Republic of Lettres."[20] This is decidedly and unapologetically the "World Empire of Letters." It is crucial for us to recognize that the primary abode and normative habitat of the Persian Prince is Persian poetry and prose—though with equally happy dwellings in the neighboring Greek, Hebrew, Pahlavi, and Arabic habitat. In the bosom of these languages and cultures is the Persian Prince born and raised. The rest, the physical world, the actual world, the battlefields of life and fate, the historical geography over which the Persian Prince presides, all come next. Before the Persian Prince went about conquering the physical world, there was a moral and imaginative world, a normative and poetic home the prince had to call and command. The literary abode of the Persian Prince in Persian, Arabic, Hebrew, Pahlavi, and Greek texts is his birthplace, hometown, country of origin, ancestral habitation. Let me give you a very specific, perhaps the clearest, example.

I cannot recall now if I read this somewhere or had it said to me by a learned person in full command of the legacy of Persian literary humanism: that if civilization as we know it were to be wiped off the face of the earth and only two books survived, Saʿdi's *Bustan* (1257) and *Golestan* (1258), humanity will be able to rebuild the civilized world on the basis of these two jewels of Persian poetry and prose alone. Contrary to the common wisdom that it is impossible to convey the beauty and elegance of Saʿdi's prose and poetry in any other language than its original, I believe that, if not the letter of his poetry, then certainly the soul of his sagacious wisdom is perfectly capable of being rendered in any number of other languages.[21] More than anything else, it is the formal confidence of these two seminal texts that first and foremost strikes careful or even casual readers. Take, for example, *Bustan*, the masterpiece he composed in 1258. Even before you start reading its ten chapters, its preamble reveals itself as a testament to grace and beauty, worthy of the Persian Prince to which it gives narrative birth, an edifice to the cultured life with the precision of the portal of a mosque or the entrance to a palace. As you start reading the book you feel privy to a royal audience—though the royalty here is not that of the actual prince to whom it is dedicated and for whom it was primarily composed but the regal elegance and grace of Saʿdi's own poetic sublimity, into which he allows you, in fact seduces you, to enter and stay and think and live and be and wonder. Imagine Shakespeare's poetic prose, Bach's cantatas, Mozart's frivolous genius, Beethoven's magisterial phrasings—and all of these by way of European examples, for we might equally go to Asia, Africa, and Latin America and point to equally beautiful signposts of those civilizations to give you a suggestion of what it means to read Saʿdi and be in his poetic presence. And all of that is the abode of the Persian Prince, where the royal audience of the icon of Persian cosmopolis has its wholesome, unitary, monadic meaning.

The poet's nom de plume was "Saʿdi" because he had named himself after the dynasty of his patron princes Outlaugh Khan Abu Bakr ibn Saʿd ibn Zangi I (reigned 1226–1260) and his son Saʿd II b. Outlaugh Khan (reigned 1260–1262). Such *takhallos*, or pen names, that abound in Persian, Urdu, and Hendi literary history point to the metamorphic character of the poet and their patron prince. The poets abandon their own names for all practical and professional purposes and become the prince they are praising, and conversely, the princely power of the ruling monarch transmigrates, as it were, into the poetic soul of the voice that praises, admonishes, educates, and at the same time procures the longevity of his good name. This metamorphic intertwining of the poet and the prince becomes a central theme of the archetype of the Persian Prince throughout history.

Very early in the prolegomena to his *Bustan*, Saʿdi tells us he has divided his book into ten chapters—Babs, as he calls them, doors or entrances. A mere glance at the very titles of these chapters shows the range of moral and ethical issues he wishes to share with his patron prince. These are the ten chapters: first is the Bab-e Adl (the Chapter on Justice) and includes Tadbir va Ra'i (Perspicacity and Sound Judgment), which is meant to instruct the prince why he should fear God and care for his subjects; second is the Bab of Ihsan (Magnanimity), for a magnanimous prince will honor the Grace of the Lord; third is the Bab of Eshq, Masti, va Shur (Love, Drunkenness and Passion), a real love, as he reminds the prince, and not a fickle and ephemeral love; fourth on Tavazoʿ (Humility); fifth on Reza (Contentment); sixth on Qenaʿat (Austerity); seventh on Tarbiyat (Education); eighth on Shokr-e bar Afiyat (Gratitude); ninth on Tubeh va Rah-e Savab (Repentance and the Righteous Path); and finally, tenth, a short chapter on Monajat va Khatm-e Ketab (Benediction and Conclusion).[22]

In a key passage in the introduction, writing about his patron prince, Saʿdi notes:

> I was not inclined to compose such a poem
> For I was not about praising kings—
> But I composed this poem in the name of the prince
> So that people of taste would say:
> That Saʿdi who was such an eloquent poet
> Lived in the time of Bu Bakr ibn Saʿd—
> It is apt if I am proud to live in his time
> The same way that our Prophet was proud
> To have been born at the time of Anushirvan.
> Protector of the Realm, of the Faith and of Justice:
> No one was like Bu Bakr after Omar—
> Towering over the mighty and the crown of the best
> Oh World: Be proud to be in his realm.[23]

The link between pre-Islamic princes, here represented by a reference to the Sassanid king Anushirvan and his own patron prince, is here associated with Saʿdi following Prophet Muhammad's example. Alluding to a Hadith in which the Prophet presumably said, "I was born at the time of the Just Ruler," this passage is emblematic of the literary habitat of the Persian Prince, in which the poet and his patron prince partake in a distant Iranian archetype that in fact predates Islam and locates Prophet Muhammad himself within a (Zoroastrian) Sassanid temporal reference.

The entirety of *Bustan*, but particularly the first chapter, can be read as a detailed mirror for a prince, educating the prince not merely on how to be just but on how to be a human being. If the first chapter is about justice, the rest of the book and the remaining nine chapters are about how to be a decent and civilized person. The first chapter is full of beautiful stories, in the midst of which Saʿdi instructs the prince to be gentle with the weak and conscious of his own mortality. He tells him about the virtues of chivalry, how to win the hearts of his subjects with kindness, and how to be a free and liberated man; he also informs the prince that there is an afterlife and that he will be punished or rewarded for what he has done in this world. He does all of these things while telling one exemplary story after another to illustrate the points he is making and, in the process, educate, entertain, and amuse the prince.

The remaining nine chapters place the prince in the larger frame of a civilized life, teaching him the contours of a fair and equitable reign, the meaning of earthly and divine love, the necessity of humility, how to be content with what God has given him, how to be patient and grateful and hope for the best, of the virtue of silence, of the horrors of talking too much, of not badmouthing people, of the full dimensions of a cultured and caring life in which judicious behavior, wisdom, and good humor are far superior to waging battles and war. Saʿdi does have a section on the education of women, which, typical of his era, is misogynistic, patriarchal, and outlandish, but still he praises a kind, caring, and competent woman, "the person whose home is peaceful and his spouse a friend, God has looked kindly upon him." He advocates monogamy, to spend a lifetime with just one woman, and warns against debauchery and overindulgence in sex. He leaves not a stone unturned, from birth through the pitched fever of youth to old years and the necessity of repentance in old age. And then he concludes with yet another sublime example of Persian poetic wisdom:

> Oh come let us rise in love,
> For tomorrow we cannot resurrect from our graves
> Don't you see in the season of autumn,
> All the trees are naked from the brutish cold.
> If a poor person were to ask for forgiveness
> The Almighty will never disappoint him—
> Don't you ever think you will be turned away disappointed
> From that door that is never closed—
> The fate will give him a royal robe
> Destiny will place fruits in his sleeves.[24]

By the end of *Bustan*, we wonder who Saʿdi wrote this book for, who his primary interlocutor, or secondary, etc., was. The book is ostensibly written for Saʿdi's immediate patron prince, as he tells us from the very beginning. But soon *Bustan* also becomes a reality unto itself. Yes, it is for the education of the prince, but for the edification of humanity at large, every single factual or fictive person here becomes a prince. The monadic disposition of the princely power here becomes an idyllic realm where reason and sanity rule supreme—as Saʿdi links the very idea of the Persian Prince to its archetypal visions.

The Persian Prince in the Persianate Cosmopolis

Sa'di's *Bustan* is a typical example of the literary abode of the Persian Prince. But where is his physical dominion, where he reigns supreme? There must also be a physical world, a geographical domain, mountains, rivers, seas, and valleys over which the Persian Prince rules. Where is that dominion of the Persian Prince?

A prince requires a principality, a princedom, a sovereign state. Where is the domain and dominion of the Persian Prince? Here, by "domain" or "dominion," I do not mean Ctesiphon, for example, for the Parthians and the Sassanids, or Baghdad for the Abbasids, or Isfahan or Istanbul or Delhi for the Safavids, the Ottomans, and the Mughals, respectively. I mean the larger imperial imaginary in which the Persian Price is at home. The domain and dominion of the Persian Prince in this sense can be variedly identified as Iranian, Persian, Persianate, Indo-Iranian, and more broadly the Islamic worlds, but by extension also the worlds of classical antiquity and the Hebrew Bible. Each one of these designations has certain advantages and certain disadvantages. The reason for that is simple. These worlds are interrelated and interpolated, and there is no artificial and forced way of separating them. More recently, the term "Persianate" has become popular with scholars of South Asia, specially of a period they identify as "early modern"—which is, of course, Eurocentric in its temporal spectrum and almost entirely meaningless on any other chronological or thematic periodization anywhere else in the world. These scholars have produced an important body of scholarship, but they have also somewhat ahistorically dragged the term mainly into the Indo-Persian direction, which is only partially correct, for it actively disregards the equally, if not even more important, domains of Central Asian, Transoxiana, the Caucuses, Asia Minor, Anatolia, the Ottoman domains, and particularly the Arab-Islamic worlds. But as I reason and theorize the idea of the Persian Prince in this book, the Hebrew Bible, the Arabic literary world, the Pahlavi texts, the Greek antiquity, and the archeology of the ancient world are all equally the provenance of this Persianate world.

In this sense, I use the term "Persianate world" in a decidedly more global sense. As it is currently used, the term has assumed a specifically North American academic provenance—a mixed blessing. In 2002, the distinguished Iranian sociologist Said Amir Arjomand founded the Association for the Study of Persianate Societies, which also published the *Journal of Persianate Studies*, and started organizing a biennial international conference in places like Tajikistan, Turkey, Bosnia and Herzegovina, India, Pakistan, Georgia, and Armenia.

More recently a conference was organized at Yale University in 2014, and a subsequent volume was edited and published in 2019 on the basis of that conference.[25] This was perhaps the best and most potent use of the term "Persianate" in a transnational and wide-ranging sense.

The term "Persianate," as well as its sister idea of "Islamicate," was originally coined by the American historian Marshall Hodgson in the 1960s.[26] He had found these terms useful in his own reading of Islamic history, but the two terms never assumed widespread acceptance or usage until recently, when a few scholars of South Asia based on North American campuses began to pick up where Hodgson had left off and started using "Persianate" in their scholarship.[27] But they abandoned Hodgson's far more universal notion of "the Persianate," which proverbially expanded "from Balkan to Bengal"—and included the territorial domains of "the Greater Iran," from Asia Minor to Central and South Asia. The most cogent and systematic treatment of this territory has appeared in the impressive work of Nile Green, *The Persianate World: The Frontiers of a Eurasian Lingua Franca* (2019). Equally important is Kevin L. Schwartz's *Remapping Persian Literary History, 1700–1900* (2020), which, without resorting to the term "Persianate," correctly takes issue with Iranian nationalist historiography and expands the domain into Central Asia and Afghanistan, which I had also done in *The World of Persian Literacy Humanism* (2012). But before these books, the prominent Czech Orientalist Jan Rypka (1886–1968) did the same in his seminal and classic text *History of Iranian Literature* (1956).

A more useful conceptualization emerged from a different angle. The eminent Sanskritist Sheldon Pollock's *The Language of the Gods in the World of Men: Sanskrit, Culture, and Power in Premodern India* (2009) offered a solid and useful idea of the "Sanskrit cosmopolis."[28] The publication of my own book a couple of years later, *The World of Persian Literary Humanism* (2012), came at a similar idea from a slightly different angle, for among my main concerns in that book was the notion of "Persian literary humanism," which I had offered for the institution of Adab and theorized historically as "cosmopolitan worldlines." I had borrowed and expanded this idea from the work of my own teacher, George Makdisi (1920–2002). In my carefully theorized trajectory of the term "Persian Adab," predicated on Makdisi's pathbreaking work on Arabic Adab, Indians, Iranians, Afghans, Tajiks, Arabs, and Turks all have equal and identical claim to the term "Persian Adab." In that book I demonstrated in detail what the term "Persian" could mean historically, conceptually, and institutionally. Soon, other scholars in the field began to expand on these ideas, and the two terms of

"Sanskrit cosmopolis" and "Persian cosmopolis" began a fruitful circulation. In his excellent essay "The Persian Cosmopolis (900–1900) and the Sanskrit Cosmopolis (400–1400)" (2019), Richard M. Eaton gives a full and admirable expression of these two concepts.[29] In this essay, he makes the following precise observation:

> What we see . . . is not evidence of an "Islamicate" world, much less an Islamic one, but of something we may more properly call a Persian cosmopolis. What I mean here is an aesthetic and literary sensibility, together with an integrated understanding of moral and social order that was informed not by religion as such, but by ideas and values that spread through the circulation of canonical Persian texts and the growth of populations that used Persian in speaking, reading, or writing.

Eaton here detects and theorizes a distinct Persian cosmopolis that has vast continental expressions. He further elaborates his point:

> Precisely because this Persianate world could be decoupled from the Muslim religion—or indeed, from any religion—that Hindu rulers such as those at Vijayanagara could so readily title themselves "sultan" in their public proclamations, or assimilate pointed arches and vaulted domes into their urban landscape. Doing so signaled their desire to participate in a transregional understanding of prestige and authority.[30]

Eaton takes issue with Hodgson for having confused Islamicate with what in fact was the Persian cosmopolis, which he also believes was far more cosmopolitan than the Sanskrit cosmopolis for the liberality of its syncretic disposition in including pre-Islamic Iranian, Persian, Islamic, and Sanskrit worlds. He even proposes a more provocative idea:

> This would appear to explain why Marshall Hodgson had confused the Persianate for the Islamicate—or indeed, most all things Persian with Islam. It also explains why art historians might think of vaulted structures in India as exhibiting an "Islamic style." . . . For it was precisely the non-religious character of this larger Persian cosmopolis that had allowed non-Muslims to participate in it so readily.

He believes most modern scholarship has missed this point, busy as it has been casting Indian history in Hindu-Muslim terms. He therefore concludes, "For such reasons the idea of a Persianate world, or Persian cosmopolis, might prove a promising conceptual key for understanding pre-modern South Asian history on its own terms—and indeed, for rescuing both Iranian and Indian history from the steel grip of nationalist historiographies."[31]

This may indeed be the case in the Indian context but would be an exaggeration in the larger Muslim world farther to the West, where the Persian cosmopolis most certainly includes the Abbasid, the Saljuqid, the Mongol, and the Ottoman domains. The idea had also proven useful for Emma J. Flatt in her beautiful new book, *The Courts of the Deccan Sultanates: Living Well in the Persian Cosmopolis* (2020), or, before her, in the work of Owen Cornwall, my own student at Columbia, in his brilliant master's thesis, "Alexander and the Persian Cosmopolis, 1000–1500" (2016), or in the work of a host of other scholars who continue to use the term "Persian" in the long and solid tradition of doyens of South Asian studies like Irfan Habib, Mozaffar Alam, Sanjay Subrahmanyam, and Sheldon Pollock. It is far more urgent but difficult to think of what has happened in terms domestic to a vast civilization like Islam or the Turkic, Persian, Indian, or Arabic component of it—for which a native and organic intimacy with the language and culture is required. My paramount task here is the systematic theorization of a concept that long predates all these anxieties of ethnic nationalism. As I use it in the phrase "Persian Prince" to theorize a specific archetype of political authority, the term carries no such anxieties. If the preference for the term "Persianate" is in reaction to the nationalist proclivities of Iranian historiography, then those who prefer "Persianate" to "Persian" might also be falling from the other side of the roof into a terrible case of Iranophobia or, even worse, Islamophobia, which in the context of Hindu fundamentalist rule in India might place these scholars in unsavory company.

I use the term "Persianate" interchangeably with "Persian," for the term "Persian cosmopolis" or my own concept of "Persian cosmopolitan worldliness" already entails "the Persianate world." In addition to my *World of Persian Literary Humanism* (2012), in a subsequent book, *Iran Without Borders* (2016), I located the very idea of Iran squarely within the larger cosmopolitan world that extends from the Mediterranean to Central Asia to India. This world, as I have extensively argued throughout my work, is always already *polyvocal* (speaks multiple languages), *polylocal* (spaces itself out from India through Central Asia and the Caucuses to the Mediterranean Basin), and *polyfocal* (navigates a heteroglossic array of discourses). In this Persianate world, people speak Greek, Pahlavi, Sanskrit, Persian, Arabic, Turkish, Armenian, Bengali, and Urdu. They live in Athens, Jerusalem, Cairo, Baghdad, Isfahan, Kashmir, and Delhi. They oscillate between theology, philosophy, and mysticism in stylized prose or poetry, in illustrated manuscripts and monumental architecture, in melodious *dastgahs*, *maqams*, *radifs*, and *qawwali* music.

The domain of my primary concern with the idea of the Persian Prince dwelling in this Persianate cosmopolis is the Persian component of the much larger expanse of the Islamic civilization, bordering with Indian, Greek, Hebrew, and Egyptian worlds—especially in the successive unfolding of Iranian, Muslim, and Roman empires in which I propose that the idea of the Persian Prince epitomized in Xenophon's *Cyropaedia* and the Hebrew Bible was seminal. Multiple major dimensions of these civilizations predate Islam by long and rich and powerful histories: Egyptian, Greek, Hebrew, Iranian, and Indian. These seminal loci of successive civilizations are rooted in their respective pre-Islamic heritage, which has left an indelible mark on their take on Islam. As a result, my focus on the figure and archetype of the Persian Prince dwells on a component of Islamic civilization that is deeply rooted in pre-Islamic, non-Islamic, Iranian imperial imaginary, which we can safely call the Persian or Persianate cosmopolis, theoretically grounded in what I have proposed as "cosmopolitan worldliness," which I had borrowed and expanded from Hans-Georg Gadamer and Edward Said. There is a structural and thematic organicity between pre-Islamic, non-Islamic, and Islamic sides of the political domain of the Persian Prince. My use of the term "Persian" or "Persianate cosmopolis" as the dominion of the Persian Prince is in this sense of a component of the Islamic civilization with active and conscious pre-Islamic and non-Islamic roots.

One could easily make a similar argument about the Egyptian, Hebrew, Greek, and Indian sites of all these civilizations, similar to what Pollock has called "Sanskrit cosmopolis" and I "Persian cosmopolitan worldliness." But in this book, and for the domain and dominion of the Persian Prince as I theorize here, I dwell on the pre-Islamic, Iranian, and ultimately Persian facets of Islamic civilization, its Persian or Persianate cosmopolis. If and when I use the term "Persianate" as a result, it is in this sense of the "Persian cosmopolis," which includes Iran but is not limited to Iran, which includes Persian but is not limited to Persian, and extends into Greek, Hebrew, Arabic, Armenian, and a host of other adjacent languages. When the eminent historian Abu Mansur al-Thaʿalibi (961–1039) wrote his seminal book *Ghurar Akhbar Muluk al-Furs wa Siyarihim* in Arabic, he was being Persianate, as long before him had Xenophon when he wrote his *Cyropaedia* in Greek, or before him those who immortalized the Persian queen Esther in the Hebrew Bible, or long after that, Ibn Muqaffaʿ when he wrote *Kelilah wa Demneh* (hereafter referred to as *Kelilah and Demneh*) in Arabic, as did countless other poets and prose stylists and historians in these and other languages. Greek, Pahlavi, Persian, Hebrew, or Arabic may have been their scholastic or humanistic language, but Persianate (as an adjective, not as a noun) was their emotive universe, their intellectual provenance, their moral imagination. As I envision and theorize the idea, the Persian Prince speaks all these languages and is at home in all these cultures.

I also use the terms "Persian" and "Persianate" interchangeably because I think that much of the whole commotion of differentiating between these two terms is misbegotten and much ado about nothing. By the time the US-based professoriat on the North American campuses have concurred on a concept, the world has moved beyond these horizons, as the territorial expanses of what such terms refer to has deterritorialized and transmuted into something else; the floating signifiers of cultures and climes do not stand still for one generation to retire and for another generation to start flexing their Oedipal muscles. Meanwhile, one must avoid attributing misplaced concreteness to the terms "Iran," "Islam," "Persia," "Persianate," etc., for all are floating signifiers. As I argued in detail in *Being a Muslim in the World* (2013), we are more defined by the varied expanse of our alterities than by our presumed identities. The legitimate litigations against nationalist historiography could very easily slip into the fetishization of its regional alternatives on, for example, Indo-Persian frontiers and as such might very well collapse into an even nastier brand of Iranophobia to replace Iran-centrism or, even worse, dangerously flirt with Islamophobia—and at the high time of Hindu fundamentalism, these are verily frightful turns in one's obsessing over one term over another.

There is more than one way to challenge nationalist historiography and posit liberating alternatives. In a succession of books that coagulated around my *Iran Without Borders: Towards a Critique of the Postcolonial Nation* (2016), I have mapped out in detail the *transnational public* sphere upon which the *postcolonial subject* has taken shape. Iran as a postcolonial nation-state is integral to that transnational sphere but not definitive to it. All such considerations in fact fade in the face of an even more urgent matter to which I shall turn toward the end of this book, when I map out the contours of the *nomadic* turn in our fragmented subjectivities. The idea of the Persian Prince has always been a Trojan horse, both legitimizing and delegitimizing, empowering and dismantling power that has laid claim to it. The circulatory of this crosscurrent of power and insurrection has been the engine of history rooted in this transhistorical idea. The idea of the Persian Prince was not propagated by doctors of law and their Shariʿah, theologians of divine dispensation and their speculations, or philosophers in search of their kings. It was the artifact of a scattered tribe of prose stylists and poets, whose own claim to authorship was already compromised by the turn of the pen they held in their hands, by what that pen wrote, and by how others hoped to read and interpret them. As Islamic scholasticism effectively sought to stabilize Islamic imperial conquests of the world, Muslims' turns to literary humanism—in Arabic, Persian, Turkish, or Urdu—did much more than challenge that imperial legalism and sustained a pluralist cultural heritage for generations to come. Contrary to early Orientalist assumptions, there is no racially dividing these two adjacent and complementary fields of scholasticism and humanism. Arabs and Persians and Turks and South Asians were as active in scholasticism as they were in humanism.

In reconfiguring the Persianate world, we also need to come to terms with the changing spatial politics of being-in-the-world—and the historical unfolding territorialities of such worlds. Here, what the French Marxist sociologist Henri Lefebvre has called "the third space" becomes crucial: first is the physical space, second is the mental space, and third is the social space.[32] Another theorist of space is equally important here: Edward Soja's notion of "Third Space" works through what he calls spatial trialectics. Third Space is both real and imagined.[33] The idea of Third Space, as I propose here for the Persianate world, is open-ended, miasmatic, cumulative, or an evolving trialectics. While Soja points to hybridity and the duality becoming trialectical and thus the third space opening up on to new horizons, I have previously proposed an interstitial space, which is hidden to both First and Second spaces to sustain the subversive power of art and literature on that in-folded and unfolding space.[34] Contrary to any attempt to fix and locate this Persianate world, it has always been an interstitial space, roaming from India to Transoxiana, Central Asia, the Caucuses, through the current border of Iran and deep into the Ottoman Empire. From Europe to North Africa, the Persianate world has had textual evidences of mobile significations. The ancient roots of this fact have to do with the imperial origins of the terms all the way back to the Achaemenid Empire, and some of it with the multicultural disposition of other Iranian empires and then the Islamic empires that have followed it. As a result, the Persian in the Persianate has intertextual presence in Arabic, Turkish, Urdu, and Bengali, which in turn implies a far more interpolated presence of proto-Iranian leitmotifs from pre-Islamic deep into the Islamic periods.[35] It is precisely that Persianate world that is enriched, conflated, and further interpolated by translations reaching from the sixth-century Pahlavi rendition of *Panchatantra* into the eighth-century Arabic of Ibn al-Muqaffaʿ's *Kelilah and Dimnah* to the twentieth-century translations of Mahmoud Darwish, Pablo Neruda, or Vladimir Mayakovsky into Persian.

The link between the worlds of Persian letters and the territories of the Persianate worlds therefore maps the immediate landscapes of the expansive highways, byways, domains, and dominions of the Persian Prince. Rooted in pre-Islamic, non-Islamic, Greek, Hebrew, Sanskrit, Sassanid, Parthian/Arsacids, Hellenic-accented Seleucids, all the way back to the mythic renditions of the Achaemenids, and informed by the Zoroastrian, Manichean, and Mazdakite traditions, the idea of the Persian Prince is an unmistakably imperial trope and as such has no anxiety peculiar to postcolonial nation-states, until it begins to dissolve in postcolonial terms—a subject to which I will now turn.

TWO

The Persian Prince Comes of Age

> He is that Prince who has been expelled from his own city,
> Wandering through seas and deserts.[1]
>
> Mehdi Akhavan-e Sales,
"Qesseh-ye Shahryar-e Shahr-e Sangestan"
[The ballad of the prince of Stoneville], (1960)

> In these globalized times of accelerating technologically mediated changes, many traditional points of reference and age-old habits of thought are being re-composed, albeit in contradictory ways. Paradoxically, old power relations are not only confirmed but in many ways exacerbated in the new geo-political context. At such a time more conceptual creativity is necessary, and more theoretical courage is needed in order to bring about the leap across inertia, nostalgia, aporia and the other forms of critical stasis induced by our historical condition.[2]
>
> Rosi Braidotti, "Writing as a Nomadic Subject" (2014)

WHY BOTHER WITH THE IDEA of the "Persian Prince" when the major country that now lays claim to the social and intellectual history that gave birth to the archetype is ruled by an octogenarian fraternity of Shiʻi clerical brothers that has toppled the last monarchy, and the last Persian prince of that monarchy lives a parasitical life in the United States, far away from his own homeland? If this historical inquiry is not to be an exercise in antiquarian curiosity, albeit in an erudite academic prose, we must see the transmutation of the figure of the Persian Prince into something else, something even more archaic and yet omnipresent, something at the very archetypal root of the Persian Prince: the prophetic voice of the poet that had historically sustained it and has now been resurrected in the visionary poetics of the postcolonial Persian poet, or what in Gramsci's language he generically called "the organic intellectual." This is precisely where the demise of the institution and the dissolution of the idea of the Persian Prince epistemically yields to the prophetic voice of the rebellious poet and brings us into the fold of our current, critical, and fragile postcolony.

The rest of my story, as a result, will shift not into the relics of defeated and discredited monarchies and their outdated princes but into the rise and resurrection of the iconic figure of the poet/prophet as the voice and vision of a forgotten past coming back to haunt a sustained history. In the detailed mapping of this transmutation from the Persian Prince onto the Persian poet, I continue to take my cue from Gramsci's "Modern Prince," in which he speculates about the transmutation of the myth of Machiavelli's *Prince* into the machinery of the political party. But from that point forward, I part ways with both Machiavelli and Gramsci and bring the archetype of the Persian Prince toward the figure of the prophetic poet to navigate the formative forces of the Persianate public sphere—which extends from India to Central Asia to Iran and, from there, deeply into the sprawling territories of the Ottoman Empire.

As I conceptualize it this way, the Persian Prince moves through the Persianate history of countries and climes from the classical to the contemporary periods like melodious variations on a constant theme. The idea is both potent and malleable. While Xenophon meant his Cyrus as an ideal typical and a mirror for princes, Machiavelli's conceptualization of his Prince was proscriptive, and Gramsci's analytical, while my idea of the Persian Prince is entirely descriptive—mapping, detailing, and theorizing its amorphous disposition to both constitute political legitimacy and, paradoxically, dismantle it. I call it "Persian" as opposed to "Arab," "Greek," "Indian," or anything else in entirely nonracialized and actively deracialized terms, and only because the provenance of its rising legitimacy is definitive to the Persianate world from the Indian subcontinent to the Iranian plateau to the Mediterranean shores. From its Iranian provenance to its Indian inspirations to its Greek theorization to its Hebrew canonization, the Persian Prince dwelled on varied and multiple planes. I call it "Prince" as opposed to "Poet" or "Prophet" or "Rebel" because the prophetic, the poetic, and the rebellious dispositions of the archetype are all potential and embedded in its princely desires. In this domain the Persian Prince is polygenderous—male, female, or both or neither—a phenomenon particularly pertinent in the Persian language, for here we do not have gender-specific pronouns. It is therefore an archetype, a Weberian ideal type, or in the shape of a Platonic Form, which in Arabic and Persian we have translated as *muthul*—the plural of *mathal*, meaning "archetypal similitude." As I theorize it here, it is, in short, the most potent unit of analysis in Persianate and Islamic political thought. It is precisely for that reason that in order to detail its analytical contours I must navigate the idea through a myriad of poetic, literary, historical, and aesthetic texts and sources to flesh out its enduring parameters. This polylocality of my investigation will also help prevent taking the changing parameters of the idea as an indication of its "purity" or "impermeability." The idea is entirely permeable, syncretic, and amorphous.

From the Persian Prince to the Prophetic Poet

To come to terms with this later transformation of the idea of the Persian Prince far away from the ruling states, we too will have to overcome the crucial but limited insights of Gramsci and recall a later gestation of Machiavelli's *Prince*, decidedly different from Gramsci's, and look at the way the eminent German philosopher Ernst Cassirer (1874–1945) rearticulated it in the aftermath of the rise of German Nazism and European fascism, when he wrote his seminal (and posthumously published) text, *The Myth of the State* (1946). The insights contained in this text came our way long after Gramsci, when Cassirer had escaped the terror of the Nazis and spent the last part of his life teaching at Yale University in the United States. While in exile from Germany and with the consequences of European fascism fresh in his mind, Cassirer wrote his final book, in which he traces the emergence of the myth of the state and offers a crucial insight on Machiavelli's *Prince*, almost a decade after Gramsci's passing in 1937.

In his book, Cassirer considered Machiavelli the first European philosopher to have a clear conception of the state as a reality sui generis, a unique and unprecedented aspect of his political philosophy. Machiavelli's theory of politics, Cassirer proposes, was not immoral but amoral. He proposed that Machiavelli's theorization in *The Prince* had little to do with the figure of Cesare Borgia, whom he feared more than admired; to the degree that he did admire Borgia, it had more to do with his having revealed to him the true nature of politics: the rise of an autonomous state severed from the rest of society. What fascinated

Machiavelli, according to Cassirer, was not Cesare Borgia but *"the structure of the new state* that had been created by him."[3] Cassirer then further clarifies:

> Machiavelli was the first thinker who completely realized what this new political structure really meant. He had seen its origin and he foresaw its effects. He anticipated in his thought the whole course of the future political life of Europe. It was this realization that induced him to study the form of the new principalities with the greatest care and thoroughness. He was perfectly aware that when compared to former political theories this study was to be regarded as a certain anomaly and he apologized for the unusual course of his thought.[4]

What Cassirer had seen in Machiavelli's *Prince* was not just "the future of the political life of Europe" but also the future of the political life of the world at large that Europe had conquered and colonized. However, like most other European philosophers, Cassirer was blind to that fact.[5] Be that as it may, Cassirer's is a vastly different reading of Machiavelli's *Prince* than the one offered by Gramsci. It was this matter-of-fact and amoral (not immoral) separation of state from the rest of the lived reality of those ruled by the state that was the issue. The state had become a reality sui generis, and its interests had become an end unto themselves, separated from the commonweal, from the nation that had been falsely annexed to the state and made the chimerical construct of the nation-state. Contrary to Gramsci, who as a Marxist wanted to take over the state, Cassirer did not want to use any political party to control the state, for in the form of Nazi Germany he had already seen the monster that could emerge.

The predicament of Germany under Nazism and Europe under fascism in general were but a taste of European colonialism around the globe—as seminal theorists of colonialism like Aimé Césaire had diagnosed and theorized. Cassirer's disillusion with the very idea of the state, and thus his critical reading of Machiavelli's *Prince* (which effectively supersedes Gramsci statist reading), is the occasion when the state finally becomes a chimeric construction entirely contingent upon itself. Yet, faking rootedness in the nation to feign legitimacy, as a result, resonates very well with my post/colonial reading of the sublimation of the idea of the Persian Prince as far away from the figure of a ruling monarch and deep into the floating phantom of a prophetic poet whose very existence is ipso facto the dismantling of any state that might lay false claim to the figure of the Persian Prince—for the poet has already appropriated its archetypal provenance.

In much of the colonized world, the colonial and postcolonial state had become the replica of the monster both Machiavelli and Cassirer had seen in their respective diagnosis, covering between them almost half a millennium of European and Eurocentric history. The nations were thus effectively bifurcated from the state and going their own ways, as the state became the Leviathan that fed on itself. Here is when, in the Persianate world, the three concomitant figures of the Persian Prince, the Persian Prophet, and the Persian Poet revealed themselves to have been in fact coterminous from their very inception. The ancient Iranian poet/prophets Zoroaster, Mani, and Mazdak thus resurfaced at the roots of the archetypal construction of the Persian Prince. Much later in history, at the dawn of colonial modernity, the princely and the prophetic were subsumed under the poetic, and thus the figure of the Persian poet was resurrected outside the dynastic habitat and entered the emerging public spheres. In short, we need to pay much closer attention to the figure of the Persian poet as the focal point of where the embedded archetypes of the Persian Prince and the Persian prophet come together under European colonial duress.

In the Persianate world, the dominion of the Persian Prince proper, the rise of a succession of prominent poets began to occupy the central place of the imperial archetype in the heart of the emerging transnational public spheres, at a time when the ruling dynasties had all but lost their legitimacy. From Fatemeh Qorrat al-Ayn (circa 1814–1852) to Muhammad Iqbal (1877–1938) to Sadriddin Ayni (1878–1954) to Nima Yushij (1897–1960) to Khalilullah Khalili (1907–1987) to Abolqasem Lahuti (1887–1957) to Forough Farrokhzad (1934–1967), just to give a few towering examples from multiple countries, we are in the presence of the representatives of these rebel/poets, in their respective public spheres, now reconfigured as postcolonial nation-states. The dissemination of the figure and institution of the Persian Prince and the eventual rise of the prophetic voices of these rebel/poets coincide with the global topography of transnational public spheres and the formation of the postcolonial subject to people these nations. These prophetic voices have historically been fragmented beyond the fictive frontiers of the anticolonial nationalism of the nation-states—where the former imperial boundaries of the Persian Prince were by now the domain of the Persian poets. If these prophetic poets are brought together and to full collective consciousness, the fragmented postcolonial nations regain their shared memories in the voices of their rebellious poets. The figure of the Persian Prince was thus resurrected in the figurative disposition of the rebellious Persian poet, who began to articulate the vision of the other than the real. This resurrection early in the postcolonial period brings back the memories of the rebellious disposition of early Persian prophets of the early Islamic Iran, when revolutionary characters like Babak Khorramdin (circa 795–838), Sunpadh (thrived circa 755), and al-Muqanna' (died circa 783) had led uprisings against their Arab conquerors.[6]

There is no one definitive but multiple decisive turning points in the transmutation of the figure of the Persian Prince into the prophetic voice of the post/colonial Persian poet, when the institutional authority of the imperial archetype eventually dissolves and yields its power and authority to the revolutionary voice of the rebel/poet surfacing on the gendered public sphere of the era.[7] Sometime in the middle of the nineteenth century, two seminal figures, a minor Qajar prince and a major revolutionary poet, appeared on the tumultuous history of their homeland as two iconic voices and visages of this prophetic resurrection of the Persian Prince. If we are to look at them together, one hailing from the beleaguered Qajar aristocracy and the other from the stagnant Shi'i scholasticism, we can see where and how and why the mythic figure of the Persian Prince was now at the threshold of a new moral and normative dispensation.

Tahereh Qorrat al-Ayn (circa 1814–1852) was a poet, a liberation theologian, and a revolutionary leader from a prominent clerical family who would join the most radical revolutionary movement of her time, the mid-nineteenth-century Babi uprising, which occurred in Iran and parts of the Ottoman territories.[8] She was married off to her first cousin, as was the custom of the time, but she deeply resented the marriage and divorced her husband the first chance she had. While still in Najaf with her husband, she became attracted to the radical ideas of Shaykh Ahmad Ahsa'i (1753–1826), the leading liberation theologian of his time, and eventually joined Ali Mohammad Shirazi, known as Bab (1819–1850), who was putting a radical interpretation of Ahsa'i ideas to revolutionary work, leading an uprising against the religious establishment and the Qajar monarchy.[9] In the course of a political gathering in Northern Iran, Qorrat al-Ayn publicly unveiled herself and led a major flank of the Babi battalion against the Qajar monarchy. She was arrested and jailed and asked to repent. She did not and was executed in 1852. Just a generation before her, as indeed during and long after her, a woman like Tahereh Qorrat al-Ayn would be effectively incarcerated inside her gender and her role as a daughter and wife and mother, and condemned to a secluded and protected life to her dying day. She was not the wife of an emperor, or the daughter of a monarch. She entered, redefined, and gendered a revolutionary agenda on the platform of a public sphere effectively all by herself. In her short but extraordinary life, in her gifted poetry, in her scholastic command of a liberation theology, Tahereh Qorrat al-Ayn was the resurrection of the Persian Prince on the tumultuous battlefields of the fateful nineteenth century—furthest removed from any royal court that she sought to bring down, and yet the "queen" of a far more significant and enduring polity than the crumbling Qajar monarchy could claim. It is a fateful spectacle to see how the archetypal figure of the Persian Prince as the epitome of political authority metamorphoses in the figure of a prophetic poet, a liberation theologian, and a radical revolutionary woman like Tahereh Qorrat al-Ayn.

Tahereh Qorrat al-Ayn's male counterpart would be Jalal al-Din Mirza Qajar (1827–1872), a minor Qajar prince born to royalty but who soon emerged, in his short but effective life, as a potent revolutionary poet totally in tune with the tumultuous spirit of his age. Though the transmutation of the figure of the Persian Prince into a prophetic poet was more a symbolic and allegorical resurrection than a literal one, still in the figure of Jalal al-Din Mirza we are present in the historic moment when the Persian Prince becomes the prophetic voice of a rebellious poet. Born and raised in Tehran, Jalal al-Din Mirza was the son of Fath Ali Shah Qajar (reigned 1797–1834), who grew up bilingual, speaking Persian and French in the royal court. Judging by his exquisite command of the Persian language, he was a deeply cultivated prince who was equally at home with the reformist and revolutionary aspirations of his time extending from Iran (in fact the royal court) to Central Asia to the Caucuses to Russia and from there to the Ottoman territories and Europe. In the two almost contemporary figures of Qorrat al-Ayn and Jalal al-Din Mirza, the prototype of the Persian Prince is ushered into the revolutionary age of local, regional, and global transformations of the time.

The Persian Prince Begins to Speak in Heteroglossia

The crucial work of Jalal al-Din Mirza is his book *Nameh-ye Khosrovan*. The title of this text is of seminal importance. It literally means the "Book of Kings," so it can be translated as "The Shahnameh," alluding to Ferdowsi's classical text of the same title, with *Khosrovan* standing for "Shahs" and *Nameh* for "Nameh." *Khosrow*, which means "king," is the cognate of Kisra and Caesar. Jalal al-Din Mirza opts for the Persian word *Khosrow* to give his book a decidedly archaic tone. Much has been made of his "anti-Arab" sentiments in this book—and indeed there is a vertiginous racist sentiment that animates many similar texts of the period. But much of these references are to the Arab invasion of the Sassanid

Empire in the seventh century, and in this respect, he equates the consequences of that invasion to that of Alexander before them and the Mongols after them. What holds these three distinct events together is their invasion and occupation of Iran, not their racial distinctions from Iranians. What drives the book is an appeal to the imperial legacy of Iran and thus a bitter critique of the three crucial defeats of Iranian armies by Alexander and the Arab and Mongol conquests. Of his projected four volumes of *Nameh-ye Khosrovan*, only three were published. The first volume (1868) covers pre-Islamic history to the collapse of the Sassanid dynasty in 658 CE; the second volume (1870) the Tahirids to the Khwarazmids; and the third volume (1871) the Mongol invasion to the Zands, the dynasty just before his own. The fourth volume as a result would have been about the Qajars; perhaps his silence was meant as the tabula rasa of the rising revolutionary spirit of his time.[10]

In addition to being paired with Qorrat al-Ayn, the same Jalal al-Din Mirza should also be placed next to another key transformative figure, Mirza Fath Ali Akhundzadeh (1812–1878), slightly his senior, a towering transnational public intellectual, a pioneering playwright, and in this particular case the author of a seminal text called *Maktubat*, in which we have precisely the evidence of this institutional transformation of the archetypal figure of the Persian Prince into the prose and politics of a new gestation. Born and raised in Shaki (known until 1968 as Nukha), Azerbaijani, Mirza Fath Ali Akhundzadeh emerged as a leading intellectual of the time, thriving in his native Azeri and literary Persian, as well as his impeccably fluent Russian, which he commanded with remarkable ease. We know that Akhundzadeh's "mother was descended from an African who had been in the service of Nader Shah, and consciousness of this African element in his ancestry served to give Akhundzadeh a feeling of affinity with his great Russian contemporary, Pushkin."[11] His biographical provenance, cultural pluralism, and deeply rooted Persian literary humanism all point toward the figure of Akhundzadeh, who was a seminal intellectual in Azerbaijan, the Caucuses, Central Asia, and ultimately Russia as the epicenter of his life and upbringing. The fateful encounter between Jalal al-Din Mirza Qajar in Iran and Akhundzadeh in Azerbaijan opens up the Persian cosmopolis into the active dominion for the resurrection of the Persian Prince in the towering figures of the emerging public intellectuals, poets, prose stylists, and dramatists who were recasting the politics of their age. Geographically we are in the familiar territories of the Persian Prince, where the Qajar, the Russian, and the Ottoman domains interpolate. But the political and revolutionary sentiments of the age are all evident in the emerging transnational public spheres among these empires and far from the royal courts.

Akhundzadeh's *Maktubat* (Correspondences, 1865) is his major literary work, which consists of a series of fictitious letters exchanged between two imaginary princes. The provenances of these two princes are crucial for us to recall here—an Indian Prince in Iran and a Persian Prince living in Egypt. Equally important is the heteroglossia of the whole fictious performance, where in the Turkish version of the letters Akhundzadeh says he is not the author but the translator of the original exchanges that were in Persian, and in the Persian version he says the original book was in Turkish! The exchanges were reported to have been between the Indian prince, Kama al-Dowleh, and the Persian prince, Jalal al-Dowleh, and the text is a powerful denunciation of religion and politics of the time. According to the scholars of this text:

> His [Akhundzadeh's] intention was to have the letters published in both languages in Paris, with the help of [his colleague and collaborator] Mirza Yusuf Khan; the Turkish edition was to be distributed in Turkey and Egypt, and the Persian, in Iran, Central Asia and India. The plan was never executed, and the Russian translation of the letters, made in 1874 by the Orientalist Adolf Berge, was rejected by all the publishers to whom it was sent in St. Petersburg. The fame of the letters seems to have been restricted in the lifetime of their author to those individuals, chiefly in Iran, to whom he sent handwritten copies.[12]

By using this fictitious epistolary plot, Akhundzadeh could speak critically of the status quo in the form of these four letters, three by the fictitious Indian Prince Kamal al-Dowleh, "the son of Aurangzeb," writing from Tabriz in 1863 to the Persian Prince Jalal-Dowleh, who resides in Egypt, and the one letter he receives in response.[13] Perhaps intentionally, all these dates and characters are entirely ahistorical and Akhundzadeh kept adding to and appending the letters.[14] The result is a powerful epistolary work of fiction in which two Persian/Indian princes bring Iran, India, and Egypt together and recast them as critical public spheres as they seek to save their respective homelands. Keep in mind that the author of all these letters is an Iranian-Azerbaijani-Russian public intellectual actively engaged in reimagining the very figure of the Persian Prince. The allegorical figure of the Persian Prince is being actively recast in these writings into the figure of a progressive critical thinker and revolutionary activist seeking to liberate their homelands in three interrelated loci: in India against the British, in Iran against the Qajars, and in Egypt against the Ottomans.

In 1870 Jalal al-Din Mirza sends his *Nameh-ye Khosrovan* to Fath Ali Akhundzadeh, and this marks the beginning of an enduring friendship. The relationship between Akhundzadeh and Jalal al-Din Mirza as two prominent intellectuals of their time in effect replicates the relationship between the two fictive princes in *Maktubat*, to the degree that some had falsely assumed that in fact the historical Qajar prince Jalal al-Din Mirza was the model for the fictious Jalal-Dowleh. In this exchange between Akhundzadeh and Jalal al-Din Mirza, a number of crucial languages of the region come together—Persian, Turkish, Russian, and Arabic—marking the multicultural heteroglossia in which the Persian Prince is now actively at home as the archetypal figure pivots from the royal habitat at the court into the battlefields of anticolonial and anti-tyrannical modernity.

The relationship between Jalal al-Din Mirza and Akhundzadeh points to something even more crucial, the symbiotic relationship between two seminal periodicals of the early Constitutional Period: *Molla Nasraddin*, published in Azeri first in Tiflis (1906–1917) and then in Tabriz (1921) and Baku (1922–1933), and the other, *Sur-e Esrafil*, published in Persian in Tehran (1907–1909), and then in Switzerland (1909). The dialectic of Azeri-Persian (deeply informed by Russian and Arabic) that happens between *Molla Nasraddin* and *Sur-e Esrafil* (which often mirror each other) points to a crucial configuration of the decidedly transnational public sphere upon which the transfiguration of the figure of Persian Prince into a rebel/poet takes place and surfaces. Here is where the term "Persian" or "Persianate" reveals itself as entirely non-ethnic and freely floating from East to West, where the historic provenance of the Persian cosmopolis is somewhere entirely amorphous—somewhere ranging from the Indian subcontinent to Central Asia, the Caucuses, Iran, and the Ottoman territories. These two periodicals fed on each other and reciprocated each other's synergy. The relationship was not imperial or territorial but entirely syncretic and aterritorial, porous and mobile, bypassing censorship and dodging the political persecution by Iranian, Ottoman, and Russian authorities alike. This points to the parapublic disposition of the sphere that imperceptibly held them together. The space was dialogical and included hidden Russian and an allusion to Arabic. This heteroglossia animated much of the Central Asian and the Caucasus interactions with Iran and its revolutionary dynamics. That makes the public and parapublic spheres where the public intellectual emerges inherently cosmopolitan in tune with the Persian cosmopolis it now politically inflected and replicated in Central Asia, in the Caucuses, in Egypt and the rest of the Arab world, and in the Indo-Pakistani domains.

This historic metempsychosis of the figure of the Persian Prince—from the habitual abode of the royal court into a sojourner of truth on borderlines of languages and lexicons, countries and climes, nations and their narrations, their proses and politics—is where the prophetic soul of the visionary poet who had initially informed the archetype comes back to reimagine its worldly habitat. A *dyadic* disposition now takes over the idea of the Persian Prince somewhere between nations and the states that lay false claim to them, between every two languages that come to inform the poet of revolt against tyranny and colonialism, as the ancient archetype altogether abandons the ruling regimes of power and reenters the collective unconscious of the polity, the commonweal, the rebellious nations. The *monadic* presence of the Persian Prince at the heart of varied and successive empires now collapses, and in the dyadic domain of the postcolonial nation-states altogether exits the ruling states and comes to the public and parapublic spheres and resumes its prophetic voice of the rebel/poet. In this dyadic state, the Persian Prince is reminded of its repressed poetic voice and vision that had hitherto, in its monadic state, been delegated to the court poet to articulate and theorize. The prince and the patron become one and the same as they both exit the royal court and join the precarity of the people they once ruled, and thus deprive the ruling regimes of any pretense to political legitimacy. The rebellious poet now retrieves that prophetic voice, and the Persian Prince begins to speak a vastly different prose and enact a diametrically oppositional politics.

The Persian Prince at the Intersection of Race, Gender, and Ethnicity

As you can see, I am now carrying the archetype of the Persian Prince across and through multiple empires, from the pre-Islamic to the Islamic to the post-Islamist eras, into the colonial encounter with European imperialism, and down to our own postcolonial times. Because of the necessarily *longue durée* spectrum of my project, in both the general and the specific sense of the term, before and after the French Annales, the idea of the Persian Prince as a result has to be tested through a variety of conceptual clarifications. The rise of the rebel/poet on a gendered and transnational public sphere, as I argue in this book to have been predicated on the archetypal premise of the Persian Prince, requires an immediate attention to the epistemic foregrounding of what I mean by the "Persian Prince."

Because I predicate the term "Persian Prince" on Machiavelli's Prince and Gramsci's "Modern Prince" and wish to extend the idea into the much larger Iranian and Islamic contexts, both the term "Persian" and the term "prince" require a clarification as to how I use them. Upon our entry into the colonial and postcolonial worlds, one context exudes ethnicity with "the Persians" and the other the gender-specific "prince," as opposed to "princess." Right from the outside, it is imperative to de-ethnicize and degender these two terms—for I use the term "Persian Prince" as a reference to an archetype, a myth, as Gramsci would say, an allegory, a literary trope—not a gendered human being, a person, a man, a woman, or anything else in between. It is therefore neither a term of ethnic designation, as opposed to Arab, Turkish, Indian, or Chinese for that matter, nor a gendered monarch—man, woman, or otherwise. When both Machiavelli and Gramsci were theorizing the idea of "the prince," they were not referring to an Italian prince or a European prince or, indeed, a Persian Prince. Nor did they mean a male prince or a female princess—and indeed neither do I. Gramsci altogether argued for the transformation of the figure of the prince into the organism of a political party, and I intend to expand upon his argument into uncharted postcolonial domains, where the archetype of the Persian Prince first disseminates into the public sphere and then resurrects into the figure of the poet-prophet. Moreover, the terms *shahzadeh* or *shahryar*, the words for "prince" in Persian (into which in fact Machiavelli's *Prince* has been translated), is gender-neutral and can refer to either a prince or princess. In Persian, we do not have gender-specific pronouns. This is one of the glories of Persian language, that we do not know if the subject is male, female, or anything in between. This is not to deny the fact that the overwhelming majority of Persian monarchs and princes have been male but rather to point out that the term "Persian Prince" as I use it here is an archetypal construct, a potent political myth, not a gendered person. I intend for the term to refer to a persona, an archaic mask, not a person, male or female.

The same holds true for the term "Persian." In my book *The World of Persian Literary Humanism* (2012), I radically altered the Orientalized, ethnicized, nationalistic, and essentialist reading of the term. In this book I have mapped out, in extensive historical and literary detail, four phases in the reading of the word "Persian" and have systematically de-Orientalized and de-ethnicized it. I begin by demonstrating how the earliest implications of the word "Persian" indeed begin with a sense of *ethnos* early in the Islamic period, when tribal Arab patrimonialism invoked similar responses from their Iranian subjects; then turn into *logos* about the time of Ferdowsi, when the primacy of the Persian language asserts itself; before it becomes *ethos* at the time of Saʿdi, when the ethical propensity of Persian literature overcomes its linguistic disposition; and ultimately into what I have called *chaos*, in the aftermath of the encounter with the European colonial modernity and the rise of a postcolonial public sphere. This dynamic and organic reading of the word "Persian" leaves little room for ahistorical appropriation of it into ethnic nationalism or, conversely, Iranophobic reactions to it.

Today the rampant spread of ethnic nationalism has deeply compromised our understanding of Islamic (including Arabic, Persian, Turkic, Indian) cultures in their irretrievably pluralistic, nonbinary, and interpolated historical provenances. Ethnic nationalism is of course a categorically colonial bourgeois legacy reflecting back on early Islamic history, distorting its innate and dynamic forces and factors, its own multiple and successive empires over much of the civilized world. Throughout my scholarship, I have done my share of disentangling such false binaries between Persians and Arabs; or Arabs, Persians, and Turks; or Arabs, Persians, Turks, and Indians; or, even more egregiously, between Sunnis and Shiʿis. These much later racialized binaries have affected our understanding of such crucial episodes in early Islamic history as the Shuʿubiyyah movement, which has been falsely racialized and read as a sign of ethnic hostilities between Persians and Arabs or else between "Aryans" and "Semites"! These were and remain all Orientalist phantasies of their own dominant racial and racist theories. One can add the even thornier question of trying to parse the Turkic, Persian, and Islamic dimensions of such seminal dynasties as the Ghaznavids, the Ottomans, or the Safavids, or Sanskrit and Persian cosmopolitanism. Retrieving and mapping out the historical vicissitudes of an archetype like the Persian Prince is categorically irrelevant to such anxieties.

My use of the term "Persian" in "Persian Prince" relies on a far more complicated understanding of the term I have already spent a whole book explaining—in which the word becomes radically de-ethnicized and deracialized and revealed as a floating signifier. My understanding of the Shuʿubiyyah movement, for example, is not in ethnic terms at all—that Persians or Iranians, or "Aryans" (as some Orientalists even put it), were revolting against Arabs, or "Semites." To me the Shuʿubiyyah movement was the rise of a pluralist and cosmopolitan culture based in Baghdad that included but was not limited to Iranians. It brought together Arabs, Iranians, Turks, and their respective Zoroastrian, Jewish, Christian, and Muslim literary heritage, prose stylists, and poets into a revolutionary effervescence. As such, it was expressed against the remnants of not just the tribal patrimonialism of the pre-Islamic and early Umayyad periods but also the aristocratic elitism of the Sassanids and the Byzantines. The Abbasid period saw the height of the Shuʿubiyyah movement not because of any "Persian influence" but because of the intensification of the urbanization of the powerful empire, for which reason Baghdad, their capital, was the epicenter of the movement. Meanwhile, the Turkic, Mongol, and Indian elements came together to recast from the Ghaznavids and Ilkhanids periods all the way to the Ottomans, the Safavids, and the Mughals, which had their own distinct signature on Islamic political thought, with markedly syncretic forces among Indian, Islamic, and Iranian elements. One might even go further into Maghrib and see similar and additional syncretic forces in action in North Africa and the Iberian Peninsula. My articulation of the archetype of the Persian Prince is therefore not at the expanse of any of these factors but seeks to add an entirely neglected (or else falsely ethnicized) political force, in manner and matter, normative rulership and moral imagination. When Machiavelli and Gramsci after him theorized "the Prince," no one accused them that their theorization was glorifying or even privileging Italy and disregarding the French or the Germans or the English. They were theorizing an archetype, a "myth," as Gramsci would later say. So do I plan to do in this book with the idea of the Persian Prince.

There are multiple discursive, literary, aesthetic, and analytical paradigms, ranging from India to Iran to Ottoman to Arab frames of reference, that explain the ideological foregrounding of Muslim empires, none of which is at the expense of the others. To understand the ways in which Islamic empires, from the Abbasids to the Saljuqids to the Mughals to the Safavids to the Ottomans, evolved and held on to their dominions, we need to consider key aspects of their political rule: their apparatus of legitimacy, their varied and interpolated political cultures. My contention here is not to dismiss or diminish the significance of Arabic sources, Arab dynasties, or sources of legitimacy emerging from Arab and Islamic thoughts—or from India, for that matter, or the Mongol or Ottoman empire. My references to the Persian Prince and Persian sources or pre-Islamic Iranian lineage are all to propose a crucial force in our understanding of Islamic history as Islamic history. Whatever pre-Islamic ideas—Iranian, Egyptian, Indian, Greek—entered the Islamic world were all effectively Islamicized in a much larger frame of moral and political imagination. There has been an enormous emphasis on Arabic sources over the past decades in understanding Muslim empires, and justly so, and I have done my own share of work in this field from the earliest stages of my own scholarship. But here in this particular project, I am after something else, after documenting and arguing a missing link, and then bringing that link to our own contemporary time as I investigate the plight of the category of the Persian Prince in the colonial and postcolonial periods. In mapping the contours of a Persian cosmopolis or a Persianate world within the larger Islamic frame of reference, this idea needs careful consideration.

That brings us to the crucial question of gender, which is much more important than the mere presence of a few powerful women among the ruling elites in the Islamic and Persian worlds. Through such recent works of scholarship as those of Leslie Peirce in her *Empress of the East: How a European Slave Girl Became Queen of the Ottoman Empire* (2017) or Ruby Lal's *Empress: The Astonishing Reign of Nur Jahan* (2018), we have solid evidence of the fact that some women from elite families occasionally commanded enormous political power in the Islamic worlds. But the far more serious question of gendered politics must be considered in this examination of the figure of the Persian Prince. I have brought attention to the Saljuq queen Tarkhan Khatun in my book *Truth and Narrative: The Untimely Thoughts of Ayn al-Qudat al-Hamadhani* (1999) and to the revolutionary figure of Tahereh Qorrat al-Ayn in my *Shi'ism: A Religion of Protest* (2011). It is this latter figure that should be given a more prominent presence in the formation of a gendered transnational public sphere where the transformation of the archetypal figure of the Persian Prince into the public sphere and the persona of the poet/prophet—and not to "the political party," as Gramsci presumed for his own particular political reasons—assumes catalytic significance. The contours of the gendered politics of this public sphere are where the precise dialogical nature of this transmutation becomes evident. It is precisely this dialogically gendered disposition of the public sphere in the aftermath of the encounter with European colonial modernity that will recast the category of "the Persian Prince." As an archetypal figure, as a result, and as I intend to theorize the figure in this book, "the Persian Prince" is not gendered, but the transnational disposition of the public sphere on which the figure of the Persian Prince is resurrected into a poet/prophet is most emphatically gendered.

What further complicates the figure of "the Persian Prince" is the gendered disposition of the polity that emerges in the aftermath of its encounter with European colonial modernity. In *Shi'ism: A Religion of Protest* (2011), I detailed how the post-Safavid public sphere from which the postcolonial nation eventually emerged had become polygendered, most emphatically in the nineteenth century, through such revolutionary figures as Tahereh Qorrat al-Ayn (circa 1814–1852). To her exceptionally important figure, which I have already detailed, we need to add the importance of other crucial figures like Taj al-Saltaneh (1883–1936) and Bibi Khanom Astarabadi (1858–1921), two pioneering women's rights advocates. But at the same time, the archetype of the Persian Prince should not be reduced to the heteronormativity of a bourgeois gendered morality either. The archetype of the Persian Prince is not gender-specific. It is a floating signifier, in race, gender, and ethnicity. It is a chameleon, a myth, an archetype. The multiracial, multiethnic, and decidedly non-heteronormative gendered domains of the Persian Prince point to the pluralistic, always multivariant disposition of the archetype as it emerges from its archaic certainties and steps into the modernity of its colonial encounters.

The "Withouts" and the "Returnees": The Nomadic Prince of the Persian Gulf

The archetype of the Persian Prince spoke multiple languages as it roamed over a vast territory from India to Central Asia to Iran to Ottoman territories. The heteroglossia of the Persian Prince, definitive to its universalizing proclivities, has always been embedded in the emerging sites of the Persian cosmopolis, which by this time was squarely evident in Central Asia, not just in the Indo-Persian or any other exclusive domain. The idea of the Persian cosmopolis must always be considered ambulatory, mobile, and even "nomadic" in the sense of cultivating new and untested territories of knowing and being, a dialectic of identity and alterity that has never remained constant. Initially we can think of this nomadic disposition of the Persian cosmopolis in the course of its encounter with colonial modernity in Ibn Khaldun's terms in his *Muqaddimah*, in which he proposes a dialectic of social formations between Bedouin and sedentary cultures through which each civilization cultivates the particularities of its *Asabiyyah*, or collective consciousness.[15] But we must then move from Ibn Khaldun toward a conception of the "nomadic," which is more in the sense of the syncretic and rebellious disposition of cultural formations and moral imaginaries that defy and dismantle stable and mechanical solidarities. The epicenter of the Persian cosmopolis has historically moved from Central Asia to Greater Khorasan to what is today Tajikistan, Afghanistan, Iran, and the Indian subcontinent, and from there westward toward Baghdad and contemporary Iraq, then north into Asia

Minor, modern Turkey, and the Caucuses. At the dawn of the Muslim encounter with European colonial modernity, the Persian cosmopolis was more established in Mughal India than it was in Safavid Persia, in which scholastic Shi'ism had become dominant. This ambulatory conception of the Persian cosmopolis reveals its historic organicity far better than assuming it sedentary and exclusive to any particular imperial or postcolonial domains.

A quick look at some seminal poets and their locations and spheres of influence with lasting political consequences into the nineteenth century should make this ambulatory disposition clear. If we take only the iconic poets on the wider Persian cosmopolis in mind and begin with Nur ad-Din Abd al-Rahman Jami (1414–1492) in Herat, and move to Abdul-Qadir Bedil (1642–1720), Mirza Asadullah Khan Ghalib (1797–1869), and Muhammad Iqbal (1877–1938) in the Indian subcontinent, we come down to Tahereh Qorrat al-Ayn (circa 1814–1852) in Qajar and the Ottoman territories and Sadriddin Ayni (1878–1954) in Central Asia, at which point we must include literary pioneers and essayists like Zeyn al Abedin Maragheh'i (1840–1910) in the Russian, Ottoman, and Iranian territories, Mirza Habib Isfahani (1835–1893) and Mirza Aqa Khan Kermani (1854–1897) in Istanbul, revolutionary activists like Seyyed Jamal al-Afghani (1838–1897) all over the Muslim world and in Europe, Mirza Malkam Khan (1834–1908) in London, and poets like Abolqasem Lahuti (1887–1957) in Iran and Central Asia, a trajectory that brings us to literary scholars like Hassan Taqizadeh (1878–1970) and Hossein Kazem Zadeh Iranshahr (1884–1962) in Berlin, to literary giants like Sadegh Hedayat (1903–1951) in Mumbai and Paris, down to the earliest pioneers of cinema like Khan Bahadur Ardeshir Irani (1886–1969) in Mumbai, and finally to towering literary scholars like the Egyptian Abdelwahab Azzam (1894–1959), who devoted his fruitful life to introducing the Arab world to the masterpieces of Persian poetry. This ambulatory spacing through and around the world of Persian literary humanism maps the contours of where the Persian poetic intuition of transcendence meets its fresh worldly challenges.

This ambulatory disposition is all preliminary to the peripatetic lives of an entire generation of travelers from the four corners of the Persian cosmopolis who traveled across the globe and kept a detailed account of what they saw and what they thought. Their mobile lives and musings were the definition of the nomadic lives they led and the monumental body of syncretic prose they produced. In *Reversing the Colonial Gaze: Persian Travelers Abroad* (2020), I studied more than a dozen of these travelers and detailed how their discipline of thought or quest for truth outside the boundaries of nation-states had generated a provocative new prose. I challenged the conventional assumption that these travelers "went to Europe" and demonstrated, chapter and verse, that they were in fact going around the world (including but not limited to Europe). It was the nomadic disposition of their emerging thoughts that was of paramount importance to me. Earlier, in *Iran Without Borders: Towards a Critique of the Postcolonial Nation* (2016), I had mapped out the fact that the very idea of "Iran" as a nation-state was dreamed outside its current borders, in a globalized Persian cosmopolis that could not be confined to any given country. In *Persophilia: Persian Culture on the Global Scene* (2015), I had also detailed the contours of the transnational public sphere on which European philosophers, artists, poets, painters, mystics, and literary scholars had made the Persian cosmopolis integral to the European bourgeois public sphere. This was a two-way street, I argued, the result of which was the circularity of the globalized labor and capital being translated into the circulatory disposition of the public sphere they had generated. In subsequent generations, varied and potent poets like Vladimir Mayakovsky from Russia, Faiz Ahmed Faiz from Pakistan, Nazem Hekmat from Turkey, Pablo Neruda from Chile, and Aimé Césaire from Martinique all came together to craft a body of poetic voices that were at home in a homeless world. In this world the indivisible "monadic" European subject of Leibniz had become a mere imperial construct, a fiction, as Gilles Deleuze would later argue, revealing its far more "nomadic" alterity, where the received worlds are not all the existing worlds that give birth to stable selves. This is not to fetishize nomadism but to borrow the metaphor to mark the homelessness of the postcolonial subject and to explore infinite possibilities outside the limited European philosophy.

The prospect of this nomadic subject growing on the fertile grounds of the enduring archetype of the Persian Prince takes us closest to what Deleuze and Félix Guattari theorize as nomadic, both literally and figuratively, as distinct from the royally sedate mode of knowing and being, which is far more transitory than stable. The condition of nomadic knowing and being is obviously anxiety-ridden, and uncanny, where identity is contingent on alterity and where the familiar constantly becomes foreign, as the foreign becomes familiar. There is no sense of fixed belonging here; all that was territorial has become deterritorialized, and characters are composite and cultures crisscross. Deleuze and Guattari detailed this nomadic subject in *Nomadology: The War Machine* (1986). But it is in the works of another eminent philosopher that the concept achieves its most detailed treatment.

The gifted and iconoclastic feminist philosopher Rosi Braidotti has in such seminal works as *Nomadic Subjects: Embodiment and Sexual Difference in Contemporary Feminist Theory* (1994) and *Transpositions: On Nomadic Ethics* (2006) dwelled on sustainable subjectivity as a condition of flux, of becoming and overcoming. Her insights are of immense importance in understanding the condition of nomadic subjectivity far beyond her own immediate concerns. In Braidotti nomadic theory, drawing on Deleuze, Foucault, and Luce Irigaray, among others, Braidotti engages with issues of sexual difference and embodied subjectivity and the all-too-crucial issue of post-secular citizenship. In her effectively deterritorialized reconceptualization of being human, Braidotti seeks modalities of life force located somewhere in between territories. Her notion of nomadic subjects thrives on alterity instead of identity. As she puts it succinctly: "My lifelong engagement in the project of nomadic subjectivity has been partly motivated by the conviction that, in these globalized times of accelerating technologically mediated changes, many traditional points of reference and age-old habits of thought are being re-composed, albeit in contradictory ways. Paradoxically, old power relations are not only confirmed but in many ways exacerbated in the new geo-political context."[16] Braidotti thus advocates for "conceptual creativity" and "theoretical courage" in order to detect the transformation of our subjectivities. "The philosopher in me believes that a new alliance between philosophy, the arts and science is a crucial building block for this qualitative shift of perspective. The writer in me, on the other hand, continues to muse about the complex ways in which the imaginary both propels and resists in-depth transformations."[17]

This is all music to the ears of a postcolonial subject who is the product of a colonial condition that has experienced such lives long before it occurred to the European philosopher of the nomadic subject. On the colonial edges of European modernity that has now finally hit the cul-de-sac of nomadism, these lived experiences begin with the fateful calamity of encounter with the European conquest of time and space on their broken back. In my reading of nomadic subjects, they dwell on renegade texts, texts that do not belong to any particular discipline, field of study, or territory of libraries that are easily identifiable, for they are forming their own *overworlds* on conflating parapublic spheres. These overworlds are so visible they cannot be seen, for we habitually assimilate them backward to the world we already see and know. In these overworlds, the postcolonial subject on the site of the transnational parapublic sphere is ipso facto nomadic.

It is on the deterritorialized premise of this nomadic subject formation that I propose that the transmutation of the Persian Prince into the post/colonial rebel/poet takes place and effectively dwells and thrives. I would posit that this condition of nomadic subjectivity, as Braidotti has ably theorized, is in a constant state of flux and was becoming evident on its colonial sites long before it was theorized on its advanced capitalist stages. The colonial subject was desubjected from the get-go, for we were objectified (like our minerals and archeological relics) to be the knowable world to the European knowing subject. On the nomadic fact and imaginary of our colonial desubjection, we were always becoming something else, something other than ourselves, something outside ourselves. As I argued in my *Corpus Anarchicum: Political Protest, Suicidal Violence, and the Making of the Posthuman Body* (2012), the posthuman body is the condition of subjectivity here where our fragmented agency lacked a body to inhabit. On the colonial site the nomadic subject has always thrived on this condition of precarity. We did not have to wait for the condition of advanced capitalism at its fictive centers for that precarity or composite disposition of the knowing and conquering subject to finally reveal itself. Both the deterritorialized and nomadic subject were the very state of our coloniality. The subjective bricolage that is just beginning to be theorized on its European philosophical premises had been definitive to the predicament of the post/colonial subject. We did not have to wait for the Holocaust to realize that the European subject was a disastrous proposition. We lived that holocaust in the incremental and global disposition of the European colonial conquest of our worlds.

Our historically desubjected subjectivity exposes the systematicity of the epistemic violence that has been perpetrated on any and all notions of totality, as they deterritorialized and reterritorialized in and out of their contexts. The evidence of this precarity, this nomadic subjectivity upon which the Persian Prince becomes aware of its prophetic voice and altogether abandons the royal court, are what in my work I have called *renegade texts*—texts such as José Martí's "Our America" (1891), W. E. B. Du Bois's *The Souls of Black Folk* (1903), George Padmore's *How Britain Rules Africa* (1936), Muhammad Iqbal's *What Should Then Be Done O People of the East; Traveller* (1936), Aimé Césaire's *Discourse on Colonialism* (1955), James Baldwin's *Notes of a Native Son* (1955), Frantz Fanon's *Wretched of the Earth* (1961), Jalal Al-e Ahmad's *Gharbzadegi* (1962), Malcolm X's *Autobiography* (1965), Edward Said's *Orientalism* (1978), and V. Y. Mudimbe's *Invention of Africa* (1988). Such renegade texts are the living memories of the precarity, of the nomadic whereabouts, of our subjectivities.

Here we see how the advent of colonial modernity, the unfolding national sovereignty, and the resurrection of the Persian Prince in the figure of the post/colonial poetic persona all come together to configure the schemata of the rebel/poet as the "unacknowledged legislator" of history, though not in a romantic but in fact in a very realistic sense. The formative disposition of the Persian Prince in the classical period is a crucial foregrounding for this later transformation. The figure of the Persian Prince therefore has both a period of gestation for its formative rise and a period of resurrection in its postcolonial phase. The rise of the Persian Prince thereby extends from the pre-Islamic into the Islamic period, while it is in the course of the Muslim encounter with colonial modernity that the archetype loses its institutional legitimacy and dissipates into the public sphere, and definitive to that domain, it resurrects into the figure of the rebel/poet. Although the Persian cosmopolis was divided into multiple dynastic empires, the postcolonial Persianate space divides into multiple nation-states, and thus the organicity of the Persian poet begins to disassemble into Afghan, Pakistani, Iranian, or Tajik poets. But even thus fragmented, still the figure of the Persian poet appeals to the same inaugural humanity that the mythic Keyumars had initiated—the first man, the first king, the first prophet. In his or her poetic voice, the Persian poet reenacts that inaugural moment. The distant echoes of this inaugural prophetic voice inform the organicity of the postcolonial poet in whatever postcolonial boundary he or she may find his or her voice.

What I am proposing here in effect is the fusion of the two seminal Gramscian ideas of "political party" and "organic intellectual" into the resurrection of the figure of the Persian Prince as the "Modern Prince" as the rebel/poet recollecting the prophetic voice and visage that was evident in the originary figure of the Persian Prince as the genesis of the archetype—though the crucial warning of Cassirer casts the poetic voice outside the institutional power of the ruling states. In other words, these turns from Machiavelli to Gramsci to Cassirer enable us to see the organicity of the political authority of the Persian Prince rooted in not entirely the political domain but the metaphysical provenance of the polity the prince reclaims, and thus the proclivity for the talismanic power of poetry or poetic prose and the tendency toward the archaic aura of "pure Persian"—an entirely liturgical presupposition rather than factual evidence. With the dissolution and resurrection of the Persian Prince into the prophetic voice of the politically engaged poet, something even more radical takes place in the territorial domain of their subjectivity, for it becomes so radically aterritorial that the term "Persianate worlds" (in plural) will have to roam from India to Iran to

Central Asia to the Caucuses to the Ottoman territories, and thus become completely mobile, polyphonic, and ultimately nomadic. Here, therefore, we must abandon the sedentary and territorial politics of Machiavelli, Gramsci, and Cassirer and turn to the eminent theorist of the nomadic subject, Rosi Braidotti. The crucial move from Machiavelli to Gramsci becomes even more radical in the move from Gramsci first to Cassirer and finally to Braidotti.

The nomadic subjectivity of Braidotti, however, has a colonial blind spot, a vision of the subaltern of the subaltern—again to turn to Gramsci for one of his seminal ideas—of which she is unaware and for which the faded figure of the Bidoons in the Persian Gulf areas is the most compelling case. Who are the Bidoons? Bidoons are "non-citizens," or citizens without citizenship, or "illegal residents," a whole spectrum of oxymoronic designations referring to men and women who have fallen deeply into the cracks of postcolonial nation-state formations. The Bidoons (short for "Bidoon Jinsiya," meaning "without nationality" in Arabic), we are told by officials paying attention to these homeless people, "are a stateless Arab minority in Kuwait who were not included as citizens at the time of the country's independence or shortly thereafter."[18] The term and the fact to which it refers, however, extend far beyond the tiny state of Kuwait or the ethnized assumption of their being "Arab" and spread far and wide into the farthest corners of the Persian Gulf, the Arabian Sea, and the Indian Ocean, and thus include Iranian, Indian, African, Pilipino, Sri Lankan (all of them in quotation marks), and a whole spectrum of other "guest laborers" who lack citizenship in any specific postcolonial nation-state, of which Kuwait is a prime example here. "The situation of Bidoon in Kuwait," we read in the same report, "is only one manifestation of a regional problem, with 500,000 people believed to be Bidoon across the Gulf region." Even that number, 500,000, is not entirely reliable—for the condition of being "Bidoon" extends to the oxymoronic designation of "stateless citizens" or "illegal residents" being applied to all of them. These stateless men and women are simply called "Bidoon," literally "without," meaning "without nationality." But they are more than "without nationality," they are entirely "without"—they have become an absolute and irrevocable *preposition*. They are without identity, ipseity, alterity, personhood.

To these Bidoons we can also add a similar group known as the Muʿavedin (the Returnees). These are the Iraqi citizens whom the ruling state in Iraq had considered Iranians and forced to return to Iran, while in Iran they were considered Iraqis and treated as refugees, and they were mostly bilingual in Arabic and Persian. These posthuman bodies, if we are to use Braidotti's language, referred to as "the Withouts" or "the Returnees," are the human debris of colonial conquests, manufactured borderlines, and postcolonial nation-building projects. They are in fact the return of the repressed of the colonial conditions, where humanity at large are all and all remain as Bidoons and Muʿavedin, fallen in between cracks, nomadic in not only a literal but also, even more compellingly, an allegorical sense.

As it has been theorized from Deleuze to Braidotti, the philosophical articulation of nomadic subjectivity is predicated on a mode of deterritorialization that is here evident literally on the colonial ground zero, with the Bidoons and the Muʿavedin as its prime examples. Historically, the location of the Persian cosmopolis and the knowing subjects it has enabled has never been sedentary but ambulatory on the borders of Iran and its environs, between Iran and the Indian subcontinent, or Iran and Central Asia, or Iran and the Caucuses, or Iran and the Ottoman territories. The Persianate world has always been mobile and circumambulatory, porous and interlaced. Today, the ground zero of that world is in the Persian Gulf region and particularly in the migrant and stateless laborer roaming from South India to East Africa to the coastal towns and harbors of the Persian Gulf. Stripped of all its royal pretenses, and roaming as Agamben's *homo sacer* in a nomadic world beyond and through any and all borders, the Persian Prince today dwells around the waters of the Persian Gulf, inhabiting the deterritorialized posthuman bodies of the stateless migrant laborer, for they are "Without" and the "Returnees," the homeless souls, who are, like the *Dead Souls* (1842) of Gogol's masterpiece, alive but not living, present but absent, just like Palestinians who do not exist in their own homeland. The People of Without, or the People who have Returned from somewhere to nowhere, nomadic in the very quintessence of their non-being. From the mighty palaces of kings and sultans to the prophetic voice of the rebel/poets to the sinking boats of refugees, the deterritorialized nomadic subjectivity of the Persian Prince has mapped out its prolonged and persistent political history.

By the time we get to our designation of the nomadic subject, we notice that a crucial pattern has emerged: the systematic and historical transformation of the Persian Prince from a *monadic* figure of its archetypal royal provenance into a *dyadic* disposition, where at the moment of its encounter with colonial modernity it resurrects as a prophetic poet overcoming its royal configuration, and ultimately into a *nomadic* sojourner of political truth at home in no habitat. The same monadic, dyadic, and nomadic triangulation might also be detected and suggested as operative in the three figures of the *prince*, the *prophet*, and the *poet*, that the imperial archetype has traversed vicariously through these figures and keeps them morally alert and normatively apocalyptic. I have already identified the *monadic* phase with Zoroastrianism, the *dyadic* with Manicheaism, and in its subversive disposition the *nomadic* with Mazdakism. I can now further add that when I use this terminology, I am thinking through specific Persian concepts corresponding to these terms so that by "monadic" we understand *yeganeh*, by "dyadic" *doganeh*, and by "nomadic" *biganeh*. *Ganeh* or *guneh* here means "kind" or "species," so *yeganeh* means one of a kind, *doganeh* two of a kind or binary, and *biganeh* "without match," which is why in modern Persian it means "stranger." The monadic (*yeganeh*), dyadic (*doganeh*), and nomadic (*biganeh*) trajectories of the prototype of the Persian Prince, as I propose here, have deeply rooted Iranian predicates in Zoroastrian and its Manichean and Mazdakite offshoots of the First Prophet, the First Human, the First and Archetypal Being. While the archaic origin of the idea of the Persian Prince was monadic, its dualistic offshoot in Manichaeism was the pretext of the dissolution into dyadic dualism of the future nation-state upon which the Persian Prince splits into the mirror images of the prophet/poet, recalling the binary twins of the prince/poet, in its later gestations, while the revolutionary offshoot of Manichaeism in Mazdakism would be the prototype of its nomadic resurrection much later. These archetypal tropes have always been actively dormant in the collective imagination of the Persian cosmopolis; while we may have recognized them successively and diachronically, they have been evident and omnipresent concurrently and synchronically.

Ibn Khaldun, Al-Thaʿalibi, and the Idea of the "Longue Durée"

It is by now quite obvious that in this book I am concerned with a major idea in Persian and Islamic political thought (with extended inroads into the Greco-Roman and Jewish and Christian domains) over and through a *longue durée* perspective; for that reason I will not be limited only to Persian mirrors for princes but will in fact cover a vast spectrum of sources that share one crucial feature: their simultaneously literary and political prose. My intention is to examine both these aspects at the same time. This detection of politics in the poetics, and the poetics in the political, has been a trademark of my scholarship and it is definitive to this book. My contention is that some of these literary sources have been read mostly for political purposes, their literary disposition disregarded or repressed. The latter aspect has a catalytic impact on the formal disposition of the politics these texts entail. Here I aim to unpack a major, but by no means the only, imperial ethos in the making and unmaking of Muslim and Persianate empires, and from there, the thematic transfiguration of the Persian Prince from a royal provenance deep into its uncharted future territories. I therefore put a particular literary twist on the idea of the longue durée to demarcate the poetic politics of the history that is otherwise lost to episodic and dynastic historiography of the classical or contemporary kind.

Historically we must keep in mind how the belles lettres and literary disposition of the prose and poetry of articulating the characteristics of the Persian Prince emerged from the courtly culture of their provenance and entailed the legitimizing power of their poetic vision of the world. This is in marked contrast to the scholastic disposition of Islamic law (performed in Arabic, Persian, or Turkish), which had an equally commanding authority over Islamic culture but through the decidedly legalistic control of the human body and behavior. The literary discourse of the Persian Prince (performed in Arabic, Persian, Turkish, or Urdu, or indeed in Greek or Hebrew) gave its prose and poetry a literary, almost liturgical power—and all of that via a humanism that had decidedly asserted itself dialogically against legalistic scholasticism. This will bring my reading of the actively deracialized and degendered archetype of the Persian Prince closer to Gramsci's designation of Machiavelli's prince as a myth. My contention is that the vicissitude of time and narrative does in fact have enduring and catalytic effect on the prototype of the Persian Prince, especially so in the aftermath of the Muslim encounter with European colonialism, when the archetype completely abandons the royal courts and reenters the battlefields of a new history. But even before that, in its varied encounters with Arab, Mongol, Indian, and Turkic dynasties the archetype has had a dialectical interface with its multifarious political environments—and therefore has never remained "pure," always syncretic and dialogical. The way I read it, the Persian Prince is primarily a literary trope, a poetic construct, and precisely for that reason, it has the potential to unfold like a floating signifier. As a floating signifier, the archetype goes through various iterations in a range of cultural contexts thanks to the successive patronage of the Samanids, the Ghaznavids, the Saljuqids, the Mongols, the Ottomans, the Safavids, and the Mughals. This is so precisely because of the potent ideological force of the Persian Prince as it has thematically unfolded over a very long period of history. My opting for a longue durée narrative therefore has both a mythological and a theoretical set of reasons behind it.

I mean the idea of the Persian Prince as a conceptual chameleon recasting the discourse of Islamic statecraft and governance around and through a theoretical reorientation that has been missing from other studies on the subject. The historical vicissitude and political consequences of this archetype must be mapped out and theorized in a sustained and prolonged timeframe. This is not, of course, to suggest that the idea of the Persian Prince is the missing panacea that will tell us everything we need to know about Islamic political culture. That is not the point. Indian, Greek, Ottoman, Mongol, Arab, and Islamic components of Islamic political thought are all equally important. My focus here is on the central archetypal figure of the Persian Prince, which we can detail, map out, and theorize as a crucial dimension of this multifarious political culture without diminishing the significance of other factors. The making of Islamic political culture has a whole universe of paradigms that have come to it from India to Iran to the Greek, Hebrew, Ottoman, and Arab frames of reference—none of which is at the expense of the others. Islam, as I have always said, is a dialogical proposition. The idea of the Persian Prince is only one such dialogical paradigm. What is entirely unique to this study is my holding constant the idea of the Persian Prince as I run it through a decidedly and consciously longue durée, tracking its vicissitude from pre-Islamic to Islamic to post-Islamist gestations.

My successive references to Xenophon, Erasmus, Machiavelli, Gramsci, Cassirer, and finally Braidotti in European contexts of the past 500 years are for not only heuristic and comparative purposes. Gramsci's take on Machiavelli in his *Prison Notebooks*, what has reached us as "The Modern Prince," offers an extraordinary occasion to rethink his pioneering thoughts on progressive politics in postcolonial contexts—where I intend to trace the resurrection of the Persian Prince in its full subversive force. In *Persophilia: Persian Culture on the Global Scene* (2015), I mapped out a panoramic view, from classical antiquity and biblical sources to our own time, the manners of such cross-fertilization of what Edward Said called "traveling theories." This is another occasion to do the same with Xenophon, Machiavelli, Gramsci, and beyond. Machiavelli's ideas in his *Prince* did not remain constant, and subsequent theorists, especially Gramsci and Cassirer, updated them for their own particular circumstances—and the same holds for my idea of the Persian Prince in a parallel course. This will inevitably bring together multiple fields of scholarship in an active cross-disciplinary prose. As is evident in two of my recent books, *Europe and Its Shadows: Coloniality After Empire* (2019) and *The Emperor Is Naked: On the Inevitable Demise of the Nation-State* (2020), it is no longer possible to disregard the cross-disciplinary fact of much of our scholarship—in which we must traverse borders and timelines beyond limited disciplinary formations. The result of all these is a different kind of longue durée historiography, in which a singularly important idea—in this case the archetype of the Persian Prince—requires rethinking much historical and disciplinary compartmentalization.

Crossing over such limitations, in this book I trace the dissolution of the figure of the Persian Prince from the ruling class altogether leaving the state apparatus and coming to sustain the sovereignty of first the nations but eventually the "multitude" (as Hardt and Negri theorize it) and the domain of their common—all through their poets and intellectuals active in its public and parapublic spheres. This Gramscian move (though in a postcolonial key beyond his immediate concerns) requires a radical reconfiguration of Habermas's seminal work on the bourgeois public sphere, and of course a global articulation of Hardt and Negri's multitude.[19] In mapping out such epistemic and theoretical foregrounding of the public spheres in which my idea of the Persian Prince asserts itself, the significance of economic, military, and other material forces remains constant, but so does the predominance of a literary and poetic culture that has foregrounded the moral imagination. Ruling dynasties spent significant resources to sustain court culture, gathering learned poets, philosophers, and artists, commissioning the writing of their histories and training their successors. This was never at the expense of more material forces of history that were at work—it was integral to them. Alexander the Great and Julius Caesar slept with a copy of Xenophon's *Cyropaedia* under their pillows! Their daggers and swords must have been in close proximity too. Keeping the idea of the Persian Prince constant as a floating signifier over a longue durée, all other such forces become material in their poetic and aesthetic forces.

In European historiography the idea of the longue durée was developed by the French Annales school to mark their preference for long-term historical structures over short-term and episodic courses of events and in an attempt to discover hidden and subterranean forces and factors beyond the dynamics of the visible life cycles. Pioneered by historians like Marc Bloch and Lucien Febvre and actively theorized by Fernand Braudel, the historical school incorporates social and economic histories and points to, as Braudel did in his magisterial work *The Mediterranean and the Mediterranean World in the Age of Philip II* (1949), the tension between mountain dwellers and plains dwellers, with their different cultures and economic models, as a basic feature of Mediterranean history over thousands of years. This was a marked return to an earlier generation of European historians like Jules Michelet, Leopold von Ranke, Jacob Burckhardt, and Fustel de Coulanges in his seminal study *The Ancient City: A Study on the Religion, Laws, and Institutions of Greece and Rome* (1877). It is in the same genre that one might read Max Weber's book *The City* (1921). Longue durée historiography, as a result, comes closer to sociological observations about history than the more limited disciplinary notion of episodic, national, or even regional histories. Such modes of thinking are active exercises in historical hermeneutic.

This useful notion of the longue durée has extended resonances (not precedence or genealogy) in Islamic and pre-Islamic historiography long before the French Annales and perhaps philosophically best represented in Ibn Khaldun's classic *Al-Muqaddimah* (1377), where, like Vico and Hegel after him, he looks for long-term cyclical structures over short-term scales, teasing out slowly evolving motifs such as what he calls *"asabiyyah."* The same is also evident (though in a different analytical register) in Abu Mansur al-Tha'alibi's (961–1039) monumental book that has reached us with multiple titles, including *Tarikh Ghurar al-Siyar, Al-Ghurar fi Siyar al-Muluk wa Akhbarihim, Ghurar Akhbar Muluk al-Furs wa Siyarihim, Ghurar Muluk al-Furs,* and *Tabaqat al-Muluk*—the common feature of all these titles is a reference to the Persian monarchy and the lives of the monarchs before and after the advent of Islam.[20] To be sure, Tha'alibi was a universal historian with a penchant for pre-Islamic Iranian heritage for whom history began with the first Persian king, Keyumars, and lasted through his own time. But still, there was something specific about his prose. Composed at the height of the Ghaznavid Empire (977–1186), this seminal text revolves around Tha'alibi's reconstruction of the history of Persian kings, and then traces them back to the creation of humanity, with the Persian mythological monarch Keyumars as the very first human being, then up to his own ruling monarch. The book is a history but also in effect a mirror, for the mention of any ancient king is an occasion to describe their court, ceremonies, and rituals—how they ruled, their apparatus of power and authority, the wisdoms and injunctions they followed and left behind, their battles, their defeats, their victories, and their causes, what they did best and what wrongs they committed. The book is also a masterpiece of literary eloquence—bringing into a superior Arabic prose the ancient wisdom of Iranian imperial heritage. In Tha'alibi's capable hands, memorial history, literary panache, and mirrors for princes all come together to stage the figure of the Persian Prince as the archetype of imperial rule—and thus my extending the idea of the longue durée to his treatment of history. "People are contingent on their time," he writes early in his book, "and time is contingent on Sultans, and Sultans after God are contingent on kings." He further adds, "There is no Din/Religion except through kings and no Donya/World except with them."[21] According to scholars of the text, only the first half of the work, up to the caliphate of

Abu Bakr, has survived, and of that only the section covering pre-Islamic Persian history has been published. It was written between 1017 and 1021, and it extends the logic and rhetoric of Persian monarchy throughout Islamic history. A fusion of the Annales school and Thaʿalibi's historiography shows how the early pre-Islamic vision of the Persian Prince, as I theorize in this book, runs across Islamic history to his and our own contemporary times.

The historical circumstances under which such texts are composed are quite important. Al-Thaʿalibi commenced composing this text following the instructions of Abu al-Mozaffar Nasr ibn Naser al-Din Abu Mansur Sabuktigin, the ruling Ghaznavid emperor Sultan Mahmoud's brother. That Thaʿalibi begins with Keyumars (or Gayomart), the first mythic Persian King and the first human being—or, more accurately, "the sixth of the heptad in Mazdean myth of creation, the protoplast of man, and the first king in Iranian mythical history"[22]—and ends with his own reigning monarch places the entirety of human history (including the Hebrew prophets and even Prophet Muhammad) within the context of Iranian mythology. Al-Thaʿalibi's history is global and includes China, India, the Roman Empire, and the Muslim caliphs as well. Al-Thaʿalibi's book seems to have identical sources as the *Shahnameh* of Ferdowsi, which was composed slightly earlier. Thus, in both prose and poetry we have towering figures of the period mapping out their contemporary history right at the birth of Persian imperial cosmogony.

My initial question—How did Muslims rule the world for as long as they did and how did they lose it?—has by now taken a long and winding path. After an initial comparative turn to Xenophon, Machiavelli, and Gramsci's thoughts on the idea of the (Persian) Prince and the Modern Prince, I began my inquiry by hoping to see and show the role of Persian theories of governance and statecraft rooted in pre-Islamic Iranian empires in that rule—and that consideration, in turn, led me to the articulation of the idea of the Persian Prince as an imperial archetype. By offering both an expansive administrative apparatus and the theoretical foregrounding of imperial rule, pre-Islamic Iranian empires, from the mythologized Achaemenids to the historical Sassanids, were the very blueprints of Muslim dynasties from East to West, including Arab, Iranian, Indian, and Turkish empires that relied on that archetype. How would the preeminent Persian poet Saʿdi Shirazi (1200–1291) in the thirteenth century know about the Sassanid emperor Anushirvan and what he said to his son on his deathbed—and even more importantly, how did such stories become emblematic and metaphorical of the very idea of justice in Muslim empires? Why does Saʿdi say "I have heard" and not "I have read" when citing the Sassanid monarch—factual or fictional? Whence and wherefore this prolonged history, literary and oral, in which the wisdom of pre-Islamic imperial pedigree reaches deeply into Muslim lands and informs the most important literary masterpieces that had sustained the moral imagination of multiple Muslim empires on a balance of poetics and politics, ethics and statecraft? For the rest of this book, the wisdom of Sa'di will remain my guiding light:

> *Boro pas-e darvish-e mohtaj dar ...*
>
> Go and look after the needy poor—
> For the king has his crown from those he rules;
> If the king be a tree those he rules are the root—
> The tree, my son, is strong by virtue of its roots![23]

Part Two

THE RISE OF AN ARCHETYPE

THREE

On the Histories, Geographies, and Iconographies of Muslim Empires

> As long as this world has existed, people have sought to procure knowledge, as they have praised wisdom, and considered wise words the most precious legacies, for in this world the more a people respect knowledge the mightier and more refined they will be. When human beings realize that nothing will remain forever they will strive to leave a good name behind and make sure their good reputation is not lost, and they do so by way of building monuments, erecting citadels, conducting chivalrous acts, with good humor and courageous deeds, and to assure that knowledge is disseminated, leading people to innovations, just as Indian kings did by ordering the writing of Kelilah and Dimnah, or the works of Shaunaka, or Ramayana and Mahabharata.[1]
>
> Abu Mansur Ma'mari, *Shahnameh Abu Mansuri* (957 CE)

IN 1920 THE EMINENT IRANIAN SCHOLAR Mohammad Qazvini (1876–1949) edited a critical edition of the introduction of an old prose Shahnameh known as Abu Mansuri's *Shahnameh*—a work that evidently predated the composition of Ferdowsi's *Shahnameh*, which was delivered in sublime poetry, early in the eleventh century. In his learned essay on the subject, Qazvini gives a detailed account of the provenance of this precious text.[2] This was a time when scholars of his generation and rank worked closely with Shahnameh manuscripts, a fact we learn because he tells us how readers of such manuscripts occasionally came across a short prose introduction to the Persian epic. These introductions are of three types, Qazvini informs his readers, composed in 957 CE, in 1425 CE, or, in his estimate of a third similar introduction, sometime between these two dates, while the more famous *Shahnameh* of Ferdowsi was completed in about 1010 CE. Between 957 and 1425, therefore, we have the masterpiece of Persian epic heritage articulated in at least four interrelated gestations—three in prose, one in poetry, all gathered between two covers of multiple provenances.

We owe it to the impeccable scholarship of Qazvini, who discovered that this earliest prose introduction to Shahnameh, dating back to 957, had nothing to do with the long poem version of Ferdowsi's; it is in fact the introduction to an older prose version, of which the rest has been lost. Qazvini then uses this occasion to trace the origin of attention to pre-Islamic Persian royal heritage back to Abdullah ibn Muqaffaʿ's (circa 721–759) translation of the iconic Sassanid text *Khwaday-Namag* from Pahlavi to Arabic, in about 759. The original Pahlavi version and Ibn Muqaffaʿ's Arabic translation of this text have alas been lost, Qazvini tells us, but there are numerous references to it in other contemporary and later sources. Qazvini also informs us that there were additional such Arabic translations from pre-Islamic Iranian sources by other near-contemporary authors of Ibn Muqaffaʿ but they too have disappeared except for references to them by other writers. Qazvini emphasizes the extended presence of these sources in later Arabic histories like the classical texts of al-Tabari, al-Maqdisi, Ibn Qutaybah, al-Masʿudi, al-Biruni, and al-Thaʿalibi.[3] In fact, while this entire genre of pre-Islamic Iranian historiographical mirrors was being translated into Arabic, their Persian versions were also being collected and published in prose and poetry in Iranian domains proper long before Ferdowsi's iconic text, such as the *Shahnameh* of the eminent Samanid poet Abu al-Moʾayyad al-Balkhi.[4] What becomes clear from all this discussion is the active presence of pre-Islamic sources of imperial sovereignty in Pahlavi, Arabic, and modern Persian versions from the earliest decades of the Arab conquest of the Sassanid Empire. The historical assemblage of these seminal texts informs the literary provenance of the towering figure of the Persian Prince as the archetype of supreme political power.

Qazvini proceeds to give us an exhaustive list of the other prose and poetry versions of the *Shahnameh* that were produced before Ferdowsi put pen to paper and wrote his own exquisite version that outshined all the rest. What is most evident in the examples that Qazvini cites is that there was ample royal demand—both in Baghdad, the capital of the Abbasid Empire, for the Arabic versions; and around the Muslim world, to the East, for the Persian version of these pre-Islamic Iranian mirrors for princes. The list of these texts ultimately brings Qazvini to the *Shahnameh* of Abu Mansuri, commissioned by a certain

Abu Mansur ibn Abd al-Razzaq al-Tusi (died 962), a prominent dignitary during the Samanid reign in Khurasan.[5] Qazvini tells us that this prose Shahnameh—the entire text of which, save for this brief introduction, has disappeared—is the basis of Ferdowsi's *Shahnameh*, excepting the passages he cites from another poet, Abu Mansur Ahmad al-Daghighi (died circa 976), who had started his own composition before Ferdowsi. However, soon after the composition of Ferdowsi's monumental masterpiece, previous versions began to fall out of favor and eventually disappeared—with the exception of this short preface, which, thanks to the iconic power of Ferdowsi's epic, has survived to reach us. So, like a Matryoshka doll, as it were, Ferdowsi's epic carried within itself small memorabilia of its prose origin, a fact we are aware of because of the meticulous scholarship of Mohammad Qazvini. The text of Ferdowsi's *Shahnameh* as we now know it is therefore the archeological site of its own literary and poetic origins in a much older, pre-Islamic Iranian heritage of mythic, heroic, and historical narratives of who and how ruled the civilized world.

From the body of the introduction to this lost prose *Shahnameh* itself, we learn that the Abbasid caliph al-Ma'mun, the son of Harun al-Rashid, had a majestic and royal demeanor. One day he was sitting consulting with his advisers and mentioned that kings should do the best they can to leave a good name behind. His secretary, Abdullah ibn Muqaffaʿ, who was in attendance, said that something had remained from the Sassanid emperor Khosrow I, Kisra Anushirvan (reigned 531–579) superior to anything else left behind by other kings: the book that he had ordered to be brought from India by his vizier Borzuyeh and translated into Pahlavi as *Kelilah and Dimnah*. Caliph al-Ma'mun asked for this book and ordered Ibn Muqaffaʿ to translate it into Arabic. This very story, though apocryphal—Ibn Muqaffaʿ had been murdered around 760, long before Caliph al-Ma'mun (reigned 813–833) ascended the Abbasid throne—eventually reached the Samanid ruler Nasr ibn Ahmad (reigned 914–943), who in turn ordered the book to be translated into Persian and asked his court poet, Rudaki, to render it in Persian verse. This account then reaches Amir Abu Mansur Abd al-Razzaq, who was of noble descent and too wished to leave behind a similar book. So he ordered Abu Mansur al-Maʿmari to convene a conference of all the learned men of Khurasan, which led to the eventual composition of the *Shahnameh*,

> So that men of knowledge would study this book and learn all about the culture of kings, the nobility and the learned men, the proper decorum of the royal court, the foundations of their behaviors and good rituals,

and how to dispense justice and manage the affairs of the empire, its army and how it should wage battles achieve conquest, conduct warfare, attack at night.⁶

From these stories, factual or fictional, we learn how such recollections about Persian monarchs of the Sassanid and earlier empires not only informed the political cultures of Muslim caliphs and sultans but also offered them a prototype of rulership as well as a mode of historiography that becomes emblematic of how Muslim history is recalled and recorded. What is evident from these precious early sources making their ways from Pahlavi, Sanskrit, and Greek into Arabic and Persian is that learned courtiers were looking around the globe—to ancient Iran, India, and Greece in particular—for pre-Islamic blueprints of imperial statecraft. With a text like *Kelilah and Dimnah*, the works of the celebrated Sanskrit sage Shaunaka, Sanskrit masterpieces like *Ramayana* and *Mahabharata*, or such Pahlavi texts as *Khwaday-Namag*, Muslim rulers were actively searching for ways to imagine themselves legitimately sitting on their thrones—while their court chroniclers were learning the prose and politics of telling their stories. The Qurʾan, to be sure, and the Prophetic Hadiths were emerging as definitive to Muslim statecraft, but at the same time, pre- and therefore non-Islamic sources were also actively on the horizon, informing the selfsame statecraft from a whole different angle of vision. It is equally important to recall that in addition to Iranian, Indian, and Byzantine examples, the Greek sources exemplified by Plato and Aristotle, and equally so by Xenophon's *Cyropaedia*, were in neighboring provinces of each other as Muslim empires seized the moment to rule the world with a posture of legitimacy.

The Iranian Lineage of Muslim Imperial Historiography

The significance of Ibn Muqaffaʿ as a literary prose stylist in the era of the early Abbasid Empire (750–1258) can scarcely be exaggerated. Abu Muhammad Abdullah Ruzbeh ibn Muqaffaʿ (circa 721–757)

> was of noble Persian stock and bore the name Rōzbeh/Rūzbeh before his comparatively late conversion to Islam from Manichaeism ... a fastidious man of refined manners, steeped in the traditional culture of the old Persian nobility, yet ever observant of the values of Arab society. In the purity of his Arabic he outshone members of the Arab ruling class, and in generosity and hospitality he seems to have tried to outdo them.

During the tumultuous transition between the demise of the Umayyads and the rise of the Abbasids he was arrested, tortured, and murdered by his political enemies.[7]

Among Ibn Muqaffa''s voluminous work, his translation of *Kelilah and Dimnah* from Pahlavi to Arabic, as well as his translation of *Khwaday-Namag*, a classic account of pre-Islamic Persian kings, princes, and warriors, are the most notable. The rich and diversified historiographical body of the pre-Islamic period is of course not limited to *Khwaday-Namag*, all of which reaches the threshold of the Islamic period, for "by the end of the 6th century, a national history of Iran existed in the royal archive at Ctesiphon." And the nature of this historiography was of course not "impartial" (if there is any such thing): the historian was decidedly "an upholder and promoter of the social, political, and moral values cherished by the Sasanian élite."[8] More than just the substance, the moral imaginary and political parlance of these pre-Islamic Pahlavi sources made their ways into the emerging Arabic historiography.

Ibn Muqaffa''s Arabic translations of *Kelilah and Dimnah* and *Khwaday-Namag* (one from India and the other from Iran) do not just become the prototype for Abu Mansur al-Ma'mari's Persian prose version of the *Shahnameh*, which in turn becomes the basis of Ferdowsi's masterpiece, but in fact their respective Sanskrit and Pahlavi provenances become the prototype for Islamic historiography as such. Ruling princes like the Abbasid caliph al-Ma'mun and the Samanid Amir Mansur sought to learn from these sources how to manage their own dynasties and empires. In his prose introduction to the *Shahnameh*, Abu Mansur al-Ma'mari offers a section-by-section treatment of how such mirrors for princes, or "histories" of an imperial order, ought to be written, and how their stories interpreted. He also offers a geographical division of the world into seven climes, at the epicenter of which is Iranshahr, which runs from the Oxus River to the Nile River. Here he adds, "Of all the seven climes, Iranshahr is the most noble, in every art."[9] China, India, and Egypt are in the immediate neighborhood of Iranshahr, where the mythic figure of the First Man, Keyumars, is identified with the biblical Adam and whose history becomes foundational for dynastic histories all the way to the Parthians and the Sassanids, bringing the line of Persian princes down to his patron, Abu Mansur Abd al-Razzaq.[10] In these earliest staccatos of Persian prose, we are in fact reading the grammatical syntax and morphology of Islamic historiography in general. If we were to consider the seminal text of Islamic history in al-Tabari's (839–923) *History of the*

Prophets and Kings, we see the presence of these mythic Persian rulers, down to Jamashid and his adaptation of the story of Adam and Eve. The composition of all these masterpieces of Islamic historiography occurs in the aftermath of Ibn Muqaffaʿ's translation of *Kelilah and Dimnah* and *Khwaday-Nama*, to which these Muslim historians had either direct or mitigated access.

The same is the case with the other major Muslim geographer and historian, al-Masʿudi (circa 896–956), "the Herodotus of the Arabs," whose remarkable knowledge of pre-Islamic Iranian mythologies and histories became definitive to his worldviews. In two of his seminal works, *Muruj al-Dhahab wa Maʿadin al-Jawahir* (The meadows of gold and mines of gems) and *al-Tanbih wa al-Ashraf* (The book of notification and verification), we read him as beholden to pre-Islamic Indian and Persian heritage; he also laments that much of this heritage has been lost and explores what is left. As scholars of al-Masʿudi's work tell us:

> His account of pre-Islamic history suggests that human beings can grasp essential truths about nature and society without help from divine revelation. In the *Muruj* he begins his survey of ancient civilizations with India, the first nation to establish a social order based on philosophical teachings. In the *Tanbih*, he begins with the Persians, who attained the highest form of political organization possible before Islam: "Their territory was vast, their history long, their dynastic succession unbroken, their administration efficient, their lands prosperous, and their subjects well cared for." Only when they neglected religion (of whatever form) and the administration of justice did the ancient empires collapse.[11]

As is evident in these seminal works of Islamic and world history, the rise and expansion of Islam and Muslim empires happened in the broad daylight of history, a history that was already very old and conscious of what had happened long before Prophet Muhammad declared himself a Divine Emissary, founded a soon-to-be globalized religion, and eventually had followers who dispatched massive armies of conquest to overcome the two major imperial orders of the time, the Byzantines and the Sassanids. Egypt, Iran, India, and China were the principal domains of civilizational consciousness prior to the rise of Islam. From the earliest periods, Muslim historians were fully aware of these pre-Islamic empires and were influenced by the accounts that had reached them of their domains; thus, they became the carriers of their memories well into the Islamic period. Islamic history in effect becomes an extension, a variation on the theme of these pre-Islamic imperial *longues durées*. Particularly important to Muslim historians, as evident in both al-Masʿudi and al-Tabari, were India and Iran, one for its civilizational forestructure and the other for its imperial world order.

The transition from the pre-Islamic to Islamic period was contingent not only on these seminal historical narratives. There was other more material evidence too. Over the past two decades, we have been witness to an impressive body of scholarship in this field. In *Imperial Matter: Ancient Persia and the Archaeology of Empires* (2016), Lori Khatchadourian draws our attention to the significance of the material world in the making of an imperial order. This is not a mere matter of military conquest but is written into the fabric of objects, from daily utensils to symbolic monuments. With a particular emphasis on ancient Persian empires, she offers insightful ways to understand imperial orders. For Khatchadourian, it is not just various archeological relics that need to come together for us to understand an empire, but varied scholarly discourses, which produce "a uniquely archeological approach to explaining both the perdurance and the fragility of imperial sovereignty."[12] She is quite conscious of the fact she is bringing the oddity of ancient Persia to bear on contemporary critical discourse about colonialism and imperialism. She then spends the rest of her learned book on what she calls "satrapal condition," extending the old Persian word for "sovereignty" to explain the significance of ancient Persian political and religious ideas. From this premise, she proceeds with the story of Houshang in Ferdowsi's *Shahnameh* and his accidental discovery of fire and the birth of civilization as we know it today.[13] Khatchadourian's remarkable scholarship remaps the pre-Islamic and Islamic periods together to reveal a whole new topography of memory and power.

In another major study, *The Iranian Expanse: Transforming Royal Identity Through Architecture, Landscape, and the Built Environment, 550 BCE–642 CE* (2020), Matthew P. Canepa has turned his attention to how "kings in Persia and the ancient Iranian world utilized the built and natural environment to form and contest Iranian cultural memory, royal identity, and sacred cosmologies."[14] What he demonstrates is how successive Persian empires before the arrival of Islam incorporated cultural memories of Mesopotamia, Egypt, and Anatolia to map out their own imperial imprints. He convincingly argues the enduring presence of these imprints long after the Arab conquest, up through the Safavids, the Ottomans, and the Mughals. In the process, Canepa studies such thematics as "ordering the earth," "sacred spaces," and "landscapers of time and memory," in effect positing how successive imperial orders invented and reinvented their ideological apparatus of power. What this study convincingly reveals is the continuity of certain dominant pre-Islamic Iranian leitmotifs foregrounding the unfolding of Islamic history in identifiably Persian terms.

The continuity and revisioning of the memorial and material evidence extends the origin and procures the dissemination of these Iranian leitmotifs, while the successive editions, prose and poetic renditions, and Persian and Arabic translations of Pahlavi sources become in effect the blueprint and modus operandi of Islamic historiography. The very title of the major opus of the eminent Muslim historian al-Tabari, *Tarikh al Rasul wa al Muluk* (*History of the Prophets and Kings*), clearly indicates the influence of pre-Islamic Iranian factual and memorial evidence that culminates in the Persian epic of the *Shahnameh*, whose poetic power guarantees the prolongation of the mythic, heroic, and historical memories it entails. From al-Tabari to al-Masʿudi to al-Thaʿalibi and beyond, all major and minor Muslim historians followed the same pattern and paid foundational attention to pre-Islamic Iranian memories. This in effect turned Muslim historiography itself into a variation on the theme of a mirror for princes.

The extraordinary epistemic shift that has taken place by a younger generation of scholars over the past couple of decades has revolutionized the field of Islamic historiography precisely because of its attention to such crossovers between pre-Islamic and Islamic periods. Let me cite a revealing coincidence with two seminal works of scholarship. One is Sarah Bowen Savant's *The New Muslims of Post-Conquest Iran* (2015) and the other Alison Vacca's *Non-Muslim Provinces Under Early Islam: Islamic Rule and Iranian Legitimacy in Armenia and Caucasian Albania* (2017). Both these insightful pieces of scholarship, which have quite different subject matters, begin, entirely independent of each other, with an identical quotation from the eminent Arab poet al-Buhturi (died 897):

> Worries were at my stopping place, so I turned
> My sturdy she-camel toward the White Palace of al-Mada'in.
> Consoling myself with good fortune, and sorrowing
> At the traces of the camp of the clan of Sasan.
> Successive afflictions reminded me of them;
> Incidents make one remember, make one forget.[15]

At the time of writing their respective books, Vacca was teaching at the University of Tennessee, and Savant at Aga Khan University in London. There is no reason for these two scholars to have opted to open their books with the same poem by Buhturi except for the fact that the iconic presence of the ruins of the

Taq Kisra, or the Archway of Ctesiphon, the Parthian and Sassanid palace, was at the epicenter of their respective arguments—namely the legacy of Sassanid historiography (in both archaic cites and symbolic importance) in their separate fields of study. Savant's elegant argument works through the instrumentality of memory in actively remembering and selectively forgetting aspects of pre-Islamic Iranian history in order to facilitate a new modus operandi of being both Persian and Muslim in the Islamic period. Meanwhile, Vacca concentrates on Armenia and Caucasian Albania to map out the thematic continuities from the Sassanids to caliphal statecraft, as she too pays close attention to the continuity of Sassanid memory in the post-Sassanid historiography of the Islamic period.

The same spirit prevails in other groundbreaking works of scholarship in the field. Although Mimi Hanaoka's *Authority and Identity in Medieval Islamic Historiography: Persian Histories from the Peripheries* (2018) suffers from a major epistemological misconception, it offers an exceptionally insightful reading of the manner in which Persianate historiography enriches our reading of Islamic history. Her emphasis on dream narratives and dream interpretations pushes the boundaries of historiography into utterly brilliant directions. She is, however, wrong to think these historiographies are "from the peripheries." These regions are peripheries only if we falsely assume an Arab-centric, and Baghdad-centric, conception of Islamic world history.[16] If we completely abandon and overcome such faulty assumptions and falsifying prejudices, the whole spectrum of the Muslim world, from Spain to India, from Central Asia to East Africa, will open up for multiple worlds. Hanaoka's discussion of Perso-Islamic historiography, with an emphasis on Bukhara, Tabaristan, and Qom, is groundbreaking in ways that the dialectic between Persian and Arabic sources and thereby pre-Islamic Zoroastrian heritage are all kept alive and well.

In the same vein, we must read the superb scholarship of Anne F. Broadbridge's *Women and the Making of the Mongol Empire* (2018), in which we see a systematic and thorough familiarity with the vast body of Persian historiography on the Mongol Empire, particularly the works of 'Ata' Malik al-Jovayni (1226–1283), Rashid al-Din Fadl Allah al-Hamadhani (1247–1318), Mirkhwand (1433–1498), and Hafez-e Abru (died 1430), chief among others. Without this facility with Persian sources, it would have been impossible to pull off such a feat of historical excavation with the role of Mongol women in the building of their empire.[17] But even more importantly, such crucial studies extend the topography of our understanding of Islamic history deeper into Eastern domains and thus sculpt a richer reading of Islamic political culture. Similar familiarity with Persian sources leads Christopher Markiewicz into even more important insights in *The Crisis of Kingship in Late Medieval Islam: Persian Emigres and the Making of Ottoman Sovereignty*:

> In the central lands of Islam—roughly the lands between the Nile and the Oxus river—such intellectual productions were frequently expressed in Persian. To be sure, Arabic still predominated as the universal language of scholarship—especially pertaining to religious learning—but Persian was used extensively or even preferred in other learned and literary forms, including Sufism, poetry, and history writing. Indeed, the prestige of Persian is evident within court culture, even among rulers whose native tongue was Turkish or whose subjects spoke Arabic.[18]

In this book, Markiewicz concentrates on Idris Bidlisi's (circa 1455–1520) monumental *Hasht Behesht* (*Eight Paradises*), rendered in beautiful Persian prose, in which he writes about the eight founding fathers of the Ottoman dynasty. Bidlisi's book, which took him about a decade to complete, centers on the eight rulers, following the example of al-Jovayni's history. Compare Markiewicz's work with the almost exclusively Arab-centric scholarship of Tarif Khalidi in his classic and rightly celebrated work *Arabic Historical Thought in the Classical Period* (1995), in which we encounter only a passing allusion to al-Tabari's iconic book *The History of the Prophets and Kings* in a discussion of pre-Islamic Persian kings.[19] Khalidi's book is otherwise a classic specimen of scholarship on Islamic historiography, and it possesses an ease with which the wealth of Arabic Hadith, Adab, Hikma, and Siyasa are interwoven. Persian, Ottoman, Indian, North African, and Iberian domains of Muslim history are pushed aside to stage an entirely Baghdad-centric vision of Islamic history. This was all good and fine for the Arabic component of Islamic history but falls short of any understanding of the last three Muslim empires of the Mughals, the Safavids, and the Ottomans, as well as many other earlier empires, particularly the Ghaznavids, the Saljuqids, and the Mongols. The new generation of Markiewicz's scholarship simply taps a much richer vein of historiographical evidence, revealing a more detailed understanding of the Iranian component of Islamic historiography.

In his provocative new study, *Islam, Literature and Society in Mongol Anatolia* (2019), A. C. S. Peacock performs a feat of literary scholarship demonstrating how the Islamization of Anatolia during the Mongol period in the thirteenth and fourteenth centuries paved the way for the establishment of the Ottoman Empire.[20] Peacock pays detailed attention to the significance of monumental figures like Rumi and his son Baha la-Din Walad and, beyond that, the Persian translation of Tabari's *History* as well as the poetries of Nezami and Khaqani facilitate this transition under the Danishmandids (reigned 1071–1178),[21] noting that before the rise of Turkish in the thirteenth century, Persian was the primary language of Anatolian Muslims. This in effect extends the pre-Islamic Iranian provenance of the domain of the Persianate world well into the foundational premises of the rise of the Ottoman Empire.

Here we may perhaps recall the signature work of the Persian poet Khaqani (circa 1120–1199) on the iconic site of Ivan-e Mada'in, also known as the Taq Kisra or the Archway of Ctesiphon.[22] This is the same site that was the subject of al-Buhturi's poem in the ninth century, which we see Khaqani revisiting in the twelfth century. In other words, for three consecutive centuries in early Islamic history, the site of a Parthian and Sassanid royal ruin was teaching Arab and Persian poets lessons from pre-Islamic history. Here are a few lines from Khaqani's qasideh:

Han, Ey Del-e Ebrat-bin az Dideh Ebar kon Han!

Oh discerning eyes lo and behold!
Observe the Ivan-e Mada'in as if it were a mirror of advice!
Once from Tigris come and visit Ivan-e Mada'in,
And cry a second Tigris upon the soil of Mada'in....
Every groove on the battlement gives you a renewed advice—
Heed each piece of this advice most earnestly!
It is telling you: You're made of dust, we are now the dust on your way—
Step on us for a while and shed some tears....
We were the court of justice—see what injustice we had to endure,
Wait until you see what will become of tyrants.[23]

The entirety of the poem is a lamentation on the past glories of Persian empires, drawing from the ruins of the palace lessons for posterity. Khaqani particularly emphasizes the significance of justice in the Sassanid Empire and extends these learnings to his contemporaries. Thus, in material and memorial history, the Iranian lineage of the pre-Islamic ages come together to teach and inform Muslim imperial historiography. As Muslim historians write one monumental opus after another chronicling the adventures of Muslim armies, dynasties, and empires, constant remains the living memory of pre-Islamic Iranian monarchs and emperors—chief among them Khosrow I Anushirvan the Just, whose fact, fiction, truth, and myth survive to cast him as the single most important archetype of Persian princely power and authority. "I was born during the reign of the Just Ruler" is an apocryphal Hadith attributed to Prophet Muhammad. True or false, factual or apocryphal, the Hadith reveals a sentiment definitive to all-powerful Muslim rulers who wanted to appeal to the prototype of the Persian Prince. Including pre-Islamic Iranian history in Muslim historiography was not merely *chronological* but in fact *epistemological*, for such annals of world history established the narrative protype of Islamic historiography and subsequently cast the entirety of Muslim history in decidedly pre-Islamic, Iranian terms.

The Persian Prince in Muslim Robes

The universal significance of the figure of the Persian Prince, as I propose it here, is woven into the global map of Muslim empires and their histories and geographies, where the ancient Iranian archetypal figure becomes definitive to the projected legitimacy of the whole political apparatus. If we were to trace Xenophon's *Cyropaedia* all the way to its Latin gestations down to Machiavelli's *Prince* and Gramsci's "Modern Prince," a parallel European genealogy would suggest itself, as would the sustained continuity of the Persian Prince in biblical and talmudic contexts. But in the immediate Muslim vicinities, success scenes of Muslim empires were scattered throughout the known and civilized world, from the Atlantic to the Pacific; central to them all was the monarchic power of a caliph, a sultan, or an amir, all molded on the archetypal figure of the Persian Prince—with its Iranian and non-Iranian, Islamic and non-Islamic parameters. From Indian wisdom literatures, best exemplified in *Kelilah and Dimnah* to the Yassa of the Genghis Khan, were equally present next to Persian patterns of imperial monarchy, as perhaps best evident in the unfolding significance of *Khwaday-Namag*. Precisely because of this syncretic disposition of the Persian Prince, the domain of the archetypal figure was not limited to Iranian dynasties, and its varied gestations were equally evident in Arab, Turkic, and Indian domains—where the formation of dynastic and imperial dominion found the Persian Prince a readymade institution of political legitimacy. The archetype extended all the way to Spain, where the legendary Kurdish-Persian musician, astronomer, fashion designer, and gastronome Abu al-Hasan Ali ibn Nafi, known as Ziryab (circa 789–852), thrived at the Umayyad court and ceremoniously formalized their princely and monarchic reign. The world rightly remembers Ziryab as an ingenious musician and composer, but he was also the chief protocol chamberlain, teaching the Umayyads how to behave and rule like proper kings.

All these pre- and non-Islamic traces are evident in such seminal sources of Mongol and Ilkhanid history as 'Ata' Malik al-Jovayni's (1226–1283) *Tarikh-i Jahangushay (The History of the World Conqueror)* and Rashid al-Din Fadlullah Hamadani's (1247–1318) *Jamiʿ al-Tawarikh (Compendium of Histories)*. The example of the Mongol Empire is particularly crucial, for it was the vastest and most powerful example of imperial rule for which the figure of the Persian Prince becomes definitive. Indeed, the principal historians of the empire were Iranians who wrote the chronicles of the Mongol Empire not just decidedly in Persian prose but, far more importantly, on the epistemic prototype of pre-Islamic Iranian historical consciousness. And historiography, prose, and poetry were not the only sites of evident pre-Islamic Iranian heritage. The Ilkhanid summer palace at Takht-i Suleiman (circa 1275) was a celebration of pre-Islamic Iranian architectural heritage regally staged. Systematically and consistently, over the course of successive and varied Muslim empires, the centralizing archetype of the Persian Prince became syncretic with and emblematic of Arab, Turkic, Mongol, and Iranian ideas and practices.

The advent of Islam in the seventh century, however, puts a drastic twist on this constellation of formal and formative forces. The divine mission of Prophet Muhammad (570–632) inaugurated a dramatic epistemic shift in Muslim moral, metaphysical, and historical consciousness. The Prophet's divine message, his *Risalah*, was contingent on his charismatic presence and authority and, soon after his passing on the imperial orders that followed, on the political tract of his divine mission unfolding over successive historical phases and across Muslim lands. Muhammad's charismatic authority was a decisive and historic twist on Jewish and Christian traditions. But Zoroastrian, Manichean, and Mazdakite traditions were all alive and well early in Islamic history. Rebellious heterodox proclivities that soon emerged in the form of revolutionary uprisings and staged a variety of syncretic religious sentiments at times resulted in varied dynastic formations predicated in pre-Islamic Iranian heritage.

Though expressed and articulated in the Qur'an and the Hadith and in specifically biblical terms, Muhammad's charismatic authority was still reminiscent of the Iranian idea of *Farr-e Izadi*—or, more technically, *farr(ah)*, *xᵛarənah*—which, according to scholars of pre-Islamic philology, meant "glory," "splendor," "luminosity" and "shine," already "present in the Achaemenid concept of charismatic kingship."[24] This conception of Muhammad's prophetic (charismatic) authority would remain a key idea at the root of political legitimacy in Muslim dynasties.[25] Let's revisit Weber's classical definition of charismatic authority:

> The term "charisma" will be applied to a certain quality of an individual personality, by virtue of which he is set apart from ordinary men and treated as endowed with supernatural, superhuman, or at least specifically exceptional powers or qualities. These are such as are not accessible to the ordinary person, but are regarded as of divine origin or as exemplary, and on the basis of them the individual concerned is treated as a leader.[26]

Prophets are chief among the examples Weber offers before detailing how the charisma does not totally disappear but becomes objectified—one might even say "fetishized"—in the line of royal succession or in the course of dynastic formations or legal institutions and so on. Prophet Muhammad is thus reminiscent of King Anushirvan and perhaps even the origin of the apocryphal saying "I was born during the time of the Just Ruler." The inherited heritage of the charisma of the king and the revelatory disposition of the charisma of the Prophet converge, and we have the best evidence of it in the title of Tabari's seminal *History of the Prophets and Kings*. It is therefore not too far-fetched to consider the Prophet in the pre-Islamic Iranian imagination a simulacrum of the Persian Prince and effectively see him as a rebellious prince/prophet/poet. This conflated character of the persona of the Prophet, evident in the rebellious Meccan and stately Medinan phases of his mission, becomes emblematic of two contradictory but complementary visions of the Muslim Prophet/Persian Prince as both the king and the rebel.

The conflated persona of the Prophet of Islam thus begins to absorb and absolve all pre-Islamic and non-Islamic elements into its expansive iconic reconfiguration of political authority for the subsequent history of Muslim empires. The succession of empires began soon after the period of the four Rightly Guided Caliphs (632–661), with the establishment of the Umayyad caliphate (661–750) in Arabia proper, and rapidly expanded northward and eastward into the Byzantine and Sassanid territories, with Damascus as its capital. At this inaugural moment of Islamic dynastic histories, it is crucial to recall that the Sassanid Empire (224–636) lasted for almost half a millennium on Iranian (Zoroastrian) theories of kingship before the emergence and rise of Islam. No

Muslim dynasty predicated exclusively on the Prophet's Qur'anic legacy came anywhere near that longevity unless and until they actively began to incorporate Iranian, Byzantine, Turkic, Indian, Mongol, or even North African and Iberian cultural traits. The death of Prophet Muhammad and the period of the four Rightly Guided Caliphs paved the way for the transformation of the syncretized charismatic authority of the Prophet into multiple and varied Islamic theories of governance. That transformative moment was necessary and enduring but not sufficient for the vast empires that were soon to emerge. The Umayyads were followed by the Abbasid caliphate (750–1258), which moved farther north, south, then west to form the largest expansion of Muslim rule, with Baghdad as the capital. The formation of the Abbasid Empire was entirely contingent on the active adaptation of multiple pre-Islamic—particularly Iranian—modalities of imperial order, facilitated by the crucial office of the Persian vizierate of the Barmecides.

Long before the Mongol invasion and destruction of the Abbasid dynasty in 1258, with the rise of the small dynasties in the East, pre-Islamic Iranian theories of royal authority began to reassert themselves in the renewed configuration of the Persian Prince. The dynasties in the East were by now fully underway, with the establishment of Samanid Empire (819–999) and the Saffarid dynasty (861–1003) in Khurasan, which was followed and expanded into Central Asia and India under the Turkic Ghaznavid Empire (977–1186). The Ghaznavid too had been thoroughly Persianized in their courtly culture and the ideological foregrounding of their notions of political authority—as perhaps best evidenced by Sultan Mahmoud of Ghazna's famously sponsoring Ferdowsi's composition of the *Shahnameh*, begun under the Samanids. The establishment of the Fatimid caliphate (909–1171) in Egypt and the Buyid dynasty (934–1062) in Northern Iran gave a distinctly Shiʿa character to Muslim rule—in both dynasties, Persian theories of governance had metamorphosed into doctrines of charismatic leadership of the living or absent Imams. If, in the case of Prophet Muhammad, the pre-Islamic Iranian idea of *Farr-e Izadi* (the "divine gift of grace") was implicit, for Shiʿi Imams the idea becomes most explicit in the doctrine of their presumed infallibility.[27] In this very period and region, the Persian translation of the pre-Islamic Sassanid or Parthian romance of *Vis-o-Ramin* (composed circa 1050 by Fakhruddin Asʿad Gorgani) is another clear indication of the unfolding relevance of Iranian literary and political cultures in this heightened episode of Khorasani dynasties.[28] A syncretic and dialogical disposition was by now definitive to Islamic political culture, more specifically with Iranian imperial heritage when it came to political theories of legitimate governance. The figure of the Persian Prince had been fully retrieved from its pre-Islamic provenances and was evident and staged on both Iranian and Islamic political culture.

Soon, the Saljuq Empire (1037–1194) overshadowed them all in power, prestige, and territorial expansion—with patently pre-Islamic Iranian theories of governance apparent in the respective treatises of Khwajah Nezam al-Molk al-Tusi and Abu Hamid Muhammad al-Ghazali, the era's leading theorists and practitioners. It is equally important to consider the period's Arabic and Persian sources of history. Seminal examples include, in Arabic, *Al-Kamil fi Tarikh*, by Ali ibn al-Athir (1160–1233), and before that, in Persian, *Zayn al-Akhbar*, by Abu Sa'id Abd al-Hayy Gardizi (flourished circa 1050). While Ibn al-Athir in *Al-Kamil* fails to hide his disdain for "the Persians" and accuses them of arrogance and haughtiness, he devotes a major part of his history, rooted in al-Tabari's *History of the Prophets and Kings*, to the Iranian dynasties in the East.[29] In *Zayn al-Akhbar*, on the other hand, we have a solid account of pre-Islamic Iranian kings as the prototype for Gardizi's treatment of Saljuqid history, with particularly detailed accounts of Iranian and proto-Iranian Persianate dynasties and empires in the East. Even more crucial in this context is *Tarikh Al-e Saljuqs* (*History of the Seljuqs*), by Qawam al-Din al-Bundari (circa 1190–1241), the Persian translation of *Nusrat al-Fitrah wa Usrat al-Fitrah*, by the bilingual Iranian historian Imad Katib Isfahani (1125–1201), which was itself the Arabic translation of a Persian source by Anushirvan ibn Khaled ibn Muhammad al-Kashani. The major issue here is that this same al-Bundari who translated Isfahani into Persian translated Ferdowsi's *Shahnameh* into Arabic. In other words, pre-Islamic Iranian historiography and historical consciousness, all centered on the figure of the Persian Prince, continued to define the epistemic foregrounding of Islamic historical imagination at the heart of the Saljuq Empire.

With the rise of the Mongol Empire (1206–1368), we are solidly in the domain of Persian historiography, with towering figures like al-Jovayni, Fadlullah, Vassaf, and Hamdullah Mowstofi as principal narrators of the period—without which we would be at the mercy of phantasmagoric tales of Marco Polo's "Travelogue"! Equally important in this era is the paramount significance of Nasir al-Din al-Tusi's (1201–1274) *Akhlaq-e Naseri* (*Nasirean Ethics*), which consists of three essays, on ethics, economics, and politics. The story of this major Persian treatise relevant to the idea of the Persian Prince is quite crucial. The work is based on the Arabic text of Ibn Miskawayh's (932–1030) *Tahdhib al-Akhlaq wa Tathir al-A'raq* (*Refinement of Morals and Cleansing of Ethics*), but as Nasir al-Din al-Tusi tells us, he soon realized a mere translation will not do and began to compose his text based on what he thought was important. Even more importantly, the prose of *Nasirean Ethics* is thickly philosophical—befitting his status as a monumental philosopher and scientist of the age. Nasir al-Din al-Tusi's Persian text is emblematic of a more general trend in the aftermath of the Mongol destruction of Baghdad, which ushered in a major decline in Arabic as the lingua franca of intellectual production and a simultaneous ascendancy of Persian from Anatolia to the Indian subcontinent through Central Asia and the Caucuses. Although there are more minor treatises that define this period, Tusi's *Nasirean Ethics* and Saʿdi's (circa 1200–1291) *Golestan* and *Bustan* are by far the most important sources, revealing the moral imagination of the age in which the political ideas of Iranshahri (which we might translate as "Persopolitan") are in full sway, with the figure of Anushirvan as the principal patron prince of wisdom and good judgment.

From the fragments of the Mongol Empire and their Ilkhanid branch in Iranian and Muslim domains eventually emerged the Timurid Empire (1370–1507), with Herat as its epicenter. Two major sources of Timurid history are *Zafarnameh*, by Shami, and *Zafarnameh*, by Yazdi.[30] *Zafarnameh*, a biography of Timur himself, was written by Nizam al-Din Shami in 1404 and served as the basis for a later, more elaborate *Zafarnameh* by Sharaf al-Din Ali Yazdi (died 1454).[31] The numerous extant manuscript copies of this latter *Zafarnameh*, all luxuriously illustrated, are a testament to its subsequent celebrations by successive monarchs to model themselves on the archetypal example of Timur, the founding world conqueror of the dynasty, as a prototypical "Persian Prince." The most famous of these illustrated manuscripts is "the Zafarnama of Sultan Husayn Mirza," also known as *Garrett* or *Baltimore Zafarnameh*, lusciously illustrated by the legendary artist Kamal al-Din Behzad (circa 1450–1535), the head of the royal ateliers in Herat and Tabriz during the late Timurid and early Safavid Persian periods.[32] The figurative fronting of Timur as the sovereign monarch in these exquisite paintings is where the iconography of the Persian Prince finds one of its most illustrious examples. The "realistic" depictions of Timur's coronation and his army, as well as the detailed construction of the Great Mosque of Samarkand, come together as the fragmentary scenes, shots, and sequences of an epic movie. But the most spectacular document of this period is something even more powerful: Jami's (1414–1492) Alexander romance.[33] Jami's unique and beautiful Alexander romance follows those of Ferdowsi, Nezami, and Amir Khosrow Dehlavi, but precedes that of Amir Alishir Navaʾi in adopting and adapting the legendary Macedonian world conqueror into a solidly symbolic Persian Prince. The combination of Behzad's glorious paintings of Timur and Jami's rendition of an Alexander romance allows a Turco-Mongol conqueror and his Macedonian counterpart to leave for posterity the picture-perfect disposition of the Persian Prince. Alexander romances in and of themselves are prime examples of mirrors for princes in deeply moral, philosophical, and poetic renditions.

The Timurid were followed by the last three universal Muslim empires, the Ottomans (1299–1923), the Mughals (1526–1857), and the Safavids (1501–1736), then (after a couple of more minor dynasties) by the Qajars (1789–1925). A number of crucial interchanges among these three empires define this period. The locus classicus of Persian language and literary cultures moves from Iran to India, while in the Safavid domains we are witness to art and architecture reaching unprecedented heights, while at the same time, the rise of Ottoman Turkish as the imperial language of the Ottomans reaches its zenith. But the single most iconic figure of this entire period is the Mughal prince Dara Shikoh (1615–1659) and his masterpiece *Majmaʿ al-Bahrain* (circa 1655) as the epitome of a learned Persian Prince in an Indian robe. Dara Shikoh was the eldest son and heir apparent of Emperor Shah Jahan. His honorific title, Padshahzada-i-Buzurg Martaba ("High-Ranking Prince"), speaks volumes of his archetypal descent from the Persian moral and political imagination.[34] That he did not succeed his father and was murdered by his fanatical brother Aurangzeb has forever sealed his youthful image as the martyred "Persian Prince." Dara Shikoh's masterpiece *Majamʿ al-Bahrain*, composed in beautiful Persian, remains his last will and testament for its ingenious fusion of Persian (Islamic) mysticism and Indian (Vedantic) wisdom.[35] Contrary to his powermonger brother, Dara Shikoh spent his time mastering both Hindu and Islamic learning and traveled widely to study his own homeland, effectively becoming a peripatetic prince. He also began writing brilliant pieces of meditative philosophy that ultimately resulted in *Majmaʿ al-Bahrain*.

These last grand Muslim empires ultimately collapsed under the pressure of their own internal dynamics and the onslaught of European colonialism. The Mughals yielded to the British Raj, the Safavids ultimately led to the Qajars that broke down under Russian and British colonialism, and the Ottomans buckled under the pressure of European imperialism. Throughout the domains of the Persian cosmopolis, which at its height extended from India to Iran to the Ottoman Empire, Persian historiography, with its panache for pre-Islamic Iranian heritage, gathered around the figure of Anushirvan the Just, who had by then become solidly definitive to Muslim political culture. The dynamic triangulation among these three empires became the crystallization of Muslim classical heritage. The historical map of Muslim empires reveals the global expanse of multiple Islamic dynasties that ruled from one end of the earth to the next; in all of which, pre-Islamic Iranian theories of governance were variedly evident. Although Muslim dynasties had a direct claim to their Islamic (both Qur'anic and Muhammadan) pedigree, they were at the same time the *de facto* and *de jure* beneficiaries of pre-Islamic Iranian imperial archetypes that from India to Asia Minor to North Africa and deep into Muslim Spain enabled Muslim rulers to see themselves in a direct line of descent from the most ancient emperors in the deepest folds of human history. In one particularly powerful artistic tradition in Qajar Iran, the "coffeehouse painting," we see the allegorical presence of the archetypal figure of the Persian Prince extending from pre-Islamic to Islamic iconography. Although rooted in much earlier visual and performing arts, coffeehouse painting became particularly popular during the Safavid and Qajar periods. The vastly desirable visual art form emerges from manuscript illustrations into the public domain and in the form of murals, frescoes, and large canvases that provide visual props for storytelling by professional Naqqals in which the figures of Seyavash from the *Shahnameh* and Imam Hossein from *Shi'i* martyrology become a simulacrum of the Persian Prince from the pre-Islamic to Islamic periods.[36] The iconographic resemblances between these two martyrs weave together the dramatic persona of pre-Islamic Persian and Muslim martyrology, staging the tragic figure of the Persian Prince at the threshold of its encounter with European colonial modernity.

Doctrines, Theories, and Stories of Muslim Empires

How were Muslim empires held together? What theories of legitimacy, admonitory tales of bygone ages and just and unjust rulers, lofty ideas of kingship, inspiring ideals of governance, tales of cruelties and kindness, and practical administrative wisdom came together to give these empires a sense of coherence beyond sheer force and brute violence? What stories did these rulers and emperors hear or read that colored their dreams and frightened their wits to lead a semblance of a civilized world? Wild and unruly conquerors from tribal or nomadic cultures could descend upon sedentary civilizations and conquer them on horseback, but they had to come down from their horses to rule an empire.

Who and what were there to help them rule—and by what means? Such seminal Muslim philosophers and political theorists as al-Farabi, al-Ghazali, Nezam al-Molk, al-Mawardi, Al-Baqillani, Nasir al-Din al-Tusi, Fazlollah Khunji Isfahani, and many others were of course definitive to Muslim visions of legitimate rule. But there was much more to Muslim political culture than Islamic political thought in general or particularly its legal apparatus could contain or even suggest. A particularly potent brand of European Orientalists had a peculiar penchant for the legal and juridical dimensions of Islamic political culture—an aspect that was extremely important, but not to the disproportionate extent to which these scholars privileged it over Arabic or Persian humanism (Adab). This penchant for juridical texts in the Islamic context was irrespective of other equally if not more important genres of literature not just in Arabic, but in Persian, Turkish, and Urdu sources. In Arabic alone, a work like *Maqamat*, by al-Hamadhani (died 1008), or that of al-Hariri (1054–1122) was arguably more important in the formation of the political culture of their times than any learned juridical treatise on law that a meticulous but obtuse Imam might write. This is not to dismiss the historical significance of Islamic jurisprudence, but rather to endeavor to the contrary: to see the genre in the larger context of a political culture to which law was integral but not definitive. The effervescent dialogical disposition of Islamic scholasticism and humanism (as best captured by the superior scholarship of George Makdisi) is a key factor here, though it has been missed by and large by the Orientalists specializing in one field or another.[37]

This disproportionate predilection for juridical treatises and clerical tracts has progressed apace with our own time. There is a significant body of scholarship produced over the past century in which seminal Muslim political theorists, particularly jurists, theologians, and philosophers, have been closely studied by way of mapping out the expansive contours of Muslim political thought. Antony Black's *History of Islamic Political Thought: From the Prophet to the Present* (2001) is a typical example of this new body of literature, as is Gerhard Bowering's edited volume *Islamic Political Thought: An Introduction* (2015), or before that, Mehrzad Boroujerdi's edited volume *Mirror for the Muslim Prince: Islam and the Theory of Statecraft* (2013). *The Princeton Encyclopedia of Islamic Political Thought* (2012), also edited by Gerhard Bowering, is by now state-of-the-art scholarship. More old-fashioned Orientalist scholarship continues to be productive, particularly in the trailblazing works of Patricia Crone, as in her classic, *God's Caliph: Religious Authority in the First Centuries of Islam* (1986), or more recently, *God's Rule—Government and Islam: Six Centuries of Medieval Islamic*

Political Thought (2004). The recent history of this scholarship can be traced back to Erwin I. J. Rosenthal's *Political Thought in Medieval Islam* (1958) and William Montgomery Watts's *Islamic Political Thought* (1981). In more specifically philosophical domains, Ralph Lerner and Muhsin Mahdi's edited volume *Medieval Political Philosophy* (1963) had brought together a number of original seminal texts. Later on, Mohsen Mahdi and Charles Butterworth's edited volume *The Political Aspects of Islamic Philosophy* (1992) established a solid philosophical niche in this body of scholarship. With Saïd Amir Arjomand's groundbreaking book *The Shadow of God and the Hidden Imam: Religion, Political Order, and Societal Change in Shi'ite Iran from the Beginning to 1890* (1984), a more pronouncedly Iranian and Shi'a field began to find a potent sociological expression. Abdulaziz Sachedina's *The Just Ruler in Shi'ite Islam* (1998) carried that frame of reference forward to our contemporary time. Hüseyin Yilmaz's *Caliphate Redefined: The Mystical Turn in Ottoman Political Thought* (2018) mapped out a crucial component of the field in specifically Ottoman domains. Meanwhile, Richard M. Eaton's *India in the Persianate Age: 1000–1765* (2019) and Emma J. Flatt's *The Courts of the Deccan Sultanates: Living Well in the Persian Cosmopolis* (2020) paid detailed and timely attention to similar aspects of Islamic political cultures more specifically in the Persianate domains of South Asia. This impressive body of scholarship is as revealing as it is concealing—insightful in the authors' stated objectives, and yet blinded by their own insights to the limited epistemologies of the very prose and poetry of the political work they implicate but have not read.

The rise and effervescence of this significant body of literature has surely exponentially expanded our understanding of Islamic political thoughts and cultures. Despite their extraordinary contributions to our assessment of the way Muslim empires have been theorized, there are a few issues with this important scholarship. First, by and large, they are a close examination of Muslim thinkers' actual or potential political ideas, with little to no attention paid to historical Muslim empires and what animated their political cultures. Second, until very recently and with a few significant exceptions, they are limited in scope to the Arab components of the Muslim world at the expense of Indian, Persian, and Ottoman traditions, which are in fact more expansive and enduring in theoretical and pragmatic significance. Third, there is an inordinate focus on legal and juridical texts at the expense of philosophical, moral, and literary sources. And fourth, they are fixated on ideas of statecraft and political theories, bereft of the literary and poetic disposition of the texts they examine (or, even if they occasionally do so, manhandling the aesthetic disposition of these sources in the forced interest of their political implications). Much of these studies are tone-deaf to the *manner* of the prose and poetry of a text and rush to its presumed *matters*. A serious deficiency in the enormous legacy of Arabic and Persian literary theories is a key culprit here.

Such considerations raise a more fundamental epistemological question: How are we to understand Islamic political thought? When we think of the circumstances of the rise of Islamic political thought, as indeed in the case of any other intellectual movement in the Islamic context, we must consider it in the dialogical dispositions definitive to Muslim imperial encounters with the world. This is particularly true in the context of global Muslim empires—such as the Abbasids, the Saljuqids, the Mongols, the Ottomans, the Safavids, and the Mughals—where multiple people and their cultures are brought into creative contact. Arabs, Iranians, Turks, Indians, Mongols, Africans, Europeans, and others all had their pre-Islamic cultures before they entered any Islamic domain and consciousness. Islam is the cumulative memory of multiple empires, and all those empires consisted of diverse cultures and peoples. These empires also came to an end with three premodern Muslim monarchies—the Ottomans, the Safavids, and the Mughals. One way or another, these last three Muslim empires lost and yielded to European imperial conquests, the French and the British in particular. We must consider the rise of Islamic intellectual movements—whether triumphant or triumphalist—contrapuntally and dialogically in these imperial contexts. In these contexts, the two complementary formations of scholasticism and humanism are where Islamic political thoughts are to be seen as an intellectual movement sui generis that includes but is not limited to Muslim jurists. Jurists have laid exclusive claim to being Muslim, but their claims are incorrect. The philosophers, the mystics, the literati, the poets, and the rest all have equally legitimate claims—even more so if they carry within their thoughts pre-Islamic, Iranian, Indian, Greek, or Hebrew archetypal traces.

Without an enduring attention to this dialogical disposition of Muslim political cultures, scholars are bound to swing from one extremity to another—replacing Iran-centrism, Turk-centrism, or India-centrism to compensate the Arab-centrism they legitimately criticize. There are excellent scholars like Javad Tabatabai, featured in Boroujerdi's volume, who have done major work (though mostly in Persian) in mapping out Iranian political thought. However, Tabatabai is fixated with the fictive finality of the Iranian domain, whereas pre-Islamic Iranian or Indian or Hebrew or Greek ideas were not limited to Iran in their enduring influences, nor was Iran "immune" to Indian, Arab, Greek, Hebrew, and Islamic thought.³⁸ Yes, Nezam al-Molk had paid focused attention to pre-Islamic Iranian leitmotifs of royal rule, but so had a whole slew of Arabic-writing historians, ranging from al-Tabari to al-Thaʿalibi and Ibn Qutaybah al-Dinawari and beyond.³⁹ Iranian notions of royal rule were not limited to Iran either—they extended all the way from India to Greece to the heart of the Hebrew Bible. Such falsely racialized and ethnicized readings of Islamic or Iranian political culture are fundamentally flawed and entirely ahistorical—disregarding the contrapuntal, dialogical, and metamorphic character of both Islamic and Iranian political thought or any other variety. My detection and proposal of the Persian Prince as an imperial archetype is not limited to Iran, nor is Iran devoid of non-Iranian influences in Indian, Greek, or Arab and Islamic thought. There is also an additional problem: the abusive reading of literary texts. Scholars who in Boroujerdi's volume have paid serious attention to poets like Saʿdi have two issues with their encounter with the seminal Persian poet: one is offering a political scientist's view of a master lyricist without the slightest sense of irony, and the other is the introduction of such entirely unfamiliar and anachronistic concepts as "secularism." Saʿdi was not secular, whatever that alien idea may still mean these days, in the age of "post-secularism." Saʿdi was a Persian Muslim poet. Exemplary in his conceptual precision and detailed awareness of the Persianate world in Boroujerdi's edited volume is the essay by Saïd Amir Arjomand in which he takes to task the nomocentricity of Islamic law, and the entire coterie of Orientalist tradition that has championed it in Europe and the United States, as the defining moment of Muslim political cultures.⁴⁰ But the legitimate reaction to this enduring Orientalist proclivity should not swing in the other direction to privilege Iranian and Persian sources and must, as I propose in my articulation of the idea of the Persian Prince, account for the plurality of traditions that have historically combined to give the Iranian archetype its metamorphic Muslim robes. Indian, Iranian, Greek, Turkic, Mongol, Arab, and Islamic sources all come together to define the repressed or evident archival effervescence of the Persian Prince.

The issue is not the fictive purity of any branch of political thought—Iranian, Indian, Greek, Hebrew, or Islamic. The issue is the genre of literature and the politics of the prose they have staged, whether in Arabic, Persian, Turkish, or Urdu. As Saïd Amir Arjomand correctly points out (but does not elaborate on), texts such as *Kelilah and Dimnah* and *Golestan* have been definitive to Islamic political cultures extending from India to the Mediterranean. How did it happen that these seminal texts yielded their historical and factual power and authority over an obscure treatise by Ibn Taymiyyah, or even Ibn Rushd or al-Farabi? When we read a text like al-Tusi's *Akhlaq-e Naseri*, it is the dynamic he sustains among the three discourses on ethics, economics, and politics that is most crucial, not the fact that he wrote it in Persian. Other at least as important indices of Islamic political cultures include a Sufi allegory like Attar's *Conference of the Birds*, a comparative meditation like *Majmaʿ al-Bahrain* by Dara Shikoh, a coffeehouse painting, or a romance like *Vis-o-Ramin*, ad infinitum, and most empathically, an epic like *Shahnameh* or *Garshasp-nameh*, or popular stories like *Sandbad-nameh*, known as *Syntipas* in its Greek version. So perhaps here we might be tempted to make a distinction between "Islamic" and "Muslim" theories of power and authority—if the jurists' claim on "Islam" in its entirety is to be taken seriously. Not everything Muslims have thought has been Islamic, in the bizarre and ahistorical claim that legal theories have led on the word, and not everything Islamic has had serious or enduring significance for Muslims. Pre-Islamic Indian, Iranian, Hebrew, and Greek sources have played equally if not more important roles, as has an obscure treatise by a learned Islamic jurist. Stories that kings, caliphs, and sultans actually commissioned, their courtiers read, their storytellers recited, their poets versified, their artists illustrated—this is where the political cultures of the empires dwelled.

Why is it that most of these advice literatures are full of stories and only implicit injunctions or admonitions? Because these stories were popular, entertaining, and yet full of wit and wisdom. Muslim empires were held together at least as much by these narratives as by those legal treatises and juridical speculations excavated by generations of European Orientalists and now repeated and theorized by scholars of Islam, to the conclusion that an Islamic state is a moral contradiction in terms and a political impossibility! This practice of privileging and overinterpreting this evidentiary archival body is flawed. We must actively remember the robust and healthy interface between Islamic scholasticism and humanism. This is not to disregard the enormous reactionary role that court panegyrists have played in stabilizing tyrannical dynasties but rather to shift the focal point of our critical judgment to the critical balance between humanism and scholasticism.

In the vast and variegated composition of Islamic political thought, of course central is the text of the Qur'an as the word of God, the revelation, followed by the Hadith, or the words and deeds of the Prophet in the course of his life as exemplary conducts. The combination of the Qur'an and Hadith posits a charismatic nucleus of moral and binding memories that has remained preciously dear to generations of Muslims. In what Muslim jurists call *Ijmaʿ* (consensus), and *qiyas* (legal analogy), we have the judgment of the Muslim community and the word of reason added to the other two canonical sources of Islamic jurisprudence. The result of all this is the formation of the Islamic scholasticism that ranges from legal to theological discourses and that has been mostly (but not always) on the side of the ruling power and has constituted the nomocentrism of law in juxtaposition to the logocentrism of philosophy, the homocentrism of mysticism, and the cratocentrism of political thought. On the opposite side have emerged varied forms of Muslim humanism as the combination of the genres of Adab, Andarz, and Akhlaq—varied forms of literary imagination that placed the royal court as its locus classicus. These genres were literary in character and culture, and as such any abusive reading of them that disregards their aporetic disposition does them irreparable epistemic violence. These factors and forces were mapped out historically in both classical and contemporary periods, and in Persian, Arabic, Turkish, and Urdu. In the classical case this was the result of a dialogical disposition, where law, theology, mysticism, philosophy, art, architecture, and sciences cohabited, cross-referenced, and contested one another, while in contemporary times this was also dialogical in the context of the overriding metaphor of "Islam and the West"—which brings us to the point of post-Islamism, the collapse of the fictitious twin towers, and the rise of the current dysfunctional and amorphous empire.[41]

Now, let's go back to the rhyme and rhythm of Muslim empires before the dawn of European colonial modernity. Within these deeply dialogical, multicultural, and cross-referential contexts, altogether too much attention has been paid to figures like Abu Yusuf (died 798), al-Farabi (died 950), or al-Mawardi, as well as to the works of other jurists, theologians, or philosophers for their latent or manifest political ideas; that is all fine and important, yet they are all too limited in their implications and localized in their abstractions. Far more important, if we are to remain limited to theoretical sources rather than opening up, as we must, to literary and poetic discourses in terms domestic to their aesthetic imagination, I contend that to understand Muslim imperial rule we consult the Persian works of al-Ghazali, Nasir al-Din al-Tusi, and especially Nezam al-Molk al-Tusi, who actually ran a vast empire of his time. This is so not because they wrote in Persian as opposed to Arabic, but because what they said became central to the imperial apparatus of power to which they had access. There is a difference between theoretically speculating on the nature of political authority and actually running an empire. And there is a reason why, although the authors of these texts were bilingual, they wrote their treatises on rulership in Persian: they were addressing Persian-speaking royal courts. They were partaking in pre-Islamic Iranian, Indian, or Greek legacies of imperial rulership. But whether they wrote in Persian or Arabic or Turkish, or recasted ancient Arab legacies in contemporary dynastic terms, they were still drawing from a pre-Islamic Iranian, or Indian, or Greek tradition that informed their theoretical speculations about and pragmatic recommendations for ruling an empire. All their conceptions of imperial rule came from pre-Islamic and non-Islamic Iranian, Roman, Indian, or Egyptian legacies—and it is within these legacies that the archetype of the Persian Prince found its ancient habitat and unfolding relevance. No Arab, Turkish, Indian, or even Iranian dynasty was the passive recipient of such imperial pedigree. Authors such as Ibn Muqaffaʿ and poets like Ferdowsi no doubt cast their mythic and historic memories in terms palatable to their ruling kings and caliphs. But still the potent archetype of the Persian Prince remained constant, conversant, dialogical, descriptive, and proscriptive at one and the same time.

My major bone of contention here is that the pre-Islamic Iranian origin of stories and theories of just and legitimate governance was the root of all Muslim rules, both logically and dialogically, regardless of whether the storyteller or theorist wrote in Persian, Arabic, or Turkish. In only one such text—Fakhr al-Din Asʿad Gorgani's eleventh-century masterpiece *Vis-o-Ramin*, an exceptionally popular and widespread romance rooted in Sassanid and perhaps even Parthian legacies—do we have more evidence of pre-Islamic imperial culture than a whole library of legal gesticulations about Khilafah and Imamah. My idea of the Persian Prince as an archetypal category is by definition syncretic and amorphous, metaphoric and metamorphic, and the only reason we call it "Persian" instead of Turkish or Arab or Indian is factual evidence of the pre-Islamic imperial history of Persia, which goes back to the Achaemenid Empire and its archetypal presence in Greek antiquity and biblical heritage (which in turn becomes integral to the Qurʾan itself). Greek, Iranian, Indian, Hebrew, and Egyptian sources as a result are the root of this theoretical articulation of the idea of the Persian Prince—for which reason Alexander romances in Persian are among the best literary sites of the articulation of the archetype. Cyrus, Ahasuerus, Artaxerxes, and Darius, as well as of course Queen Esther, were household names in Greek antiquity and to the ancient Hebrews. The sudden rise of Prophet Muhammad and the spread of Islam in the seventh century did not put an end to that fact, and it will have to be understood in that context. At the same time,

Herodotus (484–425 BCE) was the chief chronicler of the Persian Empire in about 430 BCE. Xenophon's *Cyropaedia* (circa 370 BCE) was the vehicle of his moral and political philosophy—predicated on a creative recasting of the Persian Prince. There is perhaps a reason why Aeschylus's *Persians* (472 BCE) was the only surviving play of his otherwise lost trilogy. As late as the time of the Platonist philosopher, historian, and essayist Plutarch (circa 46–119 CE), Persians were still a dominant theme in his *Parallel Lives* and *Moralia*. For Arab and Muslim chroniclers, the memories of the Sassanid Empire added to, rather than detracted from, these much more ancient histories, which had placed pre-Islamic Iranian heritage at the forefront of their political imagination.

The simple fact is that throughout Muslim lands, Islamic political thought rooted in Qur'anic and Hadith literature was by definition within the Islamic period, namely in the aftermath of the Arab conquests of the seventh century. There is no, nor can there be, any "Islamic" political thought before that crucial century. The origin of the Iranian theories and stories of governance, on the other hand, is of course entirely pre-Islamic and, transmitted through factual or mythic memories, goes deeply into the Sassanid period (224–651 CE) and all the way back to the Achaemenid period (550–330 BCE). These syncretic ideas and stories were eventually translated, transmitted, sublated, mythologized, and metamorphosed into the Islamic period and, combined with Indian, Greek, and Hebrew legacies, deeply influenced all varied Islamic political thought of the subsequent centuries, not just in the Arab world—which is really limited to the Umayyad and early Abbasid periods—but throughout the vast expanse of Muslim empires, all the way from India to Central Asia to Iran to North Africa and the Iberian Peninsula and ultimately the Ottoman regions, then deeply into the Arab world that the Ottomans ruled.

In this context, the Abbasid dynasty (750–1258 CE) was the prototype for subsequent caliphal power in the Muslim world, and the central administrative apparatus of the empire was formed entirely on the Sassanid model and implemented by the capable Iranian ministerial family of the Barmecides, who traced their origin to Buddhist priests in pre-Islamic Iran. By the time of the rise of the Saljuqid Empire in 1037, the Abbasids had yielded much of their power to the mighty authority of a Turkic dynasty run by chief Iranian minister Nezam al-Molk on a mostly pre-Islamic Iranian model. Even before that, the rule of the Fatimids in Egypt (909–1171) and simultaneously the rise of the Buyids (934–1062) in Northern Iran had dismantled the power of Sunni theories of governance in patently Shi'i charismatic terms. Although the formation of Abbasid caliphal rule was indebted to the Barmecides, the decline of the family's political fortunes had given rise to alternative empires and dynasties that were partaking in a more patently obvious representation of pre-Islamic Iranian imperial heritage. But even at the height of Abbasid caliphate, in addition to the Barmecide family, the palpable presence of other recent Zoroastrian converts in the mid-eighth century were becoming exceedingly powerful at court—carrying with them a pronounced pre-Islamic Iranian heritage:

> The family of Nawba<u>k</u>t is said to have claimed descent from the Kayanid hero Gēv, the son of Gōdarz. . . . Nawba<u>k</u>t first appears as an astrologer in the entourage of the second ʿAbbasid caliph, Manṣūr (136–58/754–75), under whose influence he converted from Zoroastrianism to Islam. . . . He was associated with Māšāʾallāh in selecting the proper astrological moment (30 July 762) for laying the foundations of Baghdad . . . and he advised Manṣūr concerning the revolt of Ebrāhīm in Šaʿbān-Šawwāl. . . . Abū Sahl's original name was Persian: <u>K</u>ᵛaršād Māh Ṭaymāḏā Mābāḏār <u>K</u>osrevā Behšād. . . . The occurrence of the sun and the moon as the first two elements in his name probably indicates that Abū Sahl was born before Nawba<u>k</u>t's conversion from Zoroastrianism.⁴²

All these crucial and defining elements have been delegated to curiosities and oddities of the early Islamic period by generations of European Orientalists and their later Muslim and non-Muslim followers in the interest of disproportionately favoring the clerical ulema (Sunni and Shiʿa, Arab and Iranian alike) and their legalese disposition as the defining institutions of "Islam." Two interrelated factors have given inordinate significance to legal theories of political power in Islam: European Orientalism and European colonialism. While because of their own Christian and Jewish predilections European Orientalists paid excessive attention to Arabic or Persian legal sources, in response to European colonialism Muslim reformists, revolutionaries, and critical thinkers too were instrumental in the destruction of their own multifaceted cosmopolitan cultures in the hopes of generating a singular site of resistance that had turned to formal legalism and fetishized ritualism. Here, Iranian, Turk, and Arab reformists and revolutionaries were equally to blame. The prophet of them all was in fact Jamal al-Din al-Afghani (1838–1897), an Iranian Shiʿi who masqueraded as an Afghan Sunni and became the leading force in agitating pioneering Egyptian reformists like Mohammad Abduh and his followers. The more agitated and defensive these reformists became, the more they turned the cosmopolitan universe of Islamic legacy into a fetishized clericalism. The articulation and rise of "secularism" (which became a fanatical ideology of its own) further opposed and thus exacerbated this obsessive formalism, devoid of the rich and diversified body of Muslim historical experiences. The "puritanical" Wahhabism and Salafism of the period cast a long and lasting shadow on the entirety of Muslim historical experiences. Muslim reformers and revolutionaries were far more destructive of gutting their own moral and intellectual heritage than the Orientalists could ever be. Islamic scholasticism (including legalism) in both Arabic and Persian has always been checked and balanced by the equally powerful literary humanism of these very languages.

Mirroring the Persian Prince

Until very recently, one of the very few scholars of Islamic political thought who paid close and extensive attention to Persian material was the eminent British Orientalist A. K. S. Lambton (1912–2008). In a major essay in 1970, she informed her readers as follows:

> Mirrors for princes are an important and characteristic branch of Persian *belles lettres*. Many of them are written in elegant and pleasing prose and illustrated by anecdotes and stories which, at their best, are graphic and revealing pictures of contemporary society. It is not, however, the literary aspect of mirrors which I wish to consider in this paper, but rather the political ideals put forward in them. I have selected a number of typical mirrors, some of which are well-known and others not so, to illustrate these ideals, which hold an intermediary position between the theory of the jurists on the one hand and the philosophers on the other. All three set forth the divine nature of ultimate sovereignty.[43]

There is a minor categorical issue and a much more serious epistemic matter with this introductory paragraph in an otherwise deeply learned essay. The minor issue is that here Lambton disregards the category of mystical (Sufi) literature, in which political issues were also addressed. The juridical, philosophical, and mystical discourses were variedly and occasionally even simultaneously engaged in the active theorization of political authority. But the far more important epistemological issue is that Lambton says she will disregard "the literary aspect of mirrors" and address only their "political ideals." She is quite right that these mirrors are excellent examples of Persian belles-lettres and have distinct stylistic and literary aspects to them, but she is wrong that their political dimensions can be examined independent of these poetics. The two are intrinsically interrelated. These texts are the products of a refined courtly environment, and their literary flair is integral to their political prowess. The *juridical* and *philosophical* discourses Lambton has in mind here must in fact be approximated to the *literary* and *poetic* dispositions of the literature she mentions and not the other way around. We should read those juridical and philosophical texts for their literary tropes and narratological dispositions, not to perpetrate the epistemic violence of political scientists on those literary and poetic sources. My articulation of the Persian Prince as an imperial archetype decidedly underlines the literary and poetic dispositions of the sources I examine to balance and compensate for the historically inordinate and disproportionate attention European Orientalists and Muslim Islamists have paid to juridical and scholastic texts. The reason for that is simple: the institutions of literary humanism (Adab) have been as important in defining and mirroring the Muslim moral and political imagination of their time as those of Islamic scholasticism. European Orientalists and Muslim Islamists have distorted this fact. My articulation of the figure of the Persian Prince is the occasion to restore and reclaim this crucial balance.

With these two sets of observations in mind, we can read and learn much from Lambton's informed work. In the history of Islamic political thought, three sorts of thinkers have usually written on politics: the jurists, the theologians/philosophers, and the mystics. The literary humanists, Lambton is right, stand somewhere in the midst of those three institutional discourses—above them even, beyond their scholastic reach. For jurists, politics is the administration of Islamic law (Shari'ah) in a Muslim territory; for philosophers, politics is the path to absolute happiness (Sa'ada) attained by the wisdom of a philosopher/king; and for the mystics, as we see in the cases of the Ottomans and the Safavids, the worldly life is a manifestation of the Divine Will to power. For literary master stylists, politics is the normative manifestation of the sublime and the beautiful in the aesthetic elegance of moral justice—which is precisely why their beautiful and elegant prose and poetry stand in and of themselves for the truth of justice they wish to convey, the virtuoso performance of their rhyme and rhythm effectively and symbolically marking the universal and cosmic sense of justice they wish to project. Justice is beautiful, and the beautiful is just. If for jurists it was the *juridical*, for philosophers the *philosophical*, and for mystics the Divine aspects of politics that decided their takes on power, for court poets and literary stylists it was the beauty and elegance of their prose and poetry, as well as their appeal to the superior senses of human intellect, that inspired them to address political matters in literary terms. Among all these figures, the literary stylist, particularly the poet, was the closest to the ruler in physical and political proximity—having access to his heart and mind at one and the same time. In paying close attention to these mirrors, Lambton unfortunately completely disregards the poets, while Saʿdi in his *Bustan*, Rudaki in his panegyrics, or Ferdowsi in his *Shahnameh*, among scores of other seminal poets and prose stylists, are far more important than scores of jurists, philosophers, and even mystics put together. To be sure, there is a beautiful part of *Masnavi* in which Rumi gives us a mise-en-scène of where people close to the Prince stand.

> Kings have a habit
> You may have heard:
> Warriors stand to their left
> For the heart is located to the left of the chest,
> The learned and the scribe stand to their right
> For we write from right to left.
> They place the mystics right in front of them
> For they are the mirror of the soul and even better than mirror.[44]

But this very beautiful description itself, and the mystique of its power, is precisely in its sublime poetry. The singular difference between poetry and poetic prose and all other discourses of power and politics is the sustained dissonance between what they sign and what they signify. What they sign is clear and concise, but what they continue to signify beyond their designated royal court is something beyond the control of even the poet himself.

How were Muslim empires held together? We need to understand the range and the limits of any one of the discourses addressing that question. There is no single theory of governance or polity to have held such vast and varied successions of empires together, for Islam itself is a deeply varied and multivariant phenomenon. While the jurists have had an almost exclusively legalistic take on politics, and the philosophers were in a prolonged conversation with Plato and Aristotle's conceptions of the philosopher/king and the political apparatus of legitimacy, the prose stylists (including historians) and poets writing in the genre of mirrors for princes or otherwise were deeply influenced by pre-Islamic Indian, Hebrew, and Iranian (Sassanid in particular) ideas and ideals of benevolent kingship, moral rectitude, and above all justice and fairness. If Islam as a juridical apparatus informs the jurists, and Greek philosophy is at the forefront of the philosopher's conception of politics, the prose stylists and poets represent the enduring influence of pre- and non-Islamic political ideas, in which the wisdom literature from India was always evident. It is not until the rise of the ingenious work of Shahab al-Din Yahya ibn Habash al-Suhrawardi (1154–1191) that pre-Islamic Iranian themes enter and revolutionize his philosophical discourse. It is therefore perhaps not surprising that most of these mirrors for princes, as a particularly potent genre, whether written in Persian or otherwise, were meant to be used by the reigning monarchs within the larger Muslim realms, all the way from Transoxiana to India and Mesopotamia to Iran and the Ottoman territories. Iran was by no means the only place where these mirrors were written or read and put into practice, nor was Persian the sole language of their delivery. From Spain to India, in Persian as well as in Arabic and Turkish, these mirrors have been the site of articulating these pre-Islamic ideals. The overriding pre-Islamic Iranian conceptions of rulers and their subjects are evident in all these sources. The Sassanid provenance of the political ideas expressed in these mirrors, and the fact that the overwhelming majority of them were written and put to use within Persianate domains, makes this genre of political writing of immediate consequence in its Iranian, Indian, and Ottoman contexts proper, but of equally enduring importance in the larger Islamic context, which includes but is not limited to the Arab world.

How might we best characterize the central princely figure paramount in all these imperial contexts? Definitive to the political ideals and narrative integrity of these mirrors has been the notion of the divinely ordained authority of the king, the *Farr-e Izadi* of the Persian Prince, and his equally providential predisposition toward justice and fairness in his realm. These qualities are essential, not accidental, to his legitimacy. In being directly concerned with realpolitik, these mirrors for princes at times reveal an astonishing degree of pragmatism, realism, and straightforward instrumentalities of statecraft—while simultaneously exuding the moral and ethical aspects of their enterprise. Their literary overtone is paramount regardless of the social status or aristocratic background of their authors. We have ruling monarchs, aspiring princes, aging statesmen, learned philosophers, passionate mystics, meticulous theologians, meticulous legalists, competent scribes, and boring bureaucrats as well as master literary stylists and poets, among those interested in writing such mirrors. The most enduring of these authors have been their best storytellers, as evidenced by their simultaneous concern with matters of political expediency, the primacy of justice, and the elegance of prose and poetry. In prose and poetry, from the

Shahnameh (circa 1010) of Ferdowsi, to *Qabus-nameh* (circa 1080) of Kaykavus ibn Vushmgir, to *Nasihat al-Muluk* (1109) of Ghazali, to *Bustan* (1257) of Sa'di, to *Kherad-Nameh-ye Iskandari* (composed between 1468 and 1485) of Jami—to name just a few landmarks—the Persianate world has been the site of a singular articulation of the Persian Prince. The rulers and monarchs for whom these mirrors were composed are long since gone and forgotten. What has remained and continues to resonate is precisely the aesthetic sublimity of these texts, which still commands and demands attention. It is the prophetic poetry they invested in the figure of the Persian Prince that has survived to this day. A terrible epistemic violence has been perpetrated on these texts by scholars who have disregarded their poetry and hurriedly rushed toward their politics.

These mirrors emerged under specific historical circumstances and because of their authoritative voice and imperial diction were put to immediate political use. As such, they both convey a sense of transhistorical wisdom that informs and animates them all and mark the pragmatics of the daily politics as practiced by kings, sultans, and their administrative retinues. Mirrors for princes developed adjacent to philosophical treatises, theological articulations, mystical reflections, and juridical tracts on politics, and are thus effectively in conversation with these complementary sources of inspiration, which places Greek philosophical wisdom face-to-face with Qur'anic and Hadith sources. Reason and revelation, one may thus summarily suggest, informed Islamic political consciousness, and yet they both in turn inform the mirrors' narrative tensions. The literary aspect of these texts, however, takes over and gives them their distinct characteristic and royal diction. There are therefore multiple discourses at the heart of these mirrors for princes that animate their prose: (1) Greek political philosophy (Plato and Aristotle in particular), (2) Islamic theology and jurisprudence (the Qur'an and the Hadith in particular), (3) Muslim mystical sensibilities and genealogies, and (4) a collectively received conception of pre-Islamic Iranian political ethos and practices (that of the Sassanids in particular). Mirrors for princes are informed by all these discourses but are not reducible to any one of them.

Beginning with the monumental figure of Ibn Muqaffa''s (died 757) *Adab al-Kabir* and *Adab al-Saghir*, the Sassanid court, both in reality and in its active reimagination in the post-Sassanid Muslim world, plays a crucial role in providing repeated models for a just and enduring kingship. The same is true of an entire genre of mirrors generically known as *Kitab al-Taj* in early Islamic history, which also considers the divine origin of the king's authority, on the Sassanid model, as the conditio sine qua none of political legitimacy. With the writing of Kaykavus ibn Iskandar ibn Qabus ibn Vushmgir's *Qabus-nameh* (1083), the Persian provenance of the mirror for princes assumes its most evident example. Taken together, we can now see how these mirrors held Muslim empires together: by their distillation of the theories and practices of governance directly rooted either in the Qur'an and Islamic ideals, or else in the variedly Islamized pre-Islamic ideas of primarily Persian but also Indian, Greek, and Hebrew origins. Pre-Islamic Iranian dynasties, particularly the Sassanids (226–650), remained definitive to almost all major Muslim empires. This is why in the pages of Sa'di's *Bustan* we encounter his poetic rendition of the most famous of the Sassanid emperors, Khosrow Anushirvan, and from his lips we learn:

> *Keh bakhshayesh arad bar ommidvar . . .*
>
> For the king will be forgiving to the supplicant,
> Hoping for the forgiveness of the Almighty—
> He would not like harm coming people's ways
> For he fears harm coming to his own kingdom—
> And if this were not to be second nature to him
> No one would be safe in his kingdom.[45]

The key issue here is whether the poetics of these passages override their politics, or the other way around. What began with Lambton's albeit conscious disregard for the poetic and literary force of these texts ultimately resulted in yet another major Orientalist, Patricia Crone, altogether doubting their authorial authenticity, as in her learned obsession with denying that al-Ghazali was the author of his *Nasihat al-Muluk!*[46] The question here is not whether to compare and contrast the infinite superiority of the scholarship of Jalal Homa'i, who prepared the critical edition of al-Ghazali's *Nasihat al-Muluk*. The question is something entirely different. It is total disregard for the hermeneutic fact and the poetic authority of the text itself, whoever may have authored it. This bizarre Orientalist twist of entirely casting doubt on the authorial authenticity of a text when attributed to a prominent figure like al-Ghazali, more than discrediting the text itself, exposes the literary blindness of the Orientalist herself. These learned scholars have gone on a wild-goose chase of discrediting an author, while the text itself stares them in the face. This generation of Orientalists, true to form, is quite evidently litigant literalists, like their kindred souls among the Wahabi Salafists—deaf, dumb, and blind to the textual authenticity of what they read, let alone the poetics of the prose they habitually misread. It is impossible to disregard the fact that these Orientalists have learned their "Oriental languages" as adults in universities and can afford no emotive affinity for the poetics and the aesthetics of the text they thus dismember.

Let's think this through for a moment. In understanding the hermeneutic ambience of a text, the eminent Italian semiotician and hermeneutician Umberto Eco famously distinguished among three forms of "intentions" in a text: *the intention of the author (intentio auctoris), the intention of the text (intentio operis)*, and *the intention of the reader (intentio lectoris)*.[47] Whoever the author of *Nasihat al-Muluk* was and whatever his intention may have been are entirely tangential to the fact of the text itself, which has survived the test of time and the sustained course of its manuscript histories. The same holds for Roland Barthes's by-now proverbial idea of "the death of the author," which has theoretically liberated the text from the claims of any presumed authorship.[48] The scholarly world, Muslim and non-Muslim—minus this militant Orientalist—has attributed *Nasihat al-Muluk* to al-Ghazali. So that is a textual fact, if not a biographical fact. Between Eco and Barthes, all the Orientalist had to do was to look around and allow the text to breathe in fresh air. It makes no difference whether indeed al-Ghazali wrote the book, as we believe he did, or whether someone else wrote it and put al-Ghazali's name on it. Constant remains the text itself, its manuscript variations, and the world of its hermeneutic triangulations among its presumed author, its textual evidence, and its varied readership, including the epistemic violence of its Orientalist readership. But such theoretical literary concerns are farthest removed from the minds of Orientalists when they try to decipher an "Oriental text." The more important point here is the factual and hermeneutic necessity of allowing for the literary and poetic dispositions of the text to underline its politics. From disregarding poetics to discrediting authorial authenticity, what generations of Orientalist scholars have done, to not just this particular text but any and all texts they have examined, is perpetrate irreparable epistemic violence on what they wasted their lives trying to understand.

This literary disposition of the political text is as applicable to poetic sources we examine as to those in stylized prose, as much in the genre of belles-lettres as in varied forms of historiography. The prominent example of Rashid al-Din Fadlullah Hamadani's seminal history, *Jamiʿ al-Tawarikh* (*Compendium of Histories*), for one, points to inconspicuous sources where the ideal and archetype of the Persian Prince has had enduring resonance beyond the genre of mirrors for princes. In an excellent recent doctoral dissertation, Stefan T. Kamola has fully demonstrated how "beyond the monolithic and uncritical use of the *Jamiʿ al-Tawarikh* that dominates modern scholarship on Mongol and Ilkhanids history... [this text was instrumental in] the difficult process of transforming the Mongol Ilkhans from a dynasty of foreign military occupation into one of legitimate sovereigns for the Perso-Islamic world." This extraordinary insight does precisely what is most needed to open up the historiographical text for its literary significance. Kamola points to

> a full range of Persianate cultural responses to the experience of Mongol conquest and rule through the life and work of the most prominent statesman of the period. Drawing on the example of cultural projects undertaken in the early decades of the Ilkhanate, Rashid al-Din canonized a narrative of Ilkhanid history in which his patrons embodied a model of sacred kingship that adhered both to contemporary intellectual trends in the Middle East and to Mongol dynastic traditions emphasizing descent from Genghis Khan. This new model, which first enters political discourse in the writing of Rashid al-Din in response to the vacuum of authority created by the fall of the Abbasid caliphate, laid the groundwork for later Timurid, Safavid and Mughal court ideologies.[49]

Kamola's apt perspective shows how historiographical tropes entail crucial ideological forces. What would have significantly furthered his insight is if he had been exposed to the groundbreaking work of Hayden White, *Metahistory: The Historical Imagination in Nineteenth-Century Europe* (1973), where he maps out the manner in which the prose and prosody of historiography in four main tropes of metaphor, metonymy, synecdoche, and irony are the vehicles of such hidden significations. The moral of the story here is how the vastest empire in human history was made legitimate by a monumental work of historiography in which, in the form of a historical narrative, the reign of a deeply alien invading army was systematically incorporated into Muslim dynastic cultures. Through the intermediary institution of the figure of the Persian Prince, we are witness to the systematic domestication of an alien power. Such a feat would not have been possible without the instrumental function of Persian literary cultures, in which Rashid al-Din Fadlullah seemed to be writing a mere work of history, while his contemporary Saʿdi was driving the figure of the Persian Prince deeply into Muslim consciousness—as he consistently civilized the otherwise brute machinations of power.

Makon ta tavani del-e khalq rish . . .

Never hurt those you rule,
For if you did you'll uproot yourself—
If you wish to have a straight path,
That is the path of the righteous who nourish hope and fear—
Naturally the reasonable person
Hopes for good and is fearful of evil—
If you found these two qualities in a king
You'll have a haven in his kingdom.[50]

It is perhaps important to recall at this point that this fusion of history and theory is definitive to the works of Niccolò Machiavelli as well, where we see him in his *Discourses on Livy/Discorsi sopra la prima deca di Tito Livio/Discourses on the First Ten Books of Titus Livy* (circa 1517) combine political history and philosophy, projecting what he believes can be learned from other eras to elucidate contemporary politics. Anticipating by centuries Nietzsche's short essay "On the Use and Abuse of History for Life" (1874), Machiavelli saw history as useful only to the degree that it could help our understanding of current events. He frequently turned to the Romans and other civilizations as exemplary models for his own time. Cyrus plays the same exemplary role for Machiavelli that Anushirvan plays for Muslim historians—the model of judicious and effective leadership. Moses, Cyrus, Romulus, and Theseus are among Machiavelli's favorite examples.[51] This exemplary model extended to his own contemporary time, when, in expectation of Charles VIII's 1494 invasion from France, he alludes to Friar Girolamo Savonarola's prediction in 1492 that "a new Cyrus" would appear from beyond the mountains.[52] The idea of the Persian Prince is consistently evident in Machiavelli's articulation of his Prince. The reason for that is the identical imperial archetype of the Persian Prince in both European and Islamic historiography.

Empires and Their Discontent

As I propose and theorize here, the Persian Prince embodies not just a royal identity, it is also a rebellious alterity. It is as much a position of power as it is a postulate of defiance. It is a paradoxical term: it is both itself and its other, its own light hiding its own shadow. It is a pharmakon—a poison and a cure, a prince and a rebel, a poet and a prophet, a legislator and a revolutionary. The rebellious figure of the Prophet in Mecca was like a Persian Prince, and the powerful legislator he became in Medina was also a Persian Prince. Early in Islamic history such terms of denigration and derision as *Zindiq* or *Majus* or *Rafezi* were synonymous with *Molhed* and *Kafir*, meaning "infidel" and "apostate." But the abusive terms "Zindiq" and "Majus" referred specifically to Manichaean and Zoroastrian oppositional figures whose ideas and actions did not dovetail into the dominant ideologies of imperial power and its jurists and historians. The Zindiq and the Majus were also the mirror image of the Persian Prince in power. The term "Zindiq" in particular refers to the subterrain undoing of the imperial order, of the caliphal claim to power, of the entire edifice of Islamic law legislating and legitimizing the ruling tyrannies.[53] The rebel dwelling in such subversive terms as "Zindiq" has always been the Persian Prince in bondage, in disguise. There are any number of indications of the undoing of the imperial order, perhaps best exemplified by the sectarian and rebellious uprisings against every single dynasty, but the poet in bondage is in and of itself the hidden force of rebellion against the prose of history that sought to stabilize injustice.

The names of three prominent Zindiqs, or apostates in the more generic sense, come together in early Islamic history to mark the anxieties of Arab historians and jurists about the threat they posed to their imperial powers and the scholastic orthodoxy that acts as their effective ideologies of domination over a vast empire: Abd Allah Ruzbeh ibn Daduya, known as Ibn Muqaffaʿ (721–757), Abu al-Hasan Ahmad ibn Yahya ibn Ishaq al-Rawandi (827–911), and Muhammad ibn Zakariya al-Razi (854–925) are usually recognized as the most prominent of these early Zindiqs, meaning either Manichean or, more generically, rebellious and subversive thinkers.[54] There is a glaring commonality among these three eminent intellectual figures of early Islam: they were all Iranians, and they were all accused of being Zindiqs (Manicheans) for their iconoclastic and subversive ideas that doctors of law and chroniclers of royal courts considered dangerous to their rules. Ibn Muqaffaʿ was a master prose stylist chiefly responsible for translating major literary works from Middle Persian Pahlavi to Arabic; al-Rawandi was monumental in Muʿtazilite theology and ultimately denounced all forms of religion, becoming a notorious figure as evidenced in his *Kitab al-Zomorrod (The Book of Emerald)*; and Razi was an even more monumental figure in the history of science, medicine, and philosophy.[55] That Europeans soon discovered and translated him, Latinizing his name as "Rhazes" or "Rasis," is an indication not of his significance but of Europeans catching up with civilized science and philosophy.

The generic term "Zindiq," or "Majus," as evident in these and many other recent Iranian converts, like the celebrated poet Bashar ibn Burd (714–783), was used by Arab historians to designate a whole range of subversive thoughts and practices that were ultimately evident in the massive uprisings by the impoverished peasantry and urban poor against the cruelties and tyrannical rule of both the Umayyad and Abbasid caliphs.[56] In the aftermath of the murder of Abu Muslim, who had led the Abbasid revolution against the Umayyads, a succession of mostly peasant uprisings emerged with syncretic revolutionary ideologies mixing Zoroastrian and Islamic leitmotifs, among them those of Sunpadh, al-Muqanna, Ustadhsis, and Babak Khorramdin, that rattled the foundations of the Abbasid dynasty and Islamic juridical orthodoxies. This succession of uprisings in the northern mountainous regions was a clear indication of the continued prevalence of Zoroastrian ideas in the early Islamic period. In the rebellious figures of these prophetic figures, the archetypal Persian Prince assumes its earliest manifestations in prophetic visions. From this point forward the figure of the Persian Prince is a paradoxical icon in which dwells both the ruling monarch and his rebellious shadow: the rebel, the prophet, the poet. Not a single period in Islamic history within or outside Iran has ever been devoid of such serious rebellious uprising under mostly syncretic, proto-Zoroastrian, Manichean, Mazdakite, and eventually proto-Shiʿite tropes. Integral to the imperial allegory of the Persian Prince has always been its rebellious opposite, a poet to its prince, a rebel to its power, a prophetic voice to its royal chorus, marking not just a figure in power and authority but a bandit in rebellion, a Zindiq to his tyrannical pieties.

FOUR

The Persian Literary Provenance of Muslim Empires

Our august ancestors have considered Justice one of Four Essential Virtues, and have therefore established upon it the very foundation of our worldly affairs and our Other-Worldly Day of Judgement. They believed [as we believe the Noble Prophet has said], "It is with Justice that Heaven and Earth are stabled," and considered themselves the agents of [God Almighty's command in the Qur'an that] "Verily Allah has commanded Justice and Kindness." ... But the practice of our Contemporaries these days is that such a behavior is the worst thing possible, and that Justice can cause countless calamities, and have offered clear proof of that. They maintain that the foundation of monarchy, and rulership, and being a master is in fact violence, for unless someone is feared he will not be followed, and everyone would become equal, and the whole order of things will fall apart, and the structure of the ruling regime will therefore collapse. If someone, God Forbid, were to be Just, and were not to beat up people and kill them, and then confiscate their properties, and then go ahead and get drunk and start harassing people and screaming at them, people will not fear him, and then the subjects will not follow the order of kings.[1]

Ubayd Zakani (died 1370), Akhlaq al-Ashraf
[Ethics of the nobles] (1339–1340)

"WHEN AND WHY DO MEN OBEY? Upon what inner justifications and upon what external means does this domination rest?" This key question—at once political, psychological, and philosophical—was asked by Max Weber in his seminal essay "Politics as a Vocation" (1919) and reverberates throughout world history.² The question is so seminal it is almost ahistorical. But site-specific and historical it will have to be made in order for it to be meaningful.

The Persian provenance of Muslim empires, caliphates, sultanates, and all other small and large dynasties was both de facto and de jure. There were two major institutions that linked Islamic political thoughts and practices to their pre-Islamic Persian sources: the literary genre of Andarz-nameh (advice literature) and the political office of the vizierate. Through the intermediary office of the vizierate, the very word, concept, and institution of which are believed to be Persian, the Islamic institutions of caliphate and sultanate, as perhaps best represented in the Abbasid (Arab) and Saljuqid (Turk) dynasties, were predicated on the Persian prototype of imperial monarchy metamorphosed into new Islamic forms. To be sure, the political cultures of the vast spectrum of Muslim empires were not limited to their Persian aspects, nor indeed was the regional and global spectrum where the idea of the Persian Prince was at work limited to Muslim empires. No doubt the Byzantine Empire and the Indian, Turkic, Mongol, and Arab patrimonial practice were equally important at various stages of Muslim empires, as indeed the idea of the Persian Prince was correspondingly at work in Indian, Greek, Roman, European, and Hebrew contexts. But still the theoretical modality and the archetypal blueprints of Muslim empires included considerable Persian elements in their institutional origin, as they were Islamic in ideological articulation and contained pre-Islamic Iranian elements in their archaic memories.

In the works of political theorists like Khwajah Nezam al-Molk al-Tusi, Imam Muhammad al-Ghazali, Nasir al-Din al-Tusi, and Qabus ibn Vushmgir, this proclivity for the Persianate provenance of politics was quite palpable, while in others it assumed more Islamic garbs. While at the Abbasid court this Persianate modality of imperial rule thrived in the Islamic lexicon, during the Mongol (Ilkhanid) Empire it dovetailed with Genghis Khan's Yassa; conversely, with Persianate (Samanid) and Turkic (Ghaznavid and the Saljuqid) dynasties it took such boldly Persian forms as Ferdowsi's *Shahnameh*, but in its Shi'ite gestations (the Buyids and the Fatimids and later the Safavids) it was sublated into the charismatic authority of the Ruler/Imam. The last grand constellation of Muslim empires—the Ottomans, the Safavids/Qajars, and the Mughals—were collectively Persianate in the blueprint of their imperial dispositions—with Ferdowsi's *Shahnameh* and varied renditions of the Alexander romance (Iskandar-nameh) as the key icons of this political Persianism.

To switch register in the same key, two prominent scholars carry the proud name of "al-Jovayni"—one is Imam al-Haramayn Abd al-Malik al-Jovayni (1028–1085), a towering Shafi'i jurist and theologian, and the other 'Ata' Malik al-Jovayni (1226–1283), an eminent historian of the Mongol Empire. They were both Persian—although one wrote primarily in Arabic and the other primarily in Persian. They were both politically engaged—though in two diametrically opposed proses. But the impact of the historian was infinitely more lasting than the passing import of the jurist. While we must fully recognize the significance of scholasticism as an ideological foregrounding of Islamic political thought, in this book I am making a case for the equally enduring significance of literary humanism in the selfsame political culture. The central administrative apparatus that enabled and enacted this enduring tradition was the office of the vizierate, an institution with a penchant for literary humanism. The archetypal figure of the Persian Prince remains at the epicenter of this expansive political culture—both its humanism and its scholasticism, at one and the same time. This is what I will detail in this chapter.

Stories, Histories, Old and Unfolding

In *Jawame' al-Hekayat wa Lawami' al-Revayat* (*Collection of Stories and Illustrious Narratives*), Sadid-al-Din Mohammad Awfi (died circa 1232) tells us the story of the Persian emperor Yazdegerd entrusting his newborn son Bahram to an Arab prince named Nu'man to raise as a proper Persian Prince. Nu'man, in turn, appoints three wet nurses to attend to the infant. These three nurses had come from three noble families: "One Arab, the other Iranian, and the third Turk, so that Bahram would be raised with Arabic eloquence (Fasahat), Persian courage (Samahat), and Turkish chivalry (Shoja'at)."[3]

This little story is delightfully instructive in a number of significant ways, first and foremost, perhaps, that the education of a Persian Prince is entrusted to an Arab Prince. This is not a paradox. This is parallax—looking at the same phenomenon from multiple angles. Then comes the all-important fact that three wet nurses, or mother figures, from three noble families are the true carriers of their royal cultures. After that come the beautiful stylistic formations of three adjectives—Fasahat, Samahat, and Shoja'at. The Arabic verbal form creates contrapuntal formal affinities among the three complementary cultural dissonances that these noblewomen invest in the Persian Prince. This is followed by the multicultural fact of the Persian Prince's upbringing, that at least three cultures—Arabic, Turkish, and Persian—must come together to raise a proper Persian Prince. The result is the syncretic ideal of the prince, which would be compromised without any one of its components. We are here made privy to the early education of a Persian Prince in decidedly multicultural and multilingual heteroglossia, so that the Prince would rule the Persians, Arabs, and Turks in their respective languages and cultures. The subconscious model of all this is of course Cyrus, who ruled Egypt in Egyptian ways, the Jews based on their religion, and Iran and the rest of the world in whatever ways they preferred, so far as all remained obedient to his rule. In order to be politically cogent and authentic, the Persian Prince had to be culturally syncretic and inauthentic. There is no "pure" Persian Prince or "pure" Persian idea of sovereignty. Everything from India to the Mediterranean Basin, from Central Asia to the India Ocean, is decidedly syncretic, multicultural, polyphonic. The idea of the Persian Prince assumes the kaleidoscopic colors of its linguistic and cultural habitat, the Persian language. It welcomes, hosts, and acclimates any foreign word or idea that comes its way. The rich and fertile ground of Persian literary humanism, here best represented by *Jawameʿ al-Hekayat* itself, is therefore the moral habitat of the Persian Prince as a potent force in Islamic political culture.

The *Jawameʿ al-Hekayat* of Awfi, as this precious text is affectionately known, and from which this story has reached us, is a document of extraordinary significance in our understanding of the Persian literary provenance of the Muslim empires in which the archetypal figure of the Persian Prince has thrived. It consists of countless stories and anecdotes from four corners of the Muslim and non-Muslim world in which historical facts and fictional narratives intertwine to create a third compelling prose where the two genres yield to a compelling literary diction entirely its own. Among the sources that Awfi had at his disposal were *Ghurar Akhbar* of Thaʿalibi, *Khwaday-Namag* of Ibn Muqaffaʿ, *Siyasat-nameh* of Nezam al-Molk, *Qabus-nameh* of Qabus ibn Vushmgir, and *Aghraz al-Siasah* of Zahiri Samarqandi—all of which, along with his own personal travels and observations, combine to create this treasure of seminal significance.[4] The geographical location of the author is also quite crucial. Awfi was born and raised in Bukhara but traveled to and studied in Transoxiana, Khorasan, and India, with sojourns to Samarkand, Marv, Herat, Lahore, and Delhi. Fearful of the pending Mongol invasion of his homeland, by 1220 he had emigrated to India and sought refuge in local courts when a ruling prince sponsored his composition of *The Jawameʿ al-Hekayat*. The book is a marvel to behold and read. It is such stuff that Muslim and Persianate political culture are made on.

As best evident in Awfi's *Jawame' al-Hekayat*, the Persian provenance of Muslim empires ultimately takes us to the political and perforce literary and poetic domains of their homes and habitat. Muslim empires were held together by the expansive moral imagination at the heart of this literature and not solely or exclusively by the legal treatises of punctilious jurists. The task is to look for the shifting balance between scholasticism and humanism throughout Islamic history. If we were to consider not just a few hallmarks of Persian mirrors for princes but look at the much larger and more critical mass of literature that expands into Akhlaq (ethics) and Andarz (advice) domains, we can begin to see the contours of what we might call the *collective subconscious* of these texts in terms beyond their specific localities and deeper into what has animated these genres and their authors. Over the past century, psychoanalytic and literary theory thinkers ranging from Sigmund Freud, Carl Jung, and Jacques Lacan to Walter Benjamin and Fredric Jameson have been exploring aspects of what they call the *collective, optical,* or *political* subconscious of texts.[5] Through and beyond all these theoretical speculations, over the past few decades I have been particularly preoccupied with the literary subconscious of these texts that entails their politics but is not reducible to it—and in fact altogether goes against the grain of their politics. I have on occasion also stipulated this collective unconscious as these texts' *intuition of transcendence*. Beyond the reach of the passing Orientalist mediation of these works and that of area specialists who have followed, we have finally arrived at a point when such theoretical considerations might guide our more serious encounters with these texts and the world they have informed, animated, and entailed. The study of these texts neither began with European Orientalist curiosities and colonial interests nor indeed ended with them. European Orientalism was but a passing phase in our understanding of these texts. For better or for worse, that epistemic phase is over. Far richer and more open horizons lie ahead.

The moral imagination embedded in the collective subconscious of these seminal texts pointing to their intuition of transcendence is where our hermeneutic horizons lie—and where the archetypal figure of the Persian Prince dwells, at the very heart of Muslim empires. Navigating through that critical mass, we see how the idea of the Persian Prince configures an amorphous, omnipresent, and miasmatic character—dwelling in these texts and ruling over countries and climes, dynasties and empires, from the minds of poets and prose stylists to the peacock thrones of ruling houses. The figure of the Persian Prince is metamorphic, a chameleon in action, a floating signifier roaming from the

Persian and other mirrors for princes all the way back to the Greek *Cyropaedia* or Iranian *Khwaday-Namag* or the Pahlavi and post-Pahlavi renditions of the Indian origins of *Kelilah and Dimnah*. Hidden and manifest throughout all these sources is the *collective subconscious* of the texts, where the idea of the Persian Prince dwells and dreams. If we are to understand how this imperial archetype works, we need to take a walk through its literary and poetic habitat. In power or in rebellion, the idea of the Persian Prince is tapping into a reservoir of non-Islamic, pre-Islamic, Islamic, and later even post-Islamic domains and, though fluent in multiple languages, has a penchant for Persian. Above all, the Persian Prince is a storyteller and loves to listen to and tell stories. It has a poetic disposition, and that poetry has a philosophical force of its own.

Kaleidoscopic Mirrors for the Persian Prince

The exemplary case of Awfi's *Jawame' al-Hekayat* shows in Persian prose that where the Persian Prince finds a most hospitable habitat, fact and fiction coalesce to produce a tertiary space where history and story meet to expand the horizons of being. Let's take a casual metaphoric stroll through that habitat and see what we see in that world—for the devil of the Persian Prince is in the details of his literary and poetic habitat. The literary humanism that maps the details of this habitat offers a kaleidoscopic vision of the colorful ways in which the Persian Prince has been conceived.

As one point of departure among many others, let's take a seminal figure like Ibn Miskawayh (932–1030), a towering thinker of the Buyid period—a renowned member of the literati, a moral philosopher, a medical scientist, and a recent convert from Zoroastrianism who, though multilingual, wrote his major works in Arabic.[6] The Buyids were an Iranian (Shi'ite) dynasty of Daylamite origin who ruled over Iraq and much of Iran from 934 to 1062 CE. There were a number of other Iranian dynasties in this region and period that were rooted ideologically in the revolutionary uprisings of the post-Abu Muslim period and became relatively autonomous from the Abbasid caliphate in the years leading to the Saljuqid dynasty. Historians of the Buyid period inform us that Ibn Miskawayh was a close friend (*nadim*) of Abu Mohammad Hasan Mohallabi (died 963), the vizier of the Buyid amir Mo'ezz al-Dawlah (died 967). Ibn Miskawayh was prolific in his capacity as a court secretary (*dabir*) in the Buyid court and to his patron prince.[7] He is best known for *Tajareb al-Umam wa Ta'aqeb al-Hemam* (*Experiences of Nations and Consequences of Ambitions*), a work that reveals a deeply moral and philosophical attitude toward history. Among his other works is *Javidan Kherad* (*Sophia Perennis*), which has been Arabized as *Kitab al-Hikmah al-Khalidah* (*Book of Eternal Wisdom*). This book is his Arabic rendition of a Persian original called *Javidan Kherad*, which can be traced back to the Pishdadid king Houshang and is also known as *Kitab Adab al-Arab wa al-Ajam* (*The Book of the Customs of Arabs and Iranians*). The seminal text brings together Persian, Greek, Indian, and Arabic ancient wisdom and can alone be studied as solid evidence of the active and systematic transmutation of pre-Islamic Iranian wisdom literature as it combined with its neighboring traditions and gathered around the figure of the Persian Prince. But perhaps his most famous book is *Tahzib al-Akhlaq wa al-Tathir al-Aʿraq* (*Refinement of Character and Purification of Cultures*), a treatise on moral philosophy. The bilingual and multicultural character of Ibn Miskawayh's polyphonic presence during the Buyid period marks the fertile ground upon which the Persian Prince finds much moral ground.

It is this latter book of Ibn Miskawayh, *Tahzib al-Akhlaq*, that almost a century later reaches the hands of the eminent Muslim philosopher Nasir al-Din al-Tusi (1201–1274), who, following the instructions of his patron prince Nasir al-Din Abu al-Fath Abd al-Rahim ibn Abi Mansur, the Nizari Ismaili governor of Quhistan, starts translating it from Arabic into Persian. However, he decides this text is not sufficient and vastly expands and improves upon it, producing a magisterial text, *Akhlaq-e Naseri* (*Nasirean Ethics*). Eloquent summations of Indian, Iranian, Arab, and Greek philosophies and wisdom literatures, these two texts in turn anticipate and reflect back on each other's tones, and as such mirror each other's configuration of justice and equanimity bestowed on the figure of the Persian Prince—one written in Arabic but taking full advantage of Persian and Pahlavi sources, and the other decidedly in Persian (even if al-Tusi was eminently qualified to write in Arabic, as is clearly demonstrated by his other works in both philosophy and the astronomical sciences).[8] Nasir al-Din al-Tusi later revised *Akhlaq-e Naseri* to make it more compatible with the wishes of his other patron prince, the Mongol warlord Hulagu, and thus in his prose overrides the sectarian limitations of the time between the Shiʿi and Sunni, the Arabic and Persian, and the Iranian and Mongol variations in his contemporary political culture. Whether performed in the Arabic of Ibn Miskawayh or the Persian of Nasir al-Din al-Tusi, both texts continue to center the moral education, edification, and royal disposition of the Persian Prince they are positing to educate and enable to rule.

Cut by a few decades and moving to India, we are now in the presence of Amir Khosrow Dehlavi (1253–1325), who in his version of the Alexander romance turns the Macedonian world conqueror into a mystical hero engaged in the epic conquest of his own mortal soul. In this exquisite romance, Amir Khosrow was already in the company of and conversation with two even mightier elders of his profession—for both Ferdowsi (died circa 1020) and Nezami (died circa 1209) had already perfected the genre long before Amir Khosrow was a twinkle in his parents' eyes. Among Ferdowsi, Nezami, and Amir Khosrow, and soon to be joined by the other towering figure, Abd al-Rahman Jami (1414–1492), the genre of Alexander romance, in both prose and poetry, was already solidly established as the modus operandi of turning the adventurous Macedonian general into a perspicacious Persian Prince.[9] In Persian romances, Alexander emerges as a wise and learned prince who surrounds himself with philosophers and roams the globe in search of eternal life, thus cutting a figure similar to the Platonic philosopher/king.[10] In recent and even more comprehensive studies of Persian and other Alexander romances, the Macedonian warrior turned Persian Prince becomes the metamorphic figure of a varied spectrum of moral imagination, from a prince to a prophet to a philosopher/king.[11] In the larger expanse of these Alexander romances, one can in fact detect the earlier imperial imagination of the Achaemenid Empire finding a multicultural genre in which to remap itself.[12] Al-Tusi's philosophical Persian in his *Akhlaq-e Naseri* here resonates with Amir Khosrow's poetic diction, as the abstract disposition of just and judicious governance is wedded to the worldly meanderings of an honorary "Persian Prince"—a version of Alexander who thrives in Persian diction and Aristotelian wisdom.

As the figure of the Persian Prince moves from genre to genre and from locale to locale, keeping his Persian literary habitat refreshingly joyous and commemorative, the world around it by now may have thought all was settled in terms of how the archetypal figure of the Persian Prince was to be perceived and idealized, defined and located. Then something extraordinary happens. In the interval between the end of the Abbasid Empire in 1258 and the rise of the Timurid Empire in 1370, the chaotic anxieties of the time produced two iconic poets who have left behind a remarkable body of literary and poetic evidence for us to consider. The legendary satirist, poet, and moralist Ubayd Zakani (died 1370) produced a book in prose he called *Akhlaq al-Ashraf* [Ethics of the nobles] (1339–1340), in which he both mimics and subverts the whole genre of mirrors for princes. More than two centuries before Machiavelli and in a satirical form that is the jewel of Persian prose, Zakani dismantles the lofty prose of the advice to the monarch that had come before him and exposes its dark underbelly. By doing so, Zakani suddenly puts the entire genre of mirrors, as well as Akhlaq and Andarz, under erasure. Universally celebrated for his masterpiece political satire *Mush-o-Gorbeh* (*The Mouse and the Cat*), Zakani came from a noble Arab family who had moved and settled in Iran. By opting for a satirical prose, Zakani enabled a hidden power of the Persian language to expose the hypocrisy of the ruling elite and dismantle false pretenses. Treating the work as a typical treatise on ethics, he divides *Akhlaq al-Ashraf* into seven chapters: Wisdom; Courage; Chastity; Justice; Generosity; Patience; and Being Modest, Truthful, Kind, and Forgiving. Each one of these chapters is in turn divided into two parts: *Mazhab-e Mansukh*/The Abandoned Path and *Mazhab-e Mokhtar*/The Preferred Path. In the first part he cites the thoughts and prescriptions of leading moral philosophers, and in the second part he outlines what is actually done by the ruling elite. The crux of his sublime sense of humor is captured in a passage like this:

> Iranian kings like Zahhak the Arab, and Yazdegerd the Evildoer who are now adorning the top layers of hell, and those who followed them, so far as they were engaged in tyranny their fortune was rising and their kingdom prosperous. When it came to Kisra Anushirvan, who because of the stupidities of his imprudent advisers opted for justice, in a short while his citadels collapsed, and the Zoroastrian temples where they worshipped suddenly crumbled, and their very traces disappeared from the earth.[13]

Right next to Ubayd Zakani we must place his contemporary, the incomparable lyricist Khwajah Shams al-Din Muhammad Hafez-e Shirazi (1315–1390), whose sublime lyrical poetry entails a potent subversive political force unlike any other. Oddly enough, though Ubayd Zakani and Hafez were contemporaries and lived in Shiraz, there is no evidence to suggest that they were aware of each other's presence. What is evident is the deeply troubling time they both lived in, between the collapse of Baghdad in 1258 and the rise of Timur in 1370—or, more specifically, between the end of the Ilkhanid dynasty in 1335 and the rise of the Timurids in 1370. This period, between the death of Sultan Abu Said, the last Ilkhanid ruler, and the ascendancy of Timur, was a tempestuous era dominated by corruption among the aristocracy and clergy alike. Such minor dynasties as the Inju (1304–1357), the Jalayirids (1335–1432), and the Muzaffarids (1314–1393) frame the tumultuous era of Zakani and Hafez. As Abbas Iqbal Ashtiani, the eminent historian of the period, puts it bluntly, the period was

> a time when the mother of a ruling monarch was openly engaged in adultery, and the wife of another member of the aristocracy brutally murdered her husband while he was asleep because he had imprisoned her

lover, and the wife of yet another prince coveting her own brother-in-law seduced him to divorce his own wife, and yet another king personally blinded his own father to sleep with his mother, and yet another monarch openly ordered his generals to divorce their wives so he could sleep with them and then compose poetry in their praise.[14]

With that historical background, we can understand the political dimension of Hafez's poetry much more poignantly—and see in what particular terms the very ideal-typical conception of political authority, and with it the figure of the Persian Prince, is being critically balanced. Here is a sample:

Do yar-e zirak-o az badeh-ye kohan do-mani...

A couple of refined friends and two bottles of seasoned wine—
A peace of mind, a book, at the corner of a meadow—
I won't give this for the whole world and the world to come—
Though I am constantly chased after by one group or another—
For whoever gave the corner of solitude for the treasure of the world,
Sold the Egyptian Joseph for a pittance in return—
Come here, for the glitter of this world would not diminish
With the asceticism of someone like you or the atrocities of someone like me—
Go and gaze in the mirror of the wine cup and decipher what's yet to come
For no one remembers such a strange happening—
From the tornado of these events we cannot even imagine
Upon this garden ever bloomed a Rose or a Jasmine—
From all the poisons that have blown on this flowerbed
It's a miracle we can still smell a flower or see the color of a Jasmine—
Do be patient, my heart, for the Almighty will never abandon
Such a precious jewel to an evildoer—
The times are out of joint from this calamity, Hafez—
Where is a philosopher's thought or a Brahman's sagacity?[15]

What is at work here is a fusion of beautiful lyrical poetry, a preference for ennobling solitude, and yet the towering moral imagination from which Hafez details the calamities of his time. This fusion will remain definitive for the lyrical imagination, which will entail the future undoing and redoing of the Persian Prince. Under the bright and bold sunshine of Hafez's lyrical poetry, not just the corrupt political leaders of the time and their clerical enablers but the whole discourse of Islamic legalism that was their ideological raison d'être is put on notice. In yet another similar ghazal, Hafez recites:

Yari andar kas nemibinim yaran ra cheh shod?

> We can't see friendship in anyone. What happened to friends?
> When did friendship come to an end? What happened to companions?
> The water of life has darkened. Where is the auspicious Khizr?
> Roses are bleeding. What happened to the winds of spring?
> No one says friends have the right to friendship—
> What happened to those who prized justice? What became of friends?
> This was the city of lovers and the abode of kind people—
> When did kindness come to an end? Where did just princes go?
> For years now no ruby has come out of the mine of magnanimity—
> What happened to the rays of sun and the commotion of wind and rain?
> The ball of triumph and generosity is cast in the field—
> No one comes to play. What happened to all the warriors?
> One hundred thousand flowers bloomed and not a single bird is singing—
> What happened to the robins? Where did all the sparrows go?
> The Venus is not composing any beautiful melodies anymore. Has its lute burned?
> No one yearns to be drunk. What happened to the drunkards?
> Hafez, no one knows such secrets of the divinity, be quiet—
> Whom are you asking what has happened to our time?[16]

The breathtaking beauty of this ghazal captures the fear and frustration of the age and yet keeps alive the dream of what is sublime and beautiful, just and right. Hafez praises three ruling princes of his time—Shah Sheikh Abu Ishaq Inju, Shah Shojaʿ, and Shah Mansur Muzaffar—but is critical of the tyrannical Amir Mobarez al-Din Muhammad.[17] Hafez is consistently wary of career opportunist clergy and the corrupt and tyrannical aristocracy, any and all figures of power and authority, raising his critique of these figures to an aesthetic elegance and poetic precision that will remain iconic for posterity. What was the reach of Hafez's Persian poetry? Ahmed Sudi Bosnevi (died circa 1592–1598), the Bosnian translator and commentator of Hafez and Saʿdi into Ottoman Turkish, is to this day a seminal figure because of how far and wide the Shirazi saga was read and loved and was definitive to being a Muslim in the world. Embedded in both Hafez's and Zakani's poetry and prose is the fact that the ideal of the Persian Prince was not a monolithic proposition of state legitimacy but a contested domain of engagement with what is just and beautiful.

Keeping this exceptionally crucial episode in mind, let us move forward to a radically different genre and a slightly later period and revisit the archetypal figure of the Persian Prince in the extraordinary text of *Salaman and Absal* of Abd al-Rahman Jami (1414–1492), who brings a whole history of mystical romance to new poetic heights and offers us a unique occasion to see the cosmogonic order of the prototype in an entirely different environment.[18] The origin of this romance between a prince and his nursemaid likely goes back to Indian or perhaps Greek or Hebrew sources, and finds its earliest expressions in Islamic contexts, beginning with a version by the polyglot Nestorian Christian translator Hunayn ibn Ishaq (809–873) in Arabic, then in a philosophical treatise by Avicenna and Nasir al-Din al-Tusi, followed by Ibn Tufail in his philosophical romance *Hayy ibn Yaqzan*, before it reaches Jami's hands in his *Haft Awrang*, which is dedicated to local and regional princes. Jami's *Salaman and Absal* was dedicated to Sultan Uzun Hasan Aq Qoyunlu (1423–1478), the Turkman prince of Tabriz. When Edward Fitzgerald translated *Salaman and Absal* into English, Jami's poetic rendition found a global readership.[19] Jami himself gets it from Hunayn ibn Ishaq, and in his Persian poetic rendition the archetypal figure of the Persian Prince finds a widely cosmic and cosmopolitan character. It is precisely that character in Jami's rendition of this allegorical story that frames the idea of the Persian Prince in a cosmogonic disposition. The key to this kaleidoscopic mirroring of the Persian Prince roaming through Persian literary humanism is precisely this oscillation between a deeply realistic and critical take by Hafez and Zakani and a highly cosmogonic and idyllic disposition of the archetype as emerges in Jami's masterpiece.

In Hunayn ibn Ishaq's version, which Jami Persianizes into one of the greatest literary masterpieces of all time, we read how an ascetic king named Hermanos, the son of Heraql, rules over Egypt, Greece, and Byzantium, is infinitely wise and ascetic, and avoids intimacy with women.[20] His prolonged asceticism notwithstanding, he finally desires to have a son, though without indulging in intimacy. His wise vizier, Aqliqulas, arranges for a son to be born to him via magical (artificial) insemination, and places his semen inside a Mandragora plant from which Prince Salaman is born. In gratitude for the birth of his son, Hermanos orders the construction of the pyramids. Salaman grows up and falls madly in love with his wet nurse Absal. His father is angered by this love, and Salaman and Absal run away from his court and country. Through his access to extraterrestrial forces, the king finds out where they are and makes them fall even more in love but without being able to consummate their passion, at which point the desperate lovers decide to kill themselves by drowning. But the king saves his son and lets Absal die. Salaman is inconsolable. The wise vizier appears to Salaman and vows to bring back Absal. He asks Salaman to wear Absal's clothing and spend forty days in isolation in a cave; an apparition of Absal then appears, and continues to appear repeatedly to Salaman for another forty days. After this, the Form of Venus presents herself to Salaman, who has now fallen madly in love with Venus and, through this love, assumes the capacity to become a proper Prince. At this point, we learn:

> Salaman ascends the royal throne and acquires immense fame. By his command, his story was written on seven gold tablets, and invocations to the planets on seven other tablets, likewise of gold. The tablets were placed in the pyramids. After the two deluges, of Water and of Fire, had descended, the divine Sage, Plato, appeared. He was told that exalted sciences and precious treasures lay hidden in the pyramids; he made a journey to visit them, but the kings of those days would not allow him to open them. Hence he bequeathed to his pupil Aristotle the task of gaining access to them and benefiting from the teachings of the spiritual sciences deposited there. Aristotle seized the opportunity of Alexander's Oriental campaign. Together they went to the pyramids, and Aristotle opened their thresholds by the power of the secret bequeathed to him by Plato. Alexander was able to bring out only the tablets on which the story of Salaman and Absal was inscribed. After that, the doors closed. [21]

Hunayn ibn Ishaq tells us he has translated the story from Greek into Arabic, and Jami then renders his Arabic prose into Persian poetry. The question is not how Jami had access to this story, which has been part and parcel of the Islamic intellectual repertoire, but what happens to it when he renders it into a sublime Persian poetry, in which the figurative schemata of the Persian Prince reconnects to its cosmic order, uniting Greek, Byzantine, Egyptian, Arabic, and Persian leitmotifs. Jami does this Persianization through a very simple, elegant, and opportune poetic twist. Soon after he begins the story of the Greek king Hermanos and compares him with Alexander, he introduces his grand vizier and describes how the two were inseparable in their endeavors to procure justice in the realm—at which point he asserts that an infidel king who rules his kingdom with justice is better than a Muslim king who rules with injustice. He then opens a subordinate clause in which he tells us:

> God Almighty told David the Prophet:
> Inform your people, O you judicious sage!
> When people speak of Persian kings,
> They will always be remembered for their good deeds—
> Although they were Fire-Worshippers in their Faith,
> Justice and Righteousness were their Deeds—
> For centuries the world was in peace and prosperity because of them,
> Their subjects were immune to the injustices of tyrants—
> Their subjects were at peace from suffering
> Because of justice, they lived in peace.[22]

The invocation of this ancient prototype and that cosmic order is made more meaningful if we recall that Jami composed *Salaman and Absal* soon after the tumultuous Mongol interval that had resulted in the revolutionary Sarbedaran uprising (1337–1381) in Khorasan, in Jami's own neighborhood, and how that tumult was reflected in the work of the eminent poet of the period, Ibn Yamin (1286–1368). The relative peace and prosperity in which Jami lived and thought and composed his masterpieces is predicated on the turbulent period of Ibn Yamin's poetic heritage. In Ibn Yamin's commitment to the Sarbedaran revolutionary uprising, a rebellious movement informed by Shi'i-Sufi doctrine, we detect one of the earliest occasions in which a Persian poet becomes the eloquent voice of an emancipatory cause.[23] Naser Khosrow Qubadiani (died circa 1070) would be an even earlier case of a towering Persian poet and philosopher totally committed to the Isma'ili cause. These earliest manifestations of the rebellious Persian poet as the alter ego of the Persian Prince would later be resuscitated in the active transformation of the archetypal figure back into its poetic and prophetic foregrounding.

A few generations later, with the *Majma' al-Bahrain* ("Where the two seas meet," though usually translated as "Confluence of the two seas") of the Mughal prince Dara Shikoh (1615–1659), we see the figurative persona of the Persian Prince uniting with the wise philosopher usually standing by his side. This seminal text on comparative mysticism—bringing Islam and Hinduism together—consists of a short treatise in Persian composed circa 1655. *Majma' al-Bahrain* is a compelling account of pluralistic affinities between Sufi and Vedantic wisdom exploring the epistemic harmony of Islam and Hinduism and, by extension, other religions.[24] Dara Shikoh writes from a position of royal power and intellectual authority, though with an impeccable humility befitting his moral standing. He says he is writing this treatise for his own household (Ahl-e Bayt) based on his own intuitions and taste and could not care less about the masses of both groups.[25] As becomes evident in this work, in Dara Shikoh the two positions of the philosopher and the prince, or the prince and the prophet, have come together, dropping the sword and picking up the pen. Dara Shikoh here is both Hermanos and Aqliqulas, Alexander and Aristotle, Anushirvan and Bozorgmehr, the courageous warrior and the wise philosopher, fused together.

By the time we get to the late Ottoman period, the figure of the Persian Prince is ready to encounter the European colonial modernity in closest geographical proximity to it—with a major twist away from ethical edification toward practical obstacles to the moral order of things. In *A History of Ottoman Political Thought up to the Early Nineteenth Century* (2018), Marinos Sariyannis offers a detailed account of Ottoman political texts that include fifteenth-century Persian political thought. On this score, Sariyannis observes:

> By the end of the sixteenth century, a specifically Ottoman genre, a version of *adab* or "mirrors for princes" in which advice was explicitly concrete, addressed to very specific problems, and which emphasized institutional rather than moral deficiencies, had reached maturity. Apart from these formal characteristics, the most striking feature of this genre was its view of the present as an era of disorder, a condition that could be mended only if certain shortcomings were addressed and, more often than not, departures from established custom were abolished.[26]

This is the moment of reckoning that begins to dawn on the figure of the Persian Prince dwelling in these mirrors for princes and all other relevant genres in its varied and adjacent domains, from the Indian subcontinent to Central Asia, the Caucuses, Iran, and the Ottoman territories. Before we reach this decisive point, and as we navigate through these classics of Persian and Persianate texts, we are witness to one solid streak of evidence. The collective unconscious of these texts, as I see and propose here, is the evidence of their repressed but still common denominator, dwelling on the fact that they are all performed in Persian prose or poetry or both, with regular sojourns into Arabic, Urdu, and Ottoman Turkish. Central to this collective subconscious is the haunting and haunted figure of the Persian Prince, the archetypal figure of a just and divinely graced savior that forms the forestructure of their narratives, the archetype configured as the youthful deliverer, the hero, as perhaps best evidenced in a tragic figure like Seyavash in Persian mythology or Dara Shikoh in Persianate history, one mythic and the other historical but both iconic, underpinning and foregrounded in the subconscious mind of these moralists. The particular aspect of this collective subconscious is that it is split in half: half-mythic, half-historical; half-legitimizing, half-delegitimizing itself; one half in power, the other half effectively or metaphorically challenging it. The result of this creative conflict is the engine of much of the Persian force in Islamic history.

None of these moralists, performing in multiple genres, evident in differing proses, roaming through conflated prosodies, and active in adjacent environs, was in a position of power the way the prominent Saljuqid vizier Nezam al-Molk was. But still, in mapping out the discourse of political legitimacy, these moralists were actively thinking through the metaphysics of a moral imagination otherwise hidden to their counterparts among the Muslim jurists. It is in these genres that the figure of the Persian Prince moves through Persian, Arabic, Turkish, and Urdu, while the varied proses remain steady in their form—revealing the disposition of genres as substance, as social action. There is a symbolic interactionism at work here, so that these texts perform two simultaneous functions: they do what they say they are doing (legitimizing power), and they are at the same time the evident sign of their own undoing. They are aware that what they preach is not what is, and as such they are both identity and alterity, informing their patron prince how to be a "Persian Prince" yet detailing how a prince is undone—which, in the case of Ubayd Zakani, becomes satirically explicit—literally juxtaposing the ideal and the real.

As mirrors, these texts have therefore two sets of images: one in front and the other in reverse. They tell the prince what to do and tell the world what is yet to be done—and they do both at the same time. They are at once themselves and their own otherwise. This reverse image was implicit until Zakani in satire and Hafez in frightful lyrical precision made it explicit. As such, we can see how mirrors can be transhistorical and polyvocal social acts. Zakani and Hafez are the return of the repressed, the collective subconscious becoming conscious once in satirical and then in lyrical terms. Thus they reveal how the Persian Prince is both the subject and the object of the text; in the guise of praising him, the moralists are in fact dwarfing him. In his *Mind of the Moralist* (1959), Philip Rieff theorizes this condition of moral sublimation in a post-Enlightenment context—in which the cultural mandates of interdictions against transgressions were in need of a deity outside the ecclesiastical or rabbinic order.²⁷ The same, however, is true here, with these mirrors positing a counter-metaphysics—a worldly metaphysics, a material manner of self-transcendence that was not in need of any Muslim clerical order to accredit or sustain it. These moralists were by and large Muslim—though with a strong Zoroastrian, Manichean, or even Mazdakite proclivity open to Indian, Greek, or Hebrew wisdom—but not "Islamic," if the word were allowed to be totally claimed by doctors of law, the legal theorists and jurists who were mostly (but not categorically) providing the jurisprudential underlining of Muslim empires without a sense of paradox or self-doubt. These moralists were supreme ironists, and this irony reaches potent satirical heights in Zakani and lyrical effect in Hafez, who spells out in unequivocal terms what is otherwise implicit in the whole genre of these mirrors: that they were the moralists of immoral power, fully aware of how power works and seeking to tame it by exposing its futility, fragility, alterity.

In the collective subconscious of these texts is embedded the minds of the moralists who composed them, and this is where their sustained historical intertextuality procures the archetypal continuity of the Persian Prince. The intertextual disposition of these texts, or the relationship between their hypertextuality and hypotextuality, as Gérard Genette called them, marks the collective subconscious they form. The result is a kaleidoscopic constellation of mirrors for the Persian Prince itself to behold. In his seminal work *Palimpsest*, Genette distinguishes between two types of hypertextual deformations—what he calls "transformation" and "imitation," in which he defines hypertextuality: "Every successive state of a written text functions like a hypertext in relation to the state that precedes it and like a hypotext in relation to the one that follows. From the very first sketch to the final emendation, the genesis of a text remains a matter of auto-hypertextuality."²⁸ We can think of Alexander romances in these terms, or else in terms of Persian translations of Arabic sources, Arabic translations of Pahlavi sources, poetic renditions of prose sources, or vice versa, as the condition of this hypertextuality that in turn generates a cohesive and transhistorical collective subconscious for these texts in which the Persian Prince has happily or haphazardly dwelled.

The Metamorphic Characters of the Prince and the Philosopher

The paradoxical disposition of the Persian Prince as an archetype that both enables and questions the power of its person and persona has conditioned the key position of the vizier as a seminal force in rendering Muslim empires both morally and administratively possible. The presence of the persona of the vizier, a key office whether factual or fictional, enables the Persian Prince to become a dialogical character—oscillating paradoxically between a prince and a prophet, a king and his wise adviser, a patron in power and a poet in revolt. Any rebel is a potential prince, just as any prince is a successful rebel. Throughout its varied manifestations, we scarcely see the figure of the Persian Prince alone—he is always in the company of his philosopher vizier or courtly poet. The prototype is monadic in its archetypal power and authority but dyadic in its reflective disposition with a philosophical figure or a wise vizier—Anushirvan with Bozorgmehr, Alexander with Aristotle. The Persian Prince's dialogical character renders him at once princely and prophetic, philosophical and poetic, stabilizing and destabilizing. The triadic disposition of the prince-prophet-poet gathers its momentum in the archetypal figure of the Persian Prince for much of its unfolding history. The prose and poetry of their historicality holds them together. The Persian Prince is in power, aided and moderated by the philosopher/vizier by his side, praised and admonished by the Persian poet at his court, tempted by the Persian prophet beckoning him to rise. This triadic dynamic simultaneously posits the figure of the Persian Prince and turns him against his own office. When centuries later Nietzsche called his rebellious prophet Zarathustra in his iconic book *Thus Spoke Zarathustra* (1883–1885) and let loose his poetic force against the very grain of what had been called "Western metaphysics," he was tapping into this ancient thematics in Iranian political philosophy. This is in a nutshell the internal engine of the Persian pattern of Islamic history.

The dialectic between the two sides of the *de facto* and *de jure* imperium places this dynamic paradox of the Persian Prince at the epicenter of successive Muslim empires. The genre of *Andarz-nameh* (advice) literature and the institution of the vizierate are the enduring legacies of the pre-Islamic Iranian origins of the Persian Prince as an institution of legitimate authority in Muslim empires.[29] With the exception of the Umayyads (who had carried pre-Islamic Arab patrimonial tribalism to a dynastic register), from the Abbasids forward, all minor and major Muslim imperial formations—Arab, Iranian, Turkic, Mongol, and Indian—carried the signature of the office of the vizier. What informed this office were the varied gestations of the genre of Andarz-nameh. The origin of mirrors for princes, in both prose (*Qabus-nameh*, for example) and poetry (Saʿdi's *Bustan*, for example), can be traced back, as scholars like A. K. S. Lambton and others have demonstrated, to pre-Islamic Persian manuals of proper courtly etiquette, or *A'in-Nameh* and Andarz-nameh literature, and, more specifically, to the political culture of the Sassanid court. This tracing was both factual and symbolic. It actually drew on that literature but then used the occasion symbolically to offer the ruling Muslim monarch a model of just behavior they then considered ancient and tested. The Prophet of Islam, Muhammad, was believed to have said, "I was born at the time of the Just Ruler," meaning during the era of Khosrow I Anushirvan (reigned 531–579). Whether the Prophet actually said this is less important than the assumption by subsequent generations that he did. Such doctrinal assumptions built a bridge between the Islamic and pre-Islamic periods in patently political and archetypal terms.

The Zoroastrian provenance of this theory of kingship carried its metaphysical domains to a cosmogonic conception of legitimate authority that viewed the social and political order as a continuation and reflection of the heavenly order, if now cast in patently Islamic terms, with the king as the intermediary sign and symbol that connected the two worlds. Social order, predicated on the principality of justice, reflected the cosmic order and the balance necessary to keep the firmaments in motion. Injustice was a disruption in the order of things. The narrative vehicle of this bridge was the Andarz-nameh genre, rooted in the Middle and New Persian term *Andarz*— literally "advice," often given by a father, a king, a high priest, or another figure of authority, to a younger prince, but occasionally an older monarch, in the form of admonishing the person in power for lacking wisdom. Scholars of this field associate this term with another equally important word, *frahang*, referring to a proper civilized upbringing, but also with *a'in*, meaning a royal ritual.[30]

I have developed in some detail the idea of the Persian "philosopher/vizier" as a category that acts as an intermediate institution mediating between the ruling monarch and his subjects.[31] The prototype of this mirroring is that between Anushirvan and Bozorgmehr, and this model is replicated between Alexander and Aristotle, along with numerous others.[32] This mirroring effect between the Persian Prince and the vizier sustains the dialogical disposition of both characters. This mirroring interface between the patron prince and the court philosopher remains definitive throughout the heights of Islamic dynasties. Khwajah Nezam al-Molk's *Siyasat-nameh*, composed for the Saljuqid monarch Malik-Shah I, and al-Ghazali's composition of his *Nasihat al-Moluk*, presumably for the benefit of Mohammad ibn Malek-Shah, place these two seminal Iranian moralists in immediate proximity to princely power.

This mirroring or shadowy relationship between the Prince and the Prophet, or the Prince and the Poet, was informed and animated by a body of literature that was gradually and consistently transmitted via translations from Pahlavi to Persian or Arabic, from the pre-Islamic to the Islamic period. The overabundance of such sources and the attention paid to them by the leading critical thinkers of the time, as well as the canonical status they enjoyed in subsequent generations, make it quite clear that the influence and presence of pre-Islamic Persian sources in the Islamic period was crucial to the structural and ideological formations of Muslim empires as it centered on the adjacent institutions of the secretariates and vizierates. Definitive to this trajectory, which places the Prince and the Vizier, the Prince and the Philosopher next to each other, are the pre-Islamic Iranian sources that have survived the ravages of time and reached us intact and that are clear indications of the sources that eventually surface in Arabic and Persian. One such seminal text is *Kar-Namag-e Ardeshir-e Pabagan* (*The Chronicle of Ardeshir-e Pabagan*)—written in Middle Persian (Pahlavi) during the Sassanid Empire (226–651)—which tells the life story of the Sassanid king Ardeshir I and his descendants Shapur and Ohrmazd, and recounts the conquest of the empire by the House of Sasan.[33] Another major pre-Islamic text in this genre, *Nameh Tansar* (*The Letter of Tansar*), was translated from Pahlavi into Arabic by the indefatigable Ibn Muqaffaʿ, though neither the original nor his translation has survived. But a Persian translation by Ibn Esfandiar has reached us.[34] Based on these remaining texts, we see how both the sources and the substance of the Andarznameh genre assume literary and political dominance in the most formative periods of Muslim empires. Central to all these seminal sources is the composite figure of the Persian Prince and the figure of the philosopher/vizier by his side and their just and legitimate rule at the core of the Iranian theory of kingship. The character of Tansar, the Zoroastrian high priest under Ardeshir I, is prototypical of this nucleus of power and legitimacy.[35]

The presence and influence of Persian imperial heritage in the Arab and Muslim world should also be gauged by a similar presence in the literary and imperial contexts of the Greco-Roman domain long before the rise of Islam and the formation of Muslim empires. This look beyond the Arab and Islamic contexts is crucial for us in order to place the Muslim imperial heritage in a frame of reference much larger and older than they otherwise reveal. Giving a false primacy to the Arab and Islamic chronology categorically distorts and outdates the pre-Islamic Iranian heritage and places it in a prehistoric genealogy that is entirely ahistorical. *Cyropaedia*, or *The Education of Cyrus*, a fictionalized biography of Cyrus the Great (circa 600–530 BCE), is the longest text written by the preeminent Greek chronicler Xenophon (circa 430–355 BCE). This text, we might say, is the Greek version of the pre-Islamic Iranian manual of imperial rulership, as recorded, imagined, and rendered into a mirror for princes by Xenophon. It has been widely read and admired by such diverse figures as Alexander the Great, Scipio Africanus, Augustus Caesar, and Niccolò Machiavelli. "Because of Xenophon's portrayal of Cyrus as a benevolent monarch," scholars of the text inform us, "ruling through persuasion, rather than by force, the work has contributed to the reputation of the founder of the Persian empire as a righteous and tolerant king."[36] Historically, *Cyropaedia* has been more influential in European political history than Plato's *Republic*. The text is therefore the earliest recorded mirror for princes, from classical antiquity. This places the significance of pre-Islamic Iranian ideas of imperial leadership much earlier than their resurgence in the Islamic period in Persian, Arabic, and Turkish sources. It is precisely the antiquity of such texts, informing us of the ancient roots of Persian imperial heritage, that dwarfs the Arab and Muslim dynasties in institutional duration and longevity. Central to the imperial administration of the Achaemenids was the office of *hazarapati*, who might be considered the functional equivalent of a prime minister or, as the Greeks called him, the "chiliarch."[37] Later, during the Sassanid period, the office was known as *wuzurg framadar*. The antiquity and expanse of these two pre-Islamic empires foreground the centrality of the office of the vizier in the Islamic period.

This reference to classical antiquity should of course immediately remind us of the presence and deeds of Persian monarchs in the Bible. Cyrus the Great figures most prominently in the Hebrew Bible as the "anointed" prince and patron who liberated Jews from their Babylonian captivity and allowed them to rebuild their temple in Jerusalem. Cyrus is mentioned twenty-three times by name and referred to by implication several more times. The Hebrew Bible alludes to a host of other Persian kings of the Achaemenid period: Cambyses/Ahasuerus (Ezra 4–6), Pseudo Smerdis/Artaxerxes (Ezra 4:7–23), Darius the Great (Ezra 5–6), and Xerxes/Ahasuerus (Esther 1–10), and Artaxerxes (Nehemiah 1–13; Ezra 7–10). Taken together, these references form a mirror for princes in the most compelling and archetypal sense, deeply rooted in the Biblical exegesis commenting on and commemorating these passages. The Biblical presence of Persian monarchs, in combination with their echoes in Greek classical antiquity, puts the figure of the Persian Prince at the heart of European political thought and history and solidifies the figure of Cyrus the Great as the prototype of imperial rule.

Here too it is important to remember the Book of Esther in the Hebrew Bible, in which the beautiful Persian queen Ahasuerus (Xerxes I) is found in the company of her cousin Mordecai, who is in a high advisory position to counter his rival Haman's plot to murder Iranian Jews. There are a variety of ways in which the story of Esther can be read, and one of them is to view Haman and Mordecai as in fact rivals for the position of chief vizier to the Persian monarch, and to examine Mordecai's outmaneuvering of Haman to become Xerxes's chief minister. Obviously in the Hebrew Bible it is the fate of Iranian Jews that assumes paramount importance, but from our perspective here, the rivalry between Haman and Mordecai points to a larger issue of the role of ministerial power and that of the queen consort in the making of the Persian Prince.

In the next gestation of the Persian Prince with chief philosopher/vizier by his side, we see that, as the Greeks did with Cyrus the Great, the Persians did with Alexander the Great: transform him from a mere Macedonian general into an honorary Persian Prince. The fact that Alexander the Great was fond of Xenophon's *Cyropaedia* brings him and his legend into the pantheon of the Persian literary imagination, where the figure of the Macedonian world conqueror gives rise to a major genre of poetic and prose literature at the foundation of his princely adventures. The historical relations and fictional elaborations between Alexander and Aristotle further link together the iconic figure of Greek philosophers, the Macedonian world conqueror, and Persian princely mirrors. The genre of Alexander romances, or *Iskandar-nameh*, emerges as yet another Persian tradition with strong Andarz characteristics that is based on the Greek Pseudo-Callisthenes tale that through Syriac versions ultimately reaches such eminent poets as Ferdowsi, Nezami, Amir Khosrow, and Jami. The prose versions of these romances emerged as the more widespread renditions of the tale—carrying the princely figure of Alexander deep into the heart of popular prose. These texts' fictionalized and dramatized relationship between Alexander and Aristotle is the conduit for mirrors for princes, with the Alexandrian figure of the Persianized prince the model of a just, wise, and powerful monarch. The key point here is how the figure of Aristotle is turned from his historical habitat in Greece into a Persianate philosopher in the company of a "Persian Prince."

The plethora of these mirrors for princes, in which the Alexander romances now reciprocate Xenophon's *Cyropaedia* and find a new home, were not sporadic or a genre sui generis. They were rooted in robust literary traditions with an abiding concern for ethics and politics—placing the Philosopher and the Prince he served adjacent to each other. The word "Akhlaq" in the title of Nasir al-Din al-Tusi's *Akhlaq-e Nasiri* (*Nasirean Ethics*), named after the patron prince for whom it was written and to whom it was dedicated, points to a whole genre of ethics literature. A deeply cultivated genre, Akhlaq had carved itself a space between moral philosophy and belles-lettres where it was pleasant to read, and that pleasure was integral to the moral fabric of the prose. "God is beautiful and He loves Beauty!" That Prophetic tradition dovetailed well with Akhlaq literature—where the sublime was beautiful and the beautiful marked the truth. Here we see how the terms "Andarz" (advice), "Akhlaq" (ethics), and "Adab" (literary humanism) are interrelated, initially predicated on Zoroastrian teachings but eventually lending themselves to Islamic ethics and pragmatic politics, or the practice of power linked to or modulated on moral and ethical grounds. To be sure, in pre-Islamic Arabia such ideals were also celebrated but at a communal and tribal level, most certainly not on an imperial scale, which in their neighborhood was exclusive to pre-Islamic Egyptian, Indian, Iranian, and Byzantine domains. In the Islamic period proper, Greek, Indian, Iranian, and Arab ideals and ethical principles were eventually mixed together and they staged themselves as an ethical blueprint for rulers to follow.

As Lambton had rightly suspected but readily dismissed, the literary dimensions of this genre of political writings in the broadest sense of the term were the main feature of Andarz literature. This genre included the mirrors for princes, in the strictest sense of the term, but was not limited to them. Prominent figures as diverse as the historian Abu al-Fadl Bayhaqi (died 1077), the poet/philosopher/traveler Nasr Khosrow Qubadiani (1004–1088), and the mystic Abu Said abi al-Kheyr (967–1049), among others, came together with popular stories like *Samak Ayyar* (twelfth century), masterpieces of Persian prose like Sa'di's *Golestan*, works of the iconic satirists Ubayd Zakani (died 1370) and Fakhr al-Din Ali Safi (1463–1533), and countless other treasures to form the core of this politically indented body of literature. If we allow for the literary act and the courtly culture that had enabled it to present itself, the domain of the mirrors significantly expands and opens us to the entire spectrum of Persian Adab, which in turn takes us to the pre-Islamic Iranian roots of Islamic political thought. Much attention has been paid, and rightly so, to the Islamic political thought produced in Arabic, but that privileging of Arabic over Persian, Turkish, and Urdu is not only limited but in fact flawed. Two factors thus become crucial in our understanding of the archetypal figure of the Persian Prince: (1) the literary provenance of the archetype and (2) the combination of poetic and political elements that create a potent prose beyond the control of the administrative apparatus of power.

From the two complementary institutions of courtly culture and vizierate emerges the politics of royal patronage as the source of Andarz literature. The politics of royal patronage sustains the poetics of power and authority that the genre of mirrors generates and sustains. In the twelfth-century classic *Chahar Maqaleh* (*Four Treatises*, composed circa 1155), Nezami Aruzi writes of four major functions within the court quintessential to the successful rule of a prince: the Royal Secretariat, the Court Poet, the Court Astronomer/Astrologer, and the Court Physician. Here we see how the historic figure of the philosopher/vizier splits into four characters. Nezami Aruzi intended the book as a manual of courtly culture, detailing why and how these four functionaries were imperative to an effective ruler. In the words of a key scholar of this text, "In his [Nezami Aruzi's] opinion, which also may reflect the prevailing views of the time, the good order of the realm was ensured by secretaries, the perpetuation of its good name by poets, the good timing of its business by astronomers (or astrologers), and the good health of its ruler by physicians."[38] This text is therefore devoted to prescribing the qualifications of these four crucial functionaries enabling the sustained legitimacy of the Persian Prince. The text also includes established and classic sources that the author recommends students of these four fields read in order to prepare themselves for these services. By this time in the twelfth century, we see how the paramount institution of the vizierate has undergone a "division of labor," as it were, to sustain the archetypal figure of the Persian Prince in power in specific and pragmatic, yet literary and poetic terms. Aruzi's text further points to the courtly culture that had occasioned the institutional circumstances under which both narrative and substantive attention to pre-Islamic sources and ideals found a hospitable environment in the Persianate empires. The political culture of power and patronage provided the institutional basis for the continued validity and currency of pre-Islamic Iranian theories and practices of governance during the Islamic period. This institutional foregrounding of dynastic power and legitimacy became definitive to all Muslim empires, from India through Iran to the Ottoman and Arab worlds. The kaleidoscopic mirrors and their collective subconscious have by now posited a moral imagination in which the configurative archetypes of the Persian Prince and the philosopher/vizier sustain the cosmogonic universe of political authority in all Persianate dynasties and empires.

Kelilah and Dimnah *in a Metaphoric Register*

The collective subconscious of these texts and the configurative icons of the Prince and the philosopher cum vizier they posit unfold their cumulative narratology apace, spreading over an entire history of Persian literary imagination, a sphere that is the natural home of and a hospitable habitat for the Persian Prince—with palpable sojourns into Arabic, Turkish, and Urdu sites, while remembering their Hebrew, Greek, and Latin resonances. We might consider the heteroglossia and polyphonic voices of these texts expressed as a fourfold tropic, as Hayden White, in his *Metahistory: The Historical Imagination in Nineteenth-Century Europe* (1973), has theorized as four main moments of the prose of history: metaphor, metonymy, synecdoche, and irony. But before we do that, we must first recall how in her classic *Narratology: Introduction to the Theory of Narrative* (1985), Mieke Bal reminds us:

> A narrative text is a text in which a narrative agent tells a story.... The first question which arises is that of the identity and status of the narrative agent.... When ... I discuss the narrative agent, or narrator, I mean the linguistic subject, a function and not a person, which expresses itself in the language that constitutes the text. It hardly needs mentioning that this agent is not the (biographical) author of the narrative. The narrator of *Emma* is not Jane Austen. The historical person Jane Austen is, of course, not without importance for literary history, but the circumstances of her life are of no consequence to the specific discipline of narratology. In order to keep this distinction in mind, I shall here and there refer to the narrator as "it," however odd this may seem.[39]

Simple and elementary as this may sound, it has revolutionary implications for the way we read Persian literary sources for the purpose of mapping out the collective subconscious and the home and the habitat of the Persian Prince as an icon, an allegory, or more precisely an archetype, more a persona than a person. Based on this preliminary act of narrative de-authorization, I would propose White's fourfold topics as follows: (1) considering *Kelilah and Dimnah* an example of the pre-Islamic, Indian, Iranian, Arabic, Persian, and thereafter global specimen of animal fables, with the fabula here being played metaphorically; (2) the *Shahnameh* positing a simultaneously mythical, heroic, and historical poem, with the parabolic of its narrative resonances becoming metonymic to the whole archetype of the Persian Prince; (3) Sa'di's oeuvre in general, but particularly his *Bustan* and *Golestan*, as worldly-wise, aesthetically pleasing and beautiful, human-all-too-human, and performed anecdotally, and thus working through a sustained code of synecdoche; and (4) in the ironic mood, which will wait for the colonial encounter with European modernity, even if its revolutionary dispositions were readily available and evident in earlier stages of Persian literary narratology, built into the texts themselves, and staged dramatically by both Hafez and Ubayd Zakani. I propose these four crucial moments—*Kelilah and Dimnah*, the *Shahnameh*, Saʿdi's *Bustan* and *Golestan*, and the prose and poetry of Hafez and Zakani—all of which, though scattered throughout seminal episodes of the Islamic period, are yet rooted in and revealing pre-Islamic sources of Indian, Iranian, and contemporary character. *Kelilah and Dimnah* was Indian, *Shahnameh* Iranian, and Saʿdi decidedly worldly and contemporary, while Hafez and Zakani both recorded and anticipated the ironic disposition of the world to come.

The collection of animal fables we know as *Kelilah and Dimnah*, with the two jackals Kelilah and Dimnah as the principal characters, originated in India circa 500–100 BCE and eventually spread around the world as a seminal political allegory. It is based on the original Sanskrit text *Panchatantra*, but in its Pahlavi and subsequent Arabic translations and elaborations (by the inimitable Ibn Muqaffaʿ) it is much elaborated and rearticulated. It eventually reaches Persian and becomes a seminal text in the literary politics of the royal advice genre. Traveling even farther from its Indian origins and translated into countless languages, including Hebrew, Greek, Syriac, Latin, Spanish, and Italian, *Kelilah and Dimnah* became a staple of world literature. One of the first Persian versions was produced circa 1144, and ever since it has been the jewel of entertaining advice literature for shrewd statesmanship. The most famous translator of the text into Persian, a certain Nasrullah Munshi, came from a prominent family in the service of the Ghaznavid court in the eleventh and twelfth centuries. His translation is a literary creation anew and of monumental importance in the history of Persian literature, informing the very metaphoric figure of the Persian Prince, of which scholars of the text believe

> in a real sense, this language may be viewed as a literary creole, the vocabulary of which was adopted from those of its parent languages, namely literary Arabic and literary Persian. Its grammar remained Persian, but its artistic rhetorical embellishments were borrowed from the florid style of literary Arabic. Before Naṣ.|r-Allāh presented this linguistic medium upon the literary scene, it gestated for a long time in the bilingual chanceries of the Ghaznavid and Transoxianan courts. What should be stressed, however, is that the prose style of the Persian *Kalila wa Demna* did not evolve gradually from some earlier form of prose. Rather, it was invented by Naṣ.|r-Allāh, who, drawing on his own family

and administrative backgrounds, created it. . . . His innovative prose style soon dominated the literary scene and profoundly influenced every significant literary work that appeared in Persian for nearly four centuries.[40]

Here is where we see that the rise of the masterstrokes of Persian literary stylists was in fact coterminous with the princely prose in service of this genre. For this reason, the literary, the poetic, and the politics of this prose cannot be dissected and severed from one another. They are part and parcel of the same courtly culture. The Persian Prince was a poet in his court, at once praising and warning him, a prophet in both his ancestral lineage and the rebel banging at the gates to his capital.

Kelilah and Dimnah gave the Persian Prince an Indian provenance through the Pahlavi translation of Burzoe the Physician, its Arabic rendition by Ibn Muqaffaʿ, and the subsequent Persian versions by the historian and prose stylist al-Balʿami, the poet Rudaki, and ultimately the master prose stylist Abu al-Maʿali Nasrullah Munshi. The archaic disposition of the archetype came from Iran and India as well as the Greek and Macedonian roots of Alexander romances, a form that was already influenced and intrigued by Xenophon's Persianate Prince, as evident in his *Cyropaedia*. But in an exquisite historical case of literary circumambulation, *Kelilah and Dimnah* returns to India in its Persian version. Molla Husain ibn Ali Vaʿez Kashefi's *Anvar-e Suhayli* took it back to India, as it was now presented in beautiful and formal Persian in the Indian subcontinent. Though the work was named for his vizier Ahmad Suhayli, in *Anvar-e Suhayli*, Kashefi flaunted his Timurid-era prose under the patronage of Sultan Hossain Mirza Bayqura. Pairing it with Vaʿez Kashefi's other book on ethics and statecraft *Akhlaq-e Mohseni*, composed around the end of the fifteenth century, further expands Vaʿez Kashefi's influence in the political philosophy of his time. Giving a new rendition of *Panchatantra* back to its country of origin, through the Arabic and Persian *Kelilah and Dimnah* and the globalized *Fables of Bidpai* (*Pilpai*), the text of Kashefi became widely popular in India, ultimately reaching Emperor Akbar (reigned 1556–1605), who ordered his vizier Abu al-Fazl Mubarak to prepare a simpler, more easily understandable version of it, the result of which was *Ayar-e Danesh* (*The Measure of Knowledge*). In *Kelilah and Dimnah* the metaphoric disposition of the Persian Prince effectively enters the domain of animal fables.

From the vantage point of *Anvar-e Suhayli*, we can also explore Vaʿez Kashefi's other seminal works, such as *Futwwat-nameh-ye Soltani* (*Royal Book of Chivalry*), in the popular genre of heroic narratives, and *Rawda al-Shohada* (*The Garden of Martyrs*), on the tragedy of the Shiʿa imam Hossein and his companions in Karbala. In this context, we see how the iconic figure of the Persian Prince can become iconically supple and malleable and extend from popular heroic stories to the very heart of Shiʿi martyrology. We also know that "like other popular aklāq works, *Anwār-e sohaylī* was a standard examination text in the Indian Civil Service and the Indian Amy during the days of British rule."[41] This latter fact brings the thematic and literary domain of the Persian Prince up to the doorsteps of the Muslim encounter with European colonial modernity and prepares it for its imminent dissolution and subsequent resurrection.

Another major literary masterpiece closely related and similar to *Kelilah and Dimnah* is *Sindbad-nameh* (also known as *The Book of the Wise Sindbad*, *The Story of Seven Viziers*, *Seven Wise Men*, *The Book of Women's Deceits*, and *The Story of the Prince and Seven Viziers*), whose rendition by Zahiri Samarqandi in the twelfth century is a seminal example of elegant Persian prose, in which the figure of the Persian Prince finds its most metaphorical character traits. Just like *Kelilah and Dimnah*, the work consists of a master plot interrupted by multiple other stories. The master plot is similar to the story of Seyavash and Sudabeh in the *Shahnameh* and Yusuf and Zulaikha (Potiphar's wife) from the Bible and the Qurʾan, by this time totally marked by an endemic misogyny, while the substance of the text itself is on statecraft and the necessity of wisdom and justice.[42] Predicated on a whole genre of misogynistic literature, this text partakes in the plot of a young prince being entrusted to a wise vizier named Sindbad to prepare him to rule with justice; however, upon his arrival at the court of his royal father, the ruling queen seeks to seduce him and, upon his refusal, accuses him of having made illicit advances toward her. The vizier consults the stars and tells the young prince to say nothing for seven days, over the course of which seven wise viziers inform the monarch of the conceits of women. This systematic demonization of women appears in many other similar texts of the period, even in Nezam al-Molk's *Siyasat-nameh*. Of Indo-Iranian origin and yet with innumerable translations around the world, this text represents a seminal sample of the genre of the Persian Prince surviving plots and accusations to triumph over adversity. That it does so at the expense of women will remain a constant of this genre until much later, when the trait begins to reverse onto itself. But at the same time, precisely through its misogynistic traces, we might be able to read such texts in the metaphorically suggestive registers in which they are presented—in which case "women" are outlined as metaphoric tropes rather than actual human beings, as in fact the Persian Prince itself (following Bal's thinking) posits a subject rather than a character, a persona rather than a person.

The Shahnameh *as Prototype*

This brings us to the seminal text of Ferdowsi's *Shahnameh* (1010), perhaps the single most significant of the heroic tales about pre-Islamic Iranian imperial legacies, mythical kings, legendary heroes, and historical princes and princesses that reached and informed the Islamic period—and in which an entire section is devoted to the legendary figure of Alexander, making him not only a Persian Prince but in fact a metonymic specimen of the very persona of the archetype. The Persian epic thus effectively brings pre-Islamic Iranian, classical Greek, and Islamic heritage together in one seamless and masterful stroke. There is no exaggerating the power or the influence of the Persian epic in enabling, informing, and legitimizing multiple Persians and Persianate empires.[43]

Ferdowsi began composing his *Shahnameh* under a Samanid prince and concluded it for a thoroughly Persianized Turkic monarch. The text itself may have complicated the history of the Persian epic and its uses and abuses by ruling empires, but those empires turned to the *Shahnameh* for inspiration and legitimacy. Its tragic heroes, like Seyavash or Sohrab or Esfandiar, morally complicated and dramatized the figure of the Persian Prince right at the crosscurrents of Iranian imperial history and epic poetry. The *Shahnameh* thus emerged as a text unlike any other—at once consolidating and yet dramatizing the figure of the Persian Prince. It was a talisman of power and an amulet of legitimacy, a source of princely inspiration and a sought-after charm of legitimacy. It helped Persian and Persianized princes to rule with an air of royal authority and a claim to ancient lineage. The Persian epic managed to do all that while remaining aloof from them all, projecting an archetype of princely power and charisma and yet never collapsing into the historical follies of those monarchs who sought to model themselves after its prototypes. It did so by way of complicating the figure of the Persian Prince as a triumphant but ultimately tragic figure.

After the poetic zenith of the *Shahnameh*, three almost simultaneous prose texts brought this genre to a dramatic height. The composition of the *Siyasat-nameh*

(*The Book of Politics*) or, as it is alternatively named, *Siyar al-Muluk* (*Royal Prosopographies*), by the preeminent Saljuqid vizier Abu Ali Hasan ibn Ali al-Tusi, known as Nezam al-Molk (1018–1092), was a pivotal event in the history of Persianate Islamic political thought. Ruling over a vast empire from Central Asia to the Persian Gulf and from the Indian subcontinent to the Mediterranean Sea, the Saljuqs reigned for over a century and a half with a Persianate imperial system defined by Nezam al-Molk. His *Siyasat-nameh* has two crucial features: it was composed decidedly in Persian for the use of the Saljuqid Empire, and it consistently partook in pre-Islamic Iranian epistemologies of power.

Right next to this pivotal book stands *Qabus-nameh*, the iconic text written by Kaykavus ibn Vushmgir, the ruler of the Ziyarid dynasty (circa 1050–1087), for his son, in which we read a major work of Persian political thought in the form of a treatise written by a royal father to his young son in anticipation of his becoming a king one day. It is impossible to exaggerate the influence of these two texts on the subsequent political culture of Muslim empires and Persian and Persianate dynasties and consolidating the figure of the Persian Prince as definitive to them. More to the point, these texts give us solid evidence of the sustained course of Persian political thought at the service of ruling dynasties before and after their compositions. Another major text of this period is of course al-Ghazali's *Nasihat al-Moluk* (*Counsel for Kings*, 1109), solidly placed in the genre of "mirrors for princes," which combines the stories of Sassanid kings with those of Muslim rulers, fusing together political, ethical, and theological issues. The text was presumably written for the Saljuqid emperor Mohammad ibn Malik-Shah (reigned 1104–1117) or, alternatively, for Sultan Sanjar (1085–1157). These three texts, all originally written in Persian, convene to map out, in the most detailed prose that has reached us, the complete portrait of the Persian Prince, the pre-Islamic Iranian royal figure of power and wisdom that ideally holds together Muslim dynasties.

I cite these three seminal texts because they were composed in the historical vicinity of the *Shahnameh* and as such bring the literary and poetic provenance of Ferdowsi's masterpiece into fuller view. In *The Medieval Reception of the Shāhnāma as a Mirror for Princes* (2016), Nasrin Askari studies this phenomenon in admirable detail.[44] This is a meticulous examination of how Ferdowsi's epic was received, both as a mirror for princes and as a manual of statecraft and as such the metonymic significance of the text as the site of the Persian Prince. As Askari puts it correctly:

In the medieval period, the *Shāhnāma* was primarily understood as a book of wisdom and advice for kings and courtly élites, and that studying it in this context sheds considerable light on the meaning of its tales and the purport of its author. Also, as a repository of ancient Persian wisdom and advice on kingship, the *Shāhnāma* enhances our understanding of the development of major concepts related to kingship and statecraft in later Perso-Islamic literature of wisdom and advice for rulers.[45]

It is, however, crucial to keep in mind that the factual and historical implications of the Persian epic never exhausted the form's residual metonymic resonances, which kept it always at a poetic distance from such uses and abuses. One dynasty after another came around and put the *Shahnameh* to its political use, but embedded in the text and its collective subconscious also dwelled the undoing of that very dynasty—the poetics of the text undermining its politics.[46]

Saʿdi and his World

History unfolds, and with it come new masterpieces of Persian poetry and prose, but constant remains the figure of the Persian Prince as a just and benevolent ruler at the epicenter of them all. Saʿdi's *Golestan* (1258) is arguably the single most significant didactic text in the tradition of Persian literary humanism and the genre of royal advice. Saʿdi dedicated the book to the Salghurid Atabeg in the poet's native Fars, Mozaffar-al-Din Abu Bakr b. Saʿd b. Zangi, to his son, Saʿd, and to his vizier, Fakhr-al-Din Abu Bakr b. Abi Nasr. Such royal dedications did not deprive Saʿdi of his commitment to men of higher spiritual attainments, to whom he felt particularly attached. The poet's other seminal text, his *Bustan* (1257), is equally central to this genre, and offers advice and moral guidance to his learned and royal readers. Here is a definitive example:

> *Shanidam keh Khosrow beh Shiruyeh goft . . .*
>
> I have heard that Khosrow told Shiruyeh
> When his eyes were about to close upon this world:
> Be careful whatever you intend to do
> Consider the wellbeing of your subjects!
> Beware, never turn away from justice and wisdom,
> So people will not revolt against you—
> Subjects flee from a tyrant king

> Spreading his evil name around the world—
> Yes, men with swords can do much harm,
> But not as much as the sighs of women and children—
> A dim light that a widow alights
> Could very well burn an entire city.[47]

"Khosrow" here is the Sassanid emperor Khosrow II (reigned 590–628), and "Shiruyeh" is his son Kavad II, who ruled briefly in 628. I must wonder: In 1257, when Saʿdi was writing this work, how had he known about these kings; why did they surface in his poems; and, more to the point, what was the effect of invoking bygone monarchs and their princes when advising the kings and sultans of his own time as to how to rule? The figure of the Persian Prince was an archetype of legitimate Muslim rule—as he had been in classical antiquity and the Hebrew Bible—that rooted the figure in the pre-Islamic universe of royal legitimacy. There is no doubt that the figure of Prophet Muhammad and his divine mission remains central and definitive to the institution of the Muslim caliphate. But equally if not even more definitive remains the figurative archetype of the Persian Prince, which had consistently moved from the pre-Islamic to the Islamic period and characterized every subsequent monarch, sultan, shah, or even caliph or other dynastic head of an empire. While the doctors of Islamic law were clumsily speculating about the link between the Prophet's authority and the ruling sultans' vagaries, Persian, Arab, Turkish, and Indian poets, prose stylists, and moral philosophers were mapping out the real moral imagination of Islamic civilization. At the epicenter of that imagination towered the archetypal figure of the Persian Prince—ancient, aging, renewable, empowering.

One poet or prose stylist borrowed from another and expanded the cause of the just and ethical rule further, and they all pointed at a source beyond their immediate reaches and buried deep in the Persian past. By the time Khwajah Nasir al-Din al-Tusi wrote his seminal text, *Akhlaq-e Naseri* (*Nasirean Ethics*, 1235), in Persian, the very prose of Muslim historicality Saʿdi had inherited had reached the highest level of unsurpassed moral consciousness. In the learned opinion of one scholar of al-Tusi's text:

> The work offers a well-balanced overview of the main moral and intellectual positions of Islamic civilization at one of its peaks. It is a skillful blending of the Greek philosophical and scientific tradition with the Islamic view of man, society, and the universe; and the resulting synthesis represents a subtle transcending of both. As with virtually all

high-culture writing in traditional Islam, it is a work of theory, idealistic and normative in approach, and throwing light only indirectly (if at all) on actual circumstances at any point.[48]

By al-Tusi's time, this level of theoretical abstraction had become normative to the prose and poetry that Saʿdi performed to its highest aesthetic sublimity—marking a moral imagination that was neither juridical nor theological, neither philosophical nor mystical, yet deeply informed by the entire spectrum of Muslim learning and thereby articulating its own particular prose and politics. This moral imagination was integral, as A. K. S. Lambton rightly recognized, to the Persian belles-lettres, there to entertain and amuse, instruct and educate, admonish and civilize all at the same time. The highest manifestations of this moral imagination were composed in pure poetry, poetic prose, or a pleasant combination of both. They ranged from detailed prosaic of how to spy on your enemies in Nezam al-Molk's *Siyasat-nameh*, to the loftiest moral aspirations of Saʿdi, in his *Bustan* and *Golestan*—but equally evident in the little pamphlet Saʿdi wrote precisely in the genre of *Nasihat al-Moluk* (*Counsel to Kings*). Indian, Iranian, Greek, Arab, and Hebrew political ideas and practices of pre-Islamic origin eventually found their way into the discursive and institutional basis of governance in the Islamic period. They either remained ostensibly non-Islamic and performed in Persian with palpable Zoroastrian, Manichean, and Mazdakite sentiments, or else metamorphized into Arabic and Islamic garbs—in either case, they gave an aura of ancient authenticity to the royal claims of Muslim dynasties. Saʿdi's texts and the world they embody thus became the literary synecdoche of this universe, a part made to represent the whole universe in both iconic and material ways.

By the time Saʿdi reaches Ralph Waldo Emerson (1803–1882), and the towering American poet composes a eulogy for the Shirazi saint in 1847, the globality of the Persian Prince had broached new frontiers and rekindled the moral imagination of American transcendentalists.

> Be thou ware where Saadi dwells;
> Wisdom of the gods is he—
> Entertain it reverently.
> Gladly round that golden lamp
> Sylvan deities encamp,
> And simple maids and noble youth
> Are welcome to the man of truth.

> Most welcome they who need him most,
> They feed the spring which they exhaust;
> For greater need
> Draws better deed:
> But, critic, spare thy vanity,
> Nor show thy pompous parts,
> To vex with odious subtlety
> The cheerer of men's hearts.[49]

The Ghosts of Mazdakites Past, Present, and Future

The ironic mode of the collective subconscious of these constellations of texts that flourished in the prose and poetry of Hafez and Zakani kept the flame of the paradox at the heart of the archetype of the Persian Prince alive for generations to come, until the dawn of the Muslim encounter with European colonial modernity. We have an utterly exquisite text that best represents the dynamic of this paradoxical effervescence at the heart of the Persian literary imagination.

Ala' al-Dowleh Semnani (1261–1336) was a mystic of ancient and enduring wisdom who graced Persian prose of the Ilkhanid period. Among his many treatises and autobiographical accounts, there is one particularly beautiful essay he calls "Shatranjiyeh" (On chess).[50] In this short but exquisite essay, Semnani tells us he is going to reveal the secret meaning of the game of chess and not just its apparent rules and regulations. He recalls how he turned to the chess pieces themselves and asked them to tell him what each meant. The first one that becomes his master and teaches him its secrets is the pawn (*piadeh* in Persian—literally "foot soldier" or "infantryman"). The pawn tells Semnani he must learn from him how he has devoted his life to the King, standing up to protect him against his enemies. He is determined to defeat the King's adversaries, though he knows he has a dangerous path ahead of him.

> Sometimes I am scared of the Knight [*Fors* in Persian, literally "Horse"], sometimes of the Bishop [*Fil*, literally "Elephant"], sometimes of the Rook [*Rokh*, meaning "Chariot"], and the Queen [*Farzin*, meaning "Vizier"]. But if I were to persist through the board I'd be rewarded and become a vizier. So, I can sit with the King.[51]

From there the narrator goes to the Vizier and asks him to teach him his secrets. "I am the companion of the King," he says, "and I seek solitude, which is the reason I am so close to the King." Then he goes to the Elephant, the Horse, and the Rokh; each one explains its moves and the mystical meaning of its proximity to King as Truth. The King thus becomes the symbol of Truth and all other figures around him approximations to approaching that Truth.

> My dear, upon the board of life you are the majestic King; all your retinues are gathered around you like pieces of chessboard, sometimes someone attacks you like a Horse, then as a Rook. The task at hand is to play the game of life so judiciously as to reach Paradise rather than collapsing into Hell.[52]

The metaphor of chess in Semnani's treatise is put squarely at the service of the King becoming the princely figuration of the chess player, the human being that Semnani addresses directly. This investiture of princely potential in a mere pawn and the agency of choice in the unknown reader of a treatise by a mystic master becomes a simulacrum of the authority that the Persian Prince (the King on the chessboard) commands, not just as the ruling monarch but in fact as his nominal subjects, who are made princely by all the pieces moving on a level playing field.

The simple case of this fourteenth-century treatise on chess, in which the piece representing the King becomes a princely figure of authority in a human being, recasts the history of Islamic political thought away from a figurehead toward the dynamics of varied interactions with his subjects. Such entirely disregarded treatises—of which there are countless examples—occasion a serious reconsideration of the sources and genres of literature relevant to our understanding of Islamic political culture. Texts such as *Kelilah and Dimnah*, the *Shahnameh*, *Sandbad-nameh*, *Marzban-nameh*, *Chahar Maqaleh*, *Bakhtiyar-nameh*, *Bustan*, and *Golestan* are equally if not more important for a critical understanding of the literary foregrounding of Islamic political thought: they draw the dialogical disposition of the *monadic* phase of the figure of the Persian Prince and eventually yield to its *dyadic* phase in anticipation of its *nomadic* register, as is perhaps best evident in the case of the towering Ismaʿili poet/philosopher Nasser Khosrow Qubadiani (died circa 1017), who in his person brought together the Persian poet, philosopher, and sojourner of truth. Particularly in his *Safarnameh* (*Travelogue*), Nasser Khosrow performs in probing Persian prose his restless soul and nomadic mind when traveling around the world as an Ismaʿili moral philosopher and peripatetic intellectual. The schizophrenic bifurcation between "modern" and "medieval" thoughts, which is entirely alien to

Islamic history, has altogether abandoned allowing for such figures and thus eventually leads to the Orientalist dead end of the "impossible state." The Iranian, Indian, Central Asian, and a fortiori African experiences within the context of Islamic civilization was neither exceptional nor insular. These dimensions of political culture were definitive to the Islamic experience, of which the archetype of the Persian Prince is but one paramount example.

The archetype of the Persian Prince as I have articulated here underlines the rebellious disposition of the alterity of the monarch in the rebels who rise against him. There is a sustained and almost uninterrupted succession of revolutionary uprisings from the earliest stages of the Muslim conquest of Iran in which Zoroastrian, Manichean, and Mazdakite leitmotifs are most obvious and manifest. This succession begins with the Khorramites in the eighth century during the early years of the Abbasid caliphate, continues in the ninth century with the Carmatians, and reaches its zenith in the twelfth century in the Nizari branch of the Isma'ili uprisings, before it dovetails with the Sarbedaran uprisings of the fourteenth century, which connects to the Horufiyyah movement of the late fourteenth century. In short, the archetype of the Persian Prince sustains a paradoxical nucleus of the moral demand system (to use Philip Rieff's theory) in which both ruler and rebel partake in an identical frame of moral imagination. The Prince is aware of the prophetic voice in him and has dreadful dreams of the rebellious uprising against his throne, as for example Zahhak in the *Shahnameh*, who sees the rise of Fereydun in a dream before the next Persian Prince even enters his court. The same dynamic also accounts for the "Oedipal" tensions between fathers and sons—say, between Key Kavous and Seyavash or Esfandiar and Goshtasp. This paradoxical tension sustains the course of dramatic trauma at the heart of Iranian and Islamic history.

This tension between the Persian Prince as royal authority and his alter ego as a prophetic voice, a poetic justice, and a revolutionary redeemer is brought home in the singular figure of Anushirvan the Just. The central paradox at the heart of most revolutionary uprisings in Iranian history is their thematic allusions to Mazdakism as a prototype, and it is in the actual history of the proto-socialist Mazdakite movement that we see the seminal figure of Anushirvan turned upside down, from a towering figure of justice and magnanimity into a murderous tyrant, for the brutality with which the Sassanid emperor massacred Mazdakites and killed Mazdak. One of the best accounts of Mazdak's uprising comes from Ferdowsi's *Shahnameh*, in which we learn how he gets close to Kavad I and in fact becomes his vizier. There is a famine, and Mazdak advises the king. He informs people of the royal silos' whereabouts, which they subsequently storm to feed themselves. The king is enamored with Mazdak and converts to his religion, but the Iranian nobility is angered by the revolutionary prophet and plots against him, turning Kavad I's son Anushirvan against him, who in turn orders the Mazdakites summarily slaughtered. Anushirvan invites the Mazdakites to a royal banquet, kills them all, and plants them like trees upside down; he then calls Mazdak and asks him to see how the seeds he had planted have grown to trees, before having Mazdak hanged.[53]

> You will see trees the likes of which no one has ever seen,
> Nor has anyone ever heard of them from any wise men,
> Mazdak ran and opened the gate to the garden,
> Thinking he would see fruitful trees planted in an orchard—
> As soon as he opened his eye he passed out,
> Bursting into a dreadful cry,
> Kisra ordered tall gallows erected
> Hanging from it a long rope,
> He had him hanged while still alive,
> Killing the wretched man,
> Then he had him killed again with a rain of arrows
> If you are clever don't follow Mazdak![54]

This very poem is an example of how the collective subconscious of these texts sustained the rich complexities of the Persian Prince—at once positing and discrediting them. Moral philosophers, mystics, poets, and historians had a common denominator—the centrality of the stories they told, in which the facts and fiction, truth and narratives, histories and stories that nurtured them were intertwined.

In Philip Rieff's theory of culture, a moral demand system presides and animates the triangulation of what he calls the *interdictory*, the *remissive*, and the *transgressive* moments of a cultural universe. He did not consider this moral system to be Judaism, Christianity, Islam, or any other "religion." Within and beyond all these institutional constitutions of the sacred, this is how *the self* is formed and connects to *society* and, through it, to the supreme deities of the culture it represents, thereby laying claim to a soul. If Freud was the cartographer of this moral psyche of the soul, Weber was its prophetic voice, and Nietzsche (invoking the Iranian prophet Zoroaster) its rebellious prophet. This is also how the corporeal body of a culture asserts its enduring symbolic authority. In his seminal work, *The Mind of the Moralist*, Rieff sought to navigate a moral demand system in the theorist of the immoral releases from the bondage of power and authority. Rieff wanted to see how civilized life was possible after Freud, Marx, and Darwin, and it was his bold imagination that took him right into the crux of their work to detect interdictions embedded at the very center of their theorizations of transgressions. When I was his teaching and research assistant in the 1980s, in our seminars on the Pauline Epistles, Nietzsche's *Beyond Good and Evil*, Kafka's *In the Penal Colony*, Kierkegaard's *The Present Page*, and Weber's "Politics as a Vocation," Rieff drove these points home.

With Enlightenment modernity at the epicenter of his theoretical concerns, Rieff was in search of an amorphous deity, the sense of the sacred, which he self-referentially called "the Jew of the Culture," that had defied the odds and persisted to define our moral imagination. In what would be posthumously published as *Sacred Order (Social Order*, 2007–2008), a text that for years he called "The Return of the Sacred," he mapped out in meticulous detail how the sacred order had returned, as in the return of the repressed to reassert itself. Rieff was no antiquarian reactionary wishing for a restoration of theocratic authority. He lived and engaged with the fact of our diminished souls. What is evident in the mind of these moralists at the heart of Muslim moral life—which I examine here far from Rieff's concerns, even though, as my doctoral dissertation adviser, he caringly guided me through the earliest stages of my scholarship—is the dialectic of their own impossibilities, the negation of their own affirmations that they had lived a life of morality with or without the God the Muslim jurist had summoned at the epicenter of their jurisprudence. Mystics had turned the fear of that God into love, while philosophers stipulated gradations of distances between the command of God to Be and the mortal limitations of the world that was. Muslim jurists, however, could not breathe except in the immediate vicinity of the hellfire they had lit for the fear of Muslims. The paradox at the heart of that history is not merely diachronic; it is always synchronic too.

In the figure of the Persian Prince dwelling in the collective subconscious of the Persian and Persianate texts that have sustained the course of successive Muslim empires, the parameters of that moral demand system oscillated between the power of the ruling monarchs and the will of those dismantling the authority of that power. In the dynamic of that oscillation dwelled the engine of Islamic history. The paradox is that Anushirvan is precisely the opposite of what he is purported to be: not just, but actually a tyrannous mass murderer, he becomes a Janus figure facing both ways on and against the mirror of the Persian

Prince. He plants human beings upside down, and in hateful irony he tells Mazdak, at once his own alter ego and his substitutional father figure, "Come and watch the seeds you planted." And yet, paradoxically, he was being prophetic: the seeds that Mazdak planted would put down roots and flower for the rest of Iranian and Islamic history.

FIVE

In the Light and Shadows of the Persian Prince

> Thus saith the Lord to his anointed, to Cyrus, whose right hand I have holden, to subdue nations before him; and I will loose the loins of kings, to open before him the two leaved gates; and the gates shall not be shut.[1]
>
> Isaiah 45:1–4

IT IS TIME NOW to split the atom of the Persian Prince, as it were, and observe what is inside the archetype—how its very soul is formed, fragmented, animated, and made into the prototype of the human it is meant to rule and implicate. In the previous two chapters I have had the occasion to mark the internal dynamics and tensions in the composite disposition of the Persian Prince, demarcating the prophetic and poetic proclivities that underline its both reactionary and revolutionary potentials. In this chapter, I open up the expansive domain of the highly erudite courtly and non-courtly literatures guiding the moral universe of the Persian Prince into more extended and potent horizons. I have also very much limited those horizons to the Islamic contexts of the Persian Prince, with necessary allusions to its pre-Islamic Iranian and singularly crucial Greek gestations in Xenophon's *Cyropaedia*. But I now wish to reach beyond the Islamic domain and broaden the view into the wider Hebrew, Christian, Greek, and European domains. My purpose here is to show the shades and shadows and porous boundaries of the archetypal presence of the Persian Prince in the larger Persianate cosmopolis (Persepolis) as a vision of the world that enters and exits the confined geographical territorialities of Iran-Shahr, which I

FIGURE 2 "Kamus Fights Giv and Tus." Illustrated folio (263-recto) from the *Shahnama of Shah Tahmasp*, chapter 13b. Tehran, Museum of Contemporary Art.

might perhaps best visually depict with this allusion to a typical Persian painting (figs. 2 and 3). I draw your attention to the left side of the folio on the left and the right side of the folio on the right, where you see that the imaginary borders of the frames of the events depicted are at once formed and then stylistically defied, in one event entering the picture from the left, and in the other exiting the picture from the right. Similar pictures could be added where the borders are crossed at both the top and bottom of the frame. In other words, the logic and rhetoric of the visual depiction requires a border crossing of the frame, which marks the narrative limitations but iconic defiance of the borders. This is what I mean by opening up the conceptual confinements of the archetype of the Persian cosmopolis that houses the Persian Prince beyond its delimitations in specifically Islamic contexts to explore the Arman-Shahri (Utopian) proclivities of the Iran-Shahr (Persepolis). Three interrelated concepts are at work here:

FIGURE 3 "Faridun Tests His Sons." Illustrated folio (42) from the *Shahnama of Shah Tahmasp*. Attributed to Aqa Mirak, Persia, Tabriz, Royal Atelier, circa 1525–1535. Courtesy of Aga Khan Museum.

Iran-Shahri, Jahan-Shahri, and Arman-Shahri. Iran-Shahri (Persepolis) is the Persianate world that crosses borders into the worldliness of Jahan-Shahri (Cosmopolis), and thus posits the idyllic desires of Arman-Shahri (Utopia).

The archetypal gestations of the Persian Prince have a similar constellation of home, habit, and habitat. We have historically received its fullest formations in the Islamic domains, with evident and archaic forays into pre-Islamic Iranian, Indian, Hebrew, Christian, and Greek territories. In this fifth and final chapter of the second (classical) part of my book, I wish to offer the fullest account of the *monadic* archetype of the Persian Prince in its multiple and conflated territories. After this chapter, we will have to prepare for the contemporary resurrection of the archetype, after its fateful encounter with the onslaught of European colonial modernity. But as you will see in this articulation of the archetype, the signs and signals of its eventual desedimentation and deterritorialization are perfectly evident in its richest and fullest global manifestations. The task at hand is to have a simultaneous account of both its monadic disposition and dyadic proclivities as we see it through its self-universalizing power and charismatic character. The map that is in front of us navigates through multiple moral and cultural landscapes. The train is at once familiar and yet hiding some foreign territories. As you follow me on this journey you will have to be attentive to details and yet enjoy the scenery.

Definitive to the train of this navigation is the gentle deterritorialization of both Iranian and Islamic political thoughts. The idea of the Persian Prince allows us this cosmopolitan sojourn, this liberating move from the false assurances of the legal to the open-ended suggestions of the literary, the poetic, and the aesthetic; from the evident lights of Arabic and Persian prose to the suggested shades and shadows of Persianate worlds and non-Iranian climes; from the false binary of the Iranian versus Islamic to the vast vistas of the non-Iranian and pre-Islamic, widely into the Indian, Greek, Hebrew, and Christian demarcations; from the falsely fetishized spaces ("Islamic is here, Iranian there, and this is Indian," etc.) to regional and global interstitial spaces we may have always suspected but scarce cared to decipher. Here you will see the Persian Prince read Arabic, speak Greek, write in Hebrew, translate from Sanskrit, paint in high European Renaissance and Baroque styles, and yet still remain decidedly Iranian in its moral imagination.

This inward and outward move into the architecture and landscape of the archetype in and of itself is to mark the moral and material imagination that informs it far beyond the claustrophobic domains of Muslim political thinking and right at the center of lived historical experiences. To reach for the very soul of the Persian Prince, we need to keep an open mind to see the varieties of ways in which the princely advice or philosophical speculations pertaining to political authority can address themselves to the ruling class—and not to limit ourselves to the classics of the mirrors for princes.

A short ethical text composed by the eminent philosopher, scientist, and statesman Nasir al-Din al-Tusi, *Awsaf al-Ashraf* (*Attributes of the Nobles*, composed circa 1271), written for Shams-al-din Mohammad al-Joveini, a high-ranking official under the Mongol Ilkhans, takes the domain of advice literature into the heart of Persian mystical meditations.[2] This mystical domain is cosmic in its imagination, overcoming the false territories that have divided and distorted the dominion of the Persian Prince. Having already written two major treatises on moral philosophy, al-Tusi here opts for a perfect fusion of the saintly and the mundane, the worldly and the transcendent, the political and the ethical, where classical Sufi doctrines and practices are expressed in the form of ascetic principles directed at disciplining the soul of the princely elite. *Awsaf al-Ashraf* extends Sufi ideals and aspirations into moral and ethical doctrines made accessible to the ruling class. We must also remember that al-Tusi was no ordinary man. The author of two other major books on ethics, *Akhlaq-e Nasiri* and *Akhlaq-e Mohtashami*, to which he refers in his introduction to *Awsaf al-Ashraf*, he was also a towering astrophysicist and a groundbreaking philosopher and ethicist who accompanied the Mongol warlord Hulagu Khan (circa 1218–1265) on his way to conquer Baghdad and put an end to the Abbasid caliphate—after which he was instrumental in establishing the major scientific citadel of the Maragheh Observatory. We have to bear that in mind to see the significance of when, in this short text penned toward the end of his life, al-Tusi writes on faith, truth, sincerity, repentance, abstinence, piety, or the necessity of solitude and self-reflection.

In this meditative text, al-Tusi is as much admonishing himself as addressing his readers. Either way, as a moral philosopher at the service of multiple warriors, he was summoning the best of his wondrous mind to discipline an archetypal Persian Prince. The main interlocutors of such seminal texts were mostly princely patrons, the actual or potential rulers of a Muslim land. Again, we must recall that though al-Tusi was perfectly capable of writing in Arabic, the text of *Awsaf al-Ashraf* was composed decidedly in Persian, the language that had by now emerged as the most potent indication of both a pre-Islamic Iranian origin and the contemporary context of addressing it to the Persianate princely class of the dominant empires. The fact that *Awsaf al-Ashraf* was later translated into Arabic is an equal indication of its influence in non-Persian domains. In *Awsaf al-Ashraf*, al-Tusi effectively crafts the soul of the Persian Prince and attends to his spiritual journeys. The ideal Persian Prince is an ideal Human Being, squarely located within a moral universe that philosophers like al-Tusi had made real for the ideal type. *Awsaf al-Ashraf* is concise, almost formulaic, but written in sublime Persian prose and deeply rooted in a humanist tradition of disciplining the carnal soul. In this and similar texts the Persian Prince dwells and is most at home; this is where the poetic prose of moral philosophers locates the prophetic disposition and the monadic form of the imperial archetype at the heart of varied and successive empires. The halo of Nasir al-Din al-Tusi's moral imagination is where we see the Persian Prince both focused and amorphous into its adjacent territories.

From the Sacred to the Sovereign

To navigate the contours of those focused and amorphous vistas and thus come closer to the paradoxical and multivariant disposition of the Persian Prince, I now approach it from decidedly multiple and divergent angles, through the lateral reflections of the archetypal figure in varied cultural domains we have historically considered outside or adjacent to Islamic, Persian, and Iranian milieus. In the last two chapters I have had occasion to reflect on the Greco-Roman, Indo-Iranian, and Arab-Iranian angles of looking at the archetypal. To these closest neighborly interactions we might now add the Hebrew Biblical, the Western Christian, the Greco-Macedonian, and the Perso-Nordic fields. Here we will have to venture into sacred and profane, textual and hermeneutic, visual and performing arts. The point is to see the constitution of the archetypal figure through the sacred and sovereign reconfiguration of the Persian Prince in its adjacent realms, as they corroborate and expand upon each other while driving the figure of the Persian Prince far beyond the Iranian and Islamic domains, as the Persianate cosmopolis now finds decidedly Hebrew and Greco-Roman provenances. These multiple angles are necessary if we are to, as we must, liberate the idea of the Persian Prince from any false fixation within exclusionary political domains—Iranian or Islamic, sacred or secular, textual or institutional, originary or derivative.

If we were to consider Ferdowsi's *Shahnameh* or Saʿdi's *Golestan* and *Bustan* or Nasir al-Din al-Tusi's *Akhlaq-e Nasiri* as the prototypical epicenter where the Persian Prince is most at home, then Ibn Muqaffaʿ's Arabic rendition of the Pahlavi translation of the original Sanskrit sources of *Kelilah and Dimnah* would be its Indo-Iranian-Arabic field, while Abu Mansur al-Thaʿalibi's seminal history *Ghurar Akhbar Muluk al-Furs wa Siyarihim* is the leading candidate for marking its Arabic-Persian sphere. Even as much would have been sufficient to see the Indian, Iranian, and Arabic topography of the archetypal figure. If we were to add to this map Xenophon's *Cyropaedia* and its subsequent Roman and European receptions, we would be widely exposed to the transmigratory disposition of the Persian Prince. By now, before any other move, the Persian Prince has textual, poetic, literary, and historical claims to Indian, Iranian, Arabic, Greek, and by extension Hellenic dominions—locations where the archetypal figure is informing and being informed by cultural contexts beyond its Iranian and even Persianate habitat. But we still have vast expanses of cultural contexts to consider and include in where and what and how the figure of the Persian Prince has morally, imaginatively, and politically resonated with the charismatic disposition of other peoples and their histories. Picture a source of light, anything from the sun to a candle, that is both the evidence of its own incandescence and the cause of the shadows it projects precisely by virtue of its radiance. That is the visual metaphor I wish to invoke here—how the enlightened Persian Prince is imagined at the center and peripheries of a cultural map where we can no longer distinguish between its center and peripheries.

Let us now consider the Hebrew Bible and by extension the Talmud, the Midrash, and most particularly the Judeo-Persian epics and look at the Persian Prince in his Hebrew habitat. To begin with, the significance of Cyrus the Great as the archetypal Persian Prince is not limited to the canonical texts of the Hebrew Bible, the Book of Esther in particular. According to Amnon Netzer (1934–2008), the preeminent scholar of Iran in Hebrew sources, "the figure of Cyrus the Great in the Jewish sacred writings, especially in the book of Isaiah, has occupied Jewish thought through the ages. Cyrus is mentioned and discussed in passages in Talmud, Midrash, in the medieval commentaries and the Judea-Persian writings."[3] The prophet Isaiah's adulation of the Persian Prince was so lofty—"to be addressed by God as 'servant,' 'in whom my soul is well-pleased,' to be called, 'he whom God loves,' ... belonged to Abraham, Moses, David, *perhaps the prophet*"—that according to Netzer it had baffled Babylonian Talmudic scholars generations later.[4] What is crucial, again according to Netzer, is this:

The Prophet wants to instruct Cyrus also, addressing him in the language of the Mazdean cosmology that will be familiar to him:

> Though you do not know me, I arm you
> that men may know from the rising to the setting of the sun
> that, apart from me, all is nothing.
> I am Yahweh, unrivalled,
> I form the light and create the dark.
> I make good fortune and create calamity,
> it is I, Yahweh, who do all this.[5]

In other words, the Mazdean cosmology is rearticulated in the most sacrosanct Judaic renditions of it, approximating the two metaphysics of Divine authority together. The most compelling phrase here is "though you do not know me," at once gesturing humility yet positing overriding authority. This is a whole new provenance for the Persian Prince—whereby he has effectively become a Jewish prophet.

The same love of and admiration for Cyrus continues with Titus Flavius Josephus/Yosef ben Matityahu (circa 37–100), the first-century Romano-Jewish historian, and well into the Midrash, followed by similar treatment in some key Judeo-Persian texts. "The Midrash says," again according to Netzer, "Cyrus slew Belshazzar because he heard the prophecy in Daniel 5:28, and vowed that he would permit the Jews to return home with the vessels of the temple which had been carried away by Nebuchadnezzar."[6] In all these references the figure of Cyrus the Great is exalted in Hebrew sources as anointed by God, as loved by the prophets, and indeed as one of them. The point here is how the iconic figure of Cyrus the Great posits the archetypal presence of the Persian Prince in an entirely different domain—both pre-Islamic and non-Iranian in a provincial understanding of the term—for a sustained and historically palpable period of history. The Hebrew context of the figure of the Persian Prince is as, if not more, important than its Greco-Roman reception through Xenophon's *Cyropaedia*. Both these reflections, at one and the same time, liberate the archetypal figure from any ethnic, xenophobic, or sectarian claim in one direction or another. We now begin to see the universal claims of the Persian Prince (beyond any binary fragmentation) on our understanding of the political culture of multiple historical narratives.

That is even before we turn to the exquisite and precious body of linguistic and literary material we have in Judeo-Persian language and literature, as a uniquely Iranian medium of communication among Iranian Jews. The long and venerable history of scholarship in Judeo-Persian has concluded:

> Several hundred years before the emergence of a Persian Jewish literature, and prior even to the emergence of classical Persian literature, Persian documents and stone inscriptions were being written in Hebrew script. These are of historical importance for the light they shed on the development of the Persian language and in particular the language spoken by the Jews.[7]

This historical fact expands the domain of the Persian cosmopolis well into Levantine Palestine and thus places the figure of the Persian Prince well before and well beyond its Islamic or Greek provenance.

It is crucial here to note that the earliest examples of the Hebrew Biblical hermeneutics (*tafsirs*) were in fact in Judeo-Persian. The current state of scholarship in Judeo-Persian literature has documented the evidence of tafsirs of the Talmud, halakhah, midrashim, Kabbala and mysticism, philosophy, and theology and apologetics, as well as Judeo-Persian prayer books. Consider the reach of the Judeo-Persian literary domain:

> Scholars believe that the Jews of Persia were under the authority and influence of the Babylonian sages during the period of the Gaonim (post-Talmudic period, 7th to 11th century), and that teachers and rabbinical judges were sent to them from Babylon. However, Persian Jewry was not only subject to influence, but also exerted influence in the liturgical field. Emissaries were sent from Persia to the Chinese Jewish community.[8]

The widespread influence of this domain corresponds to the imperial imaginary of the Persian Empire, which of course included its Jewish communities. What is crucial here is the range and extension of the Judeo-Persian literary and scholastic discourses in which the Iranian literary imagination has a solid Hebrew presence.

The leading figure of Judeo-Persian poetry is Shahin of Shiraz, a contemporary of Hafez who preferred the genre of *Masnavi* as his medium. He composed his works in Persian but used the Hebrew alphabet. His *Musa-nameh* (*Book of Moses*, 1327), for example, is a Persian rendition of the Pentateuch that includes narratives from Exodus, Leviticus, Numbers, and Deuteronomy. Shahin of Shiraz also turned the books of Esther and Ezra into Persian poetry. His *Ardeshir-nameh* (*Book of Ardeshir*, 1333) is an epic of six thousand couplets partially based on the Book of Esther, with Ardeshir (Ahasuerus from the Book of Esther) and the biblical Esther (Hadassah) as the hero and heroine of the story.[9] In these masnavis composed on the model of Ferdowsi's *Shahnameh* is to be found the active fusion of Persian and Hebrew literary and sacred narratives—where the archetypal figure of the Persian Prince has found a powerful and exciting habitat.

The narrative structure of *Ardeshir-nameh* is quite crucial here: the first part of the epic begins with a genealogy of Iranian kings, namely the ancestors of Ardeshir, almost all of which are modeled after *Shahnameh*; the second part is "drawn directly on the Book of Esther, involves the story of love and union between Ardeshir and Nebuchadnezzar's daughter, Vaštī, and later between him and the Jewish girl Esther, who ultimately becomes the queen of Iran and delivers the Jewish people from the threat of destruction"; and the third part, which significantly diverges from the Book of Esther, is a "detailed story (about thirty chapters long) of the love between Šīrūya, a son of Ardašīr and Vaštī, and Mehrzād, a Chinese princess, whom Šīrūya meets during a hunting expedition. Enamored with the princess he departs with her to China where, following their union, Māhīār is born. After a series of adventures Šīrūya ultimately drowns in the sea."[10]

The significance of this structure cannot be exaggerated. It is as if we have discovered a whole unknown continent for the whereabouts of the Persian Prince, far away from its Indian, Iranian, Arab, and Greek domiciles. What we read here is the active incorporation of the Book of Esther into the pantheon of Persian epic poetry, which in turn expands the domain of the Persian cosmopolis deep into Hebrew literary and sacred narratives entirely independent of its Islamic constituencies. That consideration brings us to another major work of Shahin of Shiraz, *Ezra-nameh*, a rendition of the Book of Ezra, composed in 1372 with additional Midrashic and Iranian legends into Persian poetry.[11] It is here, in the *Ezra-nameh*, that the story of the Persian Prince becomes astonishingly rich and powerful. Let us consider what the scholars of this literature tell us:

> The main part of ʿEzrā-nāma deals with the story of the Cyrus the Great, who was called "God's messiah." ... According to ʿEzrā-nāma, Cyrus was born of Esther and Ahasuerus ..., king of Persia, a legend most probably created to answer two important questions that were debated and elaborated in the Talmud and the midrashim: why a gentile was elected "God's messiah" and why the miraculous delivery of the Jews from Babylonian

exile was at Cyrus' hand. In the second targum of the Book of Esther . . . Cyrus is said to be seated on the throne of the King Solomon, an honor that had not been granted to the kings of Israel. . . . The arguments and reservations expressed in the Jewish sources are not echoed in *'Ezrā-nāma*, however; Šāhīn indicated no doubt that Cyrus was Esther's son and thus, according to Jewish law, a Jew. This legendary descent also was . . . mentioned by Ṭabarī. . . . In *'Ezrā-nāma* Cyrus' birth is depicted as the gift of God, who bestowed all beauty and goodness on the child; he is presented as a godly figure of no less stature than the prophets and kings of Israel. His justice, truthfulness, and heroism are unparalleled among the kings of the world.[12]

This historic and sacred constitution of Cyrus as a Jew, a Prophet, and a King thematically expands the domesticity of the Persian Prince into his Hebraic homeland. From the Hebrew Bible to the Talmud to the Midrash to masterpieces of Judeo-Persian literature, we are witness to a bona fide non-Islamic domain of the Persian Prince where the very prototype of the Persian Prince, in the person of Cyrus the Great, is made into a Jew, and thus an entirely different shadow of the archetypal figure is cast upon world history.[13] What we are seeing here is not just the rendition of the Persian Prince in a Hebraic habitat but also the systematic Persianization of the Jewish faith and Jewish history. In comparison to the Greek habitat, in texts like Xenophon's *Cyropaedia* or Aeschylus's *Persians*, here we are talking about the realm of Jewish sacred and worldly historiography embracing the figure of Cyrus for its own doctrinal and normative reasons.

The move and the oscillation between the sacred and the sovereign marking the diversified disposition of the Persian Prince traffics apace from its Hebraic homeland into the Christian context. This gestation of a new horizon for the Persian Prince surfaces in Western Christianity, particularly with the figure of Esther, whose story goes through a visual and performing rearticulation in European arts, mapping the Christian iconography of the Persian Jewish Queen. Starting with the earliest works of the Huguenot playwright Antoine de Montchrestien, we eventually come to the following iconic pieces: Johannes Spilberg the Younger's *The Feast of Esther* (circa 1644), Jan Victors's *The Banquet of Esther and Ahasuerus* (1640s), Arent de Gelder's *Ahasuerus and Haman* (circa 1682), and de Gelder's *Esther and Mordecai* (1685). This was all predicated on a vast and pervasive medieval Christian iconography in which Esther was identified with the Virgin Mary—her intercession compared with Ahasuerus on behalf of Iranian Jews anticipating mediation on behalf of humankind. While Jewish communities around the world continued their celebrations of Esther, she was being actively Christianized and her Jewish identity de-Persianized, so much so that the biblical fact of her being an Iranian Jew became heavily overshadowed by other Christian indentations. For this reason, her configuration in the Judeo-Persian sources remains truest and closest to her biblical and talmudic character. Be that as it may, the Christianization of Esther opens up a whole new habitat for the princely Persian she biblically represents.

We have yet another compelling territory where the transcultural figurations of the Persian Prince come to European scenes directly from Greek antiquity, as in Handel's opera *Serse* (1738) or Mozart's *Magic Flute* (1791), with numerous other operatic and orchestral compositions shifting the reference from the royal figure of Cyrus the Great to the prophetic figure of Zoroaster by Gustav Mahler and Richard Strauss, among others.[14] That is all before we come to Wagner's *Parsifal* (1857) and *Tristan und Isolde* (1865), both containing allusions to their Iranian sources.[15] These sources come from Greek and occasionally Germanic or even putatively Nordic sources. The idea of Xerxes standing in front of a plane tree and singing the glorious *Serse* aria "Ombra mai fu" was almost completely taken from Silvio Stampiglia's (1664–1725) libretto for an earlier opera of the same name by Giovanni Bononcini in 1694, and, even before that, Niccolò Minato's (circa 1627–1698) libretto for Francesco Cavalli in 1654.[16] The operatic allusion of the libretto is even more distant from a far richer heritage in the Zoroastrian significance of a sacred tree.[17] Xerxes is not singing a love song; he is praying to that tree. That sacred moment has been transformed into romantic fantasy in a truly facile libretto. Examples abound: Thomas Arne's *Artaxerxes*, set to an English adaptation of Metastasio's 1729 libretto *Artaserse*; Antonio Salieri's *Palmira, regina di Persia* (1795), set to a libretto by Giovanni de Gamerra; Francesco Cavalli's *Il Xerse* (1660), and many more. In these and other operas, we are the spectators to a resuscitation of the Persian Prince and his Zoroastrian pedigree in the context of European Renaissance, baroque, and finally more modern musical compositions. The audience of these operas was initially the European aristocracy and eventually the emerging European bourgeoisie; for both audiences the figure of the Persian Prince sustained a course of multivariant meaning and significance, central to European cultural history, entirely tangential to Iranian and Islamic imaginative topographies until the later encounter with European colonial modernity.

FIGURE 4   Paolo Veronese, *The Family of Darius Before Alexander*, 1565. London, National Gallery.

Closely related to the figure of Cyrus the Great and other Achaemenid emperors in the European Renaissance imagination and later is the image of Alexander the Great, who is remembered and reconceptualized mostly through Herodotus's account of the Battle of Issus, which occurred on November 5, 333 BCE, between the Macedonian general and Darius III. This battle has inspired a number of opulent and heroic visual representations, marking the Hellenic tradition of Alexander the Great, in which the heroic figure of the Persianized Macedonian warrior becomes a central figure in European paintings. These include such works as *The Family of Darius Before Alexander* by Charles le Brun (1619–1690), in which we see the mother of Darius III Sisygambis (died 323 BCE) kneeling in front of Alexander the Great; *The Family of Darius III in Front of Alexander the Great* by Justus Sustermans (1597–1681); *Alexander the Great Marries Stateira, the Daughter of Darius, in Susa*, based on a painting by Andreas Müller (1811–1890); and *The Family of Darius Before Alexander* (1565–1570) by Paolo Veronese, among countless others (fig. 4). What again is crucial here is how Xenophon's idealization of Cyrus the Great reflects back on European artists' imagination of Herodotus's account of Alexander's conquest of Persia. Here, a simplistic reading of European Orientalism completely fails to understand the circular disposition of the surfacing of the Persian Prince in the figure of Alexander the Great.

Right here we might cut back into an exceptionally rich and powerful genre of popular Alexander romance in Persian that thrives on a kind of magic historicism comparable to what we read in *Don Quixote*, for example, and examine what it does to the tradition of European romances. The prose of this genre marks a transition from Safavid formalism to Qajarid realism.[18] The genre reveals the social spaces emerging in the Safavid period, such as coffeehouses and their murals and canvases. This is a popular version of the more formal prose and poetry of the genre that we read in Ferdowsi or Nezami Alexander romances, where the actual hero oscillates between *gojasteh* (cursed) and *qeddis* (saintly). In widely favored stories, the Macedonian warrior is Persianized and made into the son of Dara. Alexander romances, in both their formal and popular versions, are a perfect example of how a panegyric of defeat is transformed into a saga of victory, for here Alexander becomes a mythic figure when his persona is incorporated into a rogue element.[19] Scholars of these texts consider them the earliest forms of the soon-to-emerge novel.[20]

If we now pull back all the way from the original Persian habitat of the Persian Prince to its various shades and shadows in Hebrew, Greek, Christian, and European takes on classical antiquity and then return to popular Persian Alexander romances, we see a panoramic view of how the archetypal figure has been roaming from East to West, North to South, reconfiguring its moral and imaginative character and disposition. What I am proposing here is the manner in which the figure of the Persian Prince works through its de/territorialized shades and shadows on multiple sites as a warrior, a philosopher, and ultimately a poet, which requires the kind of schizoanalysis that overrides the monadic disposition of the princely self. As developed by Gilles Deleuze and Félix Guattari, initially in their *Anti-Oedipus* (1972) and then in *A Thousand Plateaus* (1980), we are moving into the transfigurative domains of the subconscious, where the historic subjection of the Persian Prince becomes self-transfigurative. Let's read this key passage from *Anti-Oedipus* and extend it to our present considerations:

> A schizophrenic out for a walk is a better model than a neurotic lying on the analyst's couch. A breath of fresh air, a relationship with the outside world.... This walk outdoors is different from the moments when Lenz finds himself closeted with his pastor, who forces him to situate himself socially, in relationship to the God of established religion, in relationship to his father, to his mother. While taking a stroll outdoors, on the other hand, he is in the mountains, amid falling snowflakes, with other gods or without any gods at all, without a family, without a father or a mother, with nature.[21]

Extending the revolutionary work of Deleuze and Guattari, we are here not in the field of historical neurosis and cultural castration but where the split/schizo is launched against the Oedipal and Oedipalized territorialities of home, habitat, locality, culture, and particularly narration. As we move across these climes, we encounter and tap into the de/territorialized and re/territorialized domains of hidden desires that escape the received prosody of our fragmented histories. The subject of the Persian Prince has by now become clearly conscious of its own desiring-machines. The subconscious of the archetype presents itself on multiple historical fields, while the performance of the split/schizo uncovers the subconscious desires toward the liberation of the creative schizo in varied social and historical fields. The centrality of this idea of schizo and schizoanalysis will become important for my argument later in the book when I trace the figure of the Persian Prince from its *monadic* to its *dyadic* and ultimately to its *nomadic* dispositions—whereby through a liberated narrative historiography of the figure of the Persian Prince I am in effect offering a history of the Iranian, Islamic, Persian, and Persianate consciousness furthest removed from both classical and contemporary territorialized fixations and toward a renewed awareness of their global configurations with a healthy and robust desiring-machine as the engine of history.

The idea of the shadow of the prince, where the philosopher and the poet echo the prophetic voice and reflect the poetic vision of the Persian Prince, places the archetypal figure itself in the shadow of the Divinity that is projected onto the archetype. In analytical psychology, the shadow archetype as an unconscious aspect of the persona is not so much unknown as in fact known too much. Carl Gustav Jung identified the subconscious of the persona with this shadow. As I envision him, the Persian Prince here knows the prophetic voice and vision of the philosopher and the poet standing by him too closely to realize they are his own shadows. They are not his dark side but his shaded sides; they are not irrational but too rational. We indeed have a perfect metaphor of this shadow in the figure of Homay, a mythical bird in Iranian mythology. Homay's auspicious shadow, Sayeh-ye Homay, becomes the source of Homay's blessings of the Persian Prince. If the shadow of Homay is thought to be cast on any ordinary human being, the divine dispensation of authority, or *Farr-e Izadi*, is believed to have descended upon that person and destined him for greatness.

The origin of Homay as an auspicious bird goes all the way back to Avesta and appears repeatedly in many classics of Persian prose and poetry; of particular significance, however, is the romance of "Homay and Homayoun" (1331), by Khwaju-ye Kermani, a love story between a Syrian prince of Iranian descent and a Chinese princess that is featured in the poet's famous *Khamseh* (*Quintet*). During a hunt, the prince sees the princess in a vision and ultimately invades China in pursuit of his dream, defeats his beloved princess's father, and wins the love of Princess Homayoun. The Syrian king, Kermani tells us in "Homay and Homayoun," is a descendant of Persian kings (Shahan-e Key), ruling over Rum and Rey, hoping against hope to have a son. Finally, he is blessed with a son who looks like the ancient Iranian kings, with a visage resembling Manuchehr and evoking Farr-e Qobad:

> From the sea of royalty, he was a pearl,
> In the firmament of rulership, he was a star—
> In dignity he was brighter than the sun—
> More delightful than a flower in flowerbed
> . . . .
>
> The king called him the Auspicious Homayoun
> Placing him on the precious eyes.[22]

What we have here is the closure of the shadow and the light, both de/ and re/territorialization of the dominion of the archetype, the joining of the auspicious Homay and the Prince who bears its name; "Homayoun Homay" means "the auspicious Homay," so the name of the Bird and the name of the Prince have come together and become each other's namesake. It is also crucial to keep in mind that later the name "Homa" becomes a female name and "Homayoun" a male name, whereas here in this masnavi, the gendered names are reversed; in a crucial battle scene, in fact, Princess Homayoun wears the armor of a prince and pretends to be a man before Homay overcomes her and the two proceed to marry and lead a happy and fruitful life.[23]

One last incident of the interplay between light and shadow should suffice to make the point: the story of a famous encounter between the Persian poet Baba Taher Oryan (circa 1000–1055) and the Saljuq emperor Tughril Beg (990–1063) marks an iconic interface between the saintly poet and the mighty emperor sometime between 1055 and 1058—a report, whether factual or apocryphal, that has immortalized this fusion of light and shadow in and about the figure of the Persian Prince.[24] A poet of exquisite quatrains, Baba Taher had earned the epithet *Oryan* ("Naked") because he had stripped himself of all worldly possessions and become the embodiment of ascetic quintessence—the exact opposite of the opulence of power. He is best remembered for his beautiful quatrains—pure sublimity in moving words, so simple, so elegant, so truthful that they have become the staple of poetic thinking throughout the Persian-speaking world. Countless imitations have sought to pay him homage, so much so that it is difficult to distinguish between his own original quatrains and those attributed to him. Based on the evidence of *Rahat al-Sudur* (circa 1205) of Muhammad bin Ali al-Rawandi, a major source of Saljuqid history, we learn of an encounter that presumably occurred between Baba Taher, two other saints—Baba Jaʿfar and Sheikh Hamshaʾ—and Tughril Beg at the height of the warlord's power and glory.[25] In the encounter, the saintly poet asks the world conqueror what he plans to do with the people he is conquering. "As you command," the conqueror says. "Be kind to them," Baba Taher responds. Then Baba Taher gives Tughril the handle of a clay jug from which he was drinking water and doing his ablutions and says, "There: I give you the rule of this world." The world conqueror tells Baba Taher to ask His Majesty for a favor in return for his blessings. "Just move over," Baba Taher says. "You're blocking the sun."

It is less important if this is a real or an apocryphal story—whether it actually happened or whether subsequent generations wished it had. What matters is the figurative encounter between an all-powerful emperor and a "naked" mystic, a man who had everything and wanted even more and a man who had nothing and wanted even less, and it is only the grace of the mystic that empowers the scene and remedies and reverses the imbalance of power. In this encounter, the ruling Prince stands between the light of the sun and the mystic poet, with the size of his shadow blocking the living light. In the encounter between the sacred and the sovereign, the source of grace and authority emanates from the mystic poet requesting the sovereign to move to let the light of the sun shine on them both. Integral to but unspoken in this recognition is the disarming simplicity of Baba Taher's poetry, in and of itself a lesson in humility, where we see how he strips, as it were, just like his epithet, Persian prose and poetry of all pretenses and has it speak the plain truth on the porous borderline of earthly and divine love. Here pure poetry becomes pure politics:

> *Beh darya bengarom daraya te binom ...*
>
> I look at the sea and I see the sea in thee
> I look at the desert and I see the desert in thee—
> Wherever I look, at the mountain or the prairies,
> All I see is thy beautiful countenance.[26]

The Persian Prince and the Making of an Iranian "Philosopher-King"

The idea of shades and shadows in which the figure of the Persian Prince has historically dwelled and spread from clime to clime instantly suggests the light that shines through and enables it—and there is no Iranian philosopher whose ideas are more epistemically rooted in the primacy and principality of light than the Master of Illumination, Sheikh al-Ishraq Shahab al-Din Yahya al-Suhrawardi (1154–1191). It is right here in Suhrawardi's philosophy where the archetype of the Persian Prince finds its most emphatic articulation as a "philosopher-king" entirely independent of the Platonic domain of this category.[27] Suhrawardi was born and raised in the northwestern Iranian village of Suhraward, traveled extensively in search of knowledge, and after settling in Aleppo, under the Ayyubids, he was accused of heresy and executed at the age of thirty-seven. He became famous for his signature *Hikmah al-Ishraq* (*Philosophy of Illumination*) with a singularly Iranian streak of what he considered "royal philosophy."

In the precious work of Suhrawardi, which has reached us in both rich and precise Arabic and astoundingly beautiful Persian, we discover the philosophical dimension and the allegorical imagination at work in our configuration of the Persian Prince as the cornerstone of pre-Islamic Iranian and subsequently Islamic political thought.[28] Contrary to the entire cast of Islamic philosophy as we have understood it so far, this cornerstone does not come solely from Greece. It also comes from around the world. With enduring persistence, much of Islamic philosophy is read as an extended commentary on Greek philosophy—with of course some legitimate reasons. Whatever the merits or the limitations of this proclivity, it can be sustained only until we get to the remarkable work of Suhrawardi, who in the span of a fruitful but tragically short life revolutionized Islamic philosophy precisely because his epistemology pulls the Greek heritage sideways and stages the most spectacular and hitherto little-known pre-Islamic and entirely non-Greek Iranian heritage.

We might consider Suhrawardi's philosophy along the same lines as Ferdowsi's epic poetry and al-Thaʿalibi's historiography, for this seminal Iranian philosopher did in philosophical terms what Ferdowsi had done for the epic and al-Thaʿalibi for the historical imagination—bringing back a rich heritage of pre-Islamic Iranian legacy to enrich the Islamic world. Placing Suhrawardi next to Ferdowsi and al-Thaʿalibi maps out a wider historical and literary imagination in which the seminal work of the Master of Illuminationist Philosophy speaks to a larger Iranian heritage in the Islamic moral, philosophical, and political imagination.[29] Indian, Iranian, Hebrew, and Greek sources came together to form a unique moral imagination in which philosophers like Suhrawardi lived and thought. Privileging any one of these sources would do structural damage to the entirety of them.

In the wide spectrum of the major traditions in Islamic philosophy, the *Mashsha'I* (Peripatetic) philosophy was almost exclusively Greek in origin, while the *Ishraqi* (Illuminationist) philosophy that Suhrawardi virtually single-handedly created during his tragically short life was deeply Iranian in its epistemological foregrounding—without compromising his non-Iranian inspirations.[30] While Peripatetic philosophers insisted on the primacy of reason and rationality, Illuminationist philosophers shifted their epistemology primarily (but not exclusively) toward intuition. In the words of the leading scholars of this philosophy:

> Illuminationist philosophy departs from Peripateticism in relation to: terminology; epistemological priority of the intuitive over the purely syllogistic; and use of constructed ontological-based meta-language of light applied to all entities in the whole continuum of reality, where existent things in each segment of the cosmos (Intellect, Soul, Matter, plus an added fourth realm named '*Ālam al-ḵayāl*, translated, *mundus imaginalis* by Henry Corbin) are said to be lights of various degrees of luminosity and are propagated from the source of being, the Light of Lights.[31]

There is a report of a putative meeting between Avicenna and Abu Said Abi al-Khayr that illustrates this distinction—after this meeting, the towering Muslim philosopher said of the iconic mystic: "I know what he sees, he sees what I know." This dialectic between *knowing* and *seeing*, between *reason* and *intuition*, become definitive to Suhrawardi's retrieval and excavation of pre-Islamic Iranian motifs in his Illuminationist philosophy. Within the context of this reconstruction of Iranian philosophy in Suhrawardi's work, the idea of the Persian Prince assumes a central and definitive significance.

Deeply rooted in pre-Islamic Iranian heritage, Suhrawardi's Illuminationist philosophy marks a decisive twist on the Greek philosophical tradition he and other Muslim philosophers had inherited. My primary concern here is with the configuration of the Persian Prince in Suhrawardi's body of work, but the implications of his philosophy are much wider and richer and introduce a serious challenge to the Greco-Arab-centric reading of Islamic philosophy. Suhrawardi's *Hikmah al-Ishraq*, his angelology, and particularly his employment of key pre-Islamic Persian princely figures into the speculative spectrum of his philosophical reflections (an impulse that probably contributed to his being considered a heretic and executed) are all vital components of this crucial turning point. It is particularly important to pay close attention not just to the treatises that Suhrawardi deliberately decided to write in Persian but to in fact see these Zoroastrian tropes deeply mapped out in his major book in Arabic, his *Hikmah al-Ishraq* (*Philosophy of Illumination*). Suhrawardi was not an accidental figure in the history of Islamic philosophy. The Zoroastrian sources of his philosophy are crucial signposts of where and what they mean for the larger context of the political philosophy of the figure of the Persian Prince. We need not choose between the Greek and the Persian, Plato and Zoroaster, as it were, in reading Suhrawardi—especially if we keep in mind that the *Cyropaedia* of Plato's contemporary Xenophon was for generations even more important than *The Republic*. Suhrawardi was ambidextrous both in writing in Arabic and Persian and also in bringing the Greek and the Iranian philosophical pedigree face-to-face in a harmonious and creative encounter. Right there in Suhrawardi's towering figure, the ethnicizing of the Arab and the Persian, or the splitting of the Greek and the Islamic, falls flat and becomes meaningless.[32]

Suhrawardi's systematic employment of Zoroastrian and Mazdean motifs in the making of his Illuminationist philosophy becomes integral to his intellective light principles written into his epistemic angelology. In doing so, he had brought the Greek and the Iranian traditions together into a unique and pathbreaking conversation that was almost entirely unprecedented. The eminent French Orientalist Henry Corbin devoted his scholarly life to navigating the pre-Islamic traces of Islamic philosophy in its Iranian context—both in Suhrawardi and after him, all the way to the twentieth century, with a particular emphasis on the sixteenth-century Safavid period, which he termed "the School of Isfahan." Corbin suggests Suhrawardi's work "aimed to restore the theosophical wisdom of ancient Persia in Islam itself, and with the resources of the pure spiritual side of Islam. Some four centuries before the great Byzantine Gemistes Pletho, Suhrawardi's work connected the names of Plato and of Zarathustra (Zoroaster) in his metaphysic of Light, in which the Platonic Ideas are interpreted by means of the Zoroastrian angelology."[33] Within the epistemic contours of that angelology, the central figure of the Persian Prince was definitive to the philosophical resurrection of Iranian kings and heroes Suhrawardi had now philosophically re-signified.

Based on Suhrawardi's philosophical oeuvre, closely examined by Corbin, and subsequently picked up by other scholars,[34] the tradition of what is called

"Hekmat-e Khosrawani" (royal philosophy) traces the origin of what it decidedly considers "Iranian philosophy" to Iranian kings—and thus its title—and reads Keyumars as the first "philosopher-king," followed by Fereydun and Kay Khosrow, and then includes other pre-Islamic Iranian monarchs and heroes such as Garshasp, Zal, Rostam, and Esfandiar in a similar vein. This royal and heroic genealogy generates an entire Iranian pedigree (among others) for Suhrawardi's Illuminationist philosophy. The crucial issue here is Suhrawardi's reconstruction of this philosophical genealogy deeply embedded in the context of Islamic philosophy centuries after the Muslim conquest. In the works of Suhrawardi we thus observe a deeply embedded knowledge of pre-Islamic Iranian philosophical heritage, which he revives and re-signifies within his own epistemology in which Avicennian philosophy, Neoplatonic legacy, and this Khosrawani (royal) tradition all come together to find a fusion in Suhrawardi's Illuminationist school. While Ferdowsi gave a poetic, and Thaʿalibi a historical twist to the selfsame traditions, Suhrawardi catapulted it into a decidedly philosophical direction. Suhrawardi thus stands in the crosscurrents of multiple philosophical traditions in which pre-Islamic Iranian "Royal Philosophy" assumes a renewed significance. The very idea of the Persian Prince as both philosopher and king here finds its most comprehensive characterizations. Precisely because of the fusion of Iranian, Greek, and other sources in his philosophy, Suhrawardi universalizes the idea of the Persian Prince in his version of the philosopher-king.

In his three major philosophical works, *al-Talwihat* (*Intimations*), *al-Mashariʿ wa al-Mutarihat* (*Pathways and Dialogues*), and *Hikmah al-Ishraq* (*Philosophy of Illumination*), Suhrawardi reaches for what he considers the *Khamirah* (quintessence) of philosophy, which for him comes from two principal sources: Greek and Iranian, one he identifies with Hermes and the other with Keyumars; from the Hermetic side it reaches Pythagoras, and from the Keyumars side it comes down to Fereydun and Keykhosrow and to his own contemporary mystics. What is crucial here is the way Suhrawardi projects a pre-Platonic Greek mythological and a pre-Islamic Iranian mythological pedigree for his way of thinking. The Iranian genealogy of the idea of the philosopher-king begins with the ideal type of Keyumars and continues uninterrupted to Suhrawardi's own time, which he stages in pure philosophical terms, with evident or latent political implications. What is crucial is precisely their abstract philosophical articulations by Suhrawardi, where Keyumars is identified as a prophetic "philosopher-king." The source of *Kayan Khurrah* (royal) charisma can manifest itself in the king as both the philosopher and the prophet. In a crucial passage from Suhrawardi's *al-Mashari wa al-Mutarihat* that Corbin translates, we see all these elements coming together.

> If that which predominates in the essential substance of the soul is the res Victorialis (al-amr al-qahri), then the Light of dawn rises on the soul in such a way that that part of the Victorial realities emanating from the constellations and from the Angels who are their theurgies, predominate in it. This is the suprasensory reality which the ancient Persians called Xvarnah ("Light of Glory," Khurrah in Persian). This is something which, having arisen from astral incandescence, remains as a dominating force in the human world; he who is invested with it becomes a hero, a conqueror, a victor. If the Light of dawn arising from the spiritual stars—pure spiritual entities of light—corresponds to the capacity of the soul in a "dimension" of desire and love, then what remains of the Xvarnah which penetrates it will be manifested by causing its possessor to take joy in subtle and refined things, by awakening in souls inclination and love toward him, by bringing men to sing his praises, for the splendor communicated to his being derives from the Angels and their beneficent theurgies, worthy of glorification and of love. Finally, if there is balance and if the qualities of light received from a sublime luminary through the intermediary of the celestial prince are superabundant in him, then he will become a magnificent king, surrounded by respect, favored with knowledge, perfection, and prosperity. And that alone is what is called the royal Xvarnah (Kayan Khurrah). In its plenitude this refers to the most majestic of categories, for it implies a perfect balance of light, besides the fact that the sublime Luminary is the gateway to all the greater ecstasies.[35]

The passage that is immediately related to this citation, which Corbin does not translate, is even more pertinent to my purpose here—where Suhrawardi identifies "the eminent philosopher Plato, and other renowned figures who followed him and whose name history has preserved" among the Greeks and then turns to what he calls "the Fahlaviun," or the ancient Iranian philosopher-kings, particularly "the Prince of the Earth" (*Malik al-Tin*, an Arabic translation of the Zoroastrian concept of "Gel-Shah," the epithet of Keyumars), as well as his followers Fereydun and Kay Khosrow.[36] While in this dual genealogy that Suhrawardi constructs the Khosrawani (royal Persian) line comes to such prominent mystic masters as Bayezid Bastami, Abu al-Abbas Qassab Amoli, Abu al-Hassan al-Kharaqani, Du al-Nun the Egyptian, Mansur al-Hallaj, from the Greek side it comes down to Pythagoras, Empedocles, and Asclepius, Dhul-Nun al-Misri, and Sahl al-Tustari; finally, from both these traditions, it eventually comes down to Suhrawardi himself.[37] It is impossible to disregard the exhilarating ecstasy of these moments when Suhrawardi seems to be sitting on top of a mountain and summoning the whole history of the known civilized world to map his genealogy of a moral philosophy from his East to his West.

Corbin continues his explorations of these themes from pre-Islamic to the later Shi'i philosophers of the nineteenth and twentieth centuries, collectively known as the school of "al-Hikmah al-Ishraq," which he had opted to translate as "Theosophy for the Orientals" or, perhaps more idiomatically, "Philosophy of Illumination," as it is more widely translated, the major theme of which surrounds several mythical kings and princes of ancient Iran, especially Keyumars, Kay Khosrow, Jamshid, and Fereydoun, who were all key figures in the Hekmat-e Khosrawani (royal philosophy) that Suhrawardi had received and reconceptualized. The historical figure of Anushirvan throughout Persian and Arabic literary and prose sources is therefore an approximation of the mythical archetypes of the "philosopher-king" that Suhrawardi had best identified and theorized. That full spectrum of theorization brings us to the all-important body of his exquisite Persian allegorical stories. Suhrawardi was beautifully ambidextrous. He wrote in both rich philosophical Arabic and bold and brilliant allegorical Persian prose. But his Persian allegorical stories are of a particularly stunning prose and disposition. Let me share a passage from one of his most powerful philosophical recitals, "Avaz-e Par-e Jibril" (The Song of Gabriel's Wing):

> Once when I had just been allowed out of women's quarters and was given some leeway from the restrictions of children, one night when the ghostly darkness was dawning from the depth of the concave sphere of the cobalt-colored sky and a darkness that was like the brother of nonexistence was covering the entirety of the lower world, I was awoken from sleep. From fear I was holding a candle and walked towards the men's quarters, where I wandered that night until the crack of dawn, when I desired to enter my father's abode.[38]

These Persian "recitals" (as Corbin correctly calls them) open up a whole new way of reading the domain of the Persian Prince in Suhrawardi's Illuminationist philosophy and his active articulation of the Persian version of the philosopher-king. In this context he introduces a key concept toward the end of one of his major treatises, *Partov-nameh* (*Book of Light*), in which he writes:

> Whoever knows Philosophy ["Hekmat"] and persists in appreciation and sanctification of the Light of Lights, as we said, he will be granted Royal Charisma ["Khurrah-e Kiani"] and Majestic Light ["Farr-e Nurani"], and the Divine Light will clothe him with glory and majesty, and he shall become a natural leader to this world and he will be granted help from the higher world, and his Words ["Sokhan"] shall be heard in the heavenly abode, and his dreams and inspirations will come to full fruition. And only God knows the best![39]

The central concepts of Royal Charisma (Khurrah-e Kiani) and Majestic Light (Farr-e Nurani; both of pre-Islamic Iranian origin) are definitive to this idea of the "philosopher-king" and his divinely ordained charismatic authority. The idea of the fabled bird Homay casting its shadow on the charismatic monarch is the mythic manifestation of this philosophical idea. But more to the point here, in his Persian allegorical recitals, Suhrawardi is in the position of having an authorial voice that speaks both of the mythic disposition of the Persian Prince and of himself, as he writes from that position of agential certitude and divinely inspired confidence. In these treatises Suhrawardi's narrative persona is that of the enlightened prophet-prince, now completely under the light of the divine gift of grace. In his Persian recitals the authorial voice of Suhrawardi stages and performs itself in full command of his prophetic voice—and as such, it obviously angers his contemporary Muslim doctors of law, as indeed, generations later, it still frustrates contemporary Orientalist Arabists who fail to understand Suhrawardi's sublime Persian. As he writes, the authorial persona of Suhrawardi is now in the full shadow of the prophetic light cast upon him. The pen that now writes is no longer the pen of the mortal Suhrawardi contemplating the nature of the Persian Prince. He has become the prophetic voice of that Persian Prince. He has connected to the First Person, the First Prince, to Keyumars, the first prophet, the first Persian Prince. His prose and poetry detail the philosophical landscape of the abode where the Persian Prince has ruled supreme from time immemorial. In this domain, Suhrawardi writes of a superlative reality he is experiencing and that is otherwise inaccessible to any mortal soul. The Light of Lights has taken possession of his pen and writes. Examples abound—here is a crucial passage from one of his masterpiece recitals, "Aql-e Sorkh" (The Red Intellect):

> One of my dear friends asked me if the birds understand each other's language? I said yes they do. The friend asked, how do you know? I said in

the beginning when the Former of Truth wanted to bring the foundation of my being into existence, He created me in the form of a falcon. In that abode where I was, there were other falcons too. We spoke with each other and we perfectly understood each other. The friend asked me, how did you then reach the current stage? I said, one day the hunters of Destiny had spread the trap of Fate, and spread the seeds of Devotion, and thus they trapped me and took me from the abode where we were to another clime, where they closed both my eyes, and set four ropes around me, and then put ten sentinels in charge of guarding me, five of them facing me with their backs turned outward, and the other five with their backs turned to me and facing outside. These five who were facing me with their backs outward kept me in the world of Wonder, so that I completely forgot whatever I knew of my original nest and the abode where I first was, so that I thought this is how I had always been.[40]

The distinction Suhrawardi makes here between a falcon and a human being is graded with states of self-consciousness, and the only position from which a pen can write these revelations with such confidence and clarity is where the Light of Lights has taken possession of it. Here in these passages, we are in the presence of the Persian Prince, as a person, a persona, a prophet, a poet, a philosopher, a philosopher-king, a master of the universe. This is all achieved by mastering the magic of the possibilities of philosophical Persian prose delivered in an allegorical register, not by any metaphysical claim or appeal to divinity. Above all, Suhrawardi is a master prose stylist. He crafts and conditions the manner in which his sublime prose is to be read. He does not demand or expect a leap of faith from his readers. You need not be a Muslim, a Christian, a Jew, a believer, a nonbeliever, an Iranian, or anything else for that matter to be able to read him. You just have to be able to read Persian, his Persian—have the ability to read him clearly and entirely on the *surface* of his prose, without imposing any outlandish "symbolic" interpretations of the sort to which he has been violently subjected by overzealous interpreters, who disregard the powerful images his prose generates and insist on the goose-chase as to the hidden meaning of it! While the Arabist Orientalists completely ignore his Persian prose, his Iranist admirers presume heavy hidden hermeneutics from him; regardless, his actual prose continues to shine as the prime example of his Illuminist philosophy. Understanding Suhrawardi's philosophy requires a semiotics of its surface signs and is furthest removed from the forced hermeneutics of its presumed hidden meanings.

Within the parameters of those semiotics, it is the virtual configurations of the Persian Prince as a philosopher-king that is the most enduring aspect of Suhrawardi's Philosophy of Light (Hikmah al-Ishraq) and Royal Philosophy (Hekmat Khosrawani). What is historically crucial to keep in mind here is how long it was before Suhrawardi, Ferdowsi, or Thaʿalibi incorporated such pre-Islamic themes in their respective philosophy, epic poetry, and historiography. The more potent and urgent political manifestations of the very same ideas had a pronounced presence in the wave of rebellious uprisings early in the Islamic period when the Umayyad dynasty was giving way to the Abbasids. As I alluded to in previous chapters, during this period we are witness to a succession of syncretic revolutionary uprisings ranging from Azerbaijan to Khorasan in Northern Iran. The uprising led by Behafarid (died 748) against the Abbasids, or by Ustadhsis (rebelled in 767) in Baghdis against the local Abbasid ruler, or by Sunpadh (died 755), by Ibn Muqannaʿ (died 783), and ultimately by Babak Khorramdin (circa 795–838) were all common in their proto-Zoroastrian proclivities.[41] The philosophical articulation of the Persian Prince by Suhrawardi, his heroic deeds by Ferdowsi, and his historical contours by Thaʿalibi all come in the aftermath of these decidedly political, indeed revolutionary uprisings. In his insurrectionary appeal, Babak Khorramdin in particular represented a much larger critical consciousness associated with the metaphysical underpinning of a religion known as "Khorramdini," rooted in the potent pre-Islamic movement of Mazdakism, for whom belief in reincarnation was definitive.[42] The ideological force of Mazdakism had survived the collapse of the Sassanids and was widely popular in the aftermath of the Arab conquest of Iran. At the epicenter of all these revolutionary uprisings was the figure of a resurrected and reincarnated "Persian Prince," now transfigured into a revolutionary persona who had come to save the world from evil with justice and equanimity. The same figure reenters Ferdowsi's epic, Thaʿalibi's history, and Suhrawardi's philosophy.

If we place the figures of Mazdak and Babak historically as they appear before Ferdowsi, Thaʿalibi, and Suhrawardi, then we are in possession of a nucleus of Iranian historiography that overrides the falsifying but common practice of dividing history into pre-Islamic and Islamic periods. Islam was no doubt a momentous event in the history of the region, but so was the content of the major thematic motifs running from pre-Islamic deeply into the Islamic periods.[43] In the same context, in Suhrawardi's philosophical articulation of this "Hekmat Khosrawani," the Platonic idea of "the philosopher-king" finds an entirety independent and different Iranian provenance, with the figure of the Persian Prince as its embodiment. Suhrawardi, in other words, was giving philosophical meaning and connotations to what Ferdowsi had put to epic poetry, Tha'alibi to historiography, and a whole succession of revolutionary uprisings into political practice. Centuries after these proto-Mazdakite uprisings, Muslim doctors of law in Aleppo were intuitively aware of Suhrawardi's subversive philosophy and its political implications and thus summarily murdered him. These three iconic figures—a poet, a historian, and a philosopher—had a common pre-Islamic reservoir of ideas and aspirations that those revolutionary uprisings also knew and had put into political practice, led by a Persian Prince in open revolt. At the epicenter of all of these discourses and praxis stood the iconic figure of the Persian Prince—heroic, wise, just, rebellious, and thus above all paradoxically both a prince and a rebel revolting against the ruling prince; precisely as such, the archetype kept renewing itself through successive metaphoric metempsychosis—pivoting its monadic origins to dyadic and ultimately nomadic proclivities. As the King in the Philosopher was pulling him towards the throne, the Philosopher in the King was whispering into his inner ear about the coming winter of a prophetic rebel banging at the gates of his citadel.

The Poet in Prison, the Prince in the Person

The idea I just put forward, that in the royal disposition of his Illuminationist philosophy Suhrawardi introduces his own authorial voice as the archetype of the enlightened Persian Prince, ultimately places the persona of the philosopher-prince on a much more personal and metamorphic stand—underlined by his Persian allegorical recitals that begin like innocent short stories and crescendo into cosmogonic metanarratives. It is here that we can return to our original question: What exactly held the idea of the Persian Prince together over its false bifurcation between pre-Islamic and Islamic ends? The simple answer bridges these two parts into another overriding narrative. Both before and after Islam, on one side of the equation was pure and undiluted power and violence of the ruling warlords, and on the other enduring wisdom and worldly advice upholding the ideals of truth, justice, and magnanimity—indispensable features for giving that brute force an aura of civility and legitimacy.

Ordinarily, the wise counsel of the vizier is what has sustained the balance between power and wisdom. The vizier could also embody the prudent part of the very idea of princedom. The figure of Bozorgmehr next to Anushirvan in the *Shahnameh* acts like the alter ego of the Persian Prince. A kind of pragmatic political philosophy, a moral code of conduct, an ethical spectrum of what was right and necessary to curtail and civilize the loutish power of the monarch were all at work here. Suhrawardi, however, gave these ideas a sustained philosophical prose that gathered the prince and the philosopher together, while Ferdowsi cast them in grand epic proportions, Tha'alibi put them into a succinct historical imagination, and the proto-Zoroastrian revolts of early Islam put them into political practice, all before a whole spectrum of Persian poets and prose stylists immortalized them in elegant literary masterpieces. What in effect we witness in these Persian princely demeanors evident in the body of literature that defined them is a creative fusion of ethics and politics, philosophy and poetry, where the prince inherits or attains pure force and naked violence and is eventually civilized through a massive and enduring body of political wisdom that comes with his reign. The fact that the most famous among this body of literature were produced in many elegant manuscripts and illustrated in the royal ateliers are added indices that they were integral to the imperial retinues of power. In the midst of Ferdowsi's tragic heroes, Tha'alibi's grand historiography, and Suhrawardi's allegorical sublation into the royal disposition of his Illuminationist philosophy, as well as the rebellious figures of Behafarid, Babak, and others, the figure of the Persian Prince had already germinated the seeds of its resurrection in the course of another fateful moment in the course of its encounters with European colonial modernity.

Before we turn to that momentous twist in the third part of this book, I must take you to a crucial subterranean site of its gestations. The archetype of the Persian Prince worked through its paradoxes and contradictions, the very engine of its endurance—the creative tensions between the philosopher and the king, between the poet and the prince, the sovereign and the rebel, or the prophet and the monarch, the humanity in him and the divinity that looked over him, and thus precisely setting the archetype against its own monadic constitution of power and authority, exposing the hidden urges of its dyadic disposition. The long history of the archetype was not all power and glory, philosophy and poetry. These very insignia and paraphernalia of power were at the very same time the indices of revolts and uprisings, massacres and mass incarcerations.

I therefore wish to conclude this chapter with a reference to a genre of literature in Persian we know as *Habsiyeh* (in Arabic we call it *Adab al-Sujun*), or "prison writing." In its classical cases, the genre of Habsiyeh consists of a succession of prominent poets who have been in prison for one reason or another, or else in forced exile from their homeland, and have kept a record of their predicaments in their body of work. In my theoretical schemata of this book, this body of prison writings connects back to the centrality of Gramsci's *Prison Notebooks* and marks a moment of creative crisis in the historical and archetypal constitution of the Persian Prince. Such world-famous examples of this genre as Marco Polo and Martin Luther are of course well known in the European contexts, as are Miguel de Cervantes, Sir Walter Raleigh, Galileo Galilei, Marquis de Sade, Lord Byron, and Oscar Wilde. Around the world we have the equally illustrious examples of Jawaharlal Nehru, Aleksander Solzhenitsyn, and Ngũgĩ wa Thiong'o. In Iran we have such prominent poets and philosophers as Ayn al-Qudat al-Hamadani, Naser Khosrow, Masoud Sa'd Salman, Khaqani Shervani, Baba Afzal Kashani, venturing all the way to Tahereh Qorrat al-Ayn in the nineteenth century, until we reach modern times, with such figures as Farrokhi Yazdi, Malek al-Shu'ara Bahar, Ahmad Shamlou, Mehdi Akhavan-Sales, Khosrow Golsorkhi, Mahmoud Dowlatabadi, Mehrangiz Kar, Shahrnush Parsipour, Vida Hajebi, and Behrouz Boochani.[44] All of these poets, philosophers, and revolutionary activists have left enduring evidence of how the legitimacy of the sovereign conceals its alterity in the moral imagination of precisely its own undoing.

The Persian Prince in power mirrors the prisoner in his dungeons, as the sovereign on his throne exudes the common person seeking the sovereignty of an indomitable soul. Echoing Suhrawardi's philosophical substitution of his authorial voice for the enlightened prince, Sa'di reminds the world that any person reading his poems is a prince once setting aside his or her obsequious desires. This is rooted in Suhrawardi's having become the very soul of the archetypal prince and performing it, while in the sixth book of Sa'di's *Bustan*, "On Asceticism," it is resurrected as the soul of all humanity:

Chera pish-e Khosrow beh khwahesh ravi...

Why should you go to the Prince obsequiously?
If you were to put aside your wanton desires, you're the Prince![45]

Part Three

THE RESURRECTION OF AN ARCHETYPE

SIX

The Resurrection of the Persian Prince Under Colonial Duress

The modern prince, the myth-prince, cannot be a real person, a concrete individual. It can only be an organism, a complex element of society in which a collective will, which has already been recognized and has to some extent asserted itself in action, begins to take concrete form. History has already provided this organism, and it is the political party—the first cell in which there come together germs of a collective will tending to become universal and total.[1]

Antonio Gramsci, "The Modern Prince" (1929–1935)

> The Amen-Bird in pain and lost
> Has flown to the end of this tyrannized land—
> Returned and forlorn—has no appetite for water or feed:
> Wondering the arrival of the day of deliverance—
> Knowing all that is hidden—among the hidden for
> He is the hidden ear of our pain-stricken world,
> Bringing together the afflicted masses—
> With the constant echoes of his Amens—
> He's healing their hopelessness
> Gathering their hidden hopes closer together.[2]

Nima Yushij, "Amen-Bird" (1951)

THE FIRST TIME I SAW REMBRANDT'S perhaps most famous painting, *The Nightwatch* (*De Nachtwacht*, 1642), I did not even know it was housed at the

FIGURE 5   Rembrandt, *The Nightwatch* or
*Militia Company of District II Under the Command of
Captain Frans Banninck Cocq*, 1642. Amsterdam, Rijksmuseum.

Rijksmuseum. I was in Amsterdam for a lecture series and was casually strolling through the galleries of the museum with a friend when we came to a small room where we noticed a larger-than-usual crowd. I was pleasantly surprised and spent the rest of the visit closely examining this startling work of seventeenth-century Dutch art (fig. 5). As I marveled at the composition and texture of the painting, I became especially intrigued by the work's more accurate alternative titles: *Militia Company of District II Under the Command of Captain Frans Banninck Cocq* and *The Shooting Company of Frans Banning Cocq and Willem van Ruytenburch*. Why would Rembrandt so majestically celebrate a "militia company" or "shooting company"? It was not just the military and militant disposition of the picture but also its radical contemporaneity that interested me. An urban militia unit, publicly known and celebrated, proud and posing for a portrait by none other than Rembrandt himself: What a feat!

The painting features a certain captain Banninck Cocq and members of his *Kloveniers* (civic militia guards), or *Schutterij*, a voluntary militia unit protecting the city against attacks and fires and such. The formation of this militia was what fascinated me most about this painting. What were they protecting the city from, I wondered. Obviously the city was quite opulent and full of rich people and their properties that needed protecting, but how had these rich Dutch accumulated their fortunes, and how could they afford to not only pay for these militia but even have their portraits done by Rembrandt? What business, what manufacturing, what industry did these rich Dutch own that they had managed to amass such wealth? Who paid for this painting, and how expensive was it? How could they afford it?

As I began to study the picture more closely, I recalled more about its historical circumstances. By this point, I knew of Simon Schama's major scholarship on Dutch culture of the period, *The Embarrassment of Riches: An Interpretation of Dutch Culture in the Golden Age* (1987),[3] but I also remembered, as my distinguished colleague Susan Buck-Morss has noted, that Schama is entirely oblivious to the source of all such wealth—which was of course Dutch colonial possessions, particularly their lucrative slave trade. Buck-Morss's exquisite critique of Schama drives the point home regarding both Schama's brilliant insights and his evident blindness in his reading of the so-called golden age of Dutch commerce and culture from the mid-sixteenth to the mid-seventeenth centuries—a commerce and culture that were parasitical to their brutal slave trade. As Buck-Morss puts it poignantly, this "golden age"

> was made possible by their dominance of global mercantile trade, including, as a fundamental component the trade in slaves. But if we follow its most excellent of modern historians, Simon Schama, whose thick description of the Golden Age of Dutch culture has become a model in the field of cultural history since its publication in 1987, we will be in for a surprise. Strikingly, the topics of slavery, the slave trade, and slave labor are never discussed in Schama's *The Embarrassment of Riches*, a six-hundred-plus-page account of how the new Dutch Republic, in developing its own national culture, learned to be both rich and good.[4]

Before long, the Rijksmuseum itself, taking the hint from the sort of critical scholarship Buck-Morss best represents and Schama glaringly lacks, mounted a daring exhibition on slavery that included some of Rembrandt's masterpieces and decided "to come clean," as Valika Smeulders, the museum's head of history, has put it. A major essay by Jonathan Jones in the *Guardian* on the occasion of this major exhibition on slavery read, "Rembrandt and Slavery: Did the Great Painter Have Links to this Abhorrent Trade?" Referring to a rich couple in one of the artworks in the exhibition, Jones wrote:

> There's a deeply troubling side to this couple's wealth—and Rembrandt may have wanted us to register that there was something amiss. [Marten] Soolmans was heir to one of Amsterdam's biggest sugar refineries, and the production of sugar at its origin point depended on slaves. From the 15th century up to the 1800s, Europe's sweet tooth was fed by the captivity, transportation and brutal exploitation of Africans on sugar plantations in the Americas and Caribbean. The "golden age" of the Dutch Republic—when Amsterdam was the world's busiest entrepôt and Dutch merchant ships traversed the world—saw the Netherlands muscling in on Iberian dominance in both sugar and slavery.[5]

What has now become evident in Buck-Morss's pioneering scholarship, the museum's own curatorial consciousness, and the press coverage of the slavery exhibition (all as one set of examples) is that there is more to the masterpieces of European art and culture than meets the eye. Through their beauty and elegance, craftsmanship and aesthetic sublimity, we also witness the screams of nations, chopped-up hands, decapitated heads, and the desperation of continents whose riches have been plundered, their inhabitants brutalized, all to make these rich people appreciate their lives and their artists. None of these diminishes an iota from the epoch-making work of artists like Rembrandt or the patrons who made it possible. But it does give further credence to that frightful insight of Walter Benjamin that "there is no document of civilization which is not at the same time a document of barbarism."[6]

The age of European empires coincides with the rise of the last three Muslim empires. More specifically, the Portuguese Empire (1415–1999), the Spanish Empire (1492–1976), and the origin of the British Empire (1497–1583) were coterminous with the Mughals in India, the Safavids in Persia, and the Ottomans in Byzantium. The Russian empire (1721–1917) came at the tail end of these empires. The global encroachment of European colonialism, and its moral and material consequences, was of course neither limited to the Dutch nor indeed confined to the Netherlands. In her pioneering study of the ideological foregrounding of British colonialism in India, *Masks of Conquest: Literary Study and British Rule in India* (1989),[7] Gauri Viswanathan extends Gramsci's idea of hegemony to show how the British used liberal English education to indoctrinate a class of educated Indians to rule over their masses. Much bolder testimonies have reached us from the logic and rhetoric of British colonial domination in India. In his famous "Minutes on Education" (1835), the English secretary at war Thomas Babington Macaulay (1800–1859) famously writes:

> I have no knowledge of either Sanskrit or Arabic. But I have done what I could to form a correct estimate of their value. I have read translations of the most celebrated Arabic and Sanskrit works. I have conversed, both here and at home, with men distinguished by their proficiency in the Eastern tongues. I am quite ready to take the oriental learning at the valuation of the orientalists themselves. I have never found one among them who could deny that a single shelf of a good European library was worth the whole native literature of India and Arabia. The intrinsic superiority of the Western literature is indeed fully admitted by those members of the committee who support the oriental plan of education.[8]

It is quite revealing that Macaulay proudly confesses he cannot read a word of Sanskrit or Arabic (or Persian, for that matter—for most probably he could not tell the difference). The confident phrase "a single shelf of a good European library was worth the whole native literature of India and Arabia," by a man who could not read a word of either, is simply the epitome of the racist arrogance that the British took to their colonies, doing to their languages, literatures, and cultures what Leopold II of Belgium did to the Congolese masses.[9] Predicated on that bold assumption, Macaulay proceeds to declare:

> We must at present do our best to form a class who may be interpreters between us and the millions whom we govern,—a class of persons Indian in blood and color, but English in tastes, in opinions, in morals and in intellect. To that class we may leave it to refine the vernacular dialects of the country, to enrich those dialects with terms of science borrowed from the Western nomenclature, and to render them by degrees fit vehicles for conveying knowledge to the great mass of the population.[10]

To a certain degree the British did manage, as did the French and other European colonialists, to train that class of comprador intellectuals to do precisely what they were meant to do. But that very global encroachment of European capitalist modernity did eventually result in widespread anticolonial uprisings, wars of independence, the rise of postcolonial nation-states, and finally varied modes of critical thinking about colonialism, anticolonialism, postcolonialism, and ultimately decoloniality.[11] José Martí's "Our America" (1891), C. L. R. James's *The Black Jacobins* (1938), Frantz Fanon's *Wretched of the Earth* (1961), Enrique Dussel's *Philosophy of Liberation* (1977), Edward Said's *Orientalism* (1978), V. Y. Mudimbe's *The Invention of Africa: Gnosis, Philosophy, and the Order of Knowledge* (1988), and Bernard S. Cohn's *Colonialism and Its Forms of Knowledge: The British in India* (1996) are among the landmarks of a sustained course of critical reflection on the mode of knowledge production that has upheld the fact and enduring legacies of European colonialism. This genre of thinking is the continued index of the global encroachment of colonialism that had preoccupied generations of anticolonial struggles.

The global condition of coloniality was rising and intensifying, overwhelming the other worldly cultures it faced, demoralizing and outmaneuvering the universalizing power of those civilizations. Even if these civilizations rose up to oppose European hegemony, they were reactive to the racialized supremacy of one overpowering self-universalizing culture. To be modern for Europeans meant to dominate the world. To be modern for the rest of the world was to become subject to that European modernity: thus the moral paradox of their colonial modernity.

Tragedy, Romance, or Epic

More recently, and benefiting from this prolonged history of anticolonial reflection, other critical thinkers have sought to detect certain themes in the whole spectrum of living and thinking through colonial experiences. In his finely conceptualized *Conscripts of Modernity: The Tragedy of Colonial Enlightenment* (2004), David Scott proposes that anticolonial stories have been read mostly as *romance* but should preferably be read as *tragedy*. Following his close reading of C. L. R. James's seminal book, *The Black Jacobins* (1938), on the iconic career of the Haitian revolutionary Toussaint Louverture (1743–1803), and Hayden White's distinctions between romance and tragedy, Scott offers a critique of the postcolonial present through his interpretation of the colonial past and anticipation of a different postcolonial future, thus proposing that *tragedy* rather than *romance* is a more potent way of reading the advent of colonialism, anticolonialism, and postcolonialism.[12] This insightful literary twist on a traumatic political drama opens up varied possibilities.

There are, to be sure, merits to this line of thinking, but Scott's almost exclusive reliance on James's seminal text and White's generic distinction limits the scope of his theorization primarily to European sources of both romance and tragedy. James was born, raised, and educated in colonial Trinidad and was steeped principally in European literature, from Aeschylus to Shakespeare to Melville, as of course was White; Scott therefore remains limited to just one book, *The Black Jacobins*, which he of course theorizes and locates brilliantly, teasing out its more universal implications. But when we open up the scope of theorization to much larger expanses of civilizational domains in Asia, Africa, and Latin America, with their own distinct literary traditions, then it is not European oscillation between romance and tragedy but far more emphatically epic that best defines the genres of how to read or reread our colonial and postcolonial experiences—particularly in far larger domains like the Chinese, the Indian, the Iranian, and the Egyptian contexts. In the Iranian context proper, the genre of epic is perhaps best exemplified in Ferdowsi's *Shahnameh* includes both romance and tragedy in far richer and more widespread variations than that of its limited Greek, Roman, and European counterparts.

A consideration of the more universal genre of the epic instead takes us to the far more crucial spectrum of Latin American and African decolonial theorists as they have outlined them as a process of moral, political, and above all epistemic liberation. This is perhaps best represented in the works of Walter Mignolo, Anibal Quijano, and Dussel in the Latin American context; or Mudimbe in the African context, namely decolonial theorists who rely on richer and more liberating literary traditions than those lamenting the tragic end of the condition of coloniality. In his pioneering text *The Invention of Africa* (1988), Mudimbe turns the whole idea of Africa upside down by way of dismantling the regime of knowledge of an entire continent he had inherited.[13] In the Latin American context, in their seminal text *On Decoloniality: Concepts, Analytics, Praxis* (2018), Walter D. Mignolo and Catherine E. Walsh also map out, in considerable detail, the contours of a systematic undoing of "Western" hegemony by way of a mode of thinking and being that actively overrides the violent imposition of one self-universalizing European project.[14] In my own work, I have offered the idea of "colonial modernity" as a paradox (neither romantic nor tragic) whose negative dialectics contain its own unfolding liberation; the same applies to the idea of the epic, which I have argued should never be limited to its European versions.[15]

In my book on the Persian epic *Shahnameh*, I demonstrated the serious limitations of the conceptualization for the genre by David Quint in his seminal text *Epic and Empire: Politics and Generic Form from Virgil to Milton* (1993), in which he divides the genre of European epics into two kinds: Virgilian epics of conquest siding with the victors (Virgil's *Aeneid*, Camoes's *Lusíadas*, Tasso's *Gerusalemme liberata*) and the countervailing epics of the defeated (Lucan's *Pharsalia*, Ercilla's *Araucana*, and d'Aubigné's *Les tragiques*). While the victorious Virgilian epic follows a linear, teleological narrative, the epic of the defeated offers an episodic and open-ended cycle. In an equally significant study, *Modern Epic: The World System from Goethe to Garcia Marquez* (1996), Franco Moretti has also offered a theory of "the modern epic" in which he seeks to account for such monumental works of modern fiction as *Faust*, *Moby-Dick*, *The Nibelung's Ring*, *Ulysses*, *The Cantos*, *The Waste Land*, *The Man Without Qualities*, and *One Hundred Years of Solitude*. These works of modern epic, Moretti argues, represent and naturalize the imperial and colonial European domination of the planet. Can the postcolonial world, we may interject, posit an epic of its own—an epic not of triumph or defeat but of resistance and resilience, of overcoming and transcending, one in which we can read the trials and tribulations of the very condition of our coloniality neither as romance nor as tragedy but as the will to resist power? Ferdowsi's *Shahnameh* is neither triumphalist nor tragic; it is self-transcendental, its politics always compromised by its poetics, its poetics grounded in its politics, for it always already combines three worlds: the world in which it was created, the world it creates, and the world in which it has been historically. It also posits and fuses three temporal epochs—mythic, heroic, and historical—whose temporal and spatial coordinates give the text a defiant character working toward dismantling the status quo but not by way of supplanting it, rather by way of liberating it in open-ended directions.

This way of reading the Persian epic, where the Persian Prince is best at home, places the archetypal text and context at the threshold of the condition of coloniality that has resulted in both revolutionary mobilization and critical theorization. The trilateral disposition of the temporal narrative of the *Shahnameh*, ranging from mythic to heroic to historical, frames the renewed reading of the epic on the emerging public sphere, where the condition of coloniality is actively and revised. The succession of the colonial, anticolonial, and postcolonial are all prelude to an eristic act of decoloniality, which is neither romantic nor tragic but decidedly epic. That means the mythic, heroic, and historical framing defines the contours of the modern epic in those terms, whereupon the postcolonial parapublic sphere the postcolonial epic rises. Thus this trilateral temporality of mythic heroic and historical provides the space where the Persian Prince is resurrected.

The Persian Prince: Rooted, Resurrected

Macaulay's pronouncement about the "oriental learning" that he could not even read is an epistemic violence (contingent on a far more physical violence) that marks the circumstances of how the archetypal figure of the Persian Prince was paralyzed into a traumatic remission and subsequent resurrection. It was a closed-circuit trajectory: the colonial officer consulted the recruited Orientalists and they concurred the Oriental books were no match for European masterpieces. The issue, of course, is not the fact that a shelf of any "European library" undoubtedly contains masterpieces of the best of human ingenuity—so do the shelves of libraries from India, Arabia, China, Iran, or Egypt. One does not come at the expense of the other. We need not dismiss any one of them to celebrate the other. The question rather is what happens when any one of these shelves is celebrated *in order to* denigrate the other. It would have been tempting to test the British secretary at war on any such European shelf to find out what exactly he knows about its contents. But here we are not in the realm of reason. We are in a moment of racist arrogance predicated on colonial conquest. If those Oriental shelves were not inferior, the Indians would be standing in London, not the British in Delhi. That is the pure logic of violence. This is precisely the moment when colonial arrogance shocks the moral imaginary of the conquered and colonized nations—either into indignant revolt or else into obsequious submission—both of which pave the way for the destruction of the classical archetypes. The central issue is the "nativization" of that body of literature the British secretary at war could not read and the very same cadre of Orientalists he cites were tasked to read and master. These bodies of literature were not "native." They were universal. It was not just the fact that Macaulay could not read the originals but the fact that the Orientalists he consulted were actively engaged in nativizing their universality.

There is a passage in Ferdowsi's *Shahnameh* that might help to drive home this point. The passage describes the moment when the mythical king Jamshid ascends the throne:

> He ascended the throne of his auspicious father,
> Like all other royal kings having a crown of gold on his head,
> He tightened his royal belt with regal majesty—
> The whole world under his full authority.
> The world was at ease with justice,
> Demons, fairies, and animals all under his full command—
> The dignity of the world was increased because of him,
> The imperial throne glowing because of him—
> "It is I," he said, with Farrah Izadi [Divine Gift of Grace]:
> "Mine is both royalty and priesthood,
> "I will put an end to evildoers,
> "I will lead the souls to light."[16]

Precisely because of the poetic and mythic power of such passages resonating in the minds and souls of the world the British were now ruling with ignorance and brutality, their meanings began to be metamorphized in more urgent and contemporary terms, where the ground zero of this resurrection becomes the para/public sphere of the post/colonial world. This is the moment when the readers of these verses become rebel/poets. The European invasion, occupation, and plundering of the (Muslim) world was no more or less violent and barbaric than the Mongol invasion before it, or the Crusaders before them, or Alexander's before them. But the experience of both Alexander and the Mongols had the far more redeeming factor of conquered nations ultimately absolving their conquerors into the civilizing force of their own cultures. This never happened with the European conquest, rooted as it was in racialized hatred and underlined with unbridled plunder. The shocking experience forced much moral and political trauma. In the case of Islam it dissolved itself into a singular site of resistance to domination; in the case of the Persian Prince it dissolved itself to resurrect into something far more potent and iconic: the Persian rebel poet.

At this point we are ready to make a Gramscian move and see the figure of the Persian Prince not as manifested in any political person or party (a king, a president, a revolutionary leader, a political organism, etc.) in or out of a royal court, but as effectively transformed into something else, something far more potent, something definitive to the fate of postcolonial nations that still remember the long history of this imperial archetype. Turning now to an examination of the inaugural site of that transformation of the figure of the Persian Prince on the postcolonial extension of capitalist modernity, we see how the archetypal figure is not turned into any political party, as Gramsci surmised in his contemporary Europe, but into the much larger domain of the postcolonial public and parapublic spheres upon which the prophetic figure of the rebel/poet is now staged. The defining parameters of the rebel/poet are rooted in the transnational para/public sphere upon which postcolonial nations are formed. The figurative transmutation of the Persian Prince was concomitant with the rise and global encroachment of European colonial modernity and the simultaneous discrediting of the Persianate royal courts. The transformative synergy of the para/public sphere that European colonial modernity had generated and sustained became the fertile ground of this transfiguration of the Persian Prince. To see how the figure of the Persian Prince resurfaced on that public sphere, we first need to dwell on the European moment of (colonial) modernity that had occasioned this formation of the transnational bourgeois public sphere, which on the colonial site included a powerful parapublic shadow to it. This is the moment when the monadic disposition of the Persian Prince dissolves into a dyadic spectrum of nations and states, people and their rulers, awaiting a prophetic voice to address a new dispensation of the archetype.

If for Gramsci the myth-prince becomes the party, for the prophetic voice of the Persian poet Nima Yushij the iconic archetype resurrects as a mythic Amen-Bird giving voice to the hidden hopes of the people he poetically imagined. For Gramsci the myth-prince meant political party, for Nima the iconic figure of a bird promising liberation. The party means the state-in-waiting, the staged ressentiment against the ruling faction, while the mythic bird signals the exact opposite of the state, for it defines and demarcates the public sphere of resistance to power. It means the open-ended promises of the nation trapped inside the state that lays false claim to it; one consolidates power, the other unleashes the unthought thought. One early in the twentieth century and the other later in the same century, Gramsci and Nima brought two different sets of political and poetic dispositions to the heritage of political power they had inherited at two sides of the selfsame colonial modernity. Gramsci was correct that the new prince "cannot be a real person, a concrete individual," but it does not have to rush to become a (reactionary or revolutionary) political party either. It can be the potent allusions, the poetic urge, and the prophetic intuition that inform all the politics and polity around it. In the face of Nima's liberating imagination, the revolutionary Italian Marxist thinker becomes positively reactionary.

False Fixations, Fresh Metamorphosis

Understanding this transformative moment does not accommodate any false fixation with canonical texts bereft of their living memories and devoid of their historical contexts because it is in the nature of archetypes to metamorphose and resurrect in varied and altered forms. In a typically erudite volume that pivots around the discourse of *Zaval* (decline) and *Enhetat* (downfall), the prominent Iranian intellectual historian Seyyed Javad Tabataba'i narrates a learned history of Iranian political thought that starts with Greek philosophy and culminates in Aristotle, before turning to their Islamic manifestations in Farabi and Miskawayh all the way to Avicenna, and then coming to its zenith in Nasir al-Din al-Tusi and beginning its "decline" in Mulla Sadra and Mulla Hadi Sabzevari in the sixteenth to nineteenth centuries, to finally crash, in his estimation, to a closure with the late Timurid philosopher Jalal al-Din Davani (1426–1502).[17]

A deeply abstract scholasticism informs this habitual (if not altogether cliché) narrative, which is typically enamored with the Greeks, Plato in particular, and ignores the fact that the very Platonic idea of the "philosopher-king" was equally undemocratic and as such had nothing to do with Tabataba'i's anachronistic conception of *Shahrvandi* (Citizenship), a framework he borrows from the French Enlightenment and catapults back to the Greeks, who had also produced the entirely imperial manifesto of Xenophon's *Cyropaedia*, which Tabataba'i completely disregards. The ideas of Zaval and Enhetat are categorically flawed because they are terminal, defeatist, and classicist, informed and animated by a certain kind of scholastic absolutism and textual determinism forgetful of history; conversely, we can consider the shift in the way Davani, for example, is received in India, because the public spheres (facilitated by trade routes) that are active or emerging in the region are transnational and extend from India to Central Asia, to Iran and the Ottoman territories.

It is precisely a disregard for this transregional world and its contingent para/public spheres that distorts Tabataba'i abstract and teleological narratives. The main culprit in Tabataba'i teleology is the Mongol invasion of the thirteenth century, which, in his estimation, brings the effervescent Iranian intellectual "golden age" of the preceding centuries to a crushing close, rescued only temporarily early in the Safavid period. He then calls for an *Agahi-ye Melli* (national consciousness) in historiography but at the same time assigns the period of "the Middle Ages," straight out of the European historiographical context, right onto Iranian history without any sense of irony. His conclusion, foregone, is the approximation of Iranian historiography to European historiography,[18] both its similarities and differences, all gathered around the two European concepts (as he admits) of *Pishraft* (progress) and *Zaval* (decline) and the binarism of Iran and Europe; typical of his generation of intellectual historians, it sustains the thematic course and makes him entirely oblivious to the two adjacent sister civilizations of India and the Ottomans, and the Central Asian spectrum they shared with Iran. This historical and narrative jingoism that places an insular "Iran" and a superior "Europe" face-to-face does irreparable damage to the collective consciousness of the era, fetishizing texts out of their contexts and extracting stories out of their histories.

If we were to change the discourse from the misplaced Eurocentrism of "Progress and Decline" (Europe progressed, the rest of the world declined)[19] to the historic metamorphosis of the archetypal category of the Persian Prince or any other conceptual category integral to the Iranian and Islamic moral universe, we come to pay closer attention to the Indian reception of the selfsame Jalal al-Din Davani's seminal text that Tabataba'i marks as the moment of "decline." We know for a fact that although Davani may never have traveled to India, his books and his ideas certainly did. Davani was a prominent philosopher, theologian, jurist, and poet of his time. He was a close confidant of Qara Qoyunlu, Aq Qoyunlu, and Timurid and Ottoman rulers, and he died just before the Safavids came to power. His most important book by common consensus is his seminal work in political philosophy, *Akhlaq-e Jalali* (*Jalali's Ethics*), which he had composed on the basis of Nasir al-Din al-Tusi's *Nasirean Ethics*.[20]

In the context of the metamorphosis of the archetype of the Persian Prince, the reception of Davani's book on political philosophy in India is in fact more important than its own exquisite brilliance. We know that a certain Fathollah Shirazi was chiefly responsible for introducing Davani to Bajpur and Agra by way of bringing the Islamic philosophy of such eminent figures as Davani and Dashtaki to India.[21] The British were eager to have Davani's *Akhlaq-e Jalali* brought to India and read in Indian Islamic schools. The book was also translated into English by a certain W. F. Thompson, given the title of "Political Philosophy of Muhammadan People," published in London and Karachi, and taught at the Oriental College of Lahore. In 1839, it was also translated into Urdu. Indian scholars soon began writing commentaries on Davani's seminal text on ethics and politics. But the interest in Davani was not limited only to *Akhlaq-e Jalali*. Another major work of his, a commentary on Suhrawardi's *Haykel al-Nur* (*Shapes of Light*), called *Shawakil al-Hur fi Sharh Hayakil al-Nur* (*Angelic Forms: Commentary on the Shapes of Light*), was also of widespread interest in India and the subject of other commentaries. This sideways move of Persian works of ethics from Iran to India under British colonial occupation maps out an interstitial space that recasts the historic fate of both climes. Right here in this interstitial space is where the initial encounters take place between the latest stages of philosophical reflections on the nature and function of authority and European colonialism. As the Mughals yield to British colonial domination, the last Persianate dynasty becomes the locus classicus of the Persian Prince—where the archetype begins its historic transformations. From here and in the face of colonial modernity the imperial archetype begins to metamorphose into its future shapes and resurrect into its forgotten familiarities.

Self-Portrayals of the Persian Prince

The rapid encroachment of Russian and European empires into the Persianate world, extending from India to Central Asia to the Caucuses through Iran and to the Ottoman Empire, coincided with one extraordinary document we have, in the form of a rare autobiography by the Safavid monarch Shah Tahmasp I (1514–1576).[22] He was the son of Shah Ismail I (reigned 1501–1524), the founding figure of the dynasty and its longest-ruling monarch. Any one of these last three Muslim empires we choose—the Mughals, the Safavids, or the Ottomans— has organic links with the other ones, among them panning out a transregional constellation of public spaces and parapublic spheres. Shah Tahmasp is best known for having given refuge to the fugitive Mughal emperor Humayun (ruled 1530–1540 and 1555–1556) as well as to Suleiman the Magnificent's son Şehzade (Prince) Bayezid (1525–1561). During Shah Tahmasp's reign, Persian art and architecture reached its zenith, the most famous example being the *Shahnameh* of Shah Tahmasp, which he offered as a gift to the Ottoman sultan Selim.

Early in his autobiography, Shah Tahmasp discusses his reasons for writing the text:

> It occurred to me, Tahmasp ibn Ismail ibn Heidari al-Safavi al-Mousavi al-Hosseini, to write an autobiography of my life so that it would remain as a legacy in this world and might be a manual for my children and friends so when it reaches the dearly beloved, they might pray for me. I write it in a simple prose so they would not find fault with it and

not consider it as a pretentious and duplicitous act, and God alone is the source of success and support.[23]

As we read through his autobiography, we see how Shah Tahmasp identifies with the legendary Iranian king Fereydoun,[24] repeatedly cites the poems of Saʿdi,[25] tells us his dreams, and also interprets them for us—as, for example, when he tells us in Nakhichevan on 18 Safar 961 (Monday, January 22, 1554) he dreams of a Qurʾanic verse written in royal calligraphy on the sky,[26] or on another occasion that he dreams about four beautiful women his sister had brought to his private quarters.[27] What is crucial in this document is how the figure of the Persian Prince has become his own biographer, dreamer, and dream interpreter. Shah Tahmasp writes of his birth and upbringing, the precise day he ascended the throne, his battles and skirmishes, his political adversaries, his fears and aspirations. He believes monarchy is a divine gift, he considers the Qezelbash militia instrumental to his reign, he writes of his fears of the Ottomans, he uses Qurʾanic verses—Persian poetry, mostly of Saʿdi—plus frequent Turkish words and phrases. In short, the Persian Prince has picked up the pen from his courtly chronographers and assumed agency in his personal capacities as the king-scribe of his own realm.

Historians of the period have read Shah Tahmasp's autobiography as modeled on the Mughal emperor Babur's similar text—which is a crucial observation, for it marks the emerging transnational public sphere of the Persianate world. But compared to Babur's autobiography, the *Babur-nameh*, Shah Tahmasp's autobiography is a pedestrian piece, for the text of the founder of the Mughal dynasty is a far superior document. *Babur-nameh*, also known as *Tuzuk-i Baburi*, became an instant classic, originally written in Chagatai Turki by an emperor who had written other works on Sufism and composed his own poetries. From all we know about him, Babur was a deeply cultivated man, a philosopher-king, a poet-king, a mystic-king who, despite writing his autobiography in Chagatai Turkic, was a deeply learned Timurid prince with a solid command of Persian as well. Babur did not write his book in Persian, nor did he have it illustrated. It was Babur's grandson, Emperor Akbar (reigned 1556–1605), who had Babur's autobiography translated into exquisite Persian and then had it lavishly illustrated, using his grandfather's memoir as the foundational text of their dynasty, turning it into a mobile museum of astonishingly beautiful illustrations.[28] One of the lusciously illustrated manuscripts ordered by Akbar was subsequently vandalized and torn into pages in 1913 by colonial merchants trading in Islamic art treasures, and its pieces sold into slavery to the Victoria and Albert Museum in London, the British Library, the British Museum, the State Museum of Oriental Art, Moscow, the Walters Art Museum in Baltimore, and who knows how many other private collections. The same barbaric vandalism was perpetrated later on other masterpieces of the period, such as the equally glorious *Shahnameh* that Shah Tahmasp had ordered and sent as a gift to Sultan Selim. The destruction of these two and other manuscripts by the colonial greed of European and US museums and private art collectors is tantamount to placing a bomb in the Uffizi, Tate, or Metropolitan museums and then raiding its masterpieces for auctioneers.

Babur's autobiography begins simply and symbolically: "In the month of Ramzan of the year 899 (June 1494) and in the twelfth year of my age, I became ruler in the country of Farghana."[29] He then proceeds to give his own account of how he conquered Central Asia, down to Afghanistan and farther south to the Indian subcontinent. But there is much more to Babur's autobiography than meets the eye. In a brilliant doctoral dissertation by Tannaz Latifian Isfahani of Beheshti University in Tehran, we see how Babur in fact turns his autobiography into a celebration of an idyllic space, life in a garden, based on a sublime aesthetics, predicated on a divinely ordained architecture.[30] Tannaz Latifian Isfahan's exquisite scholarship teases out aspects of Babur's narrative imagination in which *Zendegi dar Bagh* (life in a garden) is predicated on a *Ziba-shenasi* (aesthetics) of his own making and a detailed *Vazheh-ha-ha-ye Meʿmari* (architectural lexicography). Through her close and creative reading of *Babur-nameh* we have access into the collective unconscious of Babur as he imagined his conquered realm as a garden and therefore himself as a gardener. This idyllic transmutation of the historical narrative into an iconic imagining of a beautiful and sublime life on earth is the last enduring evidence of the classical disposition of the Persian Prince retrieving and staging its subconscious archetype right into the throes of British and other European colonial conquests. In this insightful reading of *Babur-nameh* we have textual evidence of all those idyllic gardens we see in the background of Mughal paintings.

Shah Tahmasp's autobiographical *Tazkireh* and Babur's *Babur-Nameh* offer a clue as to how to read and detect the rising new archetypes of the Persian Prince, to which we might also add the simultaneous rise of Ottoman portraitures, which, after an initial recruitment of European artists like the Venetian artist Gentile Bellini, turned inward and to aesthetic traditions domestic to its own imperial imaginations. According to Ottoman art historians:

During the second half of Sûleyman's long reign, as the borders of the empire solidified, Ottoman art and architecture no longer appeared receptive to foreign models. Court ateliers began to develop a distinctly identifiable Ottoman idiom in ceramics, textiles, architecture, and, eventually in the last quarter of the century, in manuscript painting. Numerous accounts of the reigns of Ottoman sultans were composed in this period, accompanied by narrative images that eulogized the ruler as well as his court. The late sixteenth-century illustrated histories not only embodied the emergent Ottoman self-image but contributed to its crystallization through both their form and content. Patrons and authors alike began to encourage the use of their own language, Ottoman Turkish, alongside the customary Persian, to compose histories and formulated a specific visual idiom to illustrate official court chronicles.[31]

Such visual idioms were decidedly self-referential—where the Self becomes its own other. Texts in Ottoman Turkish and classical Persian, and their rich and suggestive visual allusions, were integral to one another, embedded in and implicating one another, identical in their self-referentiality to both Babur and Shah Tahmasp's autobiographical texts. In the same vein, we may also look at Lady Mary Wortley Montagu's (1689–1762) famous *Turkish Embassy Letters* as thriving on a dialogical disposition in which her encounter with Ottoman women alters her own self-perceptions and through that encounter, we at least have a mirror image of Ottoman women.[32] Because of Lady Montagu's repeated self-referential anxieties, these letters are not written from a position of power, especially given the imperial sway of the Ottomans at the time, which preempted any such power-basing narratives. If there is any Orientalism in these letters it is not an Orientalism of domination. It is an Orientalist marker of self-anxiety. The *Letters'* near contemporary, Mozart's *Abduction from Seraglio* (1782), is an Orientalism of fear and loathing, as long before them the Orientalism of Aeschylus's *Persians* (472 BCE) is an Orientalism of rivalry and admiration. Said's insights in his classic text *Orientalism* (1978) are valid but limited to a very specific period of his investigations. There are varied forms of Orientalism that entail different kinds of power dynamics.[33] The self-referentiality of the Persian Prince in visual and verbal variants extending from the Mughal to the Safavid to the Ottoman courts is paradoxically gendered in Lady Montagu's *Turkish Embassy Letters* in a crucial dyadic direction when the alterity of the Persian Prince finds a gendered rendition in English.

The Last Three Empires and Their Penultimate Princes

These varied forms of verbal and visual self-references of the Persian Prince bring us to a more historical assessment of the three penultimate figures who represented the archetype. As it has become quite evident by now, I use the term "Persian Prince" as an entirely literary trope and archetypal prototype, without any ethnic implication. The Persian (or Persianate) Prince could be Iranian, Indian, Turk, Mongol, or Arab—based on the political culture in which its dynastic power is located. What the term designates is a particular modality of power and legitimacy that has come into the Islamic period from pre-Islamic Iranian origins, resonated with its multicultural contexts, and expressed itself mostly in Persian but also in Arabic, Ottoman Turkish, or Urdu—with Xenophon's *Cyropaedia* as its Greek and subsequent Latin protypes. It is important here to keep *Cyropaedia* in mind precisely because it was done in Greek and for Greek, Roman, and later European and even North American uses, but still, it was on the model of the Persian Prince.[34] The Persian Prince therefore could even be thought of as Greek, Roman, Byzantine, and, by extension, as part of the very fabric of European monarchies claiming lineage from that Greco-Roman heritage. This is perhaps at least one reason for the many classical paintings and later operas on Persian imperial themes.

The classical articulations and varied manifestations of the figure of the Persian Prince come to a crescendo and then a concomitant crisis in the course of the last grand Muslim empires: the Mughals (1526–1540 and 1555–1857) in India, the Safavids and the Qajars (1501–1736 and 1796–1926) in Iran, and the Ottomans (circa 1299–1923) in Europe, Asia, and North Africa. Three Persianate (not Iranian but *Persianate*) princes, one might therefore say—one Iranian, one Turk, and one Indian, all modeled on the prototype of the Persian Prince—come together in this period to personify the historic predicament of the seminal archetypal figure. The valiant but ultimately doomed projects of Sultan Suleiman the Magnificent (1494–1566), the tragic demise of Prince Dara Shikoh (1615–1659), and the pioneering encounters with European colonial modernity initiated by Prince Abbas Mirza (1789–1833) mark the end of the classical Islamic imperial dynasties and with them the entire fate of the Persian Prince. In three different but interrelated imperial contexts, these three iconic figures symbolize the last princely prototypes that could have but ultimately failed to preserve the iconic figure as they had received it from pre-Islamic princely traditions.

Sultan Suleiman I, commonly known as Suleiman the Magnificent or Suleiman the Lawgiver, who, like all other Persianate kings referred to himself with the old Iranian title of "the Padishah," was the longest-ruling sultan of the Ottoman Empire (reigned 1520–1566).[35] He battled European monarchies to his west and the Safavid dynasty to his east and consolidated the rule of the Ottomans over a vast and prosperous empire. He ruled supreme over the vast, rich, and flourishing Ottoman Empire with a steadfast determination to shape the world for good. He initiated serious administrative reforms and consolidated the supreme rule of his imperial dynasty while being a generous patron of art and architecture, poetry, and literature, which all thrived under his patronage. The Ottoman Empire and the figure of the Persianate Prince at the center of it would never again see any monarch so powerful and mighty. His reign coincided with the global rise of European imperial and colonial designs in his and other Muslim empires.

During the long and mighty rule of Sultan Suleiman I, the history of the world could have gone either way. His European and Mediterranean conquests could very well have prevented the actual idea of "the West." In his reign he brought Turkic, Islamic, European, and Iranian elements together, but the symbolic figure of the Persian Prince remained definitive to the archetypal foregrounding of his imperial rule. All these imperial dynasties, from the Abbasids down to the Ottomans, used the Sassanid Empire as their blueprint—but they were also informed by any number of other ideological strands in their dynastic history. The centrality of the heavily Persianized Alexander romance in the ideological foregrounding of the Ottoman Empire is perhaps the most palpable evidence of this fact. In Suleiman the Magnificent, the archetype of the Persian Prince saw its last mighty manifestation.

Dara Shikoh was the eldest son and heir apparent of the Mughal emperor Shah Jahan (1628–1658). Dara Shikoh's official Persian title, Padshahzada-i-Buzurg Martaba ("the magnificent prince"), clearly demonstrates his significance for his realm. Prince Dara, however, was killed by his younger brother Aurangzeb in a battle of succession that marred the rest of Mughal (and by extension Indian) history.[36] The enduring images of the two brothers thus became the split figures of the Persian Prince, Dara personifying refinement, knowledge, wisdom, and the gift of grace, his brother brute and unbridled fanaticism and violence. That iconic split image was integral to the bifurcated persona of the Persian Prince. Dara lost, Aurangzeb won, and the history of India was forever changed after that fatal bifurcation of power and grace—when the figure of the Persian Prince was institutionally disfigured. Dara Shikoh was the epitome of the Persianate Prince in the context of Indo-Persian culture. The active formation of Indo-Persian civilization evident in varied forms of institutional practices, literary texts, architectural styles, and political institutions were the manifestations of centuries of interactions among multiple Central Asian, Iranian, and Indian elements in the subcontinent. Although Indo-Persian culture came to full fruition during the Mughal period, it was rooted in the much earlier period of the Delhi sultanate (1206–1526), when Muslim and Hindu beliefs and practices had come together to create a syncretic and pluralistic culture. Even before the Delhi sultanate, beginning with the Ghaznavids (1206–1526), Persianized Turkic forces had entered the Indian subcontinent. From that point forward, Persian eventually emerged as the official language of the Delhi sultanate, the Bengal sultanate (1352–1576), the Bahmani sultanate (1347–1527), and ultimately the Mughal Empire. As the lingua franca of power and poetry, the Persian language achieved one of its most glorious zeniths here in this Indo-Persian world. Dara Shikoh was the flowering achievement of this environment—its philosophy and poetry embracing its vision of the Persianate Prince.

A major measure of the dominance of the figure of the Persianate Prince in the context of the Indo-Persian culture is the abundance of the *Shahnameh* manuscripts in the region from the Timurid period forward. Centered in their capital city of Herat, the Timurids (1370–1507) eventually turned their attention away from Central Asia and southward toward northern India, where one of Timur's descendants, Babur (1526–1530), founded the Mughal dynasty (1526–1858). The Mughal rulers were legendary patrons of art, especially the exquisite art of manuscript illustrations. Under Akbar (1556–1605), manuscript production achieved the heights of its aesthetic excellence. Here Ferdowsi's *Shahnameh* assumed its historic role as a princely manual and the figure of the Persian Prince dominated the royal court as an archetype of judicious and wise rule, with Mughal rulers invariably styling themselves after this ideal. In the split between Dara Shikoh and Aurangzeb, the figure of the Persianate Prince was cut in half, its grace and wisdom were defeated, and its brute violence was triumphed over. This was an iconic turning point in the long history of the archetype.

That brings us to the third Persianate Prince of this fateful moment in the long history of its archetypal position of power and legitimacy. Prince Abbas Mirza (1789–1833) cut a caring and competent figure in a crucial moment in the history of the Qajar dynasty.[37] He was a military commander during the fateful Russo-Persian Wars of 1804–1813 and 1826–1828 as well as the Ottoman-Persian War of 1821–1823. He was a pioneering modernizer of his armed forces and civil institutions, but he died before his father, Fath Ali Shah (1797–1834), and took with him his dreams of vital reforms of state and society. Abbas Mirza was an intelligent prince—learned, erudite, competent—and yet was outmaneuvered by forces of history beyond his control. He could not withstand the military superiority of the Russians and lost all of the Qajar territories in the Caucasus with the two ignominious treaties of Gulistan (1813) and Turkamanchai (1828). Prince Abbas Mirza was the last Persian Prince who did his best to salvage his imperial dynasty through the thick and thin of a vastly changing world dominated by Russian and British imperialism. He initiated some extraordinary deeds, but he ultimately failed. With Abbas Mirza also failed the entirety of the Qajar dynasty under the pressure of European colonial conquests. The world was changing fast around the very idea of the Persian Prince, which was now going through a transformative moment in its own archetypal history.

Of these three latest examples of Persianate princes, the first personified literary virtues and political power and became a mighty sultan, the second failed to match his refined humanist philosophy with a commanding desire for power, and the third was equipped with outdated princely qualities. The three of them together mark the final demise of the Persian Prince in its classical character and transhistorical culture. These three Persianate princes paradoxically saw through some crucial changes that would eventually shift the center of political gravity away from their royal courts and place it on the emerging transnational para/public spheres upon which the Muslim world at large now commanded an integral part.

The Para/Public Spheres of Colonial Modernity

These last three specimens of the Persian Prince lost the plot to a history far beyond their control. Something seismic was happening around the globe that was shifting the very axis of world history over a whole different spectrum of social forces. European social scientists since at least Max Weber (1864–1920) have been preoccupied with the central question of what exactly "modernity," or more precisely "capitalist modernity," is and what this project actually entails. From this most basic question they have then moved to ask about and speculate on the normative parameters of society, economy, and polity following the historical courses of the Reformation, the Industrial Revolution, the Enlightenment, the French Revolution, and above all the capitalist mode of economic production that has instigated them all. While Karl Marx was busy trying to figure out the logic and insanity of it all, Max Weber had come to the conclusion that modernity was concomitant with the dawn of a categorical "disenchantment" with the world and the subsequent fragmentation of critical self-awareness into routinized modes of knowledge in different shades of rationalization. Bureaucracy was the simulacrum of modernity, the stage when a cold and calculating logic dominates social organizations, and how capitalist modernity degenerates into an "iron cage." As Weber famously put it:

> No one knows who will live in this cage in the future, or whether at the end of this tremendous development entirely new prophets will arise, or there will be a great rebirth of old ideas and ideals, or, if neither, mechanized petrification, embellished with a sort of convulsive self-importance. For of the last stage of this cultural development, it might well be truly said: "Specialists without spirit, sensualists without heart; this nullity imagines that it has attained a level of civilization never before achieved."[38]

Europeans have of course been living that future of which Weber was so frightened. The rise of fascism, the calamitous consequences of World War II, the Holocaust, and the horrors of European colonialism were such aspects Weber either did not live to see or else were beyond his European horizons. The Holocaust was an overdose of the poison Europeans had been administering to the world at large. The Holocaust would have horrified Weber, but the European colonial conquest of the world and its inhumane consequences were beyond his visions. Against this dire prospect, Habermas's classic articulation of the notion of the "public sphere" is presumed to generate possibilities of dialogical agency for the bourgeois subject—prospects of anything from "new prophets" to a "great rebirth of old ideas." In a key passage of his seminal book, *Strukturwandel der Öffentlichkeit: Untersuchungen zu einer Kategorie der bürgerlichen Gesellschaft* (The Structural Transformation of the Public Sphere: An Inquiry into a Category of Bourgeois Society, 1962), Habermas uses the example of news circulations around the globe and their relations to commerce to theorize the premise of the rise of this public sphere:

> The traffic in news that developed alongside the traffic in commodities showed a similar pattern. With the expansion of trade, merchants' market-oriented calculations required more frequent and more exact information about distant events.... The great trade cities became at the same time centers for the traffic in news; the organization of this traffic on a continuous basis became imperative to the degree to which the

exchange of commodities and of securities became continuous.... To be sure, the merchants were satisfied with a system that limited information to insiders; the urban and court chanceries preferred one that served only the needs of administration. Neither had a stake in information that was public. What corresponded to their interests, rather, were "news letters," the private correspondences commercially organized by newsdealers.... Just as... one could speak of "mail" only when the regular opportunity for letter dispatch became accessible to the general public, so there existed a press in the strict sense only once the regular supply of news became public, that is, again, accessible to the general public. But this occurred only at the end of the seventeenth century.[39]

Crucial but undertheorized in Habermas's seminal work is precisely the transnational and therefore colonial foregrounding of this public sphere. The traffic in news and commodities were, of course, traffic, with European colonies now aggressively and violently incorporated into European spheres—both commercial and cultural. What were these "distant events" except those affecting the European mercantile class in Asia, Africa, and Latin America? The "great trade cities" mapping these circulations were not just London, Paris, or Amsterdam, after all. Istanbul, Cairo, Mumbai, Hong Kong, Johannesburg, and Rio de Janeiro were also on this map.[40] The circulation of news became public only when it in effect manufactured that public. This dialectical relationship between news and public was at once coterminous and transnational. In the Muslim world, the simplification of Arabic, Persian, Urdu, and Turkish prose; the introduction of the printing machine; the rise and effervescence of the genre of travelogues; and the demand for public education were all integral to the formation of these transnational public and parapublic spheres.[41] Here and at this crucial juncture, the archetypal figure of the Persian Prince metamorphoses and transmigrates from a charismatic character in the royal court into a major dynamism in the formation of the charismatic community at the roots of the formative forces of the emerging transnational public and parapublic spheres. At this point the public sphere becomes the expansive location where actual rebellious characters begin to become definitive to the metamorphic character of the Persian Prince.

Mostly outside the Eurocentric purviews of seminal European thinkers like Marx, Weber, Gramsci, and Habermas, the colonial para/public spheres chart a whole different trajectory of social transformations. This epistemic shift from Muslim imperial courts to colonial conquests to postcolonial state formations to anticolonial uprisings and their decolonizing projects becomes the site of critical thinking, where we see how states become incidental to nations, and nations integral to the formation of the para/public spheres upon which they are founded; it recasts the archaic figure of the Persian Prince into its historic transfigurations, in which imperial sovereignty is displaced figuratively from the Persian Prince to the prophetic voice of the rebel-poets who derive their authority and legitimacy from the site of the para/public spaces of sovereignty that frames the nation and its emerging citizens. This crucial twist in my unfolding theory works through this Gramscian move, and we see how the para/public spheres and their symbolic representations are far more important than any single political party—which in fact positively becomes an impediment to progressively expansive horizons of the para/public spheres and their poetic simulacra of the Persian Prince. The Weberian "disenchantment" with the world, rooted in the Eurocentric conquest of modernity, will inevitably entail modes of re-enchantment on colonial sites of the selfsame colonial modernity where the myth-prince could not possibly remain entrapped inside party politics. The political theater was too limited for that epic drama.

From Palaces to Coffeehouses

Where exactly was the site of the resurrection of the archetypal figure of the Persian Prince as a rebel hero? There is no specific site, and the resurrection was in the collective sub/consciousness of the nations to whom the figure was definitive. Literary texts, divans of poetry, treatises on moral philosophy, popular folk epics and romances. But if we were to identify a single category of site where the archetypal character found his most potent renewal, it would be in the coffeehouses. Coffeehouses emerged as the epicenter of public spaces and public spheres throughout the Mughal, Safavid, and Ottoman territories—where, in the form of popular storytelling, mythical heroes renewed their pact with their living memories. The origins and significance of these coffeehouses are definitive to our reading of the Safavid era.[42] Serving mostly tea despite their names, these coffeehouses offered a variety of other beverages, narcotics, and a proverbial delicacy called *Ab Gusht* (meat stew meal).

Starting in the fifteenth century, coffeehouses began to surface widely in India, Iran, and the Ottoman territories as public places where customers gathered to drink beverages, smoke *nargileh*, play backgammon, converse about their daily lives, and listen to poets and storytellers. Under the Safavids, coffeehouses flourished as a major public institution.⁴³ Mostly male customers would gather to rest, relax, conduct business, drink beverages, socialize, or play cards (*Ganjafeh*) or games such as *Torna-bazi* (also known as "Shah and Vizier"). The homoerotic environment of the space was also conducive to pederasty. These coffeehouses are the Muslim origins of what would later emerge in Europe as cafés in the Ottoman Empire. In the Muslim world, these institutions were the earliest public spaces to accommodate social gatherings. "Under the Safavids," scholars of coffeehouses tell us, "coffeehouses played an important part as meeting places for artists, poets, intellectuals, and even high officials."⁴⁴ The emergence of public spaces and public spheres was of course not limited to these coffeehouses, and the larger urban design of the city of Isfahan as the prototype of other cities like Delhi or Istanbul or Cairo or Damascus was conducive to such public spaces and public spheres.⁴⁵ We also know for a fact that "from the beginning coffeehouses had been favored meeting places for scholars, poets, musicians, and Sufis. Poets, often seated on high chairs in the center of the room . . . recited their own works, as well as pieces by Ferdowsi and other great masters."⁴⁶

The center stage of these coffeehouses eventually became either murals or canvases on which famous battles of the *Shahnameh* or else those of the Shi'i martyrs like Imam Hossein and his half-brother Abbas were depicted. As historians of this institution inform us:

> In the month of Moḥarram it was customary until quite recently for mourners to reenact Imam Ḥosayn's martyrdom in a large coffeehouse with a courtyard measuring several thousand square meters; the walls would be draped in black and a pulpit erected in one corner for the rawżakᵛān (narrator of the martyrdom of Ḥosayn . . .). The rule book of the Tehran guild of coffeehouse proprietors (qahvačīān), which remained in force until 1357 Š./1979, includes special provisions for Moḥarram mourning ceremonies. . . . In Ramażān, too, many customers, particularly tradesmen, would remain in the coffeehouses all night, enjoying special recitations. The storyteller would begin his narrative on the first night of the month and finish it on the last, often accompanying it with pictures.⁴⁷

The range and provenance of these coffeehouse paintings mapped out the domains of the mythic, heroic, and historical figures in both Iranian and Islamic cultures. These heroic figures, ranging from Rostam and Sohrab to the Shi'i Imams Ali and his son Hossein ibn Ali, were familiar to their audiences but now

FIGURE 6   Abbas Al-Musavi, *Battle of Karbala*, late nineteenth–early twentieth century. New York, Brooklyn Museum.

FIGURE 7   Hassan Ismailzadeh, *Sohrab (Is Being) Killed by Rostam*. Courtesy of the Hamid Keshmirshekan Archives.

received a new spatial, public, and performative stage, with the voice of professional *Naqqals* (narrators) declaiming the hiddenmost voices of ancient heroes. These large-scale paintings had effectively brought the "miniature" manuscript illustrations out of their opulent but limited spectatorship in royal courts to a much larger and more public domain. Coffeehouses were therefore the gathering spaces for the rise and resurrection of aging heroes on the more robust and urgent public and parapublic spheres of Muslim habitats. On their canvases and among their enthusiastically gathered audiences, the Persian Prince was breathing in a fresher and more robust habitat.

> Coffeehouse paintings were a special genre of Persian folk art, showing some affinities with Persian miniature painting. Where there was enough room in the coffeehouse a storyteller, usually illiterate, would erect a screen (parda) painted with a narrative scene and explain the story to interested customers, who would reward him with money. The pictures were usually of episodes from the Šāh-nāma, for example, the tragedy of Rostam and Sohrāb or the exploits of Esfandīār, or from such romances as Yusof o Zoleykā or the lives of the Shi'ite imams. . . . Screen painters were generally specialized in such work. . . . Most were anonymous bāzār artists, but a few signed their works at the bottom.[48]

Bringing the refined and opulent manuscript illustrations out from royal courts to the public on a larger and more vividly popular scale, these canvases and murals would become the forerunners of future visual and performing arts, drama and elocution, television and cinema. The Persian Prince was no longer a matter of poetic, prose, or speculative deliberations among the political elite and their royal patrons. That the Naqqals might have been illiterate speaks highly of their locations outside the royal courts and to their gift of rhetorical storytelling—for the oral traditions of storytelling were no less rich and powerful than their counterpart, the literary arts. These canvases were visual aids to the story, as the heroes depicted on them had in effect walked out of their manuscript confinements in the royal courts and found a voice much removed from their silent literary provenance, assuming in the process a public and oral performativity. The public and parapublic spaces and spheres were expanding, the emerging nations were finding their sense of moral whereabouts, social presence, and political purpose, far from the intrigues of the royal court, as the Persian Prince was getting ready to pack his belongings, depart from these royal habitats, and find a comfortable dwelling in a far richer, more powerful public dominion and symbolic sovereignty. If we look at a manuscript illustration of the Safavid period, the Persian Prince in the form of any *Shahnameh* hero looks incredibly refined, delicate, confined to the pages of a rich and opulent book. On the walls and canvases of the coffeehouses of the same decisive period, the selfsame heroes have been projected onto a living wall, deeply into the public, and their storytellers have appeared next to them to speak their power to a new truth.

Textual Mimicry

The monadic phase of the Persian Prince was always already and in and of itself deterritorialized and awaiting fragmentation into a dyadic version of its archetype. From the fifteenth century forward, as the European imperial adventures around the world gathered momentum and began to encroach on the globe in general and on the last three grand Muslim empires in particular, we see the pivoting of the monadic archetype of the Persian Prince, as a central point of the Persianate political culture, bending toward its dyadic proclivities—where the Persian Prince begins to find a new bicoastal habitat on both its dying legacies and its living memories, its fading legitimacy in the royal courts and its resurgent alterities on the emerging transnational public spheres. It is at this point when a mode of *textual mimicry* becomes evident in treatises that continue the tradition of mirrors for princes, seemingly unaware that they have lost the plot and a new mode of signification of the iconic figure has dawned in history—and that coffeehouses are at the epicenter of it.

A seminal case in point is Mir Seyyed Ali Hamadani's (1340–1384) monumental text *Zakhirat al-Moluk* (*Treasury of the Kings*).[49] A poet and a Sufi master of the Kubrawiya order who was born and raised in Hamadan and traveled and preached widely in Central and South Asia, Hamadani became particularly prominent in Kashmir. He was a poet and a mystic of the highest order, and his *Zakhirat al-Moluk* is widely known and celebrated as one of his finest works. Much of this book, systematically adorned by Qur'anic passages and Hadith references, concerns how a Muslim ruler must conduct himself, with a detailed chapter on the duties and responsibilities of a Muslim ruler toward his Muslim and non-Muslim subjects. So far as the Muslim subjects are concerned, the king is obligated to be humble toward them, refrain from heeding rumors about their behaviors, be forgiving toward them, be just and magnanimous, refrain from entering their private quarters, understand the limits and stations of his subjects and not expect from them what they are unable to offer, respect the elderly, honor his promises, not speak angrily to his subjects, do to Muslims what he expects Muslims to do to him, try to make peace among Muslims, be forgiving of his subjects' wrongdoings, be an exemplary model for his people, intercede on behalf of his people, always side and associate with the poor and the weak and not with the rich and powerful, be attentive to the poor and the orphans in particular, protect his realm from bandits and secure the highways, build roads and bridges, construct mosques around his realm and staff them properly, and encourage good deeds and prohibit evil acts.⁵⁰

This seems to be all well and honorable for a Muslim leader to follow. The treatment of the non-Muslims, however, is a completely different story. Hamadani is very strict about what non-Muslims' rights are. They are not allowed to build new churches, temples, or synagogues in a Muslim land, and if their places of worship are ruined they are not allowed to repair or rebuild them. Non-Muslims cannot prevent Muslim travelers from staying in their places of worship, and if Muslims stay there, the non-Muslims must provide them with food and hospitality for at least three days. Non-Muslims are not allowed to spy on Muslim countries where they live, and if members of their families are inclined to convert to Islam they must not prevent them. They must respect Muslims, and if they are in a gathering and Muslims arrive they must leave and give their place to Muslims. They are not allowed to dress the way Muslims do. They are not allowed to give themselves Muslim names. They are not allowed to ride horses with saddles and reins. They are not allowed to carry swords and arrows. They are not allowed to wear rings with jewels. They are not allowed to sell wine or openly drink alcoholic beverages. They must keep the clothing habit they had before Islam so Muslims can readily identify them. They are not allowed to engage in Muslim rituals. They are not allowed to build a house next to where Muslims live. They are not allowed to bury their dead near Muslim cemeteries. When they are mourning their dead, they are not allowed to cry loudly. They are not allowed to buy Muslim slaves. Hamadani cites Caliph Omar's treatment of the "Majus" (a derogatory term for Zoroastrians) as the model for these limitations on non-Muslims living in a Muslim land.⁵¹

The anxiety evident in the punctilious precision of the Muslim legislator at work here in this text reveals the fear of the potential dismantling of the Muslim order. This short section on non-Muslims is important not just because it seeks to secure the Muslim polity against its presumed internal dangers but also because it reveals the depth of anxiety sustaining that fear when the text specifically cites Zoroastrians as infidels and unbelievers who must be tightly controlled. This radical bifurcation between Muslims and non-Muslims in this treatise, which is typical of a punishing juridical mind, is precisely what sets the obsessive legal mind apart from the generosities of the humanist, literary, poetic, mystical, and philosophical discourses—texts in which the Persian Prince is habitually (but not exclusively) at home.

But something far more important than this classic distinction between scholasticism and humanism is at work here. The emerging and expansive public spaces and public spheres were overshadowing such classic bifurcations. Texts such as *Zakhirat al-Moluk* are to be compared with far more popular epics like *Bakhtiyar-nameh, Darab-nameh, Firuzshah-nameh, Sandbad-nameh,* and *Marzban-namah*—all of which were widely loved and admired epics with a wide-ranging appeal to live audiences. There was, to be sure, a strong streak of misogyny in these popular epics. Women in these texts were represented as archetypes and allegories and were not meant to be read literally. Be that as it may, what is more crucial here is how the textual mimicry of the abstracted scholasticism of the legalese texts was outmaneuvered by the new heroes and heroines of the expanded social formations. Women were gradually entering the labor force and public spaces and were among the visible audiences of the genres. Their real presence could no longer be subjected to allegorical archetypes. The genre of mirrors for princes indeed continued apace, but in mostly nostalgic and outdated terms—at this point, the resurrecting allegories of the Persian Prince were emerging in the form of popular heroes and rebels, and soon in the form of anticolonial uprisings from India to Iran and elsewhere. The dyadic disposition of the postclassical period was now emerging, overriding the whole spectrum of scholasticism-humanism in a widely popular body of literature on one side and on the other the effervescence of the public spheres in which the figure of the Persian Prince had a whole new rendezvous with history, where it would fulfill its innermost dyadic desires.

Resubjecting the Persian Prince

The emerging resubjection of the Persian Prince in a more gender-conscious environment will have to be traced back to the effervescence of children's literature in both the classical and contemporary eras. This eventual reconstitution of the postcolonial person projecting both inward and outward the archetype of the Persian Prince was rooted in the archaic figure but now fully aware of the changing climate of its identities and alterities. With a remarkable consistency, the trajectory of this body of children's literature has extended from pre-Islamic Iran to our own time. That body of children's literature places the idea of mirrors for princes in a whole new light—as the resurrection of the Persian Prince under colonial duress recasts the postcolonial person onto the paradigmatic disposition of a renewed worldliness.

From the astonishing figure of Ibn Muqaffaʿ (circa 721–759) in the eighth century, we have received a precious treatise on the education of children, *Al-Adab al-Wajiz li al-Walad al-Saghir* (*The Short Education for the Little Child*), which, like most other texts he wrote, was based on pre-Islamic Pahlavi sources and which has fortunately reached us through its Persian translation by none other than the foremost philosopher scientist of his age, Nasir al-Din al-Tusi (1201–1274): "My son, now that God Almighty blessed me with your existence, and graced me with your life, and let you reach the age of proper education [*Adab*] capable of acquiring the arts, it is incumbent upon me in gratitude to God Almighty for this precious gift to let you benefit from my education." He then proceeds to tell his son to obey God, solidify the rule of reason in himself, tell the truth, learn to be quiet, and associate with wise people, along with a succession of similar advice, as if he were raising a prince. In short, he advises *Kasb-e Adab* ("acquire a proper education") in simple, caring, and loving terms.[52]

The original of this text and its Persian translation have survived the ravages of time and reached our own era, being re-narrated by Mirza Aqa Khan Navaʾi Nabil al-Dowlah as *Akhlaq-e Mozaffari* (1898) and brought to wider attention. In addition to this old and seminal text, a few of the masterpieces of Persian classics such as Rumi's *Masnavi*, Saʿdi's *Golestan*, and both the Arabic and Persian versions of *Kelilah and Dimnah* were staples of children's education in the Persianate and Muslim worlds. Equally important has been fourteenth-century author Abu Nasr Firahi al-Sijistani's *Nisab al-Subyan* (*Children's Dictionary*), which is a precious Arabic-Persian dictionary consistently used in children's education. In addition, the late-twelfth and early-thirteenth-century prose stylist Sadid al-Din Awfi's *Jawamiʿ al-Hekayat* (*Compendium of Stories*) has been a consistent source of both entertainment and education for children and young adults. During the nineteenth century these kinds of texts began to proliferate, as perhaps best exemplified by Mahmoud ibn Yusef Mazandarani, also known as Miftah al-Molk, in his *Taʾdib al-Atfal* (*Education of Children*, 1876), in which the author has collected and illustrated stories and narrated them in a prose suitable for children. The same Miftah al-Molk published another illustrated book for children, based on Rumi's *Masnavi*, which he called *Masnavi al-Atfal* (*The Children's Masnavi*, 1853). *Safineh Talebi*, or *Ketab-e Ahmad* (1892), authored by Abdolrahim Talebof Tabrizi early in the twentieth century, became a groundbreaking text in the modern education of children. Mirza Ibrahim Khan Akkasbashi (1874–1915), the pioneering Iranian photographer and cinematographer, wrote his delightful *Akhlaq-e Mosavvur* (*Illustrated Ethics*, 1906), a fully illustrated collection of animal fables.⁵³ That brings us to the twentieth and twenty-first centuries and the unfolding of a rich and joyous body of literature for children perhaps best exemplified by the publications of the *Kanun-e Parvaresh-e Fekri-e Kudakan va Nojavanan* (Institute for the Intellectual Development of Children and Young Adults), established in 1965.

Considering this body of literature, which effectively constitutes a mirror for young children, we may look at the very genre of mirrors for princes differently if we were to look at its technical Latin term *"Speculum regis," "Speculum principis," "Speculum regale,"* with the prime examples of them all being Xenophon's *Cyropaedia* and Cicero's *De Officiis*. The term in Persian and Arabic we ordinarily use for this genre is *"Nasihat al-Moluk"* (advice to kings), or similar terms to that effect. As I have explained in detail in previous chapters, in Persian this genre ordinarily comes under the more general rubric of *Andarz* literature or, more specifically *Adab*, which I have previously translated as "literary humanism." But if we take its Latin and Greek roots, we might consider the metaphor of "mirror" as the modus operandi of the genre.⁵⁴ This brings us to the possibility of looking at the genre as a "mirror" in both the literal and figurative sense: what is placed in front of the prince to measure and observe himself. Perhaps the most famous poetic citation of this in Persian is in the celebrated Qasideh of Khaqani-e Shervani, to which I alluded in chapter 3 and that begins with the line

> *Han, Ey Del-e Ebrat-bin az Dideh Ebar kon Han!*

> Oh discerning eyes lo and behold!
> Observe the Ivan-e Mada'in as if it were a mirror of advice!⁵⁵

We have a much larger body of prose and poetry—for example in Hafez's and Bedil's respective divans—with allusions to the mirror, especially to "A'ineh-ye Eskandar" ("Alexander's Mirror"), which was putatively made by Aristotle and mounted on a tower in Alexandria from which the surrounding areas could be seen, which was then used by poets as a metaphor of the invisible world. We have a similar legend about Jame Jam (Jamshid's Cup), alluding to the mythical Persian king's ability to see and foresee the unforeseen and the unseen. Peter J. Chelkowski's *Mirror of the Invisible World: Tales from the Khamseh of Nizami* (1975) is a solid study of the image of the mirror in a major Persian poet. The point being the object and the metaphor of the mirror is not entirely alien to Persian literary culture.

If so, then in the more recent theorization of the "mirror stage" by the French psychoanalytic theorist Jacques Lacan, both the object and metaphor of the mirror become the locus classicus where the monadic disposition of the Persian Prince splits and becomes dyadic—both itself and its alterity (its mirror image) as itself. In Lacanian theory, the "mirror stage" marks the moment or the process whereby the child recognizes itself in a mirror and thus objectifies its ego. Initially Lacan thought of this as a moment that happens early in a person's childhood, but by the 1950s, he conceived of it as a permanent stage in the dialectical formation of subjectivity, whereby a person locates and imagines himself or herself in the world. In Lacan's own words:

> I am led, therefore, to regard the function of the mirror-stage as a particular case of the function of the imago, which is to establish a relation between the organism and its reality—or, as they say, between the Innenwelt and the Umwelt. . . . The mirror stage is a drama whose internal thrust is precipitated from insufficiency to anticipation—and which manufactures for the subject, caught up in the lure of spatial identification, the succession of phantasies that extends from a fragmented body-image to a form of its totality that I shall call orthopaedic—and, lastly, to the assumption of the armour of an alienating identity, which will mark with its rigid structure the subject's entire mental development. Thus, to break out of the circle of the Innenwelt into the Umwelt generates the inexhaustible quadrature of the ego's verifications.[56]

Lacan's use of the German word *Innenwelt*, meaning "the inner world," in contradistinction with *Umwelt* or the "outer world," points to the dialectical formation of the emerging subject and the ability for the person to say "I" from, through, and beyond the mirror stage. The dialectic might also be assumed in a more historical context to be mitigated through the genre of mirrors for princes and the normative and moral facilities it enables between the prince and his world. But it was precisely that dialectic between the *Innenwelt* and *Umwelt* that would be seriously challenged by Lacan's contemporary, critical feminist Luce Irigaray.

The publication of Irigaray's *Speculum de l'autre femme* (*Speculum of the Other Woman*, 1974) put a critical spin on both Freudian and Lacanian psychoanalysis by bringing the crucial issue of gender into focus. Irigaray overturned the idea of the sexless subject, exposing its masculinist foregrounding, repositing gendering as the place of the "no subject," for in the Euro-Platonism she criticizes (and, like all other European philosophers, calls "Western philosophy") the subject is exposed to be only a male subject. She stipulates that we must first acknowledge that what she calls the "Western subject" is a male subject, then think through the female subjection, before we can allow for intersubjectivity to emerge and work. She proceeds to expose the phallocentric disposition of "Western philosophy" via multiple critical strategies among which is a bold rereading of the Platonic allegory of the cave, which she asks us to consider as a womb. "The myth of the cave, for example," she writes, "or as an example, is a good place to start. Read it this time as a metaphor of the inner space, of the den, the womb or hystera, sometimes of the earth."[57] Her radical resubjection of the female begins with that premise: "Here is an attempt at making metaphor, at trying out detours, which not only is a silent prescription for Western metaphysics but also, more explicitly, proclaims (itself as) everything publicly designated as metaphysics, its fulfillment, and its interpretation."[58] Here is where she proposes to see the cave as a speculum—which, if she were familiar with Iranian mythology, she might have instead suggested as "Jamshid's Cup," an even more provocative metaphor:

> But this cave is already, and ipso facto, a speculum. An inner space of reflection. Polished, and polishing, fake offspring. Opening, enlarging, contriving the scene of representation, the world as representation. All is organized into cavities, spheres, sockets, chambers, enclosures, simply because the speculum is put in the way. The operation is abortive naturally—since only reflection is safe and spawns misbegotten freaks, abortive products before and after the fact.[59]

Between Lacan and Irigaray, between a flat mirror and the curvature of a speculum, the subject becomes gender-specific and historical. Going back to Ibn Muqaffaʿ's Arabic text in al-Tusi's Persian translation, we may now recall how it is consistently addressed to a boy and regularly invokes the phrase "*Ey Pesar*" (Oh son!). Although on an entirely allegorical plane, the figure of the Persian Prince in its classical articulation was historicized on a decidedly male domain of subjection, despite the fact that its archetypal modality was always mythic, atemporal, interstitial, unearthly, parabolic, and proverbial. If we now allow the mirror of the Persian Prince to be seen as a speculum, or more specifically Alexander's phallic tower mirror as Jamshid's Cup, then the gendered bifurcation of the princely figure has found its way back into a postcolonial and decolonial pivoting toward resubjection. Through a creative reading of Plato's allegory of the cave, Irigaray's speculum (our Jamshid's Cup) turns the flat mirror into a concave surface on which the subject is made visible on the simultaneous dialectic of its *Innenwelt* and *Umwelt* turning to each other where the male/female dichotomy begins to reflect each other in and out despite and in spite of themselves. By now the monadic formality of the Persian Prince has metaphorically split and bent toward its own dyadic desires and organically androgynous disposition.

Another Nightwatch

The gendering of the archetype of the Persian Prince was at once a metaphoric and a historical outcome. As the Persian prince reenters history, its *Innenwelt* and *Umwelt* brace for a ravaged earth under colonial duress. I began this chapter with a reference to Rembrandt's *Nightwatch* (1642), so let me now conclude with a brief recollection of the towering Iranian poet Nima Yushij's "Nightwatch," his iconic poem "Kar-e Shab-pa" ("The Work of the Nightwatch," 1946), in which the bold and choral strokes of the Dutch painter's brushes are matched and uplifted by the brave and piercing staccatos of his kindred Persian poet's soul:

> *Mah mitabad, rudest aram . . .*
>
> The moon is shining, the river is calm,
> On the branch of the field elm the pheasant
> Has let loose her tail asleep
> But in the field the nightwatch's work is not yet done—
> Blowing in his horn now
> Banging on his drum then with his stick:
> In that frightful darkness
> There is no other sound except the clamor he makes—
> Fear is foremost, everything subdued:
> A spindle is moving—that's his figure,
> A shadow is running away—is that a boar?
> Sleepy, his eyes tired,
> He whispers to himself:
> "What a nasty, long, scorching hot night:
> My wife just died,
> My two children are hungry,
> Not a handful of rice is left in our cottage,
> "How could I console them?"

> He bangs on his drum yet again,
> In an air assorted with fog,
> On it sparkled the moonshine dust.[60]

The course of colonial modernity was always global, but it was ideologically anchored and centered in Amsterdam, London, Paris, or Brussels—in the West rather than in Istanbul, Cairo, Rio de Janeiro, Delhi, or Tehran, in the Rest. As the imperiled imaginary of global European colonial encroachment began to fade in and out of our worldly consciousness, the archetypal figure of the Persian Prince was undergoing a transmutation, leaving behind all the pretenses of the ruling states in exactly the opposite direction of what Gramsci had envisioned in his "Modern Prince," finding richer, more emancipatory prospects in the iconic, allegorical, and poetic propensities that the collective consciousness of nations and their dreams and nightmares had now made collectively im/possible. If in Rembrandt's painting his *Nightwatch* gang were watching over the wealth of nations plundered and accumulated in one European capital, in Nima's prophetic poem his solitary "nightwatch" was watching over the despair of the destitution left behind. The pain and suffering of people on the receiving end of imperial hubris, colonial brutalities, and postcolonial state violence were now unfolding in ever-wider circles, as the Persian Prince found himself on far more dangerous terrains and yet fielded poetically far more promising hopes cast on perilously uncharted territories.

SEVEN

Colonial Modernity and the Metamorphosis of the Persian Prince

Nah har keh chehreh bar-afrukht delbari danad
Nah har keh Ayeneh sazad Sekandari danad...

Not just anyone who has a delightful face knows how to steal hearts—
Not just anyone who made a mirror knows how to be an Alexander—
Not just anyone who put his hat sideways and sat arrogantly on the throne
Knows how to carry a crown like a king or command the ceremony of lordship...
There are a thousand subtle points here—
Not just anyone who shaved his head knows how to be chivalrous:
With a towering figure and a handsome countenance, just about anyone
Who became the king of the righteous
Would conquer the world if he only knew how to be just.[1]

Hafez

I know it is difficult. I was for a long time the lord's double. It was torture. It is not easy to suppress yourself to become another. Often I wanted to be myself and free. But now I think this was selfish of me. The shadow of a man can never desert that man. I was my brother's shadow. Now that I have lost him, it is as though I am nothing.... The shadow of a man can never stand up and walk on its own.

Takeda Nobukaado, in Akira Kurosawa's
Kagemusha (Shadow Warrior), 1980

IN 1969 A BIZARRE BOOK was published in Tehran, with a strange title, and an even more outlandish name for its author. *Rostam al-Tawarikh* (The Rostam of histories) is the title of the book, and Rostam al-Hokama ("the Rostam of Philosophers") the name of its author.[2] Rostam is the main hero of the Persian epic *Shahnameh*, so colloquially it means the most powerful of all things; therefore, *Rostam al-Tawarikh* means "the champion of all histories," and its author "the most powerful of all philosophers." When we begin to read the book, the author tells us his actual name is Mohammad Hashem Asef Mousavi Hosseini but that his father gave him the title of "Rostam al-Hokama" when encouraging him to write a book on his contemporary history. As for the subject of the book, it is a colloquial take on the history of the later Safavid era through the Afsharid and Zand periods all the way to the early Qajar—so it covers roughly the entirety of the eighteenth century, mapping out the trajectory of four dynasties, one after the other. This very inter-dynastic historiography was among the oddities of the book. Usually, a court historian wrote the history of that dynasty or of the whole world leading up to that dynasty, but not a history of multiple dynasties and the interstices of the period between them.

Soon a storm of controversy began to swirl around this book. Who was this author and what was he writing about? Some scholars initially suspected that this was all a hoax and the author was actually a "Babi" troublemaker, while other scholars began to dig deeper and discovered that there are only two manuscripts of this book extant, one in Germany and the other in Iran. The Babi suspicion, leveled mostly by learned Shiʿi scholars, refers to the massive revolutionary movement of the mid-nineteenth century led by Ali Mohamad Bab (1819–1850). The curiosity and the suspicion continued until one particularly committed and curious scholar, Jalil Nozari, wrote a whole book on Rostam al-Hokama and his *Rostam al-Tawarikh* and concluded that this was in fact a pseudonym for Reza Qoli Khan Hedayat (1800–1871), a renowned Qajar-period writer, poet, and tutor at the royal court.[3] Other scholars with strong anti-Babi sentiments continued to insist that the author was a Babi propagandist in disguise wreaking havoc on the sacred history of the Shiʿi faith and Persian historiography. Being called a "Babi" among devout Shiʿi scholars was like being labeled a "Commie" by Senator Joseph McCarthy in the 1950s, a sign of suspicion and distrust.

These two opposing views on *Rostam al-Tawarikh* and its author continued apace and effectively canceled each other out. The major scholar, a cleric named Rasul Jaʿfarian, insisting Rostam la-Hokama was a Babi ideologue, refused to yield that he might in fact be Reza Qoli Khan Hedayat; and Jalil Nozari, the scholar who believed it was Hedayat, refused to yield that he might be a Babi. Soon secular modernists jumped on the bandwagon and proposed that *Rostam al-Tawarikh* was in fact a pioneering text championing European modernity (of which, in their deeply colonized minds, they had a rosy and sanguine interpretation) and as such an unappreciated masterpiece of "Iranian modernity."[4]

All these controversies finally came to an end with a brilliant essay by a prominent scholar, Seyyed Ali Al-e Davood, who, in a major piece on the subject, proved chapter and verse that Rostam al-Hokama is indeed a historical figure, neither a pseudonym for Reza Qoli Khan Hedayat nor a Babi propagandist but a pioneering anticolonial thinker. "We must recognize Rostam al-Hokama among the first writers who had come to realize the terrible consequences of colonialism, and the necessity of fighting against colonizing countries."[5] This impeccable piece of scholarship set all these wayward speculations aside and went deeply and widely through the texts and manuscripts' catalogs and concluded Rostam al-Hokama was a real person, Mohammad Hashem Asef Mousavi Hosseini (as in fact he asserts in his book); that he was the author of more than sixty treatises, among them *Rostam al-Tawarikh*, which he wrote between 1779 and 1794; and that he is neither a Babi, nor a secular modernist of the northern California vintage, nor indeed a pseudonym for Reza Qoli Khan Hedayat, nor anyone else for that matter.

The Birth of the Author

When we take a few steps back from this controversy before it was resolved by one precise scholarly intervention, we see how two opposing factions have dragged the author and his text to two opposing camps, while a third has opted for a conspiracy theory of a hidden author behind the text. Shi'i historians dismiss the author as a purposefully deceitful Babi propagandist, while secular Europhiliac modernists celebrate him as a harbinger of their idea of political liberation; all the while, a conspiracy theorist begins to speculate that the author was an entirely different person. So while the Shi'a historians concentrate on the author and seek to discredit him, their secular nemeses abuse the text to have it anticipate their own secular convictions. What had remained by the wayside, demanding closer attention, was the flamboyant text itself screaming for a different reading than those afforded it. There was an author, his name was Mohammad Hashem Asef Mousavi Hosseini, his pen name was Rostam al-Hokama, and he had written a book, *Rostam al-Tawarikh*. That much was certain.

But what exactly is this *Rostam al-Tawarikh*? What kind of text is it? Is it history, a story, fact, or fiction, and how are we to read it? These scholars were all taking the text too seriously but in a wrong way. The zealot Shi'is thought it was insulting their dogmatism, secularists thought it promised their liberation, while conspiracy theorists were after the goose chase of an entirely different author. What remained behind and before all of them was the astonishing text itself, that was demanding to be read as it was written, as a literary event, a parody, a lampoon in the same genre as in Zakani's *Akhlaq al-Ashraf* (*Ethics of the Nobles*) back in the fourteenth century. But even beyond Ubayd Zakani's specific case, we have the genre of *Hazl* (lampoon), in which we have such master practitioners like Sa'di, Suzani Samarqandi, and later Iraj Mirza. *Rostam al-Tawarikh* overrides serious prose by mimicking it, for everything in this text, including its millenarianism that annoys the Shi'i scholars and its presumably early modernism that delights secular modernists, is an act of literary parody, of lampooning the received conventions of writing serious history. One must read it in the genre that extended from Zakani's satire in the fourteenth century to Ali Akbar or Iraj Mirza Dehkhoda in the twentieth century. To be sure, in Zayn al-Din Mahmud Abd al-Jalil Vasefi's *Badai' al-Waqai'*, an early sixteenth-century memoir and historical account, we do have an earlier example at the height of the Timurid period with similar nonconventional prose that might be read as a predecessor of *Rostam al-Tawarikh* in their similar bold prose, with which they mimic the dominant historiography of their times to dismantle their claims to truth. So *Rostam al-Tawarikh* is not without literary and poetic precedent. What is, for our purpose here, unique about the text is precisely its anticolonial disposition, its bold and direct critique of European colonial designs on the Iranian and Muslim world.

Rostam al-Hokama's prose is deadpan, his idiomaticity poker faced, as it were, into which we are lured even though we do not quite know what it is we are reading. The author is verbose, mimicking the prose of lofty histories of yore, but mixing it with satirical twists, writing obscenities with a formal prose, deploying turns of phrase that doubt the very thing the author is writing. We think we are reading something serious, but the prose becomes frivolous, so we think we are reading something playful, then the prose becomes macabre. We assume we are reading a book of history—after all, it is "the Rostam of all histories"—but there is a sardonic overtone to the prose that radically compromises that very assumption. A good fifty pages into the book, we learn that the author began writing the book in 1779, finished his first draft in 1784, and revised it in 1794. The book has the aura of a memoir, an autobiography. Rostam al-Hokama tells us that this book is actually his father's thoughts and he is being an amanuensis for his father, who wants to share crucial facts from late Safavid through the Afsharids, the Zandis, and to the early Qajars. But even his father is only interpreting the dreams he has seen for his son and then instructs him:

> Oh, you fortunate son, write down these stories you hear from me with utmost clarity and brevity, with such sweet phrasings that everyone, educated or otherwise, could easily comprehend. Do not abandon the dictum of "the best discourse is the briefest and most convincing," and beware, never use difficult and complicated words that ordinary people could not understand, for it will confuse people and they will have to resort to dictionaries and encyclopedias to understand you and these books are very rare ... and call this book Rostam al-Tawarikh.[6]

So the father dreams, the father interprets, the father dictates, and the author writes. But who exactly is this father? Rostam la-Hokama introduces his father to his readers as Amir Hasan Khosh Hekayat ("Amir Hasan, the sweet storyteller").[7] This miasmatic poise of the authorial voice is cast upon the entirety of his prose. We are in the presence of a playful and confident author writing sarcastically about the crucial issues of his time. To come to terms with this narrative ploy, we need to open up the frame of our references and think in broader comparative literary terms. In Arabic and Persian contexts proper, the whole genre of *Hajv* (burlesque), perhaps best represented in the poetry of Suzani Samarqandi, with samples throughout the works of all major poets, is the foregrounding of this prose.[8] But more specifically, *Rostam al-Tawarikh* is to Persian and Islamic historiography what Ubayd Zakani's *Akhlaq al-Ashraf* is to Persian mirrors for princes—or, more broadly, even to what Cervantes's *Don Quixote* is to chivalric romance and Swift's *Gulliver's Travels* is to the utopian novel. They all infiltrate their genre and turn it upside down and make it self-conscious, exposing their manufactured conventions and clichés. The only exception is that *Rostam al-Ta Tawarikh* is mocking fact, not fiction; history, not novels. Rostam al-Hokama parodies and dismantles the genre of Persian historiography the same way Cervantes dismantles the genre of romance and Swift dismantles utopian novels.[9] In Rostam al-Hokama's hand, the romance of history becomes burlesque and its utopian delusions frightfully dystopic. A shrewd, playful, wise, and worldly author is being born on the pages of *Rostam al-Tawarikh*.

The key question is what exactly such subversive prose does to the key protagonist or the narrator of the prose. In a major essay, "Parody, Satire and Sympathy in *Don Quixote* and *Gulliver's Travels*" (2002), David Fishelov has detailed his assessment of how in two masterpieces of European literature the dismantling of the genre is coterminous with generating sympathy for their protagonists.[10]

> This dual attitude—mocking certain texts or literary conventions and sympathizing with a naive character—may be argued to mark some of the greatest parodies. In fact, one of the literary masterpieces of all time—Cervantes' *Don Quixote*—is based precisely on this dual principle: the conventions of the chivalric romance are exposed, but our hearts ache for Don Quixote. In *Don Quixote*, the novel, the connection between a critical attitude towards the conventions of a literary genre and sympathy towards the deluded human being is very intimate.[11]

The same is true with *Rostam al-Tawarikh*, in which the archaic terms of the genre of Persian historiography are staged to be dismantled, but instead of sympathizing with the protagonist we identify with the author, who effectively emerges as "the protagonist" of his own text, so that the corresponding feeling is not sympathy but identification. His authorial voice is the most pronounced dramatis persona he creates. The same is true with *Gulliver's Travels* as Fishelov reads it:

> Whereas Swift's work is first and foremost a satire, criticizing certain social norms and human modes of behavior, he also sends his critical arrows towards a specific literary and philosophical tradition, that of utopias.... To begin with, the *Travels* share a narrative structure with some exemplary utopias, especially [Thomas] More's *Utopia*. In both works we meet a traveler—Raphael in More, Gulliver in Swift—leaving Europe, arriving in an unknown country in a remote part of the earth.[12]

The same is the case with *Rostam al-Tawarikh*, which also shares similar narrative structures with classical Persian historiography, and as a result we find ourselves in the presence of a different kind of historian: Rostam al-Hokama has become the new common person, with the vantage point that of the common reader. There is a publicity to the domain of his readership that is palpably new. He is no longer writing solely for the courtiers or for the distant and abstract posterity but for his own present company. What the reversal of the genre therefore does to the protagonist/author/narrator is an open-ended realism. As Fishelov puts it:

> Both Cervantes and Swift invented a protagonist enchanted by an imaginary, fictive, literary world and this enchantment leads the character

to depart from normality. Don Quixote became a demented individual who actually saw giants in windmills. Gulliver evolved into a misanthrope, repelled by his own wife and children, enjoying conversing with horses.[13]

The same is with the author of *Rostam-Tawarikh*. His provocative diction becomes the open-ended voice of a new authorial persona in which the living history breathes—with wit, wisdom, sarcasm, feigned formalism, and cynic mockery of an entirely new vintage. This is the birth of the author of a living history, of the vanishing presence, and the very uncertainty, the fragility of his prose, concealed under a simulated narrative authenticity, announcing the birth of a new historical person in whose voice the Persian Prince has reentered a living history. Rostam al-Hokama is the voice of the new Persian Prince. The major twist with Rostam al-Hokama, just like with Cervantes and Swift, is the birth of the historical author fully present in his prose through a creative act of having his text defy convention of formal and cliché effacement of the author. Conventionally, the author of Persian and Arabic texts, with few and notable exceptions, like Ayn al-Qudat (1098–1131) in his *Shakwa' al-Gharib (Apologia)*, for example, efface themselves out of a false humility, referring to themselves as *Raqem-e in Sotur* ("the writer of these lines"), *In Aqal* ("this humble self"), or *In Haqir* ("this lowly being"), among others. Exactly the opposite happens in *Rostam al-Tawarikh*, where the author consistently refers to himself with flamboyant and effusive titles. What the scholars attending to this text could not handle was the fact that an author had an authorial audacity, and by virtue of that bold authorial voice, was dismantling the false humility of the classical authorship. In *Rostam al-Tawarikh* the historian has become historical. But—and there is the rub—precisely by virtue of that authorial voice, the normative diction of the author had become self- and other-conscious. That self-consciousness is precisely the venue from which the Persian Prince resurrects into the colonial modernity of his new environment.

Missing the parodic disposition of the prose, a leading historian of the Qajar period takes Rostam al-Hokama's critique of the British colonialism as an example of "Anglophobia."[14] But the case of Rostam al-Hokama is neither Anglophobia nor Anglophilia. It is the first fully charged critic of British, and by extension European, colonial adventures in Iran and its surrounding areas. His critique of colonialism is not a sign of psychological malady—unreasonable phobia or obsequious admiration. It is among the earliest texts of the critique of militant colonialism descending upon the non-European world. It should not be psychopathologized. Such genealogies of the rooted prose critical of European colonialism need a renewed reading to prevent them from being abused in pathologies of love and hate for the British or the Europeans in general. We are in the context of a much larger global frame of reference extending from India to Iran to the Ottoman territories, deeply into other parts of Asia, Africa, and Latin America, each of whose regions have been seriously theorized into their colonial experiences, anticolonial uprisings, postcolonial predicaments, and above all, decolonial epistemics. This is yet to happen in the mostly positivist and pedantic Qajar historiography.

The birth of a self-conscious author, the power and panache of a critical thinker bursting into the formal structure of historiography, actively turns capitalized "History" into multivariant stories and stages of the literary disposition of all acts of historiography, just as Hayden White had theorized in his seminal text, *Metahistory* (1973).[15] All of these are indices, along with the textual evidence of the rebirth of the new historical person into and through which the archetypal figure of the Persian Prince finds a renewed subjectivity with which to reenter world history. The paradox of colonial modernity had inaugurated a new episteme whereby exposure and subversion of the formal structure of historiography had begun working via overstaging its literary disposition. There is no new Persian Prince without a new Persian person, and the text of *Rostam al-Tawarikh* and its flamboyant author are among the first indices that the new Persian person is being reimagined, reconstituted, resubjected, into which the ideal-type of the Persian Prince will now healthily resurrect.

Resurrection of the Persian Prince on New Fertile Grounds

The case of Rostam al-Hokama's *Rostam al-Tawarikh*, with its provocative prose and thematic roots in earlier sources, as well as its wider domains of parody and satire around the world, marks the emergence of the living author as the chronicler of a new time and place where the Persian Prince finds a renewed significance in contemporary history. Without such vessels of formative subjectivity for the Persian Prince to rise as the modus operandi of political consciousness, the archetypal figure would not have the channels of his rebirth and resurrection. The dominant themes of *Rostam al-Tawarikh* implicate the rising colonial presence of falling empires: of successive dynasties from the Safavids to the Afsharids, the Zandis, and the emerging Qajars, of the Mughals falling to the British, anticipating the Qajars' subjugations to the French, the British, and the Russians' imperial designs, and the Ottomans to the combined forces of British and French colonial encroachment. The resurrection of the new Persian Prince could only be predicated on the metamorphosis of the classical archetype from its institutional courtly habitat back to its worldly origins. The Persian Prince is here reminded of his prophetic voice, of his poetic disposition, and through all that is drawn back to his rebellious character. There is also an ancient eschatological force at work here where the messianic figure of Saoshyant (the Savior) in Zoroastrian traditions begins to be actively remembered, though passively subsumed until the emergence of a towering Persian poet of the twentieth century, Mehdi Akhavan-e Sales (1929–1990).[16] The messianic figure of the Savior at this particular point in history finds its most potent force in the Babi movement (1844–1852). The ghostly figure of the Persian Prince is hovering over the vast vicissitude of the Persianate world from India to Iran to the Ottoman territories to reveal itself.

Here we are at the crucial moment of the transformation of the imperial archetype into the emerging political consequences of European colonialism and the active formation of national (against dynastic) sovereignty.[17] The birth of postcolonial nations in the Muslim world had by now entered its transhistorical phase, when the very idea of *sovereignty* was being recast from the figure of the monarch, the sultan, the caliph, the shah to the domain of the public weal, where final authority and legitimacy now dwelled. Muslim empires were collapsing, nations were rising, and the fragmented territorialities of these nations in confrontation with European colonial powers were actively redefining the terms of their sovereignty. Across major capitals of the Muslim world, from India through Iran deep into Central Asia and the Ottoman Empire, vast and pervasive social movements began to radically alter the moral and normative disposition of Muslim societies and the deeply entrenched organs of transnational public spheres and their contingent civil societies and communities. The simplification of Persian prose, the eventual introduction of the printing machine, the effervescence of newspapers, and a voluminous body of translations, travelogues from around the world, and rebellious prose and poetry were actively defining the terms of these transnational para/public spheres. The transhistorical figure of the Persian Prince was being "baptized" by fire.

"The People" were now the persona of "the Prince." Instead of court poets of yore praising the fictitious virtues of the monarch, their counterpart poets of these times were singing the praises and effectively constituting the very existence of the People. These rebellious, confident, and towering poets first became the voice and the vista, and eventually the very truth of those People. Poets were the singing troubadours, the happy harbingers of the coming melodies of the political truth that would inform the emerging history. The all-too-crucial conceptualization of *national sovereignty* takes place on these transnational public spheres, as they dismantled the authority of the royal court and discredited any organized political party that could lay false claim to it, thus paving the way for a new poetic voice evident in the rising prophetic echoes of the modernist Persian (and Persianate) poets—from India to Central Asia and the Caucuses to Iran to the Ottoman territories. By now the dyadic disposition of the Persian Prince had inhabited the body and soul of the vision and voice of the rebellious Persian poet confronting the misplaced binaries of nations and their ruling states.[18] As the machinery of the ruling states, as mere monopolies of violence, went in one direction, the open-ended sovereignty of nations went in exactly the opposite direction. The Persian Prince had found a happy and healthy habitat with these nations, furthest removed from the palaces of kings, sultans, and their courtiers.

Conditions were now ripe for the rebirth of the Persian Prince, the transfiguration of the figure of the prince into the public and parapublic spheres upon which the prophetic voices of immemorial days rise and resurrect the defiant melodies of the poet evident in the birth of the author for precisely the opposite reasons stated by Roland Barthes in his famous essay "The Death of the Author" (1967). At this and subsequent periods we witness the birth, not the death, of the postcolonial person, author, thinker, fighter, rebel, poet. European colonialism and its regime of knowledge and domination were being cast like a violent and pervasive net over the entirety of the globe. This is the crucial moment of the foregrounding for a future project of decoloniality. It is here that we realize the European project of capitalist modernity was a mixed blessing for Europe itself and an epistemic impossibility for the rest of the world it violently silenced and colonized. Halfway across the world, generations later, Michel-Rolph Trouillot's *Silencing the Past: Power and the Production of History* (1995) is a testimony to this historic fact.[19]

The sustained and prolonged European colonial conquest and control of the Muslim world in India, Iran, and the Ottoman territories injected a major epistemic rupture in the variegated history of Muslim and Persian political cultures and material civilizations. The onslaught of this colonial modernity for much of the postcolonial world has spelled out a systemic breakdown of civic and political lives. Far beyond the position of any shift from *romance* to *tragedy* (as David Scott proposes) in our reading of coloniality is the necessity of an even more radical epistemic shift from the postcolonial *state* toward the anticolonial *nation* and, ultimately, to the condition of decoloniality as the site of our critical thinking. That critique of coloniality and the condition of decoloniality are not exhausted by the misbegotten postcolonial state, for the nations over which they lay a false claim are deeply rooted in the effervescence and ambivalence of the transnational para/public sphere upon which these nations originally emerged. By definition, postcolonial nations are formed long before a state emerges to lay any false claim to them. States are incidental to nations, and nations are integral to the formation of the public sphere upon which they are ipso facto founded. The thematic link among the postcolonial state, the anticolonial nation, and the decoloniality of the epistemic foregrounding of a renewed reading of the Persian Prince forces open Gramsci's idea of the Modern Prince to larger and more radical possibilities.

These transnational para/public spheres upon which nations were being formed are precisely the locations where the figure of the Persian Prince undergoes its historic transfiguration, where the entire edifice of sovereignty is relocated from the figure of the person of the Persian Prince onto the figurative authority of the nation, of the people, or, more precisely, of the public weal. Social, political, and intellectual movements of the nineteenth century across the Muslim world are the *locus classicus* of this sustained course of transfiguration, where revolutionary mobilizations of one sort or another become the conduit of constituting the sovereignty of the nation—and through it the heroic figures that now personify its will. The Babi movement of the mid-nineteenth century in Iran, for example, was the most serious revolutionary challenge to the Qajar dynasty, effectively discrediting and dismantling the figure of the Qajar monarch and its historic claims on the Persian Prince. The widespread consequences of that uprising, plus the social upheavals generated by a succession of commercial concessions the ruling elite gave to the European (British in particular) colonial powers, ultimately led to the Constitutional Revolution of 1906–1911. The net result of these historic events was the organic growth and exponential expansion of the public sphere upon which the very idea of the nation was now being articulated. The sound of the bullet that Mirza Reza Kermani fired to assassinate the Qajar monarch Naser al-Din Shah in 1896 echoed and reverberated as the resounding bell of the final demise of the Persian Prince as symbolically gathered in the person of the shah. At that very moment, the arrested, incarcerated, tortured, and killed body of the shah's assassin, Mirza Reza Kermani, was the fertile premise upon which the idea of the nation as the sole substance of legitimate sovereignty was being formed. From that premise, the heroic figure of national heroes begins to gather the historic memories of the Persian Prince away from the royal court and place it back in the emerging postcolonial nation.

We are here at the presence of the birth of colonial consciousness, of the anticolonial rise of national sovereignty and the postcolonial predicates of a future project of decoloniality as an epistemic shift in rethinking the politics of emancipation. The globalized trauma of European colonialism, with its brutal racial undertones and systematic genocide in Asia and Africa, was shaking the foundations of non-European political cultures around the globe. Such reactionary reactions included the rise of nativism, Islamism, and triumphalism. But there were far more emancipatory and open-ended prospects. Under the overwhelming duress of this political and epistemic pressure, such movements were the defining moments of the active transformation of the monadic disposition of the Persian Prince as a nucleus of political organism into its own innate dyadic proclivities—when its poetics overwhelmed and redefined its politics. The birth of *nations* in the Muslim world had by now entered its transhistorical phase, when the very idea of sovereignty was being recast from the figure of the monarch, sultan, caliph, shah, and others to the opening horizons of the public weal for which the poet was the celebrated troubadour. The emerging postcolonial states were parasitical to these far more rooted developments. Muslim empires were collapsing, postcolonial nations were rising, and the fragmented territorialities of these nations in confrontation with European colonial powers were actively redefining the terms of their sovereignty. In his pioneering work *The Nation and Its Fragments: Colonial and Postcolonial Histories* (1993), Partha Chatterjee has argued how the political nationalism of state-building differs from anticolonial nationalism, effectively constituting the domain of sovereignty even before the colonial powers lower their flags and set off for their European capitals. Across major capitals of the colonized world, from India through Central Asia and Iran and deep into the Ottoman Empire, vast and pervasive social movements began to radically alter the disposition of Muslim societies and the deeply entrenched organs of transnational public spheres and their contingent civic societies. The Persian Prince was being metamorphosed and resurrected in a healthy and robust habitat.

The catalytic presence of the colonial factor caused and remained coterminous with the falling Muslim empires—as the Mughals fell to the British; the

Qajars to the combined forces and rivalries among the Russians, the French, and the British; and the Ottomans to the selfsame European imperial forces. By this point the archetype of the Persian Prince had completely lost its classical wherewithal as the world around the archetype was fast falling apart. The idea had to adapt. "Not just anyone who put his hat sideways and sat arrogantly on the throne," as the glorious Hafez had diagnosed in a powerful ghazal generations earlier, "knows how to carry a crown like a king or command the ceremony of lordship." This was back in the fourteenth century, when the internal paradoxes of the Persian Prince were widely detectable. By the nineteenth century those internal dynamics had split open under colonial duress. Generations earlier, the master lyricist had detected the intermediacies of power and ceremonies of authority. Halfway around the globe, and generations later, master Japanese filmmaker Akira Kurosawa's epic *Kagemusha* (1980) would also stage how an emperor lookalike who appeared exactly like the Japanese warlord Takeda Shingen was just a common thief, and yet King Lear, in yet another context, even after his fall from power, still had in his "countenance" that which his loyal sentinel Kent called "master." The Persian Prince too was ready and roaming for a whole new sojourn in its long and lasting history.

Revolutions and Reforms

The metamorphic Persian Prince had much larger historical domains though which to unfold and realize itself. Through its metamorphosis under colonial duress, the archetype of the Persian Prince was becoming metaphoric, metonymic, allegorical unto itself. A constellation of revolutionary uprisings defined the mid-nineteenth-century Persianate and Muslim worlds: the Indian Rebellion of 1857 against the British, the Babi movement of 1844–1852 against the ruling Qajars and their clerical supporters, plus a succession of rebellions in the Ottoman Empire of the same period.[20] The anticolonial sentiments of the period best evident in the Indian Rebellion of 1857 marked a crucial turning point in popular uprising against British and other European colonialism. The revolt began as a mutiny of sepoys of the East India Company and quickly spread to other places. The brutality with which the British quelled the uprising reverberated throughout their empire. The Mahdi movement in Sudan and Omar Mukhtar uprising in Libya are among other examples of such anticolonial mobilizations that whether triumphant or crushed had the catalytic effect of exponentially expanding the social base, economic foregrounding, and political consequences of the emerging nations, in such a way that no postcolonial state could ever lay a conclusive claim on them.

The anticolonial uprisings in India, the millenarian movement in Iran, and the revolutionary uprisings in the Ottoman territories all come together to define the fusion of two political facts, foreign and familiar despotism, and one enduring consequence: the rebirth of the archetypal monad of the Persian Prince in a dyadic disputation upon the battlefields of its contemporary history, in which the emerging ruling states parted ways with their respective nations, one devoid of enduring legitimacy, the other liberated into open-ended self-sovereignty. The colonial concoction of "the nation-state" never took root where the enduring legacies of the prototype of the Persian Prince posited an entirely different political trajectory. This triangulation of three entirely unrelated uprisings in India, Iran, and the Ottoman Empire dovetailed into an orchestration of emancipatory politics from multiple fronts. The Indian Rebellion of 1857 targeted European colonialism, the Babi movement targeted domestic tyranny and clerical corruption, and the Ottoman uprisings linked the European continent to the larger Muslim world. Meanwhile, the introduction of the printing machine, the systematic simplification of Persian and Arabic prose, the historic roots of Ottoman Turkish in both Persian and Arabic, widespread interest in the genre of travelogues, expansive horizons of translations, and the rise of the modernist Persian poetry were chief among the liberating discourses of this transhistorical moment where and when revolutionary uprisings met the rise of the new discourses.

Each one of these three sites of resurrections in India, Iran, and the Ottoman Empire against domestic tyranny and European colonial encroachments had its particular power and urgency. But right in the middle of them all, the Babi movement in Iran was of particular significance for a very historic reason. The iconoclastic presence of one singularly revolutionary woman, Tahereh Qorrat al-Ayn (circa 1814–1852), at the heart of the Babi movement for the first time genders the resurrected figure of the Persian Prince and restores its iconic nonbinary androgynous disposition—which goes back all the way to Mashya and Mashyana, the "Adam and Eve" of Persian mythology, who were born to a plant that grew out of the seeds of the primeval beast Gayomart, who was neither female nor male. Within that mythic context, in the millenarian Babi movement, Tahereh Qorrat-Ayn appears as the messianic figure of Saoshyant (savior) when the ancient archetype of the Persian Prince resurrects as a revolutionary woman. The Babi movement was founded by Ali Mohammad Bab (1819–1850), and it had a number of other revolutionary leaders, but the towering figure of

Tahereh Qorrat al-Ayn outshines them all. In my book *Shi'ism: A Religion of Protest* (2011), I discuss how she gendered the emerging public sphere.[21] But from the premise of that very gendered public sphere, Tahereh Qorrat-Ayn was walking into the metamorphic archetype of the Persian Prince and thus degendering and regendering it.

All, indeed, was not revolution and rebellion in the course of the last three Muslim empires in this twilight era of resurrection and metamorphosis for the Persian Prince. The widespread Tanzimat (1839–1876) in the Ottoman Empire eventually led to the Nahda in the Arab world and coincided with the pervasive court-initiated reforms of the Qajar period, as well as with the equally crucial but unintended consequences of the British educational reforms in India, as perhaps best evident in the education clause of the Charter Act of 1813. Under this clause, the British East India Company had to allocate resources to propagate both English literature and Christian missionaries—to teach the Indians how to gently and politely turn the other cheek while quoting Chaucer and Shakespeare, never mind the company's plundering of their homeland.

While no doubt European colonial forces had a major role in the formation of transnational public spheres in Asia, Africa, and Latin America, far more important were the developments in parapublic domains domestic to these societies. The Tanzimat in the Ottoman Empire (1839–1876), for example, or their counterparts in court-initiated reforms in the Qajar dynasty, were meant as carefully orchestrated state-sponsored modernization projects, but they effectively expanded the institutional foregrounding of a variedly enabling public domain far beyond their intended consequences. Whereas the ruling Ottoman state, as did the Qajar reforms, intended these Tanzimat as a consolidation of Ottomanism for the benefit of the ruling elite, they effectively initiated the formation, expansion, and eventual structural transformation (Habermas) of the bourgeois public sphere into neighboring Persianate domains. While the autonomy of various ethnic and racialized communities was being erased, a renewed sense of citizenship beyond the wishes or control of the state apparatus and the ruling elites was in the making. The more layered, textured, and organic became these transnational para/public spheres, the flatter, more arcane, more formalistic and devoid of meaning, and thus illegitimate appeared the figures of the ruling monarchs and their royal courts. By now the figurative posture of the Persian Prince had undergone a historic metamorphosis. "The People" and the postcolonial "person" were now "the Prince," as these poets had in turn become the troubadours of their truth.

An equally if not more important development than the Ottoman Empire's mid-nineteenth-century Tanzimat was the rise of Al-Nahda, a cultural and intellectual "awakening" that began in Egypt in the late nineteenth and early twentieth centuries but eventually spread to the rest of the Arab world. The impetus for Al-Nahda might be traced back to the critical responses to Napoleon's invasion and occupation of Egypt in 1798, which then dovetailed with the Tanzimat in the larger Ottoman territories. The combined effect of the Tanzimat and Al-Nahda was an exponential reconceptualization of the entire Arab and Muslim world in terms at once rebellious to European colonial conquests and domestic to democratic aspirations evident in the transnational public sphere that now thoroughly embraced and recast the Muslim world.

During the same period, the widespread reforms associated with two seminal Qajar ministers, Amir Kabir (1807–1852) and Mirza Hossein Khan Moshir al-Dowleh Sepahsalar (1828–1881), defined the course of numerous serious educational and administrative initiatives that had an enduring effect on the course of the Qajar dynasty before the dawn of the Constitutional Revolution of 1906–1911. There were intended and unintended consequences to these reforms: as the domain of public education expanded, so did political consciousness, emancipatory politics, ideas of representative democracy, and reformist and revolutionary potential outside the control of the royal court. The establishment of Dar ul-Fonun college in Iran in 1851, followed by the pioneering work of Haji-Mirza Hassan Roshdieh (1851–1944) in reforming outdated pedagogies, were definitive to the expansion of the public and parapublic spheres, forming and enabling a budding moral imagination in which no retrograde monarch could sit comfortably on any comfortable throne.

Revolutionary uprisings and prevalent reforms in the last three Muslim empires were coterminous with the colonial conquest of their territories and resources, when the prophetic voice and rebellious disposition of the Persian Prince finds new dramatis personae to form, inform, invoke, and inspire. While the reforms expanded the domain of the public sphere and crafted the very idea of citizenship, the revolutionary uprisings offered towering figures like Tahereh Qorrat al-Ayn to instigate and trigger emancipatory political visions to those public spheres. Poets ranging from Muhammad Iqbal (1877–1938), in the Indian subcontinent, to Aref Qazvini (1882–1934), in Iran, to Nazım Hikmet (1902–1963), in Turkey were the conduits of these revolutionary and pathbreaking sentiments. Contrary to Gramsci's Prince, the "New Persian Prince" was no political party. It had come back as the fertile ground of a public sphere where, like

Mother Earth, she could nourish and raise an entire generation of hope. The budding flowers of that earth could sing revolutionary songs in Persian, Urdu, or Turkish, but in all these and any other poetries was already ringing the resounding voice of the one and only Tahereh Qorrat al-Ayn.

The Great Reversal

How were these critical thinkers, poets, public intellectuals, revolutionaries, reformers, and the public they were crafting and informing aware of, conscious of, and communicative with one another? Definitive to the emergence, expansion, and widespread structural transformation of the transnational public sphere upon which these postcolonial nations and their polities were being defined was the appearance of a robust mass media. Predicated on the introduction of the printing machine in the early nineteenth century in Iran—even sooner in the Ottoman territories—and on the vocal demand for public education, the subsequent advent of mass media was the prime example of how these transnational public spheres were eventually formed and put to increasingly widespread use. Many of the earliest periodicals were called *Ruznamehs* (dailies), and a more politically charged supplement to them emerged as *Shabnamehs* (nightlies). While Ruznamehs were bold, openly critical, and initially published from extraterritorial locations in European capitals, Istanbul, Central Asia, Egypt, or India, Shabnamehs were underground and published domestically. Such now-legendary periodicals as *Akhtar* were published in Istanbul, *Qanun* in London, *Habl al-Matin* in Calcutta, *Sorayya* and *Parvaresh* in Cairo.[22] All these periodicals were published in simplified prose, on inexpensive papers, and widely circulated through the emerging postal system or traveling merchants, from their place of publication to far-reaching Persian-speaking domains from the Ottoman Empire through Iran and Central Asia to India.

These and many other similar periodicals offered the public (open) and parapublic (underground) spheres for the cultivation of an informed and layered transformation of the Persian Prince, from the monadic to the dyadic, from the figural to the figurative, from the person of the monarch to the persona of the rebel/poet. To be sure, it was not just the press and charged political prose but also a creative literature, a lyrical poetry, a nascent drama, and a robust travel literature that came together to enable and enrich these public spheres. The figure of the Persian Prince thus eventually metamorphosed into the figurative power of the people, the nation, the public weal to author sovereignty and offer or withhold legitimacy. The battle was decisive and the defeat of the Persianate empires final, but the figure of the Persian Prince was destined to have a resurrected public life. The relationship between two seminal periodicals of this period, *Molla Nasraddin*, published in Azeri in Azerbaijan, and *Sur-e Esrafil*, published in Persian in Tehran, is a key example of how the dialectic of Azeri-Persian marked a crucial configuration of the decidedly transnational public sphere upon which the metamorphosis of the figure of the Persian Prince into a rebel/poet took place and eventually surfaced. Founded by Mirza Jahangir Khan (1870–1908), *Sur-e Esrafil* was published between 1907 and 1909—becoming a major outlet of revolutionary thinking during the Iranian Constitutional period. Mirza Jahangir Khan was arrested and executed in 1911, and his comrade Ali Akbar Dehkhoda (1879–1956) resumed the publication of the journal from Switzerland for another three issues. But for our purposes here, the significance of the relationship between Mirza Jahangir Khan (a fallen hero) and Ali Akbar Dehkhoda (his mourning comrade) is even more significant.

Powerful evidence of the resurrection of the figure of the Persian Prince as a rebel/poet is the legendary poem "Yad Ar, Zeh Shamʿ-e Mordeh Yad Ar!" (1909), which literally brings together the fallen revolutionary and his mourning poet comrade. The refrain of this now-iconic poem is "Remember, remember that extinguished candle!" The poem was published in the last issue of *Sur-e Esrafil* from Switzerland and is dated Monday, 15 Safar 1327/March 8, 1909. This is the first stanza:

> *Ey Morgh-e Sahar cho in shab-e tar* . . .
>
> Oh Morning Bird, once this dark night
> Let go of its shady deeds—
> And from the delightful melodies of the morning
> Heads are cleared of nightly slumber—
> And as the beloved sporting a dark turban
> Has let loose her golden locks—
> The Almighty Light is fully visible
> And the Dark Iblis enchained—
> Remember, remember that extinguished candle![23]

From this point forward, the poem works as a paradox between the beauty and glory of the nature upon which the morning bird sings and the poet's recollection of his fallen friend. Scholars of this period like Yahya Aryanpour believe the poem was formally influenced by both Turkish and French poetry of the period—for Dehkhoda had full command of the Turkish scene and was in Yverdon-les-Bains, in the French speaking part of Switzerland, when composing it. The poem is also celebrated as one of the earliest occasions of emerging modernism in Persian poetry. But something else, something more archaic, is happening in the poem. In the first stanza Dehkhoda invokes Zoroastrian and Mazdaian metaphors of Yazdan and Ahriman, in the second he uses nature, in the third he turns to biblical references to Joseph in prison as well as to the Israelites leaving Egypt, and in the final stanza he turns to archaic metaphors of Arabian antiquities and the figure of Shaddad, believed to be the king of the lost Arabian city of Iram of the Pillars. In short, Dehkhoda is using varied ancient metaphors, particularly Zoroastrian, biblical Hebrew, and Arabian mythology, to place the murder of a contemporary fallen friend early in the twentieth century at the epicenter of a renewed cosmogony of mythic proportions.

What is the result? In this iconic poem, a fallen revolutionary and a mourning poet comrade have literally come together to form the dyad of a poet/rebel. Mirza Jahangir Khan had appeared in Dehkhoda's dream, as the poet tells us, meaning the dyadic personae of the rebel/poet have physically united, the Persian Prince finally splitting into the two contingent components of its archaic character. This will be repeated many times by other poets remembering and mourning revolutionary comrades, such as in the case of Aba'i (1921–1946), a young Turkman teacher and political activist who was murdered by Reza Shah's army, and the poem that Ahmad Shamlou composed for him, "Az Zakhm-e Qalb-e Aba'i" (From the wounded heart of Aba'i, 1951). In these iconic poems, the rebel and the poet become one and the same, the doppelgänger of each other. The splitting of the monadic figure of the Persian Prince into the dyadic disposition of the rebel/poet is here complete. The Persian poet is no longer singing the praise of a tyrant, hoping to civilize his barbarities. The poet has become the voice of the eternal rebel in search of justice yet to come: in a split persona, the Persian Prince in a dyadic mode remembers and retrieves its archaic origins.

The realm of this new dyad of the Persian Prince as the rebel/poet keeps expanding into former imperial domains—from India to Iran, Central Asia, the Ottoman territories, and even via Russian empress. The cosmopolitan disposition and the discursive prowess of the new polity were decidedly transnational and extended deep into the Caucuses and Central Asia. Published in Azerbaijan, *Molla Nasraddin* was perhaps the epitome of this transnational public sphere, as it was widely read across the Persianate and even the Arab and Russian worlds.

Headquartered first in Tiflis (1906–1917), then in Tabriz (1921), and finally in Baku (1922–1931), the satirical periodical was published mostly in Azari but occasionally in Russian. It was founded by Jalil Mohammad Qolizadeh (1862–1932) and featured regular cartoons in which it advocated progressive politics and cultural modernization. Its impact was particularly widespread in Azerbaijan and Iran. Crucial in the publication of *Molla Nasraddin* was the role of Jalil Mohammad Qolizadeh's wife, Hamideh Javanshir (1873–1955), a deeply cultivated and pioneering women's rights activist.[24] As a cultural couple, Mohammad Qolizadeh and Javanshir become exemplary for generations to come.[25]

Equally important in this era was the rise of modern drama and the poetic dramaturgy that it occasioned—again on the borderlines of Azeri, Persian, and Russian languages and literatures. The first playwright with a lasting influence in this crucial period was Mirza Fath Ali Akhundzadeh (1812–1878), who lived in the Caucasus and wrote his plays in Azeri Turkish between 1850 and 1855, focusing mostly on social issues, backwardness, and paths to progress. Although he was reading Gogol and Molière (both in Russian), his plays are elementary attempts to command the genre. All of his plays were translated into Persian and published in 1874. Following him was his contemporary and close follower Mirza Agha Tabrizi, the author of four comedies in Persian. Tabrizi initially considered translating Akhundzadeh's plays from Azeri Turkish into Persian but eventually decided to try his hand at writing, penning an original composition in Persian, imitating the works of Akhundzadeh.[26] Much of the influences and sources of inspiration for these plays were in fact Russian, not Western European. Even if these playwrights read Molière, they did so in their Russian translations. A synergy therefore emerges here among Russian, Azeri, and Persian in a creative heteroglossia that informs the transnational public sphere between Iran and the Caucuses.

The selfsame cosmopolitan worldliness extends to India too. Equally important in these crucial periods was an abundance of travelogues that emerged as a widely popular genre. From the late eighteenth to the early twentieth centuries, travelers from India and Iran went around the world, keeping detailed diaries of their daily encounters in a simplified Persian prose and publishing them to a widespread readership. Much of this extraordinary literature has been read exclusively for the portions that deal with Europe—damaging the importance of reading their totality. In *Reversing the Colonial Gaze*, I cover the entirety of their itineraries, showing in detail how these explorers in fact traveled and mapped out the surface of the globe and, in writing their travelogues in Persian, systematically and exponentially expanded the transnational public sphere upon which their respective readership in the Indo-Persian world received and interpreted them.[27]

The emerging public and parapublic (open and underground) spheres evident in the widespread dissemination of newspapers, travelogues, and eventually drama mapped out the wide spectrum of the moment when the monadic archetype of the Persian Prince was splitting into the dyadic disposition of itself. The historic constitution of the archetype was now yielding to the dissolution and resurrection of its imperial lineage. The colonial encounter with Europe was the key dividing factor. Gramsci's twist on Machiavelli here enables a similar turn to Gramsci himself as we reread his "Modern Prince" for postcolonial context. While for Machiavelli the figure of the prince was the epicenter of politics, rooted in his idea in Xenophon's *Cyropaedia*, for Gramsci that figure was of course anathema, and it was instead the collective body of the political party that was destined to be the organizing force of a progressive politics:

> The modern prince . . . cannot be a real person, a concrete individual. It can only be an organism, a complex element of society in which a collective will which has already been recognized and has to some extent asserted itself in action begins to take concrete form. History has already provided this organism, and it is the political part—the first cell in which there come together germs of a collective will tending to become universal and total.[28]

The sources of that living organism upstream from the political party are the public and parapublic spheres, and in this particular case the expansion of the transnational public sphere, which included aspects of what I have called and detailed as "Persophilia" plus the extensive body of travelogues I have examined in *Reversing the Colonial Gaze*. From Xenophon's *Cyropaedia* in classical antiquity on one side and the later European Persophilia of the eighteenth and nineteenth centuries on the other, the formation and vicissitude of European political thought and their structural transformations of the public sphere were rooted and evident in their take on the Persian Prince.

The multifaceted public and parapublic spheres, informed by the simplification of Persian prose, the introduction of printing machines, the varied periodicals, magazines, journals, travelogues, and memoirs published around the region and the globe in Persian, as well as the emergence of modern drama that entailed the poetic dramaturgy of the new postcolonial personae and eventually led to works of fiction and above all a modernist poetry that was rooted in these historical experiences, all resulted in a fertile ground upon which the archetypal figure of the Persian Prince eventually found a renewed historicity. Transnational public spheres and the postcolonial subject were predicated primarily on colonial economics as its modus operandi of subjection, with the Tobacco Revolt of 1890 against economic concessions to European interests as the key anticolonial event of the century.

Then followed the dividing practices, which included the reality of the bifurcation between the dominant colonizer and the subjugated but rebellious colonized, and the gendered practice of male and female, which squarely placed Iran in a sustained course of transversal relations with other nations in its immediate surroundings; the enduring result of this was what W. E. B. Du Bois called "dual consciousness": the systemic divide between the world of the colonizer and the world of the colonized, the will to dominate and the will to resist power. In the Persianate world, the political culture of the Persian Prince rose to override the Sunni-Shi'i divide within Islam—and Persian poetry emerged as the talismanic disposition of that culture, with poets like Muhammad Iqbal (1877–1938) and Nima Yushij (1897–1960), perhaps its two towering examples, eventually moving toward a prophetic voice that thrives on a new transversal subjectivity—both making a world and making it imaginable, inhabitable, knowable.

Persian prose and poetry became the singular site of this transversal subjection—crafting a new worldly intersectionality in which the postcolonial person would eventually reclaim and inhabit a new selfhood. In two of his masterpieces, *Asrar-e Khodi* (*The Secrets of Selfhood*, 1915) and *Romuz-e Bikhodi* (*Signs of Selflessness*, 1918), Muhammad Iqbal put in exquisite poetic Persian the way toward self-realization and gave it a detailed interiority. In his immediate neighborhood and soon after him in Iran, from periodicals to drama to revolutionary tracts, eventually we reach the Constitutional Period poetry of the early 1900s, which ultimately yields to the revolutionary poetry of Nima Yushij, who in form and substance turned the millennial Persian poetic heritage upside down. Nima's poetry in general, and perhaps one particular poem more specifically, is where the Persian Prince would find his modernist poetic habitat. "Padeshah Fath" (The prince of conquest, 1947) is where Nima completely recasts the very idea of the Padeshah, the King, the Sovereign, the Prince. The poem is deeply dark and troubled, like the night it begins to describe in its first stanza.

> *Dar tamam-e tul-e shab...*
>
> All through the night
> When the countless teeth of this old darkness
> Are falling, and from the depth of these conniving obscurities
> Shadows of the grave of the dead and the abode of the living
> Are mixing together—and when
> That magician of the world
> Hidden in its own magic
> Brings your slumber through your ears to your eyes:
> The Prince of Conquest is lying upon his throne—
> After a heavy, troubled night
> For a few moments of rest—
> Just like a drunk resting in his seat.[29]

The rest of the poem tells us how the "Prince of Conquest" is like a fire hiding in ashes, lost in his dreams, that he observes the misery of the world around him, fearful and hopeful at the same time. The Prince then bursts into an air-shattering laughter, from which children's worries are assuaged and cold and fireless ovens are warmed. As the light of the morning starts shining, the night is about to collect itself and leave, at which point the Prince speaks:

> These nightmares are awakening these children in vain,
> I am a refined, punctilious point in this story,
> I know how to untangle these tangled lines,
> I know well which immature soul is tired in the midst of this dark night—
> Or what feet are trembling on the narrow path.[30]

The Prince continues to give hope and assure forthcoming victory as he beseeches his people not to worry, advises them to be steady on their path, reminds them that he knows everything, good and bad. He assures them he is not dead, that he is alive and well—even if those who want to instill fear in people claim he is dead. The poem begins and ends with the twilight of hope and despair, the rising news of his death, the promise of his resurrection, as the night continues, while the Prince is resting on his throne. Is he dead or is he just asleep?

It makes no difference. We are in the twilight of hope and despair, as the dead/alive Prince is writing the autobiography of a resurrected myth—from somewhere beyond the reach of night or day, of light or darkness. Hafez had anticipated Nima's answer by about six centuries:

> With a towering figure and a handsome countenance, just about anyone
> Who became the king of the righteous
> Would conquer the world if he only knew how to be just.[31]

EIGHT

The Nomadic Fate of the Persian Prince

> Who said I am the last wise man
> On this earth?
> I am that beautiful monster
> Standing on the equator of the night
> Drowned in the purity of all
> The waters of this earth—
> As upon the horizon of whose devilish sight
> A star is about to rise—
> I have a humble cot at the end of the earth
> Where the firm rootedness of the soil—
> Just like the shimmering of a mirage—
> Relies on the deception of thirst.
> Where Man meets God...
> My home is at the end of the world
> Where dust and desolation meet.[1]
>
> Ahmad Shamlou, "Oqubat"
> [Punishment], (1960)

My lifelong engagement in the project of nomadic subjectivity has been partly motivated by the conviction that, in these globalized times of accelerating technologically mediated changes, many traditional points of reference and age-old habits of thought are being re-composed, albeit in contradictory ways.... At such a time more conceptual creativity is necessary, and more theoretical courage is needed in order to bring about the leap across inertia, nostalgia, aporia and the other forms of critical stasis induced by our historical condition. It has become like a mantra to me: we need to learn to think differently about the kind of subjects we have already become and the processes of deep-seated transformation we are undergoing.[2]

Rosi Braidotti, "Writing as a Nomadic Subject" (2014)

MUHAMMAD MEHDI IBN MOHAMMAD REZA AL-ISFAHANI, known as *Arbab* ("master," thrived in the 1860s), was a learned man, a serious and pious man, a gifted writer who came from a prominent family. He was the father of Zoka'-al-Molk I and the grandfather of Mohammad Ali Zoka' al-Molk Foroughi (1877–1942), one of the most eminent statesmen, diplomats, and literary scholars of his era, who served as prime minister of Iran multiple times—and in his spare time wrote one of the most exquisite earliest Persian histories of European philosophy. What little we know of al-Isfahani the grandfather is because of an erudite book he wrote about his hometown of Isfahan, placing it in the context of global history and the known and imaginative geography of the world. In this book, *Nesf al-Jahan fi Ta'rif al-Isfahan* (On Isfahan: The center of the world), al-Isfahani has a long chapter on the history of Isfahan in which he cites his hometown as the very epicenter of real and mythic histories.[3] The origin of Isfahan, he tells us, goes back to the time of Tahmores, the mythic Iranian king. Since Fereydoun, it has fully entered history, with the people of Isfahan helping Jamshid to overcome Zahhak; he also believes that Kaveh the Blacksmith, another legendary hero who led a revolt against Zahhak, was from Isfahan.[4] Al-Isfahani shares this information very much as a matter of fact, evidently not only to boast about his hometown. Isfahan was indeed, just as he thought, the very epicenter of the universe.

What is remarkable about this book, as with similar books about other cities in Iran or other parts of the world from India to Anatolia and beyond, is how the physical and material location of the city is linked to and embedded in the mythic and heroic phases of Persian, or Vedic, or Biblical, or Qur'anic narratives. The city has been in effect mythologized, pushed back from its lived experiences and plotted within a larger unlived memory from time immemorial. The city thus becomes part of a mythic universe whose streets and alleys, squares and monuments, from its basements to its rooftops and beyond, farther into its environmental landscape, are woven into a whole different universe. The act extends to the real peoples living in these cities, their own collective consciousness, from their daily routines, familiar and familial experiences, deeply and widely into a fictive realm, into a collective subconscious. As they begin to name their newborn children Tahmores, Fereydoun, Kaveh, Roudabeh, Farangis, Manizheh, and so on, the city and its inhabitants have suddenly become the mobile carnival of a temporal and spatial cosmos that the mind could not have otherwise reached, the imagination fathomed, or reason anticipated. To that universe there is a center, and that center, we read here in this book, is Isfahan.

Persepolis, Cosmopolis, and Utopia

Reading al-Isfahani's *On Isfahan: The Center of the World* cover to cover, something else emerges. The city becomes a literary proposition—composed of words and sentences, prose and poetry, fact and fiction, truth and fantasy. Once that happens, the city is a literary trope that taps into an even richer literary tradition. In Persian poetry we have a genre literary historians have identified as *Shahrashub* or *Shahrangiz*, literally "city-inciting"—meaning a kind of poetry that is exclusive to city dwellers, that praises or maligns a city, that identifies its various professions and industries, commerce and trades, and that indulges in sexually charged adulations of young apprentices of such professions, mixing initially social but increasingly political incitements with either cliché or occasionally provocative eroticism. There is no one particular format of this genre, and it can assume the form of Quatrains, Qasideh, Ghazal, or Masnavi. The sites where Shahrashub has been popular extend from India to Iran to the Ottoman Empire, with extensive samples in Persian, Urdu, and Turkish. That the name of the genre is Persian reveals its literary genealogy, but its Urdu, Turkish, and even Arabic versions speak to a much larger domain of popularity and influence. Masʿud Saʿd Salman (circa 1046–1121), Sanaʾi Ghaznavi (circa 1080–1141), Mahasti Ganjavi (circa 1089–1159), and Amir Khosrow Dehlavi (1253–1325) are usually considered the classical masters of this genre.[5] Here is an example of a Shahrashub from a poet named Mirza Taher Vahid Qazvini from the Safavid period describing a young Coppersmith (Mesgar) apprentice he loves:

> Thinking of my own Coppersmith
> Makes my head noisier than the shop of a coppersmith—
> Once I'm in ecstasy from the love of my Beloved
> I'd be happy even if I were to shed my skin,
> I would not mind if my bodily desires
> Were to consume me just like copper in a brazier.[6]

What makes this a Shahrashub is the way the coppersmith becomes both a factual and a metaphoric reference to an urban profession in the bazaar—where the person of a coppersmith apprentice becomes the persona of a lyrical object of desire. From these classical iterations, in all its variations—Persian, Turkish, or Urdu—Shahrashub eventually emerges as a highly political poetry. Citing the Pakistani scholar Seyyed Abdollah, the eminent Iranian literary scholar Mohammad Jaʿfar Mahjoub reports: "Shahrashub is a kind of poetry in which social change, presence or absence of chaos in a city or a country are described. It is a genre that deals with economic and political problems, or the condition of various classes, which are expressed in a satirical or farcical way."[7] One might even read these poems as urban reportage. Masʿud Saʿd Salma's famous Masnavi in this genre describes a city so well it's as if he has a documentary filmmaker roaming the city with a digital camera in his hands. The same is true of Sanai's description of Balkh. Mahasti Ganjavi's Shahrashub was so provocative and powerful that later literary historians thought she must have been a prostitute![8]

With the ruins of ancient cities like Persepolis and Ctesiphon as the prototype for these cities, the preponderance of city references in Persian poetry of these successive periods obviously points to increasing urbanization and the position of poets outside the royal courts. Real characters like a baker, a greengrocer, a carpenter, or a blacksmith now actively enter Persian prose and poetry through the Shahrashub genre. The development also brings to a particular location and urbanizes the abstract and mythic disposition of the Persian poet, the object of his or her desires, and thus perforce the subjectivity of the Persian person—the systematic subjection of the Persian Prince right into the winding labyrinth of unfolding history. It both personalizes and particularizes the mythic and historic archetypes of the Persian Prince as the prototype of the person who now speaks in and through the Persian poet. There is a pronounced eroticism in the poetics of the Persian person that thus rises in between the amorous poet and the androgynous object of his or her desires. Given that in Persian we do not have gender-specific pronouns, the object of the poet's desire could be male or female, and thus both and neither. The poetic subjection of the Persian person cum the Persian Prince at the epicenter of the Persepolis thus takes place on the nonbinary gender-neutral subjection between the historicized poet and the urban landscape of his or her new habitat. From the ancient ruins of the *Persepolis* now emerges the site of the new *Persopolis*, with the Persian poet as the troubadour of its urban legends.

At this point we are ready to make another major epistemic shift. From this premise, in the archetypal figure of the Persian Prince we may detect the nodal point at which the political universe of the Persian and Persianate cosmopolis intersects and branches out to bring together the trilateral ideals of *Iran-Shahr*, *Jahan-Shahr*, and *Arman-Shahr*. If we were to translate Iran-Shahr as Persopolis, then Jahan-Shahr would be Cosmopolis, and Arman-Shahr Utopia. By linking these three takes on the Persian cosmopolis, we can theoretically pivot toward an excavation of a genealogy of postcolonial subjectivity outside but adjacent to the European project of colonial modernity—which the world has received under colonial duress. That people around the world are not "European" is not only not enough but in fact deeply distorting, for it cross-authenticates the fiction of "Europe" and further alienates the varied cultures and civilizations from the terms of their own humanity. Beyond being a nonentity, the nature and function of the "non-European" subject is a *terra incognita* that very few philosophers and critical thinkers outside Europe have explored. To this day, V. Y. Mudimbe's seminal opus *The Invention of Africa* (1988) remains a singular achievement exploring the nature of the knowing subject and of being-in-the-world beyond Europe. Next to it, Enrique Dussel's *Philosophy of Liberation* (1980) and Gustavo Gutierrez's *Liberation Theology* (1971) have done the same in Latin American contexts. I have those models in mind when I map out the emerging post/coloniality of the Persian Prince on the fertile premise of the urban public spheres where it is now rising.

All those seminal texts by Mudimbe, Dussel, Gutierrez, Walter Mignolo, Achille Mbembe, and others were deeply engaged with Europe as their main interlocutors—as they should have been, and indeed as are my own encounters with Xenophon, Machiavelli, Gramsci, Cassirer, and Rosi Braidotti, which are for more than just heuristic reasons. That Xenophon's *Cyropaedia*, based on his reading of Cyrus the Great, was the prototype for all subsequent mirrors that ultimately reached Machiavelli and were deeply radicalized makes this entire genre a particularly European take on the prototype of the Persian Prince. This fact must be placed next to another important one: that from the time of Machiavelli forward, the European encounter with the colonial world was decidedly exacerbated.

The same historical coincidence is true of my interest in Gramsci, whose Eurocentric Marxism had completely blindsided him to the colonial site of European capitalist modernity. Kevin Anderson's *Marx at the Margins: On Nationalism, Ethnicity, and Non-Western Societies* (2016) brings that blind spot to light. The same is also true of Braidotti, whose exceptionally insightful work on the nomadic subject requires careful rearticulation on the post/colonial site. This long tradition of the European take on the archetype of the Persian Prince therefore makes the varied historical formations of the Persian cosmopolis integral to a global context facilitated precisely by the selfsame European colonialism. The attraction of initially European and subsequently American world and continental conquerors to Xenophon's *Cyropaedia* (all the way from Alexander the Great and Julius Caesar to Thomas Jefferson, John Adams, James Madison, Benjamin Franklin, and Harry Truman) was an attraction to the global consequences of the archetype of the Persian Prince. When this inner traction within European and US imperial proclivities comes back to the Persianate world, it breaks it down into its poetic and prophetic voices, as a form of the return of its repressed. We can therefore read the anticolonial struggles of nations, from the Indian subcontinent through Central Asia, the Caucuses, Iran, and the Ottoman territories, as a battle within the paradoxical proclivities of the princely and the prophetic sides of the Persian Prince.

Return of the Repressed

The return of the historically repressed under colonial duress is where the archetype of the Persian Prince begins to be decoded back into its constituent forces. Rooted in the ancient, heroic, and historical sites of Persian literary cosmogony, the monadic disposition of the Persian Prince resumed its classical phase with the active translation of Pahlavi (Middle Persian) sources into Arabic and Persian early in Islamic history. The classic texts of *Kelilah and Dimnah*, the *Shahnameh*, *The Book of Sandbad*, *Belawhar and Budhasaf*, *Vis-o-Ramin*, and *The Letter of Tansar* all originated in Pahlavi and subsequently reached both Arabic and, more crucially for our purpose here, Persian renditions.[9] All these pre-Islamic texts (of either Indian or Iranian source) brought a powerful literary impetus to the emerging historical consciousness of Persian culture and civilization, both integral to its new Islamic milieu and distinctively Iranian in its literary character. *Kelilah and Dimnah* provided a deeply rooted and cultivated Indian aspect to this constellation of the Persianate cosmopolis, while the *Shahnameh* took a vast panorama of Iranian mythology from its Avestan and Pahlavi sources and delivered them to the poetic craftsmanship of Ferdowsi. Conversely, the *Book of Sandbad* could be of Indian and/or Iranian origins. *Belawhar and Budhasaf* is a story about the life of Buddha, a tale that has reached us in both Arabic and Persian, thus placing a decidedly non-Islamic perspective on the literary heritage of the Persianate world. As for *The Letter of Tansar*, it is basically a political treatise from the Sassanid period that reached us through its

Arabic rendition by Ibn Muqaffaʿ. Such Pahlavi sources became the conduit for the transformation of pre-Islamic to Islamic gestations of the archetype of the Persian Prince in its monadic disposition.

Rooted in these texts and flowered into subsequent canonical sources of Persian literary humanism, the figure of the Persian Prince has always been entirely figurative, never real, always ideal, a prototype of legitimate power, at once mighty and commanding and yet just and judicious, now personified by a monarch, then represented by a rebel, always the subtext of poets and prose stylists at the royal courts. No particular prince, monarch, or emperor was ever the ideal thing, though they were cast against that archetypal model. Even if apocryphal, the prophetic Hadith attributed to Prophet Muhammad, "I was born at the time of the Just Ruler," a reference to the Sassanid emperor Khosrow Anushirvan, has marked the legendary justice of the archetypal monarch. Figures like Cyrus the Great, Khosrow Anushirvan, Harun al-Rashid, Shah Abbas, Dara Shukoh, and Suleiman the Magnificent have taken the stage as chief archetypes of legendary proportions. But in historical terms they have simply personified what their archetypal model has projected on to them. In being real, they personified an irreality. That dynamic dialectic between the real and ideal remains definitive to the archetype.

As a figurative ideal-type deeply rooted in the collective memories of multiple postcolonial nations, the figure of the Persian Prince is an enduring literary construct. The legends embedded in the labyrinth of such memories and the facts they have either concealed or staged have become the stuff of our current concerns and contestations about the world in which Muslims and non-Muslim rooted in the Persian cosmopolis find themselves, exercising their collective will upon this public domain they have invariably formed. It is imperative to keep in mind that introducing a wider audience of readers and interpreters to a reconstruction of Iranian (Persianate) and Islamic political thoughts is not a mere academic exercise (in futility). Such reconstructions of the figurative figures, like that of the Persian Prince, are invariably geared toward a reappraisal of the present predicament of Muslims and non-Muslims in general, how they got to be where they are today, and why certain democratic institutions are lacking in their received political cultures. To address such questions, the premise must be the historic transformation of Iranian and Islamic political thought and institutions under colonial duress within the past few centuries; even if one were to disagree with the current assessment of things, the sense of loss and despair is entirely evident and even justified. The return of the repressed in the collective

Persianate subconscious is not necessarily a liberating or perforce arresting proposition. It is a purgatorial stage in which the flow of realities might be in both and opposite directions.

To see how the figure of the Persian Prince transfigured into the public weal (very much on the model that Gramsci thought political parties the transfiguration of Machiavelli's *Prince* in his contemporary Europe), we need to go to the epicenter of its rise in literary consciousness, when the politics of power and the poetics of revolt come together and find their most formal abstractions. That literary consciousness did not just occur in a transnational public sphere out of the thin air. It was effectively recrafted over the course of the rise of colonial modernity in Persian (as it did with Arabic, Turkish, Urdu, etc.) prose and poetry, which was concomitant with the formation of the transnational public sphere that anticolonial struggles had occasioned. Classical masterpieces now began to be reread, new meanings were discovered in the poetries of Omar Khayyam, Hafez, and Rumi, while the modernist poetry of Nima Yushij and his followers was assimilated backward and forward as the literary pedigree of political defiance against colonial domination and domestic tyranny. When in 1971 the late shah of Iran celebrated the 2,500th anniversary of the Persian monarchy by standing in front of the grave of Cyrus the Great, proclaiming himself the King of Kings, and beseeching Cyrus the Great to sleep calmly, for he was awake, Ayatollah Khomeini was, at just about the same time, declaring himself *Vali-e Faqih* (Supreme Jurisconsult). Both men may have thought themselves vastly different nemeses of each other, but they were effectively pointing to the selfsame figure of the Persian Prince hidden and manifest in the deepest layers of their collective subconscious. The only trouble with this was they were appealing to a figure that had long since vacated its figurative presence and moved squarely into the public domain of political sovereignty, over which they had no effective knowledge or had made any symbolic inroads.

My perhaps counterintuitive suggestion here casts the figurative character of the Persian Prince as reverting back to its rebellious roots in the pre-Islamic and Islamic periods now in the course of its militant encounters with European colonial modernity as the prototype metamorphoses into exactly the opposite figure of the ruling regime and begins to question and subvert their power and authority. The abysmal failures of the ruling monarchs of the Mughal, the Qajar, and the Ottoman Empires to protect the boundaries of their dynastic territories, let alone lead their people to resist European colonialism, effectively neutralized and categorically severed their claims to the iconic figure of the Persian Prince.

As the ruling monarchs and sultans declined any legitimate claims to the Persian Prince, the towering presence of revolutionary rebels challenging both the ruling tyrannies who had lost all claims to legitimacy and the European colonial powers reverted the figure of the Persian Prince to its pre-Islamic origin of the prophet/painter/poet on the model of Zoroaster, Mani, and Mazdak. The ineptitude of the ruling monarchies made a monarch, a Persian Prince, of every rebellious subject of their empires, the citizen of a republic that was yet to be. Exactly the same way that early in the Islamic period in Iran the rebellious figures of Behafarid, Ustadhsis, Sunpadh, and Ibn Muqanna' resurrected the prophetic archetype of Mazdak, in the aftermath of encounters with European colonial modernity the figure of the Persian Prince metamorphosed into a prophetic resurrection of its inaugurating archetype.

The inordinate attention to the figure of the revolutionary memory of Babak Khorramdin (circa 795–838), who would revolt against the Abbasids centuries later during the Qajar and Pahlavi periods, is perhaps the clearest indication of this historic recurrence of the pre-Islamic and early Islamic Iranian archetype of rebels now encountering not Arab conquerors but those of European empires. The same is true for the mythic figure of Kaveh the Blacksmith in the *Shahnameh*, who had revolted against the tyranny of Zahhak, who now saw his name resurrected as the title of a leading revolutionary periodical, *Kaveh* (1916–1922) published during the Constitutional Period in Berlin by Seyyed Hasan Taghizadeh (1878–1970). The politically potent glorification of pre-Islamic Iran that begins earlier in the writings of nineteenth-century revolutionaries like Mirza Aqa Kermani (1854–1897) should be read in this light. It is true that their glorification of pre-Islamic Iran had a strong element of anti-Arab racism. This anti-Arab sentiment, however, had a crucial symbolic reference not to their Arab, Turk, or Indian contemporaries who shared their colonial fate but to the early Arab conquerors of the Sassanid Empire—and in this respect they were equally critical of Alexander's invasion before the Arab conquest and of the Mongol invasion after.

The desire at this point was not a return to that empire but to achieve political agency against European colonialism embedded in the historical memory of Babak Khorramdin or Kaveh the Blacksmith, rebellious characters unto which the Persian Prince had recast itself. By now the historic figure of Babak and the mythic figure of Kaveh had become entirely iconic, bringing the memories of the revolutionary rendition of the Persian Prince back from the distant past and making them available and appealing to the anticolonial struggles of a whole new generation of rebellious characters. Three leading revolutionary thinkers of this period—the same Mirza Aqa Khan Kermani and his two comrades, Sheikh Ahmad Ruhi and Mirza Hasan Khan Khabir al-Molk, were rounded up by Ottoman authorities in Istanbul and handed over to Qajar authorities to be executed in retaliation for the assassination of the Qajar patriarch Nasser al-Din Shah. The assassination of Nasser al-Din Shah in May 1896 and the execution of these three revolutionaries in July of the same year is one precise moment of the transfusion of the figure of the Persian Prince away from the ruling monarchs and royal courts and unto revolutionary thinkers and activists. This is one precise moment of metempsychosis of the Persian Prince from its archaic origins, through a vast historical expanse, down to the anticolonial struggles of nations, retrieving its prophetic and poetic points of departure.

The literary, poetic, dramatic, eventually cinematic, and other creative resurrections of the revolutionary rebel, of the iconoclastic dissident, of the rebellious hero, of "the public intellectual," now in the figure of the protagonist of a social justice cause, are the manifest remembrances of the Persian Prince that symbolically link the classical prototype of the savior prince to the inaugural moment of the early Islamic period when the proto-Mazdakite prophets on the model of Mazdak, and then followed by figures like Behafarid, Ustadhsis, Sunpadh, or Ibn Muqanna', appeared on the horizon. The romantic figure of the poet and the rebel, or the heroic figures he or she crafted or celebrated now personified the Persian Prince as the solitary messenger of truth. The prime example of the resurrection of the Persian Prince as a rebel poet can be detected in the poetic persona of a leading Iranian poet, Mehdi Akhavan-e Sales (1929–1990), who in his iconic poem "Qesseh-ye Shahryar-e Shahr-e Sangestan" (The Ballad of the Prince of Stoneville, 1960) reconfigured the archetypal icon for his own time. The epic narrative of this poem details the contemporary fate of an ancient hero, decidedly portrayed as a pre-Islamic, archaic Persian prince with Zoroastrian heritage whose comrades and courtiers have all died and turned to stone, leaving all his cries for resurrection and valiance unanswered.

Composed as a folk ballad, "The Ballad of the Prince of Stoneville" is a narrative poem, staging the heroic exploits of a fallen Persian Prince deep from the distant memories of the nation. The ballad begins with two doves sitting on a branch of an ancient cedar tree, a profoundly sacred item in ancient Iranian mythology, under which rests a tired stranger. The birds, speaking to each other like two kind sisters, wonder who this stranger is and what he is doing resting under their tree. The tired man is resting with his hands over his eyes—is he a shepherd whose flock has been devoured by a wolf? Is he a merchant whose ships have been lost at sea? Is he a forlorn lover? Who is he? The doves think they can help him find his way if he is lost. Finally, one of the sisters says the man looks like Bahram Varjavand, a Zoroastrian messianic figure appearing just before the Day of Resurrection, and predicts that other heroes will follow him, like Give, Son of Gudarz, Tus, Son of Nozar, and Garshasp, all coming to rescue his homeland from evil forces and raise the flag of justice and righteousness. The doves soon admonish each other not to make fun of this tired man with such lofty allusions and outlandish thought. When they realize that the man is actually listening to them and watching them through his fingers, they conclude:

> He is that Prince who has been expelled from his own city,
> Wandering through seas and deserts.[10]

Through the descriptions of the two doves, we come to recognize the man as a prince whose homeland has been plundered and who has tried to mobilize his nation to fight back; however, no one has answered his call, for they have all turned to stone. At this point, Akhavan-e Sales turns the poem into a jeremiad of pain and anger against theft and the plunder of his homeland. The sister doves offer the Prince a way out of his predicament: he must get up and walk to a nearby cave, where he will find a fountain. He will wash himself, perform his ablutions, pray in the name of the Six Angelic *Amshaspands*, then throw seven pebbles into a well. They encourage and promise him he has merely fallen from his horse, and not lost his royal grace. The Prince proceeds to do as the doves tell him, point by point, then asks the cave, "May I have hope for salvation?" In response, the echo of his own voice comes back at him with the last syllables of his question: "No, there is no hope for salvation." Projected as a figure like Bahram Varjavand, an eschatological savior in the Zoroastrian tradition, this allegorical Prince brings the idea and its historical implications to a full epistemic and formal circle. Giving voice to this voiceless Prince, the poet himself becomes that Persian Prince.

As is best evident in this poem, the iconic figure of the Persian Prince runs like a winding river through the near and far of a vast and transhistorical landscape. From a heroic thunder to a tragic solemnity, the Persian Prince has remained a constant allegory of power, justice, sovereignty, legitimacy, and the wish for a sublime and sacred order to the world, always desired and wished for but never fully achieved; in between that hope and that despair, it has sustained a continued relevance and potency. The crescendo of that poetics and politics of power achieved its zenith with the last three Muslim empires—the Mughals, the Safavids, and the Ottomans—and from the height of that point forward eventually began to crumble under the weight of its own internal paradoxes and the onslaught of the mighty European empires. That paradox, that the Persian Prince is both a ruling monarch and a defiant rebel, has been both the source of its metaphoric power and the condition of its historical demise. Superior technologies of commerce and conquest tipped the balance of power, and Muslims lost the global game. The thematic transmutation of the figure of the Persian Prince from a triumphant conqueror to a tragic rebel has passed through the labyrinth of public and parapublic spheres that remain the most fertile ground of its past, present, and future relevance. If not a just ruler, then a rebel in search of justice, the towering icon of the Persian Prince has found itself a niche in the very bosom of what it means to be a humble human cast in the sacred image of a divinity. The poet, the prophet, and the rebel that were always under the skin of the Persian Prince finally escape the institution and recast the archetype, liberated to return to their formative forces.

Caravan as Carnival

Where and what precisely would be the location and disposition of the new Persian Prince as the figure reconfigures itself outside the royal court, upon the public and parapublic spheres within and without all postcolonial nations, deep into the labyrinth of the history of the present? The urbanity of the Persopolis is embedded in its environmental habitat—not just the cities and towns but the deserts, mountains, rivers, seas, and valleys that connect them into a conception of a homeland.

Contingent on any conception of urbanity is of course the feeling of anomie and alienation. We can move from Ibn Khaldun's *Asabiyyah* to Durkheim's *Organic Solidarity* as the theoretical condition from which alienation results in the senses of anomie, of not being part of a whole, of being far from the crowd. The royal subject here becomes the simulacrum of the rising postclassical subjection, and the Persian Prince transforms into the simulation of the Persian Person. A range of theoretical speculations thus emerges on the constitution of the royal subject as first a monadic entity reflecting the mirror image of the Persian Prince, for the genre of mirrors for princes was not just for the prince but was also in fact for his subjects, the mirror image of the royal archetype. The Persian Prince was a literary and poetic constitution, a fixed signifier that marked variedly floating meanings. It was believed to be divinely ordained, the recipient of Farrah Izadi, the divine gift of grace. As such, the imperial archetype was a moral and mortal being bestowed with immortal attributes—a prophetic voice exuding a divinely ordained royal disposition. The Prince was the magi and the monarch at one and the same time—the priest and the prince, the king and the philosopher, the divine emissary and the royal king—with the mythical figure of Keyumars as the first human, the first king, prophet, and poet, the most proverbial Persian Prince, the very first specimen of the idea, the offspring of Mashya and Mashyana, who were born to an androgenous plant.

That was the mythic origin—and then came the split. Under colonial duress, the Persian Prince was decoded from its monadic origins into a dyadic bipolarity and split into the irreconcilable binary of the nation-state, with Manichean dualism as its archetypal prototype. Here the colonial dyad replaced the royal monad at the heart of the Persian Prince as the inaugural archetype of a political culture that had endured the test of time. But the colonial dyad of the nation-state collapses under its innate contradictions and fails to form and gel, for the Prince cannot be both the nation and the state simultaneously, the subject and the predicate of itself; thus, the dialectic between the monadic origin and the dyadic splitting sublates into the nomadic condition of coloniality, corresponding in its revolutionary disposition with the Mazdakite revolt of the late Sassanid period. The monadic subject thus fails to become the Manichean dyadic nation-state and moves to the nomadic subject of its Mazdakite memories.

Here, a theoretical comparison becomes compelling. For Deleuze, this transfiguration from Leibniz's monadic to the Deleuzian nomadic was philosophical wishful thinking, but for Braidotti it was a condition of advanced capitalist globalization. For us here on the colonial edges of the selfsame European modernity where it had occasioned the crisis of the subject, however, it was the very condition of our coloniality, which was mediated by the dyadic false alarm of the nation-state. This spinning of the triad of the Persian Prince, Poet, Prophet is therefore the condition of postcolonial subjectivity mitigated by our lived experiences from monadic to dyadic to nomadic, as best evident in the status of the Bidoons/The Without (Homeland) in the Persian Gulf regions, and Muʿavedin/The Returnees (from Nowhere to Nowhere), oscillating between Iran and Iraq. The nomadic subject, as Braidotti puts it,

> is a figuration for the kind of subject who has relinquished all idea, desire, or nostalgia for fixity. This figuration expresses the desire for an identity made of transitions, successive shifts, and coordinated changes, without and against an essential unity.[11]

That form of subjection did not have to wait for the onset of globalization and border crossings of nations. We need to have a much wider conception of nomadism (both literally and theoretically) rooted in the lived experiences of people long before the "European crisis of the subject." In his monumental study, *Nomadism in Iran: From Antiquity to the Modern Era*, Daniel T. Potts has detailed across a vast panoramic history of three millennia the central role of nomadic societies in Iranian history—from the Neolithic, Chalcolithic, and Bronze Ages through the Iron Age and Late Antiquity, from the Islamic period all the way to the twentieth century.[12] Potts takes many archeological and anthropological assumptions to task, while mapping out the earliest accounts of nomadic migrations into the Iranian plateau and the dynamics between the nomadic and sedentary formations of imperial cities. He takes issue with the assumption that some archeologists have made about the sustained continuity of current nomadic conditions in Iran, instead offering a far more provocative thesis:

> Iranologists and Iranians themselves are well aware that large numbers of the nomads inhabiting Iran since the eleventh century have not been native Iranians, often called Tats or Tajiks, but immigrant, predominantly Turkic- and Arab-speaking nomads, Iliyats in the terminology of eighteenth- and nineteenth-century literature, who originated outside the country or were descendants of ones who had.... Something changed, however, by the time of Herodotus. This change, which may be considered the first great transformation in Iranian history, was almost certainly linked to the arrival of Iranian-speaking groups on the Iranian plateau. Not only do we see the evidence of this in Herodotus, but we find the later historians like Strabo, Polybius, and Livy, drawing on accounts from the era of Alexander and his successors, consistently alluding to the presence of nomadic groups in the region. Given their names, some of these groups must have been newcomers, Indo-Iranian speakers, while others may have been indigenous groups that were pushed off their land and, with little alternative, compelled to adopt a nomadic way of life. A few centuries later the traditions preserved about the family of Ardašir I include references to "kurds," a generic term for nomads/herders that was in use long before it came to denote a specific linguistic group, and by the time of the Islamic conquest those references had multiplied.[13]

What is crucial here are the sustained crosscurrents of nomadic mobility in the Iranian plateau. The issue is not the prolonged nomadic life of peoples living inside the geographical (not even the political) boundaries of Iran, but the fluidity of nomadic life into and out of the plateau. Iranians, Arabs, Turks, Mongols, and Indians have all been moving into and out of, through and around the plateau in search of better living conditions; when they have indeed formed sedentary civilizations, then the flow of nomadic life continued to animate and enable those sedentary civilizations.

This of course brings us to Ibn Khaldun's and Giambattista Vico's respective theories of history. In his *Al-Muqaddimah*, Ibn Khaldun's cyclical conception of history, rooted in his idea of Asabiyyah (group solidary) theorizes the nomadic foregrounding of the rise of civilization.[14] For both Vico and Ibn Khaldun, there is a cyclical rotation between nomadic and sedentary cultures, accounting for the rise and fall of dynasties and empires, between nomadic razzia and settled civilizations. But in the Iranian and Central Asian context, nomadism that is identified with the rise of the Ghaznavids, the Saljuks, and the Mongols also has a more harmonious cohabitation with sedentary civilizations. To this day, that oscillation has nostalgic echoes in Persian poetry—as exhibited in a romantic temptation, a poetic haven, evident in Shamlou's famous "Nocturne":

> *Dariqa darreh-ye sar sabz o gerdu-ye pir ...*
>
> Alas, the green valley and that old walnut tree—
> That melodious song of the river
> Where the village
> On both sides of the singing torrent
> Was falling fast asleep. . . .
>
> Alas, the moonshine,
> Alas, that fog—
> That vastness that opened in front of us
> Was hiding
> The tall mountain range of the jungle
> Between being and non-being. . . .
>
> Alas, Bamdad
> So regretfully had to abandon
> The green valley and return to the city—
> For in a time vast as this
> The task of putting bread on the table
> Is as arduous as securing a noble name.[15]

FIGURE 8   Parviz Kalantari, *Kavir (Desert)*, 2005.
Courtesy of the Hamid Keshmirshekan Archives.

We have a similar sentiment in a short poem of Nima Yushij:

Man az in dunan-e Shahrestan niam . . .

I am not one of these lowly city characters,
I am the painful conscience of the mountains—
Alas, from misfortune for a while
Been trapped in your city. . . .
I am happier with life on the mountains
For I have been used to it since my childhood.[16]

In the exquisite artwork of the Iranian artist Parviz Kalantari (1931–2014), we have an even more visible effusion of the abstracted city and its stylized desert surroundings, dreamlike in its miraging effects (fig. 8). The city and the desert are here visually and aesthetically intertwined—made integral to each other. There is a serenity to the effusion of the centered urbanity and the expansive desert that surrounds and graces it. In Kalantari's work the panoramic vista is completely abstracted from all its inhabitants. There are no people, sedentary or nomadic, in sight. But the vacated space allows for both to imagine and enable each other. There is where the Persian Prince is most at home.

The figure of the nomad was never far from the sedentary disposition of the Persian Prince—and came back to the surface as it transitioned from its dyadic disposition to its nomadic memories. The final destination of the figure of the Persian Prince was to be at home in the world, to fulfill its transient nomadic destiny—from its monadic confidence on the throne, to its dyadic doubts throughout its history, to its confident nomadic assurances. If Kay Kavous was the monadic archetype, his estranged son Seyavash was the dyadic prince who left his homeland for the camp of the enemy. There, he became friend and foe of the throne at one and the same time and ultimately fathered a son, Kay Khosrow, who would go back to Iran to rule his paternal homeland; thus, with Iran and Turan, a nomadic oscillation between *Yilaq* (Summer Highland) and *Qishlaq* (Winter Lowlands) would define the destiny of the Persian Prince. The seasonal oscillation between Yilaq and Qishlaq—taken in both their actual and their metaphoric senses—gives the nomadic soul of the Persian Prince a mobile subjectivity. Here, a number of signs and symbolics deeply rooted in the Persianate subconscious come together: the regularity of transhumance between Yilaq and Qishlaq, the carnivalesque disposition of trade and pilgrimage caravans, travelogues like those of Nasser Khosrow and Saʿdi, one evident in his philosophy and the other in his literary forms, Suhrawardi's beautiful allegory *Qesseh Ghorbat Gharbiyyeh* (*The Allegory of Occidental Exile*), and its sense of nostalgia for a home.

All of these and much more come together as deeply ingrained in the collective subconscious of the Persian Prince—giving the peace of his mind the agitation of his immemorial remembrances. The genre of Shahrashub is always agitated by the political consciousness brewing outside the city, where the prospects of Iran-Shahr, Jahan-Shahr, and Arman-Shahr (real and metaphoric) come together and embrace the city from a much vaster imaginative domain around it. The repressed memories of the pastoral and the nomadic are always evident in the figure of the Persian Prince, the feats of his *Razm* (battlefield) evident in the feasts of his *Bazm* (banquet), his *Safar* (sojourns) in his *Hazar* (home), where in warfare the Prince is in effect reclaiming the Yilaq for the imperial Qishlaq. As the poet always misses the pastoral, so is the nomadic agency ascertained, neither in sedentary nor rustic sojourns but in the oscillation between all centers and all peripheries, always between here and somewhere else.

I therefore place the Persian Prince onto the matrix of home and un-home, of being *Heimlich* and *Unheimlich*, very much in the same way Braidotti places her articulation of the nomadic subject:

> The nomadic subject is a myth, that is to say a political fiction, that allows me to think through and move across established categories and levels of experience: blurring boundaries without burning bridges. Implicit in my choice is the belief in the potency and relevance of the imagination, of myth-making, as a way to step out of the political and intellectual stasis of these postmodern times. Political fictions may be more effective, here and now, than theoretical systems. The choice of an iconoclastic, mythic figure such as the nomadic subject is consequently a move against the settled and conventional nature of theoretical and especially philosophical thinking. This figuration translates therefore my desire to explore and legitimate political agency, while taking as historical evidence the decline of metaphysically fixed, steady identities.[17]

To be sure, the distinction that Braidotti makes between "political fiction" and "theoretical systems" is itself a fiction—and of course, as always, Eurocentric in its narratological presuppositions. Political fictions are theoretical systems in disguise, and theoretical systems partake in political fictions without acknowledgment. The same is true with the archetype of the Persian Prince as I have detailed it in this book—rooted in its literary tropes and staged on political battlefields and royal courts at one and the same time—"blurring boundaries without burning bridges," as Braidotti aptly puts it. The idea of the Persian Prince emerged as a mythic figure, rooted in history, performed in stylized prose and poetically, moving across countries and climes to unsettle our received conceptions of political thoughts and the literary, moral, and philosophical imagination that informs them—with its monadic, dyadic, and nomadic proclivities always lurking under its royal skin.

To see how the figurative presence of the Persian Prince has transfigured into the public weal (very much on Gramsci's model, which saw political parties as the transfiguration of Machiavelli's *Prince* in his contemporary Europe), we need to go to the epicenter of its rise in literary consciousness as a floating signifier in which the politics of its power finds its most enduring archetypal abstractions. That literary consciousness did not just occur in a transnational public sphere out of thin air. It was effectively recrafted in the course of the rise of colonially conscious and mitigated "modernity" in Persian (or Arabic, Turkish,

Urdu, etc.) prose and poetry, which was concomitant with the formation of the transnational public sphere that had occasioned it. Classical masterpieces of Persian literary traditions now began to be reread, while modernist literature and poetry were assimilated backward and forward as the literary pedigree of the rising poet as the prophetic voice of the time.

When in 1971 the late shah of Iran stood in front of the grave of Cyrus the Great and proclaimed himself the King of Kings, and when almost at the same time the late Ayatollah Khomeini theorized himself as *Vali-e Faqih* (the supreme jurist) to replace the shah, they may have thought themselves vastly different "monarchs," but they were effectively pointing to the selfsame figure of the Persian Prince hidden and manifest in the deepest layers of their mutual consciousness. The only trouble was that they were both addressing an absent interlocutor by appealing to a figure that had long since vacated its figurative monarchy and moved deeply into the public dominion of political sovereignty. The Persian poet—in this case best evident in a poet like Ahmad Shamlou or Forough Farrokhzad, who were their contemporaries—had replaced and resurrected the prophetic memory of the Persian Prince with a sovereign prophetic voice; upon this voice and vision, the open-ended individuation of the postcolonial subject now mirrored the floating subjection of the rebellious poet. From transnational bourgeois public spheres to the formation of national sovereignty upon that space now emerged the poetic voice and vision of the public artist, public poet, public intellectual—with each turn articulating the terms of that very public. The figure of the Persian Prince transmigrated from the royal court into the public sphere through the nomadic visions of its own archetypal origins.

The configurative triad of the Persian Prince, the Persian Poet, and the Persian Prophet had by now disseminated into the nomadic disposition of the postcolonial subject. The pioneering work of Braidotti on nomadic subjectivity is exceptionally rich until it reaches the limits of her Eurocentric imagination:

> Though the image of "nomadic subjects" is inspired by the experience of peoples or cultures that are literally nomadic, the nomadism in question here refers to the kind of critical consciousness that resists settling into socially coded modes of thought and behavior. Not all nomads are world travelers; some of the greatest trips can take place without physically moving from one's habitat. It is the subversion of set conventions that defines the nomadic state, not the literal act of traveling.[18]

What escapes this exquisite reading of nomadic subjectivity is the condition of coloniality (whether internal as slavery or external as conquest), which, by virtue of the physical and epistemic violence it has perpetrated upon the world, makes every human being on planet Earth a nomad, a stranger, in her and his own homeland, victim of a double-consciousness that, as W. E. B. Du Bois articulated it, is split into "two souls, two thoughts, two unreconciled strivings; two warring ideals in one dark body, whose dogged strength alone keeps it from being torn asunder."[19] That is a "nomadic subjectivity" in a nutshell, in one person, at war with herself, at odds with himself.

Let me be even more specific: we have a concept and a practice in Persian called "Chavoshi," which is quite relevant here. Chavoshi is a rhythmic song or a ballad that the Chavoshi-khans sing ahead of a caravan as it leaves on a pilgrimage. Mehdi Akhavan-Sales takes that practice and turns it into a metaphor of a far different kind of Chavoshi for a vastly different journey. Akhavan-e Sales's "Chavoshi" starts sedately and nostalgically:

> *Beh san-e rahnavardani keh dar afsaneh ha guyand . . .*
>
> Just like those sojourners we read about in legends
> Carrying the backpack of their basic necessities on their shoulder,
> Holding a bamboo shoot in hand,
> Talkative now and then quiet,
> Walking in their legendary misty solitude—
> We too commence on our road ahead.[20]

The narrator then proceeds to sing us the ballad of a journey, solitary and yet communal, in which we hear the voice of history describing three paths ahead of us: one to fame, one to shame, and one to the road of no return. The traveler chooses the road of no return, full of fear and ecstasy, and fellow travelers of poets, Iranian and foreigners. The journey becomes a sojourn to the terror of history, of tyrants from Xerxes to Omar, leading to a solitary sailing upon a distant sea away from the here and now, lost in a distant mystic past where history can be redirected.

Akhavan-e Sales's poem becomes a solitary caravan of one lone traveler leading a carnival of historic calamities behind a nation that has endured it— all in a snapshot of an entire cosmogonic memory that has come back to haunt a people. This metaphor of the caravan brings us to the threshold of poetic performativity akin to Bakhtin's theorization of "the carnivalesque," a sublimated suspension of historical reasoning through which the *nomadic nomos* of the metaphor of the Persian Prince is teased out from its *monadic mythos* through its *dyadic logos*. The Persian Prince has now come full circle, at its resurrectionary end revisiting its inaugural beginning—its mythos and logos mirroring its logos—and the enduring ethos of the archetype is now fully exposed.

Retrieving the Persian Prince for Postclassical Agency

There is no subjection in a vacuum, no agency in abstraction. European philosophers have aptly theorized the European subject in terms of their own specific historicity, as if it were global. It is not. This provincialism itself, though, is global. All theorization, all philosophy, theorizes the particular as if universal. The task at hand is not to dismantle European theorization of the subject. The task is not even to provincialize it or, more accurately, expose its provincial disposition. The task is to map out alternative histories and geographies of the soul and the self to theorize. There are only a handful of civilizations that have the historical longevity, the archaic density, and therefore the capacity to theorize the particulars of their subjections in deeply rooted and archaic terms. The Persianate world, Iran and its universe, is one of them—and the Persian prince one such archetypal construct. India, China, and Egypt are along the same trajectory of such historical cultures.

Let us take archetype for what it is, a collectively, even subconsciously inherited dream that recurs and keeps demanding an explanation, an interpretation. We call it myth, we call it history, we call it culture. Rostam is an archetype, as is the son he inadvertently killed, as is Seyavash, as is Esfandiar. The father, the son, the rebel, the poet, the prophet, the prince: all are archetypes. In this case, the three figures of the Prince, the Prophet, and the Poet were in fact coterminous from their very inception of the archetype of the Persian Prince. At the dawn of colonial modernity, the princely and the prophetic were subsumed under the poetic, and thus the figure of the Persian poet was resurrected outside the courtly habitat, then entered and defined the emerging public sphere. In imperial and dynastic cultures, it was the figure of the prince that subsumed the rest. In the fateful encounter of the archetype with European colonial modernity, neither the courtly prince nor any divine emissary could be expected to perform the task, so it was the poet that subsumed the voice and vista of the rest and took over as public purveyor of truth, the mapmaker of a postclassical agency that could no longer invest trust in any political order.

What had further complicated the figure of the Persian Prince in its postcolonial resurrection was the gendered disposition of the polity that had emerged in the aftermath of the encounter with colonial modernity. The public sphere from which the postcolonial nation emerged had become gendered over the course of the nineteenth century through such revolutionary figures as the Babi leader Tahereh Qorrat al-Ayn, the pioneering women's rights advocate and Qajar princess Taj al-Saltaneh, and the equally bold and brilliant feminist Bibi Khanoom Astarabadi. But something far more enduring and far more symbolic was also at work. Let's take the example of Suhrawardi's *Aql-e Sorkh (Red Intellect)* and what prominent novelist Shahrnush Parsipur's *Aql-e Abi (Blue Intellect)* does with it to see how the archetype of the Persian Prince as the emerging knowing subject was being imaginatively re-gendered. Suhrawardi's *Red Intellect* is squarely in the context of his Illuminationist philosophy, in which he brings together ancient Iranian, Greek, and Islamic philosophies to strike a balance between intuition and reasoning. In Parsipur's *Blue Intellect*, she puts a decidedly feminine twist on the whole idea of intellection. The fusion of two stylized proses, those of Suhrawardi and Parsipur, casts the archetype of the knowing subject back into the collective subconscious and searches for its feminine voice.

Over the course of a dinner conversation I had with Shahrnush Parsipur a few years ago, she pointed to the candle on our table and said the idea for *Blue Intellect* came from the blue part of the flame. On that occasion, she gave a short explanation of how the color of the candle flame indicates its temperature. The outer core of the flame, which is the hottest, is light blue, measuring 1400°C, while the color inside the flame is initially yellow, then orange, and finally red. The closer we get to the center of the flame, the lower the temperature will be. The red portion is just around 800°C. This paradox, that the inner core is the coolest and red, while the outer part is the hottest and blue, is where she suggested that the fusion of the feminine and the masculine come together. In her other works, such as *Tuba and the Meaning of Night* or *Women Without Men*, Parsipur has continued her work of reconceiving the Iranian myth of the creation of Mashya and Mashyana as she places herself, a knowing woman subject, at the epicenter of the narrative.

The metaphor of the Persian Prince remained constant in the most iconic literary events of the twentieth century. Houshang Golshiri's novella *Shazdeh Ehtejab (Prince Ehtejab,* 1969) tells the story of one of the last ailing princes (whom we know only as "The Prince") of the Qajar dynasty suffering from tuberculosis while repeatedly receiving news of the death of family members. The Prince spends his last days with just his estranged wife and their subservient domestic help in the magnificent but forlorn rooms of his palace, from where he recollects the glories and sufferings of his ancestors. The novella is plain, powerful, iconic in its prose, and unnerving as it unravels the terror of the ruling monarchies since time immemorial. The work was adapted into an excellent film by Bahman Farmanara in 1974—even more poignant and iconic in the brevity and power of its visual imageries.[21] A decade before this landmark novella and film, Seyavash Kasra'i's epic poem *Arash-e Kamangir* (*Arash the Archer*, 1959) turned a mythic hero into a revolutionary guerrilla fighter.

These metamorphic moments in Persian mythologies took place at a time when the last Pahlavi monarch was an outdated sovereign completely gutted of all moral imagination or political legitimacy, while his chief nemesis and ultimate successor, Ayatollah Khomeini, was a vindictive jurist who went about building a tyrannical Islamic republic in his own image. Khomeini was all the moral exactitude of Islamic law degenerated into a theocratic tyranny. Against both of them, poets like Seyavash Kasra'i and Ahmad Shamlou were the rebellious voices who boldly personified and liberated the sublimated Persian Prince. As the monadic archetype of the Persian Prince becomes the ailing Shazdeh Ehtejab, the resurrected figure becomes Ahmad Shamlou's folkloric image of the Pariya (fairies) in one poem, "Dokhtara-ye Naneh Darya" (the daughters of Mother Sea), "Pesara-ye Amu Sahra" (the sons of Uncle Prairie) elsewhere, or reappears as Pari Ghamgini (a Sad Little Fairy) in Forough Farrokhzad's iconic poem *Tavallodi Digar* (*Another Birth*, 1962). Retrieving the archetype of the Persian Prince for the postclassical age was perforce performed under colonial duress, the shadow of a hope that demanded its own Persian person in the figure of the iconic Persian Prince. As the monadic archetype turned dyadic, the hidden labyrinth of the nomadic subject emerged to reclaim the world and be at home in it. The Persian Prince thus lost his royal home to find a whole world to inhabit.

The triumphant tragedy of the figure of the Persian Prince is that he was never at home in any single narrative—from the juridical to the literary—and thus could never have dwelled in any single site: courtly decorum or revolutionary uprisings, political parties or positions of power. Except in the realm of fiction and poetry, there was always something fake about anyone who claimed the archetype, which was always at odds with itself—and the world was made better in living in that very paradox. Dreaming of democratic liberation but unable to yield to the bureaucratic discipline and ideological constraints of any political party, the new Persian Prince relieved the old archetypal oscillation between power and protest, thus opting for the much bigger but less politically efficacious abodes of liberated homelands and revolutionary nations, joggling between their unending dreams and recurrent nightmares.

In the purgatory of those nomadic passages, every potential citizen became a fictional prince—a little prince, just as in Antoine de Saint-Exupéry's *The Little Prince* (1943), which was soon translated into Persian and remains widely popular. The book follows a young, lonely prince who wanders through the cosmos visiting various planets in space, including Earth, configuring the measures of his own loneliness. The narrator's description of his first encounter with the Little Prince, when he asks him to draw a picture of a sheep, is precisely the final thought I wish to share before my conclusion, as to how I think of my own Persian Prince and the book I have written like a box to contain it.

> "This is only his box. The sheep you asked for is inside."
> I was very surprised to see a light break over the face of my young judge:
> "That is exactly the way I wanted it! Do you think that this sheep will have to have a great deal of grass?"
> "Why?"
> "Because where I live everything is very small...."
> "There will surely be enough grass for him," I said. "It is a very small sheep that I have given you."
> He bent his head over the drawing.
> "Not so small that—Look! He has gone to sleep...."
> And that is how I made the acquaintance of the little prince.[22]

CONCLUSION

The Sublimation of an Imperial Archetype

Gar zeh chashmash partov-e garmi nemitabad . . .

Even though no warming gaze shines through its eyes,
Even though no happy smile grows on its face,
Who says the Leafless Garden is not beautiful?
It tells the story of skyscraping fruit trees,
Now buried in the lowly coffin of earth.
The Leafless Garden
Smiles with bloodied tears—
Forever roams around it
Mounting on his yellow horse—with its mane flowing in the air—
The Prince of all seasons: Autumn![1]

Mehdi Akhavan-e Sales, "Bagh-e Man" [My garden], (1945)

I BEGAN THIS BOOK with a fascination. I was drawn to Machiavelli's seminal text *The Prince* (1513–1532), almost intuitively pulling it back to Nezam al-Molk's *Siyasat-nameh* (1086–1091) and even, long before that, to Xenophon's *Cyropaedia* (370 BCE). It was not until I came forward to consider Antonio Gramsci's take on Machiavelli in his own "Modern Prince" (1929 and 1935) that things began to gel, by which point I was led to thinking contrapuntally in the context of Islamic and Persian literary and political genres, discourses, and histories—in a decidedly comparative context of Indian, Greek, Hebrew, and European resonances. By now, Persian, Arabic, Indian, Jewish, Greek, Roman, and European reflections of what I had come to term the "Persian Prince" were all coming together. I therefore opted for consecutive comparative moments with Xenophon, Machiavelli, Gramsci, leading to Ernst Cassirer and coming down to Rosi Braidotti's articulation of the nomadic subject closer to our own time as the theoretical signposts of navigating the historical unfolding of the Persian Prince from its archaic origins to its contemporary metamorphosis under colonial duress. I have offered three thematic moments in the life and legacy of the Persian Prince in this longue durée—beginning with its *monadic* origins, leading to its *dyadic* splitting under colonial duress, and finally resulting in the *nomadic* dispensation of the archetype.

In this trajectory, a major thrust of European political thought from Xenophon to Machiavelli to Gramsci to Cassirer and the rest might therefore be read as a particular European take on the figure of the Persian Prince as an archetypal prototype. This opens up a major comparative prospect. Historians of Greek philosophy have widely explored the link between Plato, Xenophon, and Persia as their mutual points of reference.[2] This was of course a two-way street, and arguments have been put forward that Xerxes too modeled his imperial conquest on the blueprint of Homer's epics.[3] It is perfectly plausible therefore to consider Plato's idea of the philosopher-king modeled on his perception of the Persian Prince—informed by the same sources as did Xenophon's *Cyropaedia*. A proverbial encounter between Plato at his deathbed with a delegation of Persian *Magoi* has been a constant source of exploration between Platonic and Persian thought.[4] The point here is to take the very idea of the philosopher-king as a cornerstone of Plato's philosophy and consider it as potentially having been a Greek take on the Persian Prince, whereas in his contemporary time, Xenophon's *Cyropaedia* becomes even more precise in this trajectory, leading subsequent generations to consider the Sassanid emperor Khosrow I as the prototype of the philosopher-king. The link here could also be extended to the figure of Alexander the Great in both its Greek and Persian sources. The idea of Alexander the Great as Plato's philosopher-king is perfectly plausible given the link between the Macedonian general and Aristotle. We can also make a similar case for the presence of the idea of the Persian Prince in Indo-Persian and Judeo-Persian epics, where we see a palpable fusion of Vedic and biblical themes and the archetype of the Persian Prince.[5] This places the idea of the Persian Prince at the epicenter of a longue durée that expands from classical antiquity all the way to our own time—with major way stations along its historical unfolding. The text of *Cyropaedia* places the archetypal Persian Prince right in the provenance of both Xenophon and Plato—as the varied Hebrew texts from the Book of Esther to the choral rise of Judeo-Persian epics situate the very same archetype at the heart of Judaic tradition. An idea that brings classical Greek antiquity and the Hebrew texts to converse, as it maps the Indian, Iranian, and Islamic landscape together, scarce needs any other justification for its seminal significance.

The Persian Chaosmopolis

If we take the Platonic and subsequent European idea of the philosopher-king as one particular take on the idea of the Persian Prince, we approach other manifestations of it in its immediate surroundings slightly differently. In its European version, it rolled from its potential influence on Plato's idea of the philosopher-king to Xenophon's *Cyropaedia*, down to the Christian articulation of the just ruler, as best evidenced by Desiderius Erasmus's *Education of a Christian Prince* (1516), which eventually achieves its contemporary doppelgänger in Machiavelli's *Prince*, and from here to Gramsci's "Modern Prince" and Ernst Cassirer's critique *The Myth of the State* (1946). Shifting attention from philosophy to drama, Edith Hall has traced an even longer trajectory from Aeschylus's *Persians* through the Ottoman Empire down to the US-led invasion and occupation of Iraq.[6] Meanwhile the imperial archetype had a different destiny in the Persianate world from India to Iran to Central Asia to the Ottoman world—as it evolved both thematically and chronologically from the monadic figure of the king, caliph, or sultan, to the dyadic split between the nation and the state, to the formation of the nomadic subject as the fragmented site of the archetype. In the nomadic phase, all this history comes back together to reveal how the Persian Prince was in fact the ideal type of a human being best fitted to face and embrace the world.

The three successive stages of the Persian Prince that I articulate here on *monadic*, *dyadic*, and *nomadic* planes hold together my transhistorical longue durée both historically and thematically. The *monadic stage* is when the Persian Self and the Persian Prince are the same, when the imperial archetype holds the ruler and the ruled together as one and the same—where the Prince is the mirror of his subjects, and thus the Persian prince and the Persian person are identical. The *dyadic stage* occurs when the archetype of the Persian Prince has split into two opposing fractions, when the nation and the state have become bifurcated, separate and parting ways, a Siamese twin held together at the hips but living as two different organisms. Finally, the *nomadic stage* is when the Persian

Prince has become the atomized and digitized posthuman body of the postcolonial persona, homeless in any and all habitats, rooted in the heteroglossia of its cross-colonial boundaries, dwelling on the transnational overworld that mirrors the underworld of its wandering soul. Here the figure of the Bidoon, the migrant *persona non grata* sailing about the Persian Gulf, or the figure of the Muʿavedin, Iraqis who are thought to be Iranians, and Iranians who are thought to be Iraqis, is the final destination of the Persian Prince as a prototype, and where the Persian cosmopolis has finally become the Persian chaosmopolis, a term I build on Deleuze's "chaosmos."[7] The Persianate chaosmopolis is where the Persian Prince resurrects in the body of the migratory soul of the Persian person, its fullest subjectivity realized when realizing she and he are the prince.

Here, at the conclusion of this book, I have finally come to know theoretically what I was speculating about only thematically at the end of my book *The World of Persian Literary Humanism* (2012), when I suggested that the earliest stages of Persian literary humanism had begun with the premise of *Ethnos/Nezhad*, leading to *Logos/Sokhan*, then to *Ethos/Hanjar*, before concluding with *Chaos/Ashub*. I had offered this dialectical progression as a thematic unfolding of the internal dynamics of Persian literary humanism instead of forcing it (as is habitually done) on to a European modality of classic and modern literature. I may now conclude this book by proposing that the three interrelated figures of the Prince, the World, and the Self are concealed as incompossible for having been imagined as compossible—and thus the move from the Persian cosmopolis into the Persian chaosmopolis. The figure of the Prince contains and conceals the Royalty, the Prophetic, and the Poetic. The World the Prince inhabits is divinely harmonious with sporadic demonic interjections at its dialectical roots. The World here is not based on the model of a Christian triad of Divinity, the World, and the Selves, as it was with Kant, for example. This World is decidedly Manichean and dyadic at its cosmic roots between Light and Darkness, through constant interaction between Good and Evil. The Persian Prince is here to tilt the balance toward the Good—once as prince, then as prophet, but always as a rebel/poet. The state of the chaosmopolis is where selves and societies have become open-ended, as *monadic* subjects remembering their *dyadic* disposition before entering the moment of their penultimate *nomadic* ipseity.

A thematic and theoretical triad thus emerges, where the sublimated suspension of historical reasoning resurfaces as the *nomadic nomos* of the Persian Prince is made to recollect its inaugural *monadic mythos* through its *dyadic logos*. As nomadic subjectivity becomes the norm, the monadic myth of origin of the Persian Prince resurfaces from its subconscious habitat, having just gone through the colonial trauma of its dyadic split. This proposition I now see as the culmination of a major thrust in the sustained course of my critical thinking and scholarship. The thematic move through these phases has made all national and dynastic historiographies of old-fashioned or updated Orientalism obsolete—and organically linked together the imperial histories of Muslims and their postcolonial predicaments moving on a continuous theoretical plane. But more importantly, the postcolonial subject of my sustained investigation was now historicized, liberated from any parasitical existence on the falsely manufactured binaries between "Islam and the West," "Tradition and Modernity." A whole new vista of regional and global historiography was now in sight.

A few more moves were necessary to make my argument cohere. In *The Shahnameh: The Persian Epic as World Literature* (2019), I sought to extend the logic of that project and opted for a detailed reading of the link between the Persian epic and the multiple empires it has served up to the postcolonial age, in order to make the question of the "modern epic" more complicated as a case study of the public sphere and the postcolonial subject formation through the rise and unfolding of multiple worlds—not just the one colonially dominant and imperially manufactured world, the world about which European and US literary theorists of "World Literature" consistently theorize. In *Reversing the Colonial Gaze: Persian Travelers Abroad* (2020), I placed the formative subjection of the postcolonial person on the back of a horse or a camel or a mule or a train or a ship and followed them around the globe to map out the nomadic disposition of the postcolonial subject. With this book on the archetype of the Persian Prince, I have mapped out in detailed and specific terms the historical roots and theoretical contours of the current disposition of a postcolonial person on the edges of a nomadic posthuman consciousness. The Persian chaosmopolis that has emerged as the locus classicus of this archetype roots my historical mapping of the postcolonial person in a sustained course of historical consciousness.

The Prince, the Person, the World

We should not abandon the historical person that thus emerges as a nomadic subject on a listless leaking boat wandering in the Mediterranean Sea—a Bidoon/Without, part of the Muʿavedin (Returnees) from nowhere to nowhere. Where is that nomadic soul most at home? That chaosmopolis hosting the Persian person as a distant memory of the Persian Prince has its internal logic and rhetoric—where it is at home in a homeless soul. I have proposed the archetype of the Persian Prince as an ideal type for a protagonist claiming the pride of place on a world stage, without any specific gender, both male and female, neither male nor female, or what in Islamic mysticism eventually resurfaced as an Insan-e Kamel (perfect human being). The Alam-e Saghir (microcosm) of his or her soul reflects the Alam-e Kabir (macrocosm) of the universe we all inhabit in our own fictive way. The prototype of the first and final human, however, has much older roots in Iranian and other ancient cultures. In seeking to educate the ideal ruler, poets and philosophers partook in these ideals and imagined an Insan-e Kamel—or, in specifically Iranian terms, Gayomart/Keyumars (literally "mortal being")—the mythic, heroic, and protohistoric figure to retrieve his/her immortal image. The yearning for the Perfect Man is the yearning for the First and Final person for which the Persian Prince became a prototype, an ideal type, a nostalgic allusion. While in Islamic mysticism the Prophet, the Shi'i Imams, or the mystic saints become manifestations of Insan-e Kamel, in its Iranian origins it corresponds with Keyumars, the first human being, the very image of fragile (mortal) humanity. Here is where the Prince, the Person, and the World come together.

In his pioneering essay "Die islamische Lehre vom Vollkommenen Menschen, ihre Herkunft und ihre dichterische Gestaltung" (The Islamic doctrine of the perfect man, its origin and its poetic manifestations, 1925), the prominent German Orientalist Hans Heinrich Schaeder puts forward the bold and brilliant idea that the concept of the Perfect Man is rooted in pre-Islamic, gnostic, both Hellenistic and Iranian, conceptions of the ideal type of human being and then finds its most varied and spectacular manifestations in the figure of the Beloved in Persian lyrical poetry.[8] He examines what he calls "the ubiquitous motive of the beloved friend in Persian and Persian-oriented lyrics" and discovers its "convergence" with the old mythical motive of the "Perfect Man." He proposes that the idea of the Perfect Man became central to Islamic mysticism, identified with the figure of the Prophet, and Gnostic Prophetology, but rooted in pre-Islamic ideas of the Divine Light. This eventually reaches Shi'i Imamology too, where the doctrine of the Infallibility of the Imams reflects a similar idea. Citing the Swedish Iranologist Henrik Samuel Nyberg, Schaeder then reiterates the proposition that the idea of the Perfect Man reconnects so that "Gott, Mensch und Welt inhaltlich ganz zusammenfallen. Sie sind nur drei Aspekte desselben Begriffes, und zwar zunächst so, daß der Mensch das verbindende Mittelglied dars" (God, Man, and World completely come together in terms of their content. They are only three aspects of the same concept, initially in such a way that the human being is the connecting link).[9] His contention is that this figure later becomes the metaphor of the Beloved in Persian poetry. The proposition places the figure of the Persian Prince in its mystical and poetic rendition as a central pillar of the Persianate world through Persian poetry.

Perhaps the best metaphor for this link between the Self and the Multitude, or between the soul of the Persian Prince and the collective desire of the subjects' search for him, is immortalized in Attar's *Conference of the Birds* (1177), when the birds are looking for their royal Prince and end up discovering they have been in search of themselves, their collectivity, their own collective image, their wishful thinking. A flock of scattered birds gather together, choose hoopoe as their leader, and decide to fly to Mount Qaf to find their Prince. After much commotion and discord, a group of thirty cantankerous birds get there, land on the summit of Mount Qaf, and look for their King. All they see is a mirror and their own reflections in it.[10] They are thirty birds (Si Morgh), and all they see is "Simorgh," the legendary bird who is nothing other than its own mirror image. The birds, standing in for humans, have been in search of themselves—as have humans in search of the Persian Prince. There is no King, no Prince, no Simorgh except in their collective awareness of themselves, collective desires for a better version of themselves.

Here we might consider a key line of Hafez differently:

> *Mian-e Asheq o Maʿshuq hich hayel nist*
> *To khod hijab-e khodi Hafez az mian barkhiz.*

> There is no veil between the Lover and the Beloved
> You are the veil upon yourself, get out of the way![11]

Here Man and God conflate each other—as the Prince stands for both of them held together. The Lover and the Beloved are Man and God, the Subject and the Lord, the Person and the Prince. The figure of the Persian Prince we might consider as a concrete example of the archetype in its monadic disposition that becomes fragmented and allegorized in its nomadic destiny. The question now becomes the dynamics of this transmutation from the monadic to the dyadic to the nomadic articulations of the archetype. What dwells in this line that concludes a major ghazal is the fusion of a selfless Person and a demythologized Prince. That demythologized nucleus contains all that is unfolding in specific historical terms. This is the premonition of a new World in which the Prince and the Person have finally come together, reflecting each other, as they have always done—but this time in specifically historic, neither heroic nor mythic, terms—and thus the origin of the hermeneutics of de-authenticity at the epistemic roots of the nomadic subject.

Transubstantial Motion Toward the Posthuman Persona

How does the archetype of the Persian Prince move through its own metaphors—how does it sublimate from its monadic to dyadic to nomadic gestations? In one of his seminal essays, "Ludwig Binswanger and the Sublimation of the Self" (1966), Paul de Man dwells on a crucial essay by Binswanger, "Henrik Ibsen und das Problem der Selbstrealisation in der Kunst/Henrik Ibsen and the Question of Self-Realization in Art" (1949), which is itself predicated on an essay by György Lukács, "The Subject-Object Relationship in Aesthetics" (1917). Through de Man's reading of these two essays, he brings us to the pivotal moment when the self of an author is changed and interpreted by his or her own work or, as de Man puts it, "the monadic structure" of the work and the subjectivity of the author is posited as a "windowless monad."[12] Here, the self becomes capable of revealing its own destiny, with its implied reader, through both the fragility of a poetic transcendence and the prospect of an "involuntary ascent" and, even more provocatively, "the imaginative possibility of an upward fall."[13]

It is this inverted image of "an upward fall" that I see as best suitable to what I have been driving home with the long history and varied transmutations of the figure of the Persian Prince—as it moves from its monadic to its dyadic to its nomadic selves. The sublimation of the Persian Prince is a fusion of multiple systemic propositions that include the *sublation* of the knowing subject, the *sublimation* of the authorial voice, or perhaps more precisely "al-Harakah al-Jawhariyyah" (the transubstantial motion) of the Persian Prince. I wish to bring these three different concepts, the Freudian *sublimation*, the Hegelian *sublation*, and prominent Shi'i philosopher Mulla Sadra's revolutionary proposition of "transubstantial motion" to bear on the process through which the historical transformation of the idea of the Persian Prince has taken place. In Mulla Sadra's philosophical system, the central idea of transubstantial motion posits the contingency of existence, the transfusion of the permanent into the changing, and the categorical re-creation of infinite worlds, all leading to his theory of bodily resurrection (al-Ma'ad al-Jismani).[14] This Sadraian idea perhaps best represents how the idea of the Persian Prince moves from one stage to another.

In the case of the Persian Prince, the transformation takes place entirely in the creative imagination of rebels and poets, whether they pick up arms to right the wrong they see in their worlds or they sharpen their pencils to rewrite the history they have received.

Film, fiction, and poetry are the primary domains of this open-ended sublimation. In such ionic poems as Mehdi Akhavan-e Sales's "Shahryar-e Shahr-e Sangestan" (The prince of Stoneville, 1960), landmark works of fiction like Houshang Golshiri's *Prince Ehtejab* (1969), iconic films like Amir Naderi's *Tangsir* (1973), groundbreaking novels like Shahrnoush Parsipur's *Blue Intellect* (1994), and many others, we are witness to the systematic sublimation of the idea of the Persian Prince. When we come to a poem like Ahmad Shamlou's "Abraham in the Fire" (1973), we see how he mobilizes a whole cosmogony of ancient Greek, Iranian, and biblical metaphors to elevate the figure of a revolutionary hero into an archaic Savior, a Messiah, a Mahdi, a Saoshyant. Invoking the iconic figure of the Hebrew prophet Abraham, in this poem Shamlou celebrates a revolutionary hero, Mehdi Reza'i, by comparing him with both Achilles and Esfandiar; all of them come together in this otherwise obscure revolutionary to preside over an entirely different divinity:

> I was not a hopeless little slave—
> Nor was the way to my Paradise
> Through a goat-path of obedience and supplication.
> I needed a different kind of God
> Worthy of a creation who does not submit to a mere subsistence—
> And I created a different God![15]

This "upward fall" summons the whole history of the Persian Prince for a reassemblage of the ancient archetype. The transcultural context of varied gestations of the Persian Prince is a crucial historical one to remember here. If we were to consider Erasmus's *Education of a Christian Prince*, dedicated to Habsburg emperor Charles V, and recall that this seminal text was published just three years after Machiavelli had written (but not published) *The Prince*, then we can zoom out to a larger comparative context where we see that what began as Xenophon's *Cyropaedia* in classical antiquity also had a Jewish and a Christian rendition as a well as an Islamic one.[16] This historical unfolding of the "Prince of Peace" in turn makes the figure of the Persian Prince ipso facto a migratory and nomadic prototype—from its pre-Zoroastrian traces all through its varied Jewish, Christian, and Islamic gestations. The multiplicity of the areas in which the Persian

Prince kept rearticulating itself—in Zoroastrian, Pahlavi, Greek, Jewish, Christian, and Islamic sites—had prepared the archetype for its postcolonial, anticolonial, and ultimately decolonial dispositions millennia into its future, affected deeply by and through its traumatic encounters with European colonial modernity, occasioning its resurrection back to its formative forces.

That brings us to the emergence of the posthuman subject, for which we might consider the theoretical articulation of the figure of the *Muselmann* in Agamben's reading of the living dead in Auschwitz. In his *Remnants of Auschwitz: The Witness and the Archive*, Giorgio Agamben theorizes the idea of "bare life" and, at one point, zeroes in on the concentration camp figure of the Muselmann (plural: *Muselmänner*) as a persona representing the state of unbeing. But why would such a figure in a German concentration camp containing mostly Jewish prisoners be called a Muslim? Many scholars have reflected on this puzzle. Some have opted to read it as a reference to "muscle," for these prisoners had been driven to the point of starvation. But there are also those who have opted to read it for what it is—the German word for "Muslim." Among any number of other explanations, Junaid Rana's essay "The Story of Islamophobia" (2007) reads the word "Muslim" here as coterminous with "the Jew," one as the external enemy and the other as the internal enemy of Christian Europe.[17] Whether a Muslim outside or a Jew inside Europe, the fading figure of the Muselmann in a German concentration camp is where the bare life comes to reduce the *bios* of a human being to mere *zoe* and prepare the groundwork for the posthuman body and soul.

First and foremost, the posthuman subject is a postnational person, where no one is any longer "at home" anywhere; as the habitat of that persona, the Persianate world has become globally amorphous and scattered all over the map. Perhaps the most iconic current example of this postnational person would be someone like Behrouz Boochani (born 1983), the Kurdish-Iranian writer who was held in the Australian-run Manus Island refugee camp in Papua New Guinea between 2013 and 2017. He was eventually granted refugee status in 2020. Boochani's memoir, *No Friend but the Mountains: Writing from Manus Prison* (2019), became an international bestseller and received an array of awards and recognition. The book was written over time on a mobile phone (how apt and symbolic of the nomadic disposition of our mobile lives), through a series of text messages, and eventually translated from Persian into English by Omid Tofighian.[18]

The same sense of the Persian person rethinking and reimagining his or her nomadic presence on this planet is evident in the extraordinary work of Mohsen

Namjoo, the Iranian singer/songwriter and composer, whose music is a creative fusion of blues and rock with Persian folk music and lyrics. He was born and raised in Iran and reached artistic maturity in his homeland but fled to Europe and the United States, where his lyrics and music became decidedly syncretic.[19] In his music sings a homeless soul in search of a sense of political purpose and poetic interiority. The same is true of the postnational poetry of Esmail Khoi (born 1938), a gifted poet born and raised in Iran but forced into exile in the 1980s and who now lives in the United Kingdom. In his poetry, a bitter and angry revulsion against the fate of his homeland underlines fading nostalgic memories.

We have a different (and decidedly engrossing) texture in the films of Ramin Bahrani (born 1975), an Iranian American filmmaker whose work has emerged as a potent example of postnational cinema; it follows closely the work of another gifted filmmaker, Amir Naderi, who in his early career was a pioneering figure of Iranian cinema before he moved to Europe, the United States, and Japan. The equally postnational art of Nicky Nodjoumi, Shirin Neshat, and Ardeshir Mohassess—three globally celebrated Iranian artists who made New York their home away from home—marks the unfolding of the creative souls of the postnational persons. A renowned political caricaturist, Ardeshir Mohassess (1938–2008) was a particularly powerful artist who lampooned the Qajar dynasty (1789–1926), and through it the history of Persian monarchy, during the apex of his career in Iran during the 1960s and the 1970s. Typical of his oeuvre is this piece, in which he portrays the last Qajar prince, Ahmad Shah (1898–1930), as an entirely ridiculous tyrant sporting attire that fails to conceal his miserable claim to power and authority (fig. 9). This the final image of the Persian Prince lost to any and all glory at his outdated royal court, as seen by a self-confident, flamboyant, and worldly at-home artist who is himself the last vestige of the ancient archetype.

What such postnational works of art represent is the sublimation of the postcolonial subjection—author and artist and poet as the visionaries of a lost metaphor—into visual and performing abstractions beyond the control of even the artists themselves or the audiences they engage. As such, they project and map out the rise of the posthuman subject, as best theorized by Rosi Braidotti, detailing, as she does, the contours of the technologies and the robotics of posthumanity.[20] Where is the human on this amorphous map, and where do her alterities reside? The social construction of the human becomes even more evident in the contours of the posthuman, where the knowing subject must struggle to emerge from an unknowing subjectivity. In my *Corpus Anarchicum: Political*

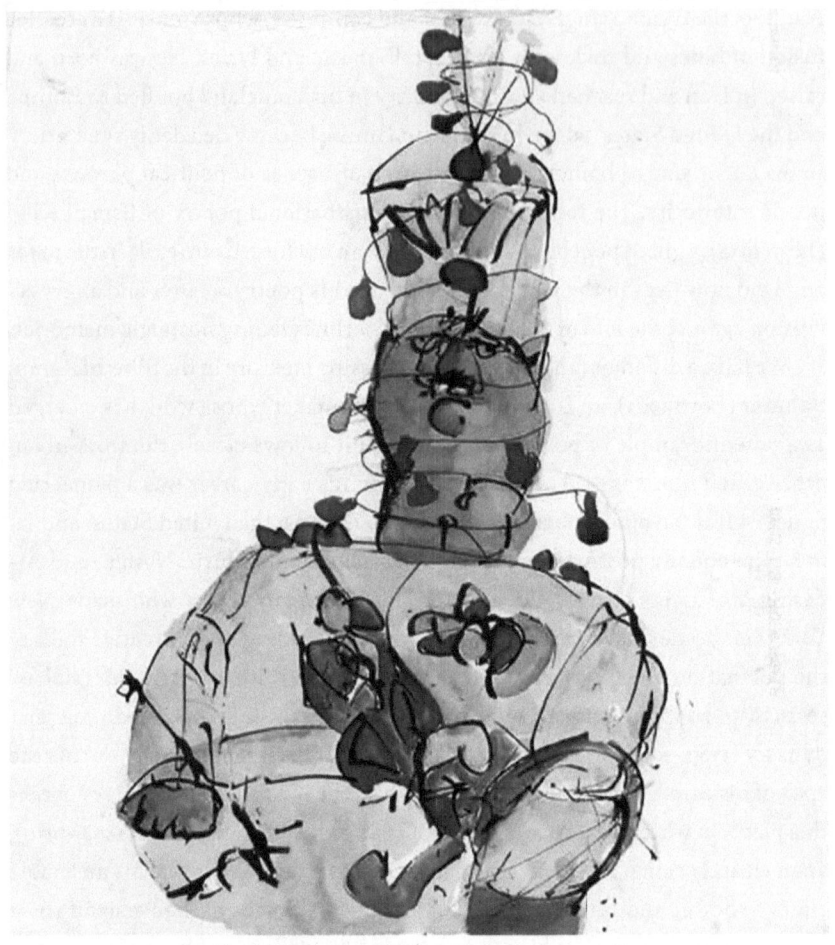

FIGURE 9 Ardeshir Mohassess, *Ahmad Shah—The Last King of Qajar*, 1980s. New York, Metropolitan Museum of Art.

Protest, Suicidal Violence, and the Making of the Posthuman Body (2012), I have explored the contours of artificial insemination, organ transplant, physician-assisted suicide, and ultimately suicidal violence as the varied modalities of the posthuman body.[21] But that posthuman body has stages to perform itself far more pleasant and hopeful to watch. If the cruel spectacles of suicidal violence are one place to mourn the failings of the posthuman body, the lost and wandering posthuman souls have far more hopeful scenes to stage their transmigratory, nomadic whereabouts.

A Persian Princess on a Whirlwind Tour of the World

As I wind down toward the end of my conclusion, let me turn to a transhistorical Persian Princess on a whirlwind tour of the global stage. In early June 2019, I was invited to Amsterdam by the Holland Festival to deliver a keynote on the occasion of an extraordinary event in the course of its annual program. That year, its program included the European premiere of *Turan Dokht*, an exceptionally daring and imaginative opera, which the festival had described as "an intercultural rewriting of Puccini's famous opera *Turandot*" (1924). *Turan Dokht* ("Daughter of Turan" in Persian), composed by the gifted Iranian musician Aftab Darvishi and directed by the Dutch dramatist Miranda Lakerveld, is an entirely new dramatic experience located somewhere between the Italian and the Persian masterpieces to which it alludes. Reaching for the Persian roots of a European masterpiece, *Turan Dokht* staged itself as indeed a beautiful tribute to both Puccini's *Turandot* and Nezami's *Haft Peykar*, which share a story about a mystifying princess.[22] In the Persian original, written in the twelfth century, the main character, King Bahram Gur, is entertained each day of the week with a story told by one of seven princesses from seven climes, corresponding to seven primary colors and seven planets. In its European version, the role of Bahram Gur is almost entirely omitted and all the operatic fantasies redirected to a powerful princess who here has become the chief protagonist.

There is, however, much more to this opera than initially meets the eye. A closer look at the long and winding history of this new Persian take on an Italian take on a German take on the Persian original shows how, in film, fiction, poetry, drama, and opera, Princess "Turandot" has become a traveling troubadour on a tour around the planet, from the Persianate and Islamic world to Europe and elsewhere. Singing songs, performing dances, staging drama, romancing love, and forming fancies of the world beneath and beyond, this Princess, of Persian origin and worldly traveled, emerged from the depth of an ancient story to adorn the finest opera houses in Europe and beyond. The modest story of *Turandot* combined with its longest journeys staged one final bravura spectacle of the fate and infinitude of the story of the Persian Prince before it was gendered, beyond its generational divides, deep into the layered subconscious of peoples and cultures around the civilized world.[23]

There are any number of places to start telling the story of *Turandot* and its global circulations, each as good as any other. In the second half of the eighteenth century, a translated version of the original Persian poem had reached the Italian playwright and leading advocate of *commedia dell'arte* Count Carlo Gozzi (1720–1806), and through Goethe it eventually reached Friedrich Schiller (1759–1805) and other European playwrights and composers. In the hands of Puccini, the central figure of Turandot emerges as a vengeful princess refusing to marry and determined to dissuade her suitors by imposing a dreadful test of their desires. In Darvishi and Lakerveld's work, the story of the princess is reimagined yet again and brought back closer to its Persian roots.[24] The Iranian composer combines classical Persian and European musical traditions for a joyously surprising rendezvous—cleverly teasing out Puccini's signature aria "Nessun Dorma" from a gracious fusion of Persian and European instruments—while bringing Nezami's masterpiece alive to her Dutch colleague's patient, learned, and cultivated directorial homage to Persian miniature tradition. The opera was a joy to watch, a deeply rooted tradition staged to be beheld. Europe and Persia had come together in a transhistorical, peaceful, joyous, celebratory, and deeply moving performing art.

The composition of the original opera by Puccini has an immediate Italian, German, and French progeny. Giacomo Puccini's *Turandot* (1926), an opera in three acts completed posthumously by Franco Alfano and set to a libretto in Italian by Giuseppe Adami and Renato Simoni, has its immediate European roots in the work of German poet and dramatist Friedrich von Schiller. Although Puccini first became interested in the subject after reading Schiller's 1801 adaptation of the play, his own opera is based on the earlier text of *Turandot* (1762) by Count Carlo Gozzi, which he had in turn received from a French translation dating back to 1675. Schiller's *Turandot: The Chinese Sphinx* (1801) was itself the result of Schiller's conversations with Goethe, who encouraged him to take on this task. In this European context, the execution of the "Prince of Persia" in the very first act of the opera is a subtextual reference to where all this operatic adventure had started. The Prince of Persia is executed to frighten Liù and give her beloved Calàf courage and cause to pick up the challenge of Turandot and sing one of his most beautiful arias, "Non piangere, Liù!"[25]

The original story of *Turandot* is based on one of seven episodes in the epic romance of *Haft Peykar* (*The Seven Beauties*, 1197), composed by the twelfth-century Persian poet Hakim Nezami Ganjavi (1141–1209). Nezami composed these seven stories in line with the seven days of the week, the seven primary colors, and the seven corresponding planets. The particular story on which *Turandot* is based is the story of Tuesday as it is told to Prince Bahram by his companion of the Red Dome, associated with Mars. In the very first line of this story, the protagonist is identified as a Russian princess. *Haft Peykar* is part of Nezami's *Khamseh* (quintet)—a masterpiece of classical Persian poetry. The five narrative poems that form this quintet are *Makhzan al-Asrar* (a didactic narrative), *Khosrow Shirin* (a love story), *Leili and Majnun* (another love story), *Iskandar-nameh* (an iconic rendition of an Alexander romance), and *Haft Peykar*. The original title of the Persian poem, *Haft Peykar*, can be translated literally as "Seven Portraits," with the figurative meaning of "Seven Beauties."

In this poem, we encounter Prince Bahram and seven princesses: from India (identified with the color black), China (yellow), Khwarazm (green), Russia (red), Maghrib (turquoise), Rum (khaki), and Persia (white). This romance part of the poem is plotted within the historical epic part of Prince Bahram. The original Persian text of this book has been as much the object of critical scholarly attention as its stories have been widely popular. A critical edition of *Haft Peykar* was produced by eminent Orientalists Helmut Ritter and Jan Rypka, edited in Prague, and printed in Istanbul in 1934. Another critical edition, by Wahid Dastgerdi, was published in Tehran in 1936. Additional critical editions followed. The entirety of *Khamseh* also received widespread translations into multiple European languages throughout the nineteenth and twentieth centuries.[26] Scholars and literati alike, composers and poets, have all been drawn to this extraordinary book, and particularly to *Haft Peykar*. Both the critical and the creative receptions of Nezami's masterpiece have been as widespread in the Persianate world as they have been in its European contexts.

At the quiet center of this epic romance, Prince Bahram is a historical figure, the Sassanid emperor Bahram V (reigned 420–438).[27] But in the story of Princess Turandot, as indeed in the entirety of *Haft Peykar*, the figure of the Persian Prince is almost completely subsumed, silenced, made tangential. We see him or learn about him only through the stories the seven princesses from around the planet, representing the whole cosmos, gather to tell. These princesses and their pavilions represent seven heavens, seven climes, the seven colors of the rainbow, and the seven days of the week. The Persian Prince (Bahram) is here the invisible epicenter of the whole universe. A whole cosmogony of planetary coordinates is gathered around these princesses and the Persian Prince they thus entertain. Many scholars have sought to read these colors symbolically and mythically—with compelling and convincing analysis. We can also read them formally and structurally. *Haft Peykar* is based on color formalism and not on color symbolism—color, calendar, and cosmogony are the key framings of the story. Both the epic and the romance it entails are ocularcentric and not logocentric, for they give manuscript illustrators clues as to how to visualize them, not how to interpret them, for the form is semiotic, not hermeneutic. Long before *Turandot* was staged and performed in European opera houses, the stories of *Haft Peykar* were "staged" and "performed" visually in exquisite manuscript illustrations in their original habitats. There is a dialectic between the visual and the verbal, fusing together the poetic of colors and the erotic of the verses they imagine.

Through *Turandot* and countless other operas, the archetype of the Persian Prince and now the seven princesses from around the world enter European opera houses. Gozzi, Goethe, Schiller, and ultimately Puccini (among many others) became the operatic and dramatic vehicle of ushering in the provenance of the Persian Prince into European contexts.[28] An earlier source before Gozzi—this time an Armenian Iranian from Tabriz—had informed them all. In 1557, Tramezzino Publishing House published a volume of Oriental tales, *Peregrinaggio di tre giovani figliuoli del re di Serendippo* (*The Three Princes of Serendip*), in which we read that a person named Cristoforo Armeno had translated it from Persian into Italian out of gratitude to Venetians. This book turns out to be from Amir Khosrow's *Hasht-Behesht* (1302), one of the five poems he composed on the model of Nezami's *Khamseh*. It eventually made it into French as well as English and German translations too. *The Three Princes of Serendip* retells the life of the selfsame Persian King Bahram V, whose stories already appear in Ferdowsi's *Shahnameh* (1010), Nezami's *Haft Peykar* (1197), and Amir Khosrow's *Hasht-Behesht* (1302), before eventually reaching Europe as *The Three Princes of Serendip* (1557) or through the collection known as *Les Mille et un jours* (*One Thousand and One Days*, 1710–1712) by François Pétis de la Croix, and from there to Gozzi (1762), Schiller (1801), and finally Puccini (1926).[29] Turandot was on a whirlwind tour of Europe and, from there, across the colonized world far from her Persianate habitat. Schiller initially recast the setting of his play from Persia to China; however, when the play was performed in Hamburg in 1802, the work was reset in Shiraz, and some of the characters were also renamed and given Persian names.[30] *Turandot* was just the tip of the iceberg, upon which sat seven planetary princesses telling the story of the Persian Prince in bold, brilliant, and provocative tales.[31]

Puccini's bit of European Orientalism, or Persophilia to be more exact, was a floating signifier, a Trojan horse. He had no idea what his opera was carrying inside its belly.³² Mesmerized by his own glorious music, Puccini was carrying a whole world inside his opera back and forth into deep past and distant future. Long before it reached Puccini, Nezami's story also appears in a mystical cast in Rumi's *Masnavi* (1258–1273) in a story called "Dezh-e Hushruba" (The fortress of forgetfulness), in which we learn there is a portrait of a Chinese princess on the wall of this fortress from which the beholder loses his mind. Three princes defy the advice of their royal father and enter this fortress, look at that portrait, fall madly in love, and travel to China to meet their beloved. Rumi takes this story, as he usually does, toward a reflection on mystical insights. There are suggestions that Edgar Allan Poe's "The Fall of the House of Usher" (1839) may have been based on this Rumi story.

Meanwhile, much later in history, and under the influence of Puccini's opera, Turandot found its way onto the silver screen. Gerhard Lamprecht's *Prinzessin Turandot* (1934) is a German comedy film starring Käthe von Nagy and Willy Fritsch. Soon, a separate French-language version of the same film appeared as *Turandot, princesse de Chine*. The script, by Thea von Harbou, includes elements of Puccini, Schiller, and Gozzi. Still later, in *Pasqualino Settebellezze/Seven Beauties* (1975), Italian filmmaker Lina Wertmüller returned to the theme of seven beauties in a landmark film starring Giancarlo Giannini, Fernando Rey, and Shirley Stoler. In 1952 Azerbaijani composer Gara Garayev composed the ballet *Seven Beauties*, based on motifs of Nezami Ganjavi's *Haft Peykar*. With Ferdowsi deep in the background, Nezami and Amir Khosrow on one side, and Gozzi, Schiller, and Puccini on the other, the figure of Turandot reigned supreme over the creative imagination of generations of artists and poets in about a dozen languages dancing around Persian.

Two pieces of literary modernism bring all of these allusions to Nezami's towering work and gendered framing of the Persian Prince to our own time: one in drama and the other in fiction, one in German and the other in Persian, and yet both focused on the role of compromised or rebellious intellectuals. A satirical and sarcastic piece, Brecht's *Turandot or the Whitewashers' Congress* (1953) was left incomplete upon his death in 1956—as was Puccini's on his own death—and did not premiere until 1969 at the Zürich Schauspielhaus. Brecht's version is also based on Gozzi's take on *Turandot*, which he had seen in Moscow in 1932—but he pushed it forward to a critical examination of the role of irresponsible intellectuals at the time of the rise of fascism.³³ Decades later, his kindred Iranian soul Houshang Golshiri (1938–2000) wrote *Shah-e Siyah-Pushan*

(*King of the Benighted*), which first appeared in an English translation (1990) under a pseudonym until it was published in its original Persian in Sweden in 2001, then subsequently translated into German and French. *King of the Benighted* is an allusion to Nezami's "Black Dome" tale from the *Haft Peykar*—which is equally preoccupied with the terrorizing circumstances of intellectuals in the Iran of the 1980s. Both Nezami and his *Haft Peykar* were being put to effective effervescence far beyond the original intentions of the master poets of yore or the virtuoso composer and his self-amusing Orientalist fantasies.

There is simply no end to how and where and why the figure of Turandot keeps resurfacing. In a bold and brilliant piece of scholarship, Angelo Michele Piemontese has suggested similarities between Turandot and Queen Esther in the Bible.[34] In Umberto Eco's *The Name of the Rose* (1980), the abductive reasoning of William of Baskerville and Adso of Melk regarding the horse Brunellus alludes to Voltaire's *Zadig* (1747), which in turn refers back to the good old translation of *Peregrinaggio di tre giovani figliuoli del re di Serendippo* (1557) by Cristoforo Armeno. The story just keeps unfolding. Puccini's *Turandot* was like a shining locomotive carrying a long train of history of European and Persian twists and turns on the Persian Prince and the princely environments to world attention, leading from Nezami's *Haft Peykar* to Amir Khosrow's *Hasht-Behesht*—from seven earthly beauties to eight gates of paradise, where heaven and earth come together and enable a towering almighty princess to overcome all princely claims to her obedience—gendering the archetype for the whole world to see. She was Russian, she was Chinese, Indian, Persian, Maghrebi, Khwarizmi, and all other hidden and quieted sisters of hers yet to come.

Precisely because such classics are texts that people mostly cite but scarcely read, they define the contours of our collective subconscious beyond false civilizational boundaries. In *Why Read the Classics?*, Italo Calvino shares his thoughts about over thirty of his preferred classics, among them Homer, Jorge Luis Borges, Dickens, and Nezami. It does not matter why these and not others. What matters is the neighborly peace in which these masterpieces come together to form a new worldly habitat. Cultures do not borrow from one another—cultures come together to form invisible sites of tertiary spaces in which they cohabit to imagine horizons beyond their immediate reach. From Nezami's *Haft Peykar* to Puccini's *Turandot* and before and beyond, we are witness to the loving memories of such moments when cultures dream of their alterities. The Persian Prince thus emerged from one world and submerged into another—afloat an archaic imagination to which there is no East or West, North or South.

Conclusion

FIGURE 10　Abbas Kiarostami, *Roads and Rain*, 2007.

The Allegory Remembers Itself

The fate of Turandot from its Persian originals to its varied European versions marks a moment of nomadic resurfacing of the Persian Prince, of the liminal sublimation of a timeless archetype. From the nomadic visitation of the archetype, we move to the active sublimation, which paves the way for the rise of the Persian Prince as an iconic allegory—where the subject of the Persian persona has dissolved onto itself, where the person has become the persona and the persona has disappeared into the fourfold frame of time and space. Here we might look at *Roads and Rain* by Abbas Kiarostami, signs but no signifiers—all transfigured into absolute abstractions of themselves where the subject has become formal, where political order has become integral to a disappearing presence and humanity has altogether abandoned the evident chaos into abstract order (fig. 10). Here we see things as the simulacrum of what they might be, in the twilight zone of the truth that abstracted reality exudes, where the Persian Prince has submerged into the most distant memories of both its origins and its destinations.

A CHRONOLOGY

GIVEN THE EXTENDED HISTORICAL PERIOD and the winding geographical scenes I travel and cover in this book as I map out the changing details of the figure of the "Persian Prince," the outline of a chronology seems to be in order. Although the epicenter of this book is the Persianate world of the past almost two thousand years, it inevitably moves back to what has artificially been called and considered the "pre-Islamic period" and, equally necessarily, into the non-Islamic sphere of the Zoroastrian, Hindu, Buddhist, Hebrew, and Greek worlds. As I have envisioned and detailed, the idea of the Persian Prince starts its active articulation in the Greco-Persian Wars of 499–449 BCE, from which the two seminal texts that matter to us are Aeschylus's *The Persians* (472 BCE), and Xenophon's *Cyropaedia* (370 BCE); the latter becomes the model for medieval European writers of mirrors for princes well into the period when Machiavelli wrote his *Prince* (1513/1552). Equally important are the Indian and Greek sources that were translated into Pahlavi, then Arabic, and then Persian, Hebrew, Syriac, Armenian, and other languages. At the same time, the sources produced in Judea-Persian were casting the Hebrew Bible into consciously Persian heroic characters and projected a whole new significance for the literature that had enabled and institutionalized the idea of the Persian Prince.

I offer the below chronology to help navigate the mapping of the book as I move from one thematic force field into another. Central to this chronology is the varied textual evidence that sustains the historical trajectory of the idea and practices of the Persian Prince in the wide spectrum of theories and institutions between Islamic scholasticism and humanism. My systematic deracialization of the concept of the Persian Prince ultimately begins to reveal its revolutionary disposition in the aftermath of its fateful encounter with the European project of colonial modernity, when the grace of the archetype completely abandons its imperial pedigree and moves squarely into its prophetic and poetic proclivities. While in the European context the capital foregrounding of their global conquest framed the eventual rise of fascism, in the Persianate context subject to that colonial conquest, exactly the opposite took place: the restitution of the rebellious disposition of the prophet-poet turned the figure of the Persian Prince into a revolutionary rebel revolting against that fascistic proclivity. For the sake of simplicity and convenience, I follow a mostly imperial chronology of Islamic and Iranian historiography but complicate the outline with allusions to non-Iranian and non-Islamic facts and figures that place this chronology in the larger frame of reference in which I have written and delivered my book.

ARCHETYPAL

The Elamites (circa 3000–530 BCE)   This is the first recorded imperial formation in the ancient Iranian and later Persianate worlds. Through successive generations of scholarship on archeological, numismatic, and codicological evidence, the earliest histories of these worlds have been reconstructed in later periods. Prior to this body of recent scholarship, in the Iranian world proper these earliest periods are cast in mythic, heroic, and subsequently historical terms. The text of Ferdowsi's *Shahnameh* as we read it today, with the figure of the Persian Prince central to its narrative thrust, is among the key surviving evidences of those worlds.

Zoroaster (circa 1000 or 1750 BCE)   The figure of Zoroaster—as revolutionary thinker, poet, and prophet—looms large over the ancient world. Although his chronology is disputed by leading scholars of the period, the impact of his teachings, the foundation of Zoroastrianism as the state religion of multiple empires, and therefore the imperial formation of the idea of the Persian Prince remains constant. What has reached us portrays Zoroaster as a revolutionary reformer, a visionary poet, and an emissary of a prophetic imagination of the world.

The Medes (694–665 BCE)   With the capital of the Medes in Hamadan (Ecbatana), we are now in full view of history, just before the rise of the Achaemenid Empire and its global conquests. Although more recent scholarship has questioned the imperial character of this tribal formation, their vicinity to the

Babylonian (circa 1895–539 BCE) and Assyrian Empires (circa 2025–609 BCE) places them in the general context of ancient Mesopotamian imperial formations in which the institution of the Persian Prince will eventually emerge.

The Achaemenids (550–330 BCE)   Founded by Cyrus the Great in 550 BCE, the empire reached its greatest extent under Xerxes I, ruling over a territory that stretched from Eastern Europe to Egypt to the Indus Valley. Greek sources are exceptionally informative about this empire. Xenophon's *Cyropaedia* (370 BCE) is singularly significant evidence of the earliest articulation of the idea of the Persian Prince. The text becomes iconic and exemplary for generations of Greco-Roman mirrors for princes. Xenophon was a student of Socrates and a contemporary of Plato, and his influence extended from classical antiquity all the way to the European Middle Ages and early modern periods. *Cyropaedia* reads today somewhere between a biographical fiction and a mirror for princes, as well as exemplary evidence of Xenophon's moral philosophy.

CLASSICAL

The Greco-Persian Wars (499–449 BCE)   Successive battles between the Persians and the Greeks became the defining signposts of the history of the region. Chief among them were the Battle of Marathon (490 BCE), the Battle of Salamis (480 BCE), and the Battle of Thermopylae (480 BCE). At this point, we encounter consolidated conceptions of the Persian Prince, best memorialized in the collective works of Aeschylus, Xenophon, and Herodotus.

The Book of Esther   Recent scholarship dates the composition of the Book of Esther in the Hebrew Bible to the middle of the fourth century BCE, during the rule of Artaxerxes III (reigned 340–338 BCE). Throughout classical antiquity, the text becomes definitive in the articulation of the figure of the Persian Prince, in the character of Ahasuerus/Xerxes. This biblical story is as significant as Xenophon's *Cyropaedia*, if not more, in the regional and global conception of the Persian Prince.

Wars of Alexander the Great (336–323 BCE)   The significance of Alexander romances in depictions of the Persian Prince can scarce be exaggerated. The Pseudo-Callisthenes Greek origin, from circa 338 BCE, was translated into Latin, but it also went through various recensions in Hebrew, Syriac, and other languages, including Persian, in all of which the Macedonian general is

Persianized all the way to having a solid standing in Ferdowsi's *Shahnameh*—as a link between the heroic and the historical.

The Seleucids (305–146 BCE)   This empire becomes a major center of Hellenistic culture, with Greek, Assyrian, Armenian, Georgian, Persian, Median, Mesopotamian, and Jewish cultures thriving in conversation and contestation with one another. The legacy of Alexander's conquests and the active Persianization of the Macedonian conqueror proceeds apace in this period. By now the idea of the Persian Prince is heavily Hellenized.

The Arsacids/Parthians (247 BCE–224 CE)   This major dynasty revived the old Iranian heritage of kingship while sustaining its Hellenistic tendencies. The eleventh-century epic romance *Vis-o-Ramin* by Fakhruddin Asʿad Gorgani is believed to have originated in the Parthian period, marking seminal literary evidence of the figure of the Persian Prince in an enduring love story that passes on the archetype to future generations.

Cicero's *De Officiis/On Duties* (44 BCE)   The publication of this seminal text marks the transition from classical antiquity to the Latin world, where Cicero reads Xenophon's *Cyropaedia* and *Oeconomicus* as providing the model and the manner in which the Greek heritage of the Persian Prince becomes emblematic of a happy, healthy, and just life.

Mani (circa 216–277 CE)   The Iranian revolutionary prophet was the founder of Manichaeism, a religion that in late antiquity brought together aspects of Gnosticism, Christianity, Zoroastrianism, and Buddhism. His historic figure personifies the prophetic disposition of the Persian prince.

The Sassanids (224–651)   The Sassanid emperors personified the Persian Prince in their vast imperial domains extending from the Indus Valley to the Mediterranean Sea. The ancient text of *Kar-Namag-e Ardeshir-e Pabagan* (*The Chronicle of Ardeshir-e Pabagan*) is one of the earliest sources of the mirror for princes that has reached us from subsequent renditions, pointing to sources even earlier than those of the Sassanid period. The figure of Khosrow I Anushirvan the Just becomes a legendary monarch in Arabic sources as the ideal of the Persian Prince par excellence. Anushirvan had a proverbial interest in history and, according to al-Tabari, studied the lives of previous Sassanid kings to learn how to better rule his realm. He also ordered the writing of *Khwaday-Namag* (*Book of Lords/Kings*)—of which the original Pahlavi is lost, but its Arabic and Persian renditions reached Ferdowsi when writing his *Shahnameh*. Translation of Sanskrit sources like *Panchatantra* into Middle Persian (Pahlavi) in this period paves the way for later translations into Arabic and Persian, through which the figure of the Persian Prince finds its Indic traces.

Mazdak (died circa 528) The Zoroastrian priest became a forceful revolutionary prophet during the reign of the Sassanid emperor Kavadh I. His socialist ideals and sizable following became a radical manifestation of the rebellious disposition of the Persian Prince.

The Umayyads (661–750) This dynasty was deeply rooted in Arab patrimonial tribalism before it encountered Indian, Egyptian, Persian, and Byzantine traditions of imperial rule during the Abbasids. The figure of Ibn Muqaffaʿ is paramount here, for he single-handedly translated major Pahlavi sources into Arabic, laying the groundwork for Arabic renditions of the figure of the Persian Prince. From the Umayyads forward, Arab patrimonialism actively begins to enter Islamic political culture and enrich the heritage of the Persian Prince.

Ibn al-Muqaffaʿ (died 760) The figure of Ibn al-Muqaffaʿ, born Ruzbeh pur-e Dadoe, towers over his contemporaries as a gifted thinker who was responsible for translating a number of highly influential pre-Islamic Pahlavi sources—including *Khwaday-Namag* and *Kelilah and Dimnah*, rooted in Iranian and Indian material—into Arabic, and subsequently into modern Persian and other languages. These sources were key in subsequent articulations of the idea of the Persian Prince.

Sunpadh (died 754) The revolutionary prophet became one among many other similar figures revolting against the Abbasid conquest of Khorasan. The iconic characters of al-Muqannaʿ and Babak Khorramdin, who also led major revolts against the Abbasids, extend the presence of these revolutionary rebels as the hidden proclivities of the figure of the Persian Prince on the historical battlefield.

The Abbasids (750–1258) Through mainly Arabic historiography of this period, a sustained narrative of the historical consciousness of Persian imperial culture feeds into the Abbasid period. Such prominent Muslim historians as al-Yaqui, al-Dinawari, al-Tabari, al-Mas'udi, al-Tha'alibi, and al-Baladhuri became the main sources of informing their readers at various imperial courts of the ways Persianate political culture ruled the world. The figure of the Persian Prince has by now become an entirely allegorical icon. Al-Tha'alibi's famous text *Ghurar Akhbar Muluk al-Furs wa Siyarihim*, for example, typifies the way ancient Persian monarchs had become proverbial to the imperial imagination of the time.

HISTORICAL

The Tahirids (821–873) Some scholars have used the term "Iranian Intermezzo" or "Persian Renaissance" to describe the period after the Arab conquest of the Sassanid Empire and before the Turkic takeover during the Saljuqid period. This interval consists of major dynastic formations like the Tahirids, the Saffarids, and the Samanids. These terms, however, are misleading and anachronistically nationalistic. These small dynasties did indeed pay closer political attention to Persian language and culture, but neither the Arab conquest in the West nor the Ghaznavid or Saljuqid takeover in the East had any serious impact on the central significance of the literary and cultural context of the Persian Prince except expanding and universalizing it. The rise and effervescence of Persian prose and poetry from Pahlavi into Arabic and then to modern Persian from the Umayyads into the Abbasid, Ghaznavid, and Saljuqid Empires is key evidence of this fact.

The Saffarids (867–1002) Both the factual and legendary significance attributed to Mohammad ibn Wasif Sagzi (died 909), Ya'qub ibn al-Layth al-Saffar's secretary and court poet, signals the central role that poets played in praising their ruling monarchs in terms conducive to the consolidation of the archetype of the Persian Prince. It was almost irrelevant whether ruling monarchs deserved the praise their poets offered them. The ideal archetype of the Persian Prince as a just and fair and equitable ruler was the primary beneficiary of that praise.

The Ziyarids (928–1043) Perhaps the most significant member of the Ziyarid dynasty was a literary prose stylist and political theorist rather than a ruler. Kaykavus ibn Iskandar ibn Qabus ibn Voshmgir, the author of the precious treatise *Qabus-nameh*, produced a landmark mirror for princes, as well as a major work of Persian literary prose, in the form of a last will and testament intended for his son Gilanshah. Composed in elegant Persian prose and delivered with erudite diction, *Qabus-nameh* (circa 1080) outlines the logic, rhetoric, and royal decorum of the Persian Prince.

The Buyids (934–989) Arguably the most spectacular figure of the Buyid period was Ibn Miskawayh (932–1030), whose *Javidan Kherad/Sophia Perennis*—Arabized as *Kitab al-Hikmah al-Khalidah (Book of Eternal Wisdom)*—became a defining moment in the philosophical articulation of the Persian Prince. The book is his Arabic rendition of a Persian original called *Javidan Kherad*, which is symbolically traced back to the Pishdadid king Houshang and is also known as *Kitab Adab al-Arab wa al-Ajam (The Book of the Customs of Arabs and Iranians)*—a seminal text that brings together Persian, Greek, Indian, and Arabic ancient wisdom.

The Samanids (875–999) Ferdowsi began working on his monumental epic the *Shahnameh* during the Samanids and finished it during the Ghaznavids. Rooted in and proud of their Iranian heritage, which they deliberately played against their Arab conquerors, the Samanids become the royal bedrock of the literary rise of Khorasan as the dynastic stage for the idea of the Persian Prince and its pre-Islamic pedigree. For millennia afterwards, the *Shahnameh* remained the mythic, heroic, and historical document for the sustained reimagination of the Persian Prince as the cornerstone of Persianate political culture. None of this ethnicized the idea of the Persian Prince, which, rooted in its Indic, Iranian, Greek, and Hebrew origins, remained a floating signifier throughout the rest of Islamic history—including in proudly Arab dynasties, who effectively embraced and enriched the idea of the Persian Prince as a foundation for their political culture.

The Ghaznavids (963–1050) Two major events of the Ghaznavid era are (1) the consolidation of Persian prose and poetry as the lingua franca of the empire and its expansion into the Indian subcontinent, and (2) the production of a major Persian history by Abu al-Fadl Bayhaqi on the history of the dynasty that became the model of literary eloquence and critical historical consciousness for generations to come. The first development solidly established the easternmost part of Muslim lands as the domain of Persianate culture, and the second foregrounded Persian as the official language of historiography for the rest of Muslim history in all subsequent Eastern empires, including that of the Saljuqids and the Mongols. Both these developments became fertile ground for the expansion of the Persian Prince as the defining moment of the political culture of the Persianate world.

The Saljuqids (Great Seljuqs, 1037–1157)   Two eminent forces in Islamic political thought, Nezam al-Molk (1018–1092) and Al-Ghazali (circa 1058–1111), defined the Saljuqid period, when this towering statesman and iconic philosopher, respectively, turned to the detailed articulation of the structure of political legitimacy based in pre-Islamic Iranian and Islamic scholastic terms. The figure of the Persian Prince stands at the epicenter of their articulation of legitimate political authority and how to preserve and justify it.

Shihab al-Din Yahya al-Suhrawardi (1154–1191)   The iconoclastic work of the Illuminationist Muslim philosopher al-Suhrawardi introduced the figure of the Persian Prince into the heart of his philosophical thinking, when he gave iconic figures of Persian mythology renewed philosophical significance. In his hands the divine gift of grace anointing the Persian Prince assumes profound philosophical significance.

The Khwarazmshahids (1097–1220)   By 1200, the Khwarazmshahid dynasty had emerged in Greater Khorasan. They succeeded in creating an empire that stretched from India to Anatolia, but this success was short-lived—they were defeated by the Mongols and became part of their vast empire. The last Khwarazmshahid ruler, Jalal al-Din Mingburnu (reigned 1220–1231), was defeated by the Mongols in 1231 but spent years in exile in India and Anatolia trying in vain to mobilize forces against them. He was murdered in 1231 in Diyarbakir by an assassin. The case of Jalal al-Din is a paramount example of how, despite his otherwise courageous defiance of his fate, a Persian Prince can lose his gift of grace and die in ignominy.

The Mongols/Ilkhanids (1256–1336)   The most illustrious poet of this period is Saʿdi Shirazi, whose compendium is a wellspring of poetic stipulation of the figure of the Persian Prince as a just and fair ruler. But it is in the figure of the poet himself that the persona of the Persian Prince is best represented as a poetic metaphor. The composition of the eminent historian ʿAtaʾ Malik al-Jovayni's

Tarikh-e Jahan-Gosha (*History of the World-Conqueror*), about the life and conquests of Genghis Khan, is a landmark event in the history of Persianate historiography. Written between 1252 and 1260, this seminal text is a masterpiece of Persian prose in which the entire edifice of the Persian Prince is brought to bear on the Mongol warlord—in very much the same way that Alexander the Great was recast and Persianized.

Shahin-e Shirazi (1300s)   Shahin-e Shirazi was a gifted Persian Jewish poet who was a contemporary of Hafez (died 1390). He is legendary for his extraordinary ability to cast biblical stories in the poetic diction of the Persian epic. In his hand, the Persian Prince finds a whole new vista in the Judeo-Persian domains, equal in its significance to the Greco-Roman traditions of *Cyropaedia*, if not more so. Shirazi's cycles from the Pentateuch include his *Musa-nameh* (*Book of Moses*, 1327), modeled on Ferdowsi's *Shahnameh*, and includes passages from Exodus, Leviticus, Numbers, and Deuteronomy. This addition of this crucial Hebrew domain to Greek, Indian, Pahlavi, Arabic, Armenian, Mongol, and Persian sites is solid evidence of the deracialized disposition of the figure of the Persian Prince.

The Timurids (1370–1506)   The singular significance of the Timurid period is the spectacular formation of the Herat School, a stylistic revolution in Persian painting under the patronage of the Timurid prince Shahrokh, the son of the founder of the dynasty Timur (Tamerlane). It was during the reign of Shahrokh's son Baysunqur Mirza (died 1433) that the School of Herat became an epicenter of an aesthetic sublimation of the figure of the Persian Prince in visual and aesthetic terms—a development that was later advanced even further during the Safavid period.

The Aq Qoyunlu (White Sheep) (1378–1508)   Uzun Hasan (1423–1478), the ruler of the Turkmen Aq Qoyunlu dynasty, looms large over a short-lived but significant dynasty that ruled over parts of Iran, Iraq, Anatolia, Armenia, and Azerbaijan. He soon arranged for a strategic alliance with the Christian emperor of Trebizond as well as for diplomatic ties with Venice, Muscovy, Burgundy, Poland, and Egypt. Such alliances were coterminous with the eventual rise of European colonial powers, who would soon enter the scene with force and alter the fate of the Persian Prince.

The Qara Qoyunlu (Black Sheep) (1380–1468)   The Qara Qoyunlu were the tribal rivals of the Aq Qoyunlu, who, under Jahan Shah (reigned circa 1438–1467), maintained a considerable degree of autonomy and power. After the Timurid prince Shahrokh's death in 1447, Jahan Shah consolidated his power over some of the Timurid domains. Two contradictory factors were at work here: a patent tribalism, and the expansion of the political domain into European power politics—facts that further complicated the idea of the Persian Prince at the threshold of its encounter with European colonialism.

COLONIAL

Bahmani sultanate (1347–1527) and Deccan sultanates (1490–1688)   These were two Persianate sultanates in the Indian subcontinent for which the central idea of the Persian Prince and the official state of the Persian language were the defining factors of their political culture.

The Safavids (1501–1722)   Perhaps the single most important social sites in which the archetypal character of the Persian Prince found potent renewal in this period were widespread coffeehouses, which had emerged as the epicenter of public spaces and public spheres throughout the Mughal, Safavid, and Ottoman territories. In the form of popular storytelling, mythical heroes now renewed their pact with their living memories when they found live and engaged audiences. This departure of the mythic heroes from illustrated manuscripts, royal courts, and court poets, all under the rising European colonial duress, splits the "atom" of the Persian Prince, as it were, back into its constituent forces. This split was never sudden, unprecedented, or irrevocable. Both a ruling Prince and a rebel could lay simultaneous claim to it—and rightly so, for they were the mirror image of each other.

Machiavelli writes *The Prince* (1513/1552)   The composition of Machiavelli's *Prince* marks a crucial point in the European context of the reception of the idea of the Persian Prince from classical antiquity and the Hebrew Bible through the Latin sources to the threshold of European political modernity. Machiavelli was fully conscious of the reception of Cyrus in classical antiquity, which in turn informed his articulation of his *Prince*. It is crucial to recall that *The Prince* was written at almost the same time as Erasmus's *Institutio principis Christiani* (*Education of a Christian Prince*, 1516), intended as advice to King Charles of Spain (the later Charles V). So during this period we have in effect two European renditions of the Persian Prince, one decidedly Christian and the other patently devoid of any religious or even moral sentimentalities. As Ernst Cassirer would later say, Machiavelli's *Prince* was more amoral than immoral. The idea of the Persian Prince as I have articulated here is as much Iranian, Arab, Indian, or Turk as Machiavelli's was Italian or Erasmus's Dutch or Spanish. They could all lay claim to it, but the archetype remains iconic, metonymic, more a persona than a person.

The Mughals (1526–1857) The figure of Mughal prince Dara Shikoh (1615–1659) and his masterpiece *Majmaʿ al-Bahrain* (circa 1655) become the epitome of a learned Persian Prince in an Indian robe. Dara Shikoh was the heir apparent of the Mughal emperor Shah Jahan. His honorific title, *Padshahzada-i-Buzurg Martaba* ("high-ranking prince"), reveals his archetypal descent from the Persian moral and political imagination. That he did not succeed his father and was murdered by his younger brother Aurangzeb has cast his youthful image as the martyred "Persian Prince," which has since become iconic for posterity. The establishment of the East India Company in 1600 and the subsequent takeover of that insatiable colonial project by the British Crown from 1858 to 1947 marks the onslaught of European colonialism into the heart of the Indian and Muslim world—over the course of which the idea of the Persian Prince goes through a cataclysmic makeover.

The Ottomans (1299–1922) The predominance of Persian as the preferred language of poetry, prose, historiography, and imperial etiquette in the course of the Ottoman Empire became a crucial conduit of making the figure of the Persian Prince dominant and even subconscious in their realm. Arabic and Ottoman Turkish were equally as if not more important than Persian in scholastic learning, but the royal culture of the court was consciously formed on Iranian imperial models, with the central figure of the Persian Prince as its blueprint. By 1683, the defeat of the Ottomans at the Battle of Vienna marked the decline of the last global Muslim empire and the eventual rise of European colonial conquest of their territories.

The Afsharids (1736–1796) The court chronicler of Nader Shah, the founder of the Afsharid dynasty, Mirza Mohammad Mahdi Khan Astarabadi composed *Tarikh-e Jahangosha-ye Naderi* (*The History of World Conqueror Nader*), which was among the first of its kind to be translated into French and English by the

British Orientalist Sir William Jones in the 1770s—marking the active colonial interests in local and regional historiographies. In his stylized prose, Astarabadi performed Persian historiography in an over-formalized register in celebration of the annual Noruz at Nader's royal court. The result was the degeneration of both historiography and the literary Persian prose into a decadent version of themselves. Astarabadi did the same when writing his other major book, *Dorreh-ye Nadereh* (*The Rare Pearl of Nader*), in which the figure of the Persian Prince in the shape of the ruling monarch is depleted of any and all political or literary grace. The prose is so utterly conflated and verbose that it marks the implosion of Persianate historiography into an irretrievably profligate decadence. By the time Nader Shah invaded northern India all the way to Delhi in March 1739, both he and his conquest were devoid of any and all meaning or glories. The grace and charisma of the Persian Prince had left his persona and moved into the much more fertile ground of its own rebellious alterities.

The Zands (1750–1794) The composition of *Atashkadeh-e-ye Azar* by the prominent literary figure of the period, Azar Bigdeli (1722–1781), in the name and honor of the founding figure of the Zand dynasty, Karim Khan Zand (circa 1705–1779), is a watershed event in which the political history of the period and the biographies of some seminal poets are brought together to mark and praise a "Persian Prince" who in fact refused all royal titles and wished to be known merely as Vakil al-Roʻaya ("representative of the subjects"). The iconic figure of the Persian Prince was now off to greener pastures in the battlefields of colonial modernity.

The Qajars (1789–1925) As the Qajars consolidated their power as the last imperial dynasty facing the onslaught of European colonialism, the rise of two seminal figures redefines the contours of the revolutionary potential of the Persian Prince. The iconoclastic figure of one singularly rebellious woman, Tahereh Qorrat al-Ayn (circa 1814–1852) genders the resurrected figure of the Persian Prince and restores its iconic nonbinary disposition. Equally important is Jalal al-Din Mirza (1827–1872), a Qajar prince who switched sides from the imperial court to the revolutionary uprising of more enlightened thinkers struggling against fanaticism, tyranny, and colonial domination. Tahereh Qorrat al-Ayn and Jalal al-Din Mirza, one from the revolutionary battlefields of the realm and the other from inside the besieged royal court, recast the revived disposition of the Persian Prince.

British Raj (1858–1947)   This was the epitome of the British (European) colonial conquest of the Indian subcontinent, marking the radical transformation of the idea of the Persian Prince into its rebellious disposition.

CONTEMPORARY

The Pahlavis (1925–1979)   In multiple scholarly and artistic forms, the figure of the Persian Prince emerges in film, fiction, and poetry during the Pahlavi period. It begins with Ferdowsi's millennial celebration in 1934, in which the nascent Pahlavi monarch Reza Shah sought to link his own reign to the archetype of the Persian Prince. In subsequent decades, however, scholars, poets, and artists began to take the icon into different, more subversive, directions—chief among which were Fereydoun Rahnema's "Seyavash dar Takht-e Jamshid" (Seyavash in Persepolis, 1966), Houshang Golshiri's *Shazdeh Ehtejab* (*Prince Ehtejab*, 1969), Bahram Beizai's "Marg-e Yazdegerd" (Death of Yazdegerd, 1982), but perhaps most potently in Mehdi Akhavan-e Sales's poetry. These all become indices of recasting the legacy of the Persian Prince in a renewed artistic and poetic pact with its rebellious origins and disposition. As both Pahlavi monarchs desperately sought but mainly failed to lay any legitimate claim to the legacy of the Persian Prince, poets, artists, filmmakers, and revolutionary icons like Mirza Kuchak Khan-e Jangali or Bizhan Jazani embodied and represented it far more effectively.

Antonio Gramsci (1891–1937)   The eminent Italian Marxist philosopher wrote his highly influential "Modern Prince" in his *Prison Notebooks*, in which he retheorized Machiavelli's idea of *The Prince* to recast it as a modern political party. My idea of the Persian Prince in its encounter with European colonialism is very much inspired by Gramsci's articulation of his "Modern Prince." In this book I have done a similar recasting but have focused more on revealing the prophetic and poetic roots of the idea of the archaic figure (nestled with its imperial proclivities) that resurface under colonial duress.

Ernst Cassirer (1874–1945)   The oeuvre of the German Jewish philosopher Ernst Cassirer in general—including his seminal 1929 book *Philosophy of Symbolic Forms*, but particularly his major posthumous book, *The Myth of State* (1946)—plays a central role in detecting and articulating the mythical (mystical) dimensions of the ruling state ideologies in its European context, against the colonial consequences of which the desedimentation of the idea of the Persian Prince into its constituent rebellious forces becomes a potent anticolonial force. Cassirer's take on Machiavelli puts a corrective lens on Gramsci's and makes the three seminal European thinkers exceptionally useful for our reading of the idea of the Persian Prince on the colonial and postcolonial scenes.

Walter Benjamin (1890–1940)   The other European thinker definitive to sustaining my critical thinking about myth is above all the ingenious German Jewish philosopher Walter Benjamin. While Max Weber had seen the dawn of European modernity as the onslaught of what he thought was disenchantment with the world, Benjamin had seen how under the condition of capitalism the very same world had crafted a re-enchantment with itself—and thereby its mythic powers had been reactivated. While German Romanticism too had called for a rebirth of mythologies, as Susan Buck-Morss notes in her seminal book *The Dialectics of Seeing: Walter Benjamin and the Arcades Project* (1989), Benjamin as a key Marxist thinker had detected the same in industrial revolution. Both Weber and Benjamin were of course primarily concerned with capitalism and not colonialism, which was materially and ideologically contingent on it. While for both Benjamin and Marx classical mythology had become "comic" so that, in the course of the industrial age, humanity parts with its past laughing, alas, we cannot afford that laughter on the colonial edges of that capitalism. So we resurrect our mythologies for sustained rebellion—even against being all too serious. Thus, the idea of the Persian Prince for me resurrects not as a comedy but as a self-subversive rebel/poet who can dismantle its own archaic origins, which is far more a political parody than a disabling satire.

The Partition of India (1947)   The end of British colonial rule over India coincided with the splitting of the country into a Hindu-majority India and Muslim-majority Pakistan—a lasting bloody legacy of European colonial conquest of the Muslim and Persianate worlds. While much attention is rightly directed to Gandhi and Nehru, the champions of Indian independence, the iconic character of Muhammad Iqbal (1877–1938) stands tall as the most eloquent visionary figure imagining the legacy of Muslim intellectual history for the Persianate world. As he wrote some of his most significant philosophical work in Persian, he left for his contemporaries and posterity a solid document of how to recast the classical figure of the Persian Prince to reimagine the Persianate polity on solid moral grounds and conceive of a visionary politics of participatory democracy.

The CIA-MI6 coup of 1953   The CIA-MI6 coup of 1953 marks the coup de grâce on any and all monarchs surviving the colonial and imperial indignity of

FIGURE 11   Abbas Kiarostami, *Roads and Rain*, 2007.

their reign on foreign intervention on their behalf. By now, the grace of the Persian Prince had completely left the graceless figure of the ruling monarch, who was left soulless and sullen in the dust.

The Islamic Republic of Iran (1979–present)   The triumph of the Islamic Republic in the aftermath of the Iranian Revolution of 1977–1979 marked the desolation of the figure of the Persian Prince as a political icon of sovereignty and its disappearance into thin air of its formative forces, its gift of grace having completely abandoned any and all positions of political power (republican or monarchical, kingly or clerical). The Persian Prince had allegorically resedimented.

Abbas Kiarostami (1940–2016)   Reverting back to its visionary recitals of the prophetic and the poetic, after two hundred years of revolutionary defiance in its encounter with colonial modernity, the ethereal elements of the Persian Prince was finally scattered into the visual shimmering of the most globally celebrated Iranian artist, Abbas Kiarostami—as the poetic verve and prophetic vision of the metaphor slithered into the aesthetic dissolution of its own recollected memories of itself.

ACKNOWLEDGMENTS

THIS IS ONE of the most joyous books I have written. Fixated on the compelling centrality of an idea, I began to read and write apace until I was done. My foremost gratitude goes to Kate Wahl, the publishing director and editor-in-chief at Stanford University Press. She quickly saw the logic and reasoning of this idea and steered my detailed proposal through its acquisition process, in the course of which I received multiple excellent anonymous reviews, for which I am grateful. After that and as I was writing, Kate stayed the course with me, read my chapters with patience and grace, and gave me back detailed thoughts. I built this book from the ground up from my laptop in New York and from her reassuring editorial office in Stanford. At the center of this book is a daring and imaginative idea I needed to handle with care. She was instrumental in keeping my mind steady and at ease!

This book is very much a COVID-19 product. It was conceived as here in the United States, and particularly in New York, we went into lockdown and resumed our professional duties online, in the immediate vicinity of our families from our living rooms; and it was finished in its first complete draft when we were just vaccinated and about to resurface to a semblance of normalcy. My younger children, Chelgis and Golchin, were the precious companions of my household chores as they dutifully attended their online schooling while I cooked for and cleaned after them and worked on this book in the intervals. My older children, Kaveh and Pardis, were only a text or a FaceTime away—busy with their own lockdown lives. This book is my children's. I was just writing it.

As I began writing, my dear old friend Mahmoud Omidsalar was, as always, my constant companion as I requested obscure texts and he found them for me.

It is a blessing to have a scholar of his stature so close to me throughout my academic career in the United States. He is an old-fashioned scholar. Like me, he reads and writes for a living.

Toqa Mohamed Badran has been instrumental in securing PDF copies of old manuscripts and recent academic papers for me. This book is much indebted to her. Arwa K. Palanpurwala took over as my research assistant and was equally helpful toward the end of preparing my book for production.

I thank Ramin Bahrani for his lifetime of unwavering friendship. I thank Ali Mirsepassi for his steadfast support and solidarity. I thank Atefeh Akbari Shahmirzadi for her quiet assurances. I thank Gil Hochberg, the chair of my department at Columbia, for her steadfast support and for her defiant sense of fairness and justice. My sincere thanks also to Sarah Cole—Dean of Humanities, Faculty of Arts and Sciences, and Parr Professor of English and Comparative Literature at Columbia—for the generosity and care of her office supporting my scholarly work.

I attended to the final stages of the editorial process for this book while vacationing in Sweden with my children. My unending gratitude to my dearest friends Afrodit Bashi and Timo Nieminen for their unparalleled grace, kindness, hospitality, and generosity in which my children and I basked as we vacationed and played and I did a bit of work.

The Persian Prince came to be with the indispensable support and serene solace of all these fine friends, entirely unbeknownst to them. I am blessed by the peace of mind I find in their company.

Hamid Dabashi
NEW YORK
Spring 2022

NOTES

PRELUDE

1. Aeschylus, *The Persians*, trans. Ian Johnston (Nanaimo, BC: Vancouver Island University, 2012), http://johnstoniatexts.x10host.com/aeschylus/persianspdf.pdf.

CHAPTER 1

1. Xenophon, *Cyropaedia*, with an English translation by Walter Miller, in two volumes (Cambridge, MA: Harvard University Press; London: William Heineman, 1914), I.i.2–3 and I.i.3–4, pp. 5–7.

2. All my citations from Saʿdi's *Bustan* are from the authoritative critical edition of the text by Gholamhossein Yusefi (edited, annotated, with an introduction), *Bustan-e Saʿdi (Saʿdi-nameh)* (Tehran: Khwarizmi Publications, 1980), 42ff. All translations from the original Persian are mine.

3. For a tongue-in-cheek review, see Roger Ebert, "Is This a Dagger of Time I See Before Me?," *Roger Ebert* (blog), May 26, 2010, https://www.rogerebert.com/reviews/prince-of-persia-the-sands-of-time-2010.

4. Reza Pahlavi adroitly kept himself in the news by following the news in his homeland and calling for uprisings on his behalf. See, for example, "Prince Reza Pahlavi Calls for Civil Disobedience, Reconstruction of Iran," *Radio Farda*, February 9, 2019, https://en.radiofarda.com/a/prince-reza-pahlavi-calls-for-civil-disobedience-reconstruction-of-iran/29760926.html.

5. See Niccolò Machiavelli, *The Prince*, trans. Harvey C. Mansfield (Chicago: University of Chicago Press, 1998).

6. Machiavelli, *The Prince*, 16–19.

7. These portraits, which include one of Salah al-Din al-Ayyubi, are available online here: Wikimedia, s.v. "Category: Cristofano dell'Altissimo," last modified September 6, 2019, 20:58, https://commons.m.wikimedia.org/wiki/Category:Cristofano

_dell%27Altissimo. Cristofano dell'Altissimo's portrait of Machiavelli is available online here: Wikimedia, s.v. "File: Portrait of Niccolò Machiavelli Cristofano di Papi dell'Altissimo.jpg," last modified May 17, 2019, 15:12, https://commons.m.wikimedia.org/wiki/File:Portrait_of_Niccol%C3%B2_Machiavelli_Cristofano_di_Papi_dell%27Altissimo.jpg#mw-jump-to-license.

8. *Encyclopaedia Iranica*, s.v., "Barbaro, Giosafat," accessed August 6, 2020, https://iranicaonline.org/articles/barbaro-giosafat-venetian-merchant-traveler-and-diplomat-venice-1413-94.

9. *Encyclopaedia Iranica*, "Barbaro, Giosafat." Scholars of visual and performing arts have also noted a link between the simultaneous theatrical traditions of commedia dell'arte and Persian Ro-Hozi theater. "It seems likely," one scholar points out, "that there is a connection between all of these forms and both *commedia dell'arte* of the late Italian Renaissance and northern European comic carnival plays based on similarity of performance themes, character types, costumes, and performance conventions." See *Encyclopaedia Iranica*, "Ruḥawżi," accessed August 6, 2022, https://iranicaonline.org/articles/ruhawzi. Occurring in the time of Machiavelli, the form brought aspects of Persian culture into his own popular culture.

10. Some more recent scholarship has, of course, challenged the traditional way of reading Machiavelli—see, for example, Erica Benner, *Machiavelli's Ethics* (Princeton, NJ: Princeton University Press, 2010), for a radically different reading of *The Prince* as in fact an ethical treatise.

11. Machiavelli, *The Prince*, 98.

12. See Antonio Gramsci, "The Modern Prince," in *Selections from the Prison Notebooks*, ed. and trans. Quentin Hoare and Geoffrey Nowell Smith (London: Lawrence & Wishart, 1971), 313–444.

13. Gramsci, "The Modern Prince," 323.

14. For my detailed articulation of the idea of the transnational parapublic sphere, expanding upon Habermas's initial Eurocentric idea, see Hamid Dabashi, *Persophilia: The Persian Culture on the Global Scene* (Cambridge, MA: Harvard University Press, 2015). Nancy Fraser and Mary Ryan have alternatively offered the term "counterpublic" to specify spaces outside Habermas's articulation of the bourgeois public sphere. I still prefer "parapublic," for both theoretical and historical reasons. Fraser's and Ryan's ideas remain limited to Eurocentric experiences, and the spaces to which I refer—underground literature, works by exiles or political prisoners, etc.—are not "counterpublic"; in fact, sometimes they are more important than the public, and thus parapublic. See Nancy Fraser, "Rethinking the Public Sphere: A Contribution to the Critique of Actually Existing Democracy," *Social Text*, nos. 25–26 (1990): 56–80, https://doi.org/10.2307/466240, and Mary P. Ryan, *Women in Public: Between Banners and Ballots, 1825–1880* (Baltimore: Johns Hopkins University Press, 1990).

15. I have documented this Persian presence in European imagination in detail in *Persophilia* (see note 14).

16. For an examination of Xenophon's *Cyropaedia* and other works as a mirror for princes, see Vivienne J. Gray, *Xenophon's Mirror of Princes: Reading the Reflections* (Oxford: Oxford University Press, 2011).

17. For more on this, see my essay "Rosa Luxemburg: The unsung hero of postcolonial theory," *Al Jazeera*, May 12, 2018, https://www.aljazeera.com/opinions/2018/5/12/rosa-luxemburg-the-unsung-hero-of-postcolonial-theory/.

18. See, for example, the essays collected in Neelam Srivastava and Baidik Bhattacharya, ed., *The Postcolonial Gramsci* (London: Routledge, 2011).

19. There is, of course, much more to Gramsci's retheorization of Machiavelli's Prince, to which I will return repeatedly in this book. For a detailed discussion of the potentials of Gramsci's idea of the Modern Prince, see Peter Thomas, "Gramsci and the Intellectuals: Modern Prince Versus Passive Revolution," in *Marxism, Intellectuals and Politics*, ed. David Bates (New York: Palgrave Macmillan, 2007), 68–87.

20. For the case for the "World Republic of Letters," see Pascale Casanova, *The World Republic of Letters*, trans. Malcolm DeBevoise (Cambridge, MA: Harvard University Press, 2007). For the case for the "World Empire of Persian Letters," see Hamid Dabashi, *The World of Persian Literary Humanism* (Cambridge, MA: Harvard University Press, 2012).

21. I have made this argument in an essay I published in the philosophy column of the *New York Times*, "Found in Translation," July 28, 2013, https://archive.nytimes.com/opinionator.blogs.nytimes.com/2013/07/28/found-in-translation/. The essay subsequently appeared in an edited volume of essays from this column, Peter Catapano and Simon Critchley, ed., *The Stone Reader: Modern Philosophy in 133 Arguments* (New York: New York Times, 2016), 84–89.

22. Saʿdi, *Bustan*, 37.

23. Saʿdi, *Bustan*, 38.

24. Saʿdi, *Bustan*, 196.

25. See Abbas Amanat and Assef Ashraf, ed., *The Persianate World: Rethinking a Shared Sphere* (Leiden and Boston: Brill, 2019).

26. See Marshall Hodgson, *The Venture of Islam: Conscience and History in a World Civilization*, vols. 1–3 (Chicago: University of Chicago Press, 1974).

27. Joseph Massad, for example, is highly critical of the terms "Islamicate" and "Islamdom." See Joseph Massad, *Islam in Liberalism* (Chicago: University of Chicago Press, 2016), 214–15.

28. An earlier rendition of Pollock's seminal thesis was offered in Sheldon Pollock, "The Sanskrit Cosmopolis, A.D. 300–1300: Transculturation, Vernacularization, and the Question of Ideology," in *Ideology and Status of Sanskrit: Contributions to the History of the Sanskrit Language*, ed. J. E. M. Houben (Leiden: Brill, 1996), 197–248.

29. See Amanat and Ashraf, *The Persianate World*, 63–83. An earlier articulation of the Persian cosmopolis by Richard M. Eaton had appeared in 2013 as "Revisiting the Persian Cosmopolis" (Tlaxcala, the international network of translators for linguistic diversity), https://www.gcgi.info/blog/423-revisiting-the-persian-cosmopolis-the-world-order-and-the-dialogue-of-civilisations.

30. Eaton, "Revisiting the Persian Cosmopolis," 64–65.

31. Eaton, "Revisiting the Persian Cosmopolis," 83.

32. See Henri Lefebvre, *The Production of Space*, trans. Donald Nicholson-Smith (Oxford: Blackwell, 1991).

33. See in particular Edward W. Soja, *Seeking Spatial Justice* (Minneapolis: University of Minnesota Press, 2010).

34. See the chapter "Interstitial Space of the Art of Protest" in my recent book *The Emperor Is Naked: On the Inevitable Demise of the Nation-State* (London: Zed Books, 2019), 118–51.

35. I developed this idea further in "Nations Without Borders," in *Global Middle East: Into the Twenty-First Century*, ed. Asef Bayat and Linda Herrera (Oakland: University of California Press, 2021), 60–76.

CHAPTER 2

1. Mehdi Akhavan-e Sales, "Qesseh-ye Shahryar-e Shahr-e Sangestan" [The ballad of the prince of Stoneville], in *Az in Avesta* [From this Avesta: Collected works], vol. 1 (Tehran: Zemestan Publishers, 1397/2018), 585–95.

2. See Rosi Braidotti, "Writing as a Nomadic Subject," *Comparative Critical Studies*, 11.2–3 (2014): 163–84.

3. Ernst Cassirer, *The Myth of the State* (New Haven, CT: Yale University Press, 1946), 134. Emphasis is Cassirer's in the original.

4. Cassirer, *Myth of the State*, 134.

5. I have extended Cassirer's insight in his *Myth of the State* into the larger postcolonial world and examined similar mystification of the postcolonial state in my book *The Emperor Is Naked: On the Inevitable Demise of the Nation-State* (London: Zed Books, 2019).

6. These revolutionary figures are the subject of a recent study by the British Orientalist Patricia Crone, *The Nativist Prophets of Early Islamic Iran: Rural Revolt and Local Zoroastrianism* (Cambridge: Cambridge University Press, 2014). There are earlier and more objective studies of this period, to which I will return later in this book.

7. The first scholar of Persian poetry to use the term "rebel/poet" was the late Leonardo P. Alishan in his pioneering essay "Ahmad Shamlou: The Rebel Poet in Search of an Audience," *Iranian Studies* 18, nos. 2–4 (Spring–Autumn 1985): 375–422. Alishan (1951–2005) was an accomplished poet and scholar who tragically died in a house fire in Salt Lake City.

8. For more on Tahereh Qorrat al-Ayn's life and significance, see Hamid Dabashi, "At the Dawn of Colonial Modernity," in *Shi'ism: A Religion of Protest* (Cambridge, MA: Harvard University Press, 2011), 159–205.

9. For a study of the Babi movement, see Abbas Amanat, *Resurrection and Renewal: The Making of the Babi Movement in Iran, 1844–1850* (Los Angeles: Kalimat Press, 2005).

10. For a detailed account of Jalal al-Din Mirza's life and legacy, see *Encyclopedia Iranica*, s.v., "Jalāl-Al-Din Mirzā," accessed August 12, 2022, https://www.iranicaonline.org/articles/jalal-al-din-mirza.

11. See *Encyclopedia Iranica*, s.v., "Ākūndzāda," accessed August 12, 2022, https://www.iranicaonline.org/articles/akundzada-playwright.

12. *Encyclopedia Iranica*, s.v., "Jalāl-Al-Din Mirzā."

13. Mirza Fath Ali Akhundzadeh, *Maktubat/Correspondences*, ed. M. Sobhdam (n.p.: Mard-e Emruz Publications, 1985). In his preamble (p. 8), Akhundzadeh's narrator

claims that his objective is legal equality and not economic equality, for he says that although philosophers have concurred that legal equality is attainable, they disagree whether economic equality is attainable in this world.

14. There is a full account of Akhundzadeh's ideas in the pioneering work of Fereydoun Adamiyyat, *Andisheh-ha-ye Mirza Fath Ali Akhundzadeh* [Mirza Fath Ali Akhundzadeh's thoughts] (Tehran: Khwarizmi Publications, 1970); on *Maktubat*, see page 110 onward.

15. See the first chapter of Ibn Khaldun's *The Muqaddimah: An Introduction to History*, trans. Franz Rosenthal, abr. N. J. Dawood, with an introduction by Bruce Lawrence (Princeton, NJ: Princeton Classics, 2015).

16. See Rosi Braidotti, "Writing as a Nomadic Subject," *Comparative Critical Studies*, 11.2–3 (2014): 163–84.

17. Braidotti, "Writing," 163–84.

18. For more details about the Bidoons, see "Bidoon," World Directory of Minorities and Indigenous Peoples, accessed August 17, 2022, https://minorityrights.org/minorities/bidoon/.

19. See Michael Hardt and Antonio Negri, *Multitude: War and Democracy in the Age of Empire* (London: Penguin, 2005).

20. The critical edition of the original Arabic and the French translation of the pre-Islamic part of the book that covers Persian monarchs was prepared by H. Zotenberg as *Des Rois Des Perses Par Abou Mansour Abd Malik Mohammad Ismayil Thaalibi* (Paris: Imprimerie Nationale, 1844).

21. Zotenberg, *Des Rois Des Perses*, 47.

22. For more on Keyumars, see *Encyclopedia Iranica*, s.v., "Gayōmart," accessed August 19, 2022, http://www.iranicaonline.org/articles/gayomart-.

23. Gholamhossein Yusefi, ed., *Bustan-e Sa'di (Sa'di-nameh)* (Tehran: Khwarizmi Publications, 1980), 42ff.

CHAPTER 3

1. Abu Mansur Ma'mari, *Shahnameh Abu Mansuri*, in *Bist Maqaleh* [Twenty essays], ed. Mohammad Qazvini (Tehran, 1984), 2:30–31. My translation is from the original Persian.

2. See Qazvini's introduction in Abu Mansur Ma'mari, *Bist Maqaleh* [Twenty essays], 1:5–6.

3. For selected passages of pre-Islamic sources of Iranian historiography translated into English, see *The "History of the Kings of the Persians" in Three Arabic Chronicles: The Transmission of the Iranian Past from Late Antiquity to Early Islam*, trans. Robert G. Hoyland (Liverpool: Liverpool University Press, 2018).

4. *Three Arabic Chronicles*, 12–14.

5. *Three Arabic Chronicles*, 18–20.

6. Abu Mansur Ma'mari, *Bist Maqaleh* [Twenty essays], 33–35. My translation.

7. For a short account of Ibn Muqaffa''s life and work, see *Encyclopedia Iranica*, s.v., "Ebn Al-Moqaffa', Abū Moḥammad 'Abd-Allāh Rōzbeh," accessed August 20, 2022, https://www.iranicaonline.org/articles/ebn-al-moqaffa.

8. For a brief introduction to pre-Islamic historiography, see *Encyclopedia Iranica*, s.v., "Historiography II. Pre-Islamic Period," accessed August 20, 2022, https://www.iranicaonline.org/articles/historiography-ii.

9. Abu Mansur Maʿmari, *Shahnameh Abu Mansuri*, 2:49–50.

10. Abu Mansur Maʿmari, *Shahnameh Abu Mansuri*, 2:71.

11. See *Encyclopedia Iranica*, s.v., "Masʿudi," accessed August 20, 2022, https://www.iranicaonline.org/articles/masudi.

12. Lori Khatchadourian, *Imperial Matter: Ancient Persia and the Archaeology of Empires* (Oakland: University of California Press, 2016), xiii.

13. Khatchadourian, *Imperial Matter*, 1–2.

14. Matthew P. Canepa, *The Iranian Expanse: Transforming Royal Identity Through Architecture, Landscape, and the Built Environment, 550 BCE–642 CE* (Oakland: University of California Press, 2020), xi–xii.

15. See Sarah Bowen Savant, *The New Muslims of Post-Conquest Iran* (Cambridge: Cambridge University Press, 2015), 1; compare with Alison Vacca's *Non-Muslim Provinces Under Early Islam: Islamic Rule and Iranian Legitimacy in Armenia and Caucasian Albania* (Cambridge: Cambridge University Press, 2017), vii.

16. See Mimi Hanaoka, *Authority and Identity in Medieval Islamic Historiography: Persian Histories from the Peripheries* (Cambridge: Cambridge University Press, 2018), 79–98. A pioneering study of this kind of work through false assumptions of center and periphery is Richard Bulliet's *Islam: The View from the Edge* (New York: Columbia University Press, 1995).

17. See Anne F. Broadbridge, *Women and the Making of the Mongol Empire* (Cambridge: Cambridge University Press, 2018).

18. Christopher Markiewicz, *The Crisis of Kingship in Late Medieval Islam: Persian Emigres and the Making of Ottoman Sovereignty* (Cambridge: Cambridge University Press, 2019), 5.

19. Tarif Khalidi, *Arabic Historical Thought in the Classical Period* (Cambridge: Cambridge University Press, 1995), 73.

20. A. C. S. Peacock, *Islam, Literature and Society in Mongol Anatolia* (Cambridge: Cambridge University Press, 2019).

21. Peacock, *Islam, Literature and Society*, 34–35.

22. For the critical edition and an excellent commentary and introduction to this seminal poem, see Mohammad Javad Shariʿat, *Aʾineh-ye Ebrat: Sharh-e Qasideh Ivan Madaʾin Khaqani* [The mirror of admonition: An interpretation of Khaqani's Ivan-e Madaʾin qasida] (Isfahan: Isfahan University Press, 1968).

23. My translation of a few lines of the poem is based on the critical edition of Ziaʾ al-Din Sajjadi, *Divan-e Khaqani Shervani* (Tehran: Zavvar, 2003), 358.

24. For more details, see *Encyclopedia Iranica*, s.v., "Farr(ah)," accessed August 20, 2022, https://iranicaonline.org/articles/farrah.

25. In my previous work, I have theorized in historical detail about the particular ways in which this Weberian conception of "charismatic" authority might be extended to an understanding of the manner in which Muhammad's prophetic mission unfolded. See Dabashi, *Authority in Islam: From the Rise of Muhammad to the Establishment of the Umayyads* (New Brunswick, NJ: Transactions Publishers, 1989).

26. See Max Weber, *The Theory of Social and Economic Organization*, trans. A. M. Henderson and Talcott Parsons, ed. Talcott Parsons (New York: The Free Press, 1947), 358–59.

27. I have greatly expanded upon this idea in *Shiʿism: A Religion of Protest* (Cambridge, MA: Harvard University Press, 2012).

28. For an excellent study of this period and region, see Elton L. Daniel, *The Political and Social History of Khurasan Under Abbasid Rule, 747–820* (Minneapolis: Bibliotheca Islamica for the Iran-America Foundation, 1979).

29. For more details, see *Encyclopedia Iranica*, s.v., "Ebn al-Atīr, ʿEzz-al-Dīn Abuʾl-Ḥasan ʿAlī," accessed August 20, 2022, https://iranicaonline.org/articles/ebn-al-air.

30. For a detailed account of Timurid-period historiography, see John E. Woods, "The Rise of Tīmūrid Historiography," *Journal of Near Eastern Studies* 46, no. 2 (April 1987): 81–108.

31. First in French and then, on the basis of the French version, an English translation of this seminal text on Timur's life and adventures was done as early as 1723. The French translation was by François Pétis de la Croix, a noted French Orientalist. For the English version, see *The History of Timur-Bec: Known by the Name of Tamerlane the Great, Emperor of the Moguls and Tartars: Being an Historical Journal of His Conquests in Asia and Europe* (1723), https://books.google.com/books?id=WoJrON1y42IC&printsec=frontcover&source=gbs_ge_summary_r&redir_esc=y#v=onepage&q&f=false.

32. For a close study of this manuscript, see Mika Natif, "The Zafarnama of Sultan Husayn Mirza," in *Papers of the Index of Christian Art* (Princeton, NJ: Princeton University Press, 2002), 211–28.

33. For an excellent study of Persian Alexander romances, see Minoo S. Southgate, "Portrait of Alexander in Persian Alexander-Romances of the Islamic Era," *Journal of the American Oriental Society* 97, no. 3 (July–September 1977): 278–84.

34. For an exquisite study of Dara Shikoh, see Supriya Gandhi, *The Emperor Who Never Was: Dara Shukoh in Mughal India* (Cambridge, MA: Harvard University Press, 2020).

35. For a critical edition of *Majmaʿ al-Bahrain*, see his selected works in Dara Shikoh, *Montakhab Athar: Resaleh Haq-Nama, Majmaʿ al-Bahrain, and Majmaʿ al-Bahrain, Upankihat Mundak*, ed. Mohammad Reza Jalali-Naʾini (Tehran: Taban, 1956).

36. For a classical study of coffeehouse painting, see Karim Emami, "Naqqashi-ha-ye qahva-khanehʾi (Coffeehouse Paintings)," *Rahnema-ye Ketab* 10, no. 6 (1967): 557–63.

37. See George Makdisi, *The Rise of Colleges: Institutions of Learning in Islam and the West* (Edinburgh: Edinburgh University Press, 1981) and *The Rise of Humanism in Classical Islam and the Christian West* (Edinburgh: Edinburgh University Press, 1990). For a comparable study in the European context, see Erika Rummel, *The Humanism-Scholastic Debate in the Renaissance and the Reformation* (Cambridge, MA: Harvard University Press, 1995). The dialectic that Makdisi implicitly follows I make explicit in my own work on Shiʿi syncretic scholasticism and Persian literary humanism. My key critical position is to balance and navigate the organicity of the relationship and its shifting balance throughout Muslim history.

38. See Javad Tabataba'i, "An Anomaly in the History of Persian Political Thought," in *Mirror for the Muslim Prince: Islam and the Theory of Statecraft*, ed. Mehrzad Boroujerdi (Syracuse, NY: Syracuse University Press, 2013), 107–21.

39. For the most recent scholarship on the figure and legacy of Nezam al-Molk, see Neguin Yavari, *The Future of Iran's Past: Nizam al-Mulk Remembered* (Oxford: Oxford University Press, 2018).

40. See Saïd Amir Arjomand's "Perso-Islamicate Political Ethic in Relation to the Sources of Islamic Law," in *Mirror for the Muslim Prince: Islam and the Theory of Statecraft*, ed. Mehrzad Boroujerdi (Syracuse, NY: Syracuse University Press, 2013), 82–106. For an earlier essay making similar arguments, see Saïd Amir Arjomand, "The Salience of Political Ethic in the Spread of Persianate Islam," *Journal of Persianate Studies* 1 (2008): 5–29.

41. I have explored this theme in detail in *Islamic Liberation Theology: Resisting the Empire* (London: Routledge, 2008). More recently, I have updated and expanded that argument in *The End of Two Illusions: Islam After the West* (Oakland: University of California Press, 2022).

42. For more information, see *Encyclopedia Iranica*, s.v., "Abū Sahl Nawba<u>k</u>t," accessed August 20, 2022, https://iranicaonline.org/articles/abu-sahl-b.

43. A. K. S. Lambton, "Islamic Mirrors for Princes," *La Persia nel medioevo: Atti del Convengo internazionale, Rome, 1970* (Rome, 1971): 419–42. Reprinted in Lambton, *Theory and Practice in Medieval Persian Government* (London: Variorum, Reprints, 1980). More recently, scholars like Saïd Amir Arjomand and Mozaffar Alam have paid much closer attention to the Persian sources.

44. Maulana Jalal al-Din Rumi, *Masnavi-ye Maʿnavi*, ed. Reynold Alleyne Nicholson (Tehran: Amir Kabir, 1984), 1:194, lines 3150ff.

45. Saʿdi, *Bustan (Saʿdi-nameh)*.

46. See Patricia Crone, "Did Al-Ghazali Write a Mirror for Princes? On the Authorship of *Nasihat al-Muluk*," *Jerusalem Studies in Arabic and Islam* 9 (1987): 167–91. Crone built a reputation for her brand of militant Orientalism, in which she consistently sought to doubt, question, denigrate, and outright insult Muslim sensibilities, most notoriously with her infamous idea of Hagarism—a framework that has been rightly charged with virulent Islamophobia. See Crone and Michael Cook, *Hagarism: The Making of the Islamic World* (Cambridge: Cambridge University Press, 1979). While this book delighted US and Western European Neo-Orientalists, who considered it "a milestone," and horrified Muslims, no one bothered to consult the history of Russian Marxist scholarship on the early Islamic period, which was infinitely more grounded in the spectrum of non-Arabic and non-Islamic sources and done with precision rather than sensationalist racist disdain. For an example, see Ilya Pavlovich Petrushevsky, *Islam dar Iran [Islam in Iran]*, trans. Karim Keshavarz (Tehran: Payam, 1971). It was a blessing to have grown up exposed to this body of solid Marxist historiography by scholars like Ilya Pavlovich Petrushevsky and Nina Victorovna Pigulevskaya long before my generation faced the militant bigotry of European Orientalists like Bernard Lewis and Crone—an approach that continues apace in the Neo-Orientalist prose of dynastic historians.

47. For more, see Umberto Eco et al., *Interpretation and Overinterpretation* (Cambridge: Cambridge University Press, 1992), 64ff.

48. See Roland Barthes, "The Death of the Author," in *Image, Music, Text*, trans. Stephen Heath (London: Fontana, 1977), 142–48.

49. See Stefan T. Kamola, "Rashid al-Din and the Making of History in Mongol Iran," abstract (PhD diss., University of Washington, 2013).

50. Gholamhossein Yusefi, ed., *Bustan-e Saʿdi (Saʿdi-nameh)* (Tehran: Khwarizmi Publications, 1980), 42ff.

51. In her crucial essay "The Two Cyruses: Models of Machiavellian Humanity and Harshness for Republican Leaders," *History of Political Thought* 34, no. 1 (Spring 2013): 19–34, Jacqueline R. Hunsicker argues there are in fact not one but two Cyruses in Machiavelli, one he gets from Xenophon and the other from Herodotus. "The Xenophontic Cyrus," she asserts, "serves as an example of humanity—albeit a complicated example—while the Herodotean Cyrus serves as an example of harshness ... a combination of the Cyruses' humanity and harshness makes for a better model for republican leaders to imitate, and urges a reeducation of a republican leader like Scipio, who was inclined only to follow the humane path of the Xenophontic Cyrus." For a more direct link between Machiavelli's *Prince* and Xenophon's *Cyropaedia*, see Waller R. Newell, "Machiavelli and Xenophon's Cyrus: Searching for the Modern Conceptions of Monarchy," in *Every Inch a King: Comparative Studies on Kings and Kingship in the Ancient and Medieval Worlds*, ed. Lynette Mitchell and Charles Melville (Leiden: Brill, 2012), 129–49. The link between Machiavelli's thoughts on classical antiquity and the figure of Cyrus in particular is the subject of extensive scholarship.

52. See Machiavelli, *Discourses on Livy*, trans. Harvey C. Mansfield and Nathan Tarcov (Chicago: University of Chicago Press, 1996), 113.

53. For one of the earliest accounts of "Zindiq" in English, see Reynold A. Nicholson, *A Literary History of the Arabs* (Cambridge: Cambridge University Press, 1907), 372–75.

54. The most important study of these three figures and the whole spectrum of apostasy in early Islamic history is in Abd al-Rahman Badawi, *Min Tarikh al-Ilhad fi al-Islam* [From the history of apostasy in Islam] (Beirut: Al-Muʾassissah al-Arabiya wa al-Nashr Li'l-Dirasat, 1980). The volume contains a few original chapters and a few translated from other sources available in English. The volume is also significant for the courage of Badawi to raise this crucial issue under censorial circumstances. There is an excellent Persian translation of this book with additional notes and a new introduction by the eminent hermeneutician Mostafa Malekian. See Abd al-Rahman Badawi, *Dar Bab Tarikh-e Ilhad dar Islam [On the History of Apostasy in Islam]*, trans. Moʿin Kazemifar (Tehran: Negah Publications, 1398/2019).

55. For an excellent essay on al-Rawandi's *Kitab al-Zomorrod*, see Sarah Stroumsa, "The Blinding Emerald: Ibn al-Rāwandī's Kitāb al-Zumurrud," *Journal of the American Oriental Society* 114, no. 2 (April–June 1994): 163–85.

56. The best class analysis of these uprisings is offered in Ilya Pavlovich Petrushevsky et al., *Tarikh-e Iran [History of Iran]*, trans. Keykhosrow Keshavarzi (Tehran: Pouyesh, 1977/1980), 190–93. See also Crone, *The Nativist Prophets of Early Islamic Iran: Rural Revolt and Local Zoroastrianism* (Cambridge: Cambridge University Press, 2012), which features an exhaustive collection of primary sources that lend themselves to a typical Orientalist historiography—devoid of historical imagination or theoretical insights. These movements were neither nativist nor local. The universality and

centrality of these movements were paramount in the multiple and interpolated worlds in which they occurred. There are two other accounts of these uprisings: 'Abd al-Husain Zarrinkub, "The Arab Conquest of Iran and its Aftermath," in *The Cambridge History of Iran*, ed. R. N. Frye (Cambridge: Cambridge University Press, 1975), 4:1–56; and in the same volume, B. Amoretti, "Sects and Heresies," *The Cambridge History of Iran*, 481–519.

CHAPTER 4

1. Ubayd Zakani, *Akhlaq al-Ashraf* [Ethics of the nobles], ed. Ali Asghar Halabi (Tehran: Asatir Publications, 1373/1994), 123–27. My translation from the original Persian. For an English translation of the book, see Obeyed-e Zakani, *The Ethics of Aristocrats and Other Satirical Works*, trans. Hassan Javadi (Washington, DC: Jahan Books, 1985).

2. Max Weber, "Politics as a Vocation," in *From Max Weber: Essays in Sociology*, trans. and ed. Hans Gerth and C. Wright Mills (Oxford: Oxford University Press, 1946), 78.

3. See Sadid al-Din Muhammad Awfi, *Jawameʿ al-Hekayat wa Lawamiʿ al-Revayat/ Collection of Stories and Illustrious Histories*, ed. Jaʿfar Shuʿar (Tehran: Sazeman-e Intesharat va Amuzesh Inqilab-e Islami, 1363/1984), 65. My translation from the original Persian.

4. For an excellent account of the significance of *Jawameʿ al-Hekayat*, see Shuʿar's learned introduction to his critical edition. Awfi, *Jawameʿ al-Hekayat wa Lawamiʿ al-Revayat*, 1–15.

5. For an extensive examination of these theories, see James Mellard, "From Freud to Jacques Lacan and the Textual Unconscious," in *Beyond Lacan* (Albany, NY: SUNY Press, 2007), 13–46.

6. I refer to him by his Arabized name, Ibn Miskawayh, though this is a misnomer. His Persian name was Abu Ali Ahmad Meshkuyeh-e Razi, for he came from the Meshkuyeh region of the ancient city of Rey.

7. For a pioneering study of Ibn Miskawayh, see Mohamed Arkoun, *Miskawayh, philosophe et historian, contribution à l'étude de l'humanisme arabe au IV/X siècle* (Paris: Librarie philosophique J. Vrin, 1970).

8. For a detailed account of Nasir al-Din al-Tusi's massive intellectual output, see "Khwâjah Nasir al-Dīn al-Tusī: The Philosopher/Vizier and the Intellectual Climate of His Times," in *History of Islamic Philosophy*, ed. Oliver Leaman and S. H. Nasr (London: Routledge, 2001), 527–84. For more on al-Tusi's scientific work, see George Saliba, *A History of Arabic Astronomy: Planetary Theories During the Golden Age of Islam* (New York: NYU Studies in NE Civilization, 1995).

9. For an excellent study of these Alexander romances in Persian, see Minoo S. Southgate, "Portrait of Alexander in Persian Alexander-Romances of the Islamic Era," *Journal of the American Oriental Society* 97, no. 3 (July–September 1977): 278–84.

10. Southgate, "Portrait of Alexander," 282.

11. See the collection of essays in *The Alexander Romance in Persia and the East*, ed. Richard Stoneman, Kyle Erickson, and Ian Netton (Groningen: Barkhuis Publishing & Groningen University Library, 2012).

12. See in particular Daniel L. Selden, "Mapping the Alexander Romance," 19–60, in *Alexander Romance in Persia and the East* (see note 11).

13. Ubayd Zakani, *Akhlaq al-Ashraf* [Ethics of the nobles], 129–31.

14. See the learned introduction by Abbas Iqbal in *Kolliyat-e Obeyed-e Zakani* [The collected works of Obeyd Zakani], ed. Parviz Atabaki (Tehran: Zavvar Publications, 1342/1963), 38. My translation from the original Persian.

15. See Parviz Natel Khanlari, ed., *Divan-e Hafez* (Tehran: Khwarizmi Publications, 1359/1980), 1:952, ghazal no. 468. My translation.

16. Khanlari, *Divan-e* Hafez, 344, ghazal no. 164.

17. For a pioneering study of the time of Hafez, see Qasem Ghani, *Bahth dar Athar va Afkar va Ahval-e Hafez* [On the life, thoughts, works, and circumstances of Hafez], 2 vols. (Tehran: 1321/1942).

18. One of the best essays on Jami's *Salaman and Absal* is by the eminent Afghan scholar Allamah Abd al-Hay Habibi (1910–1984), "*Salaman and Absal Jami va Savabegh-e an*" [*Salaman and Absal* and its sources], ed. Mohammad Isma'il Moballegh (Kabul: Anjoman Jami, 1343/1964).

19. See Abd al-Rahman Jami, *Salaman and Absal: An Allegory*, trans. Edward Fitzgerald (London: J. W. Parker and Son, 1856).

20. For a detailed discussion of Jami's rendition of this much-older story, see Iraj Dehghan, "Jāmī's Salāmān and Absāl," *Journal of Near Eastern Studies* 30, no. 2 (April 1971): 118–26.

21. I take this account of Hunayn ibn Ishaq's version from the pioneering work of Henry Corbin, *Avicenna and the Visionary Recital*, trans. Willard R. Trask (New York: Pantheon Books, 1960), 210–19. For a detailed critique of Corbin's take, see Peter Joosse, "An Example of Medieval Arabic Pseudo-Hermetism: The Case of Salāmān and Absāl," *Journal of Semitic Studies* 38, no. 2 (Autumn 1993): 279–93. This is a typical Orientalist exercise in futility—much-detailed eruditions casting doubt on the original version of Hunayn ibn Ishaq, to no conclusive result. After a detailed discussion of the "pseudo-Hermetica," the text of Ibn Ishaq's magnificent story, Jami's Persian poetic version, and Corbin's provocative interpretations remain intact. For all we know, Hunayn ibn Ishaq may have written the story all by himself, but maybe he did get it from an original Greek or another version. The fact is the textual evidence of this story, which extends from Hunayn ibn Ishaq all the way to Jami, with variations culminating in Avicenna and other Muslim intellectual luminaries. That trajectory remains valid and crucial.

22. For this citation, I used the most recent critical edition of Jami's *Haft Awrang*. See Nur al-Din Abd al-Rahman Jami, *Masnavi Haft Awrang*, 2 vols., ed. Jabolqa Dad Alishah et al. (Tehran: Dafter-e Nashr-e Miras-e Maktub, 1378/1999), 1:406. My translation from the original Persian.

23. For more on the connection of Ibn Yamin to the Sarbedaran uprising, see Soheila Hosseini, "Ibn Yamin: Parchamdar-e A'in Futwwat-e Sarbedaran/Ibn Yamin/The Standard-bearer of the Sarbedaran Chivalrous Doctrines" (Sabzevar, 1394/2015).

24. See Mohammad Dara Shikoh ibn Shah Jahan, *Majma' al-Bahrain* [Where the two seas meet], ed. Mohammad Reza Jalali-Na'ini (Tehran: Taban Publishers, 1335/1956).

25. Dara Shikoh, *Majma' al-Bahrain*, 2.

26. See Marinos Sariyannis, *A History of Ottoman Political Thought up to the Early Nineteenth Century* (Leiden: Brill, 2018), 186.

27. See Philip Rieff, *Freud: The Mind of the Moralist* (New York: Viking, 1959).

28. Gérard Genette, *Palimpsests: Literature in the Second Degree*, trans. Channa Newman and Claude Doubinsky (Lincoln: University of Nebraska Press, 1982/1997), 394–95.

29. For two classical studies of the institution of the vizierate, see Abbas Iqbal, *Vezarat dar Ahd-e Salatin-e Bozorg-e Saljuqi* [The vizierate during the time of the great Saljuq sultans] (Tehran: Tehran University Press, 1958), and A. K. S. Lambton, "The Wazirate," in *Continuity and Change in Medieval Persia: Aspects of Administrative, Economic and Social History, 11th–14th Century* (New York: Bibliotheca Persica, 1988), 28–68. Equally informative is S. D. Goitein's "The Origin of The Vizierate and Its True Character," in *Studies in Islamic History and Institutions* (Leiden: Brill, 2010), 168–93. Goitein is suspicious of the Iranian origin of the office of the vizierate and ascribes it exclusively to an Arabic and Islamic provenance. Even so, the fact remains that the Abbasids were heavily reliant on the Nawbakhtis and Barmecides, the two prominent families of high-ranking officials and viziers who were ostensibly Iranian and in fact from thinly disguised Zoroastrian and Buddhist origins.

30. For a detailed essay on the Andarz genre in both the pre-Islamic and Islamic periods, see *Encyclopedia Iranica*, s.v., "Andarz," accessed August 22, 2022, http://www.iranicaonline.org/articles/andarz-precept-instruction-advice.

31. See Hamid Dabashi, "Khwājah Naṣīr al-Dīn al-Ṭūsī: The Philosopher/Vizier and the Intellectual Climate of His Times," in *History of Islamic Philosophy*, ed. Seyyed Hossein Nasr and Oliver Leaman (London: Routledge, 1996), 527–84. I have further expanded on this idea in a subsequent essay, "The Philosopher/Vizier: Khwaja Nasir al-Din al-Tusi and the Ismaʿilis," in *Mediaeval Ismaʿili History and Thought*, ed. Farhad Daftary (Cambridge: Cambridge University Press, 1996), 231–46.

32. I have additionally explored the dialogical relationship between Anushirvan and Bozorgmehr in an article in Persian. See Dabashi, "Farhang Siyasi-ye *Shahnameh*: Andisheh Siyasi-ye Filsuf/Padeshah dar Saltanat Khosrow Anushirvan" [The Political Culture of *The Shahnameh*: The Political Idea of the Philosopher/King During the Reign of King Anushirvan], *Iranshenasi* 2, no. 2 (Summer 1369/1990): 321–41.

33. For more on this text, see *Encyclopedia Iranica*, s.v., "Kār-nāmag Ī Ardašīr Ī Pābagān," accessed August 22, 2022, http://www.iranicaonline.org/articles/karnamag-i-ardasir.

34. A detailed study of all these pre-Islamic sources was done by the late Ahmad Tafazzoli in his posthumously published *Tarikh-e Adabiyat-e Iran Pish az Islam* [The history of literature in pre-Islamic Iran], ed. Zhaleh Amuzegar (Tehran: Sokhan Publications, 1376/1997). Equally important is another pioneering study by Mohammad Moʿin, *Mazdayasna va Adab-e Farsi* [Mazdeism and Persian literature] (Tehran: Tehran University Press, 1326/1947), which traces aspects of Zoroastrian themes in Persian literature of the Islamic period.

35. Ehsan Yarshater questions the validity of Arthur Christensen's belief that this Tansar is identical to Abarsam, another dignitary at Ardeshir's court. See *Encyclopedia*

Iranica, s.v., "Abarsām," accessed August 22, 2022, https://iranicaonline.org/articles/abarsam.

36. See *Encyclopedia Iranica*, s.v., "Cyropaedia," accessed August 22, 2022, http://www.iranicaonline.org/articles/cyropaedia-gr. For the classic translation of the original Greek, see Xenophon, *Cyropaedia*, trans. Walter Miller (Cambridge, MA: Harvard University Press, Loeb Classical Library, 1914).

37. See *Encyclopedia Iranica*, s.v., "Achaemenid Dynasty," accessed August 22, 2022, https://www.iranicaonline.org/articles/achaemenid-dynasty. Here, we read: "Their chief was the *hazārapati* or chiliarch, who, as the 'second after the king' . . . usually controlled the whole army. How far this official's power as a sort of 'prime minister' went in Achaemenid times, is not sure, since the evidence to this effect is more recent." See also *Encyclopedia Iranica*, s.v., "Chiliarch," accessed August 22, 2022, https://iranicaonline.org/articles/chiliarch, and s.v., "Framadār," accessed August 22, 2022, https://iranicaonline.org/articles/framadar.

38. See *Encyclopedia Iranica*, s.v., "Čahār Maqāla," accessed August 22, 2022, http://www.iranicaonline.org/articles/cahar-maqala.

39. Mieke Bal, *Narratology: Introduction to the Theory of Narrative* (Toronto: University of Toronto Press, 1985), 16.

40. See *Encyclopedia Iranica*, s.v., "Kalila wa Demna II. The Translation by Abu'l-Maʿāli Naṣr-Allāh Monši," accessed August 22, 2022, http://www.iranicaonline.org/articles/kalila-demna-ii.

41. See *Encyclopedia Iranica*, s.v., "Anwār-e Sohaylī," accessed August 22, 2022, https://iranicaonline.org/articles/anwar-e-sohayli. For a comparative assessment of *Kelilah and Dimnah*, *Anvar-e Soheili*, and *Ayar-e Danesh*, see Mehdi Hadi, Abolqasem Radfar, and Ruhollah Hadi, "Moqayeseh *Ayar-e Danesh* ba *Anvar-e Suhayli* and *Kelilah wa Demneh*" [Comparison of *Ayar-e Danesh* with *Anvar-e Soheili* and *Kelilah and Dimnah*], *Kohan Nameh Adab Parsi, Pazhuhesh Gah Olum-e Insani va Motaleʿat-e Farhangi* 6, no. 3 (Fall 1994/2015): 37–58.

42. The text of *Sindbad-nameh* was originally edited in 1948 by Ahmet Ateş (1913–1966). See Zahiri Samarqandi, *Sindbad-name*, ed. Ateş (Istanbul: Milli Egitim Basimevi, 1948). There are other critical editions of the text as well.

43. For a detailed account of these aspects of the Persian epic, see Dabashi, *The Shahnameh: The Persian Epic as World Literature* (New York: Columbia University Press, 2019).

44. See Nasrin Askari, *The Medieval Reception of the Shāhnāma as a Mirror for Princes* (Leiden: Brill, 2016).

45. Askari, *Medieval Reception*, 5.

46. I further develop this point in *Shahnameh: The Persian Epic*, 159–87.

47. Gholamhossein Yusefi, ed., *Bustan-e Saʿdi (Saʿdi-nameh)* (Tehran: Khwarizmi Publications, 1980).

48. See *Encyclopedia Iranica*, s.v., "Aḵlāq-e Nāṣerī," accessed August 22, 2022, http://www.iranicaonline.org/articles/aklaq-e-naseri.

49. From Ralph Waldo Emerson, "Saadi," in *The Complete Works of Ralph Waldo Emerson*, vol. 9 (Cambridge, MA: Riverside Edition, 1911), 136–41. First published in October 1842 in *The Dial*.

50. For a critical edition, see Ala' al-Dowleh Semnani, "Shatranjiyeh" [On chess], in *Mosanaffat-e Farsi*, ed. Najib Mayel Heravi (Tehran: Sherkat-e Intesharat-e Ilmi va Farhangi, 1369/1990), 323–28.

51. Semnani, "Shatranjiyeh," 324.

52. Semnani, "Shatranjiyeh," 328.

53. See Abolqasem Ferdowsi, *Shahnameh*, ed. Jalal Khaleghi Motlaq and Abolfazl Khatibi, bk. 7 (Tehran: Markaz-e Daʾerat al-Maʿaref Bozorg-e Islami, 1386/1997), 69–86. My translation of the original Persian.

54. Ferdowsi, *Shahnameh*, 80.

CHAPTER 5

1. The Bible, King James version, Isaiah 45:1–4, https://www.kingjamesbibleonline.org.

2. There are countless manuscripts and numerous printed versions of this text, among them Nasir al-Din al-Tusi, *Awsaf al-Ashraf* [Attributes of the nobles], ed. Abolfazl Moradi (Rasta) (Tehran: Ayat Ishraq Publications, 1396/2017). For my reading of this seminal text, I have also relied on a previous critical edition by an eminent scholar of al-Tusi, Haj Seyyed Nasrallah Taqavi, which he prepared and published in Berlin with the calligraphy of Mirza Hossein Khan Seifi Imad al-Kuttab, in Khwajah Nasir al-Din al-Tusi, *Awsaf al-Ashraf* (Berlin: 1306/1927).

3. Amnon Netzer, "Some Notes on the Characterization of Cyrus the Great in Jewish and Judeo-Persian writings," *Acta Iranica* 2 (1974): 35.

4. Netzer, "Cyrus the Great," 40. Emphasis added.

5. Netzer, "Cyrus the Great," 41. For more recent scholarship on the figure of Cyrus the Great in Hebrew sources, see Jason Sion Mokhtarian, "Rabbinic Depictions of the Achaemenid King Cyrus the Great," in *The Talmud in Its Iranian Context*, ed. Carol Bakhos and M. Rahim Shayegan (Tübingen: Mohr Siebeck Verlag, 2010), 112–39. Even more detailed references are in Mokhtarian, *Rabbis, Sorcerers, Kings, and Priests: The Culture of the Talmud in Ancient Iran* (Berkeley: University of California Press, 2015). The most eminent scholar in this field was the late Yaakov Elman (1943–2018), a professor of Talmud at Yeshiva University who was deeply influential in cultivating the field of Irano-Talmudic studies. See Azadeh Ehsani Chombeli, *Moses and Garšāsp, Ardašīr and Herod: Narratives of the Babylonian Talmud in Their Iranian Context* (Costa Mesa, CA: Mazda Publications, 2020), for the state of scholarship in this extraordinary field.

6. Netzer, "Cyrus the Great," 42.

7. See *Encyclopedia Iranica*, s.v., "Judeo-Persian Communities IX. Judeo-Persian Literature," accessed August 23, 2022, https://iranicaonline.org/articles/judeo-persian-ix-judeo-persian-literature.

8. *Encyclopedia Iranica*, "Judeo-Persian Communities."

9. See *Encyclopedia Iranica*, s.v., "Ardašīr-Nama," accessed August 23, 2022, https://iranicaonline.org/articles/ardasir-nama-a-matnawi-of-six-thousand-couplets-in-persian-by-sahin-sirazi-a-jewish-persian-poet-of-the-8th-14th-century.

10. As detailed in *Encyclopedia Iranica*, "Ardašīr-Nama."

11. See *Encyclopedia Iranica*, s.v., "'Ezrā-nāma," accessed August 23, 2022, https://www.iranicaonline.org/articles/ezra-nama.

12. *Encyclopedia Iranica*, "'Ezrā-nāma."

13. For recent comprehensive scholarship on Cyrus the Great, see Reza Zarghamee, *Discovering Cyrus: The Persian Conqueror Astride the Ancient World* (Washington, DC: Mage Publications, 2018).

14. I have explored these operas further in *Persophilia: Persian Culture on the Global Scene* (Cambridge, MA: Harvard University Press, 2015), 124–35.

15. See Max Unger, "The Persian Origins of 'Parsifal' and 'Tristan,'" *The Musical Times* 73, no. 1074 (1932): 703–5.

16. For the most recent scholarship on Handel's *Serse*, see Corbett Bazler, "The Comedies of Opera Seria: Handel's Post-Academy Operas, 1738–1744" (PhD diss., Columbia University, 2012), 19–79.

17. For more on the significance of trees in Zoroastrianism, see *Encyclopedia Iranica*, s.v., "Dera<u>k</u>t," accessed August 23, 2022, https://iranicaonline.org/articles/derakt.

18. See the learned introduction to *Eskandar va Ayyaran* [Alexander and vagabond warriors], ed. Alireza Zakavati Qaraguzlu (Tehran: Nashr-e Ney, 1383/2014), 9–17. This, according to the editor of this volume, is an abridgment of a seven-volume *naqqali* by Manouchehr Khan Hakim.

19. I have developed this theme in detail in my book *The Shahnameh: The Persian Epic as World Literature* (New York: Columbia University Press, 2019).

20. See Alireza Zakavati Qaraguzlu, *Eskandar va Ayyaran*, 9–15.

21. See Gilles Deleuze and Félix Guattari, *Anti-Oedipus: Capitalism and Schizophrenia*, trans. Robert Hurley, Mark Seem, and Helen R. Lane (Minneapolis: University of Minnesota Press, 1983), 9. "Lenz" is a reference to the novella fragment by Georg Büchner (1836) in which Jakob Lenz, a friend of Goethe, is the subject of the story.

22. Khwaja-ye Kermani, "Homay and Homayun," in *Khamseh*, ed. Saʿid Niaz Kermani (Kerman: Daneshkadeh Adabiyat va Olum-e Insani, 1330/1991), 282–84.

23. The same cross-dressing happens in Ferdowsi's *Shahnameh*, during the battle between Gordafarid and Sohrab, from which Khwaju Kermani may have taken the idea. I explore the transgender character of these events in *Shahnameh: The Persian Epic*, 150–60.

24. See *Encyclopedia Iranica*, s.v., "Bābā Ṭāher ʿOryān," accessed August 23, 2022, http://www.iranicaonline.org/articles/baba-taher-oryan.

25. See Muhammad bin Ali al-Rawandi, *Rahat al-Sudur va Ayat al-Surur dar Tarikh-i Al-i Saljuq*, ed. Muhammad Iqbal (Leiden: Brill, 1921), 99–100.

26. For a critical edition of Baba Taher's quatrains, see Baba Taher Oryan, *Do Beyti-ha ye Baba Taher* [The quatrains of Baba Taher], ed. Vahid Dastgerdi (Tehran: Nashr-e Partov, 1373/1994). My translation from the original Persian.

27. For an introduction to Suhrawardi's philosophy, see Hossein Ziai, "The Illuminationist Tradition," in *History of Islamic Philosophy*, ed. Seyyed Hossein Nasr and Oliver Leaman (London: Routledge, 1995), 465–96. Hossein Ziai has another, more comprehensive work, *Knowledge and Illumination: A Study of Suhrawardi's Hikmat al-Ishraq* (Atlanta: Scholars Press, 1990).

28. For more recent scholarship on Suhrawardi in Iran, see Gholamhossein Ibrahimi Dinani, *Shoʻaʻ-e Andisheh va Shuhud dar Falsafah Suhrawardi* [The radius of thought and intuition in the philosophy of Suhrawardi] (Tehran: Hekmat Publications, 1393/2014).

29. For a pioneering assessment of Suhrawardi's political thoughts, see Hossein Ziai, "The Source and Nature of Authority: A Study of al-Suhrawardi's Illuminationist Political Doctrine," in *The Political Aspects of Islamic Philosophy: Essays in Honor of Muhsin S. Mahdi*, ed. Charles E. Butterworth (Cambridge, MA: Harvard University Press, 1992), 304–44.

30. For a comprehensive study of Suhrawardi's allegorical writings, see Taqi Pournamdarian, *Aql-e Sorkh: Sharh va Taʾvil-e Dastanha-ye Ramzi Suhrawardi* [The red intellect: Explanation and interpretation of Suhrawardi's allegorical stories] (Tehran: Sokhan Publications, 1390/2011).

31. See *Encyclopedia Iranica*, s.v., "Illuminationism," accessed August 23, 2022, https://iranicaonline.org/articles/illuminationism.

32. An excellent example of paying critical attention to pre-Islamic Iranian aspects of Islamic political thought is Seyyed Javad Tabatabaʾi's *Dar-amadi Falsafi bar Tarikh-e Andisheh-ye Siyasi dar Iran* [A philosophical introduction to the history of political thought in Iran] (Tehran: Daftar Motaleʻat Siyasi va Beyn-al-Melali, 1367/1988). Though a pioneering study of political thought in Iran, the work has two serious problems: (1) it is devoid of historical context and is fixated on abstract ideas, and (2) it thrives in a false binary, a presumed opposition between Iranian and Islamic factors, as if these were two monolithic entities devoid of historical presence in larger regional and global contexts that extend from Indian to Hebrew, Greek, Roman, and even North African and Iberian contexts.

33. See Henry Corbin, *Spiritual Body and Celestial Earth: From Mazdean Iran to Shiʻite Iran*, trans. Nancy Pearson (Princeton, NJ: Princeton University Press, 1977), 110. Corbin has other sources dealing with the same subject. See Corbin, *Sohravardi d'Alep, fondateur de la doctrine illuminative* (Paris: G.-P. Maisonneuve, 1939), and *Les Motifs zoroastriens dans la philosophie de Sohravardi* (Tehran: Editions du Courrier, 1946). In more recent scholarship, Suhrawardi's Greek sources are more emphasized. See John Walbridge, *The Leaven of the Ancients: Suhrawardi and the Heritage of the Greeks* (Albany: State University of New York Press, 2000). This false bifurcation between the Greek and Iranian aspects of Suhrawardi's philosophy is of course entirely useless. His physical location and moral imagination were literally smack in the middle of both worlds and many other worlds, and none came to him at the expense of any other. We need to fathom a whole different geography based on the fact of his philosophy and not assimilate him forward to the Eurocentric or Iranocentric imagination of his commentators. Meanwhile, in a review of Walbridge's book, Dimitri Gutas (*Arabic Sciences and Philosophy* 13 [2003]: 303–9), completely rejects Suhrawardi's having any serious knowledge of Greek philosophy and thus dismisses the whole premise of Walbridge's argument. In between Greco-centric Walbridge et al. and Iranocentric Corbin et al. stands Suhrawardi's own monumental work itself, using what he needed from both the Greeks and the Iranians to produce his own exquisite philosophy, in which the figure of the Persian Prince shines empathically.

34. For a comprehensive study of Suhrawardi's oeuvre, see Mehdi Amin Razavi, *Suhrawardi and the School of Illumination* (London: Routledge Sufi Series, 1995).

35. I cite this central passage from Suhrawardi's *al-Mashari' wa al-Mutarihat*, which Corbin translates as "Conversations," in *Spiritual Body and Celestial Earth*, 125.

36. Shahab al-Din Yahya Suhrawardi, *al-Mashari' wa al-Mutarihat* [Pathways and dialogues], in *Majmu' Mosanaffat-e Sheikh al-Ishraq*, ed. Henry Corbin, vol. 1 (Tehran: Académie Impériale Iranienne de Philosophie, 1976): 502–3.

37. Corbin, *al-Mashari' wa al-Mutarihat*, 502–3.

38. Shahab al-Din Yahya Suhrawardi, "Avaz-e Par-e Jibril" [The song of Gabriel's wing], in *Majmu'eh Asar-e Farsi-ye Sheikh-e Ishraq* [Collected Persian works of the Master of Illumination], ed. Seyyed Hossein Nasr, vol. 3 (Tehran: Académie Impériale Iranienne de Philosophie, 1976), 209–10. My translation from the Persian original. There is an excellent English translation of these Persian allegorical stories by W. M. Thackston, Jr., *The Mystical and Visionary Treatises of Suhrawardi* (London: Octagon Press, 1982). But I prefer my own translations.

39. Shahab al-Din Yahya Suhrawardi, "Partov-nameh" [The book of light], 81. My translation from the Persian original.

40. Shahab al-Din Yahya Suhrawardi, "Aql-e Sorkh" [The red intellect], 226–27. My translation from the original Persian.

41. For a pioneering study of these movements, see Gholam Hossein Sadighi, *Les mouvements religieux iraniens au IIe et au IIIe siècle de l'hégire* (Paris: Les Presses modernes, 1938).

42. Among the earliest studies of these movements is Gholam Hossein Sadeghi's *Les mouvements religieux iraniens*.

43. In his pioneering study *Mazdayasna va Adab-e Farsi* [Mazdaism and the Persian literature] (Tehran: Tehran University Press, 1326/1947), the late Mohammad Moin has provided the widest spectrum of such continuities between the pre-Islamic and Islamic periods of Persian literature in the widest sense of the term.

44. For a pathbreaking study of this prison literature, see Valiollah Zafari, *Habsiyeh dar Adab-e Farsi: Az Aghaz-e She'r-e Parsi ta Payan-e Zandiyeh* [Prison writing in Persian literature: From the beginning to the end of the Zand period] (Tehran: Amir Kabir, 1364).

45. Gholamhossein Yusefi, ed., *Bustan-e Sa'di (Sa'di-nameh)* (Tehran: Khwarizmi Publications, 1980), 146.

CHAPTER 6

1. Antonio Gramsci, *The Modern Prince and Other Writings* (New York: International Publishers, 1957), 137.

2. Nima Yushij, "Morgh-e Amin" [Amen bird], in *Majmu'eh Asar-e Nima Yushij* [The collected works of Nima Yushij], ed. Sirus Tahbaz (Tehran: Nashr-e Nashr, 1364/1985), 606.

3. Simon Schama, *The Embarrassment of Riches: An Interpretation of Dutch Culture in the Golden Age* (New York: Vintage, 1987).

4. Susan Buck-Morss, "Hegel and Haiti," *Critical Inquiry* 26, no. 4 (2000): 823. Buck-Morss later expanded this essay into a book, *Hegel, Haiti, and Universal History* (Pittsburgh, PA: University of Pittsburgh Press, 2009).

5. See Jonathan Jones, "Rembrandt and Slavery: Did the Great Painter Have Links to this Abhorrent Trade?," *Guardian*, February 9, 2021, https://www.theguardian.com

/artanddesign/2021/feb/09/rembrandt-slavery-slave-trade-marten-soolmans-oopjen-coppit. For more on the exhibition itself, see "Slavery: Ten True Stories," Rijksmuseum, accessed August 24, 2022, https://www.rijksmuseum.nl/en/whats-on/exhibitions/past/slavery.

6. Walter Benjamin, "Theses on Philosophy of History," in *Walter Benjamin, Illuminations*, trans. Harry Zohn, ed. Hannah Arendt (New York: Schocken Books, 1968), 256.

7. See Gauri Viswanathan, *Masks of Conquest: Literary Study and British Rule in India* (New York: Columbia University Press, 1989).

8. Thomas Babington Macaulay, "Minute, Dated 2nd February 1835," *Islamic Studies* 54, nos. 3–4 (2015): 240; citing H. Sharp, ed., *Selections of Educational Records, Part 1, 1781–1839* (Calcutta: Superintendent, Government Printing, 1920): 109.

9. For one frightful account of the European genocide of Africans, see Sven Lindqvist, *"Exterminate All the Brutes": One Man's Odyssey into the Heart of Darkness and the Origins of European Genocide* (New York: New Press, 1997).

10. Macaulay, "Minute, Dated 2nd February 1835," Selections of Educational Records, 116 (see note 8).

11. Early in his seminal text *Colonialism in Question: Theory, Knowledge, History* (Berkeley: University of California Press, 2005), 3–33, Frederick Cooper offers a detailed history of this trajectory of critical thinking in colonial studies.

12. David Scott, *Conscripts of Modernity: The Tragedy of Colonial Enlightenment* (Durham, NC: Duke University Press, 2004), 9–14.

13. See Y. V. Mudimbe, *The Invention of Africa: Gnosis, Philosophy, and the Order of Knowledge* (Bloomington: Indiana University Press, 1988).

14. See Walter D. Mignolo and Catherine E. Walsh, *On Decoloniality: Concepts, Analytics, Praxis* (Durham, NC: Duke University Press, 2018).

15. I first developed this idea of "colonial modernity" in detail in my *Iran: A People Interrupted* (New York: New Press, 2008).

16. Abolqasem Ferdowsi, *The Shahnameh*, ed. Jalal Khaleqi Motalq (New York: Bibliotheca Persica, 1366/1987), 41. My translation from the original Persian.

17. Seyyed Javad Tabataba'i, *Zaval-e Andisheh-ye Siasi dar Iran: Goftar dar Mabani Nazari Enhetat-e Iran* [Decline of political thought in Iran: A discourse on the theoretical foundations of the downfall of Iran] (Tehran: Kavir Publications, 1383/2004).

18. Tabataba'i, Decline of political thought, 353–69.

19. On this point, see the brilliant argument of Amy Allen in *The End of Progress: Decolonizing the Normative Foundations of Critical Theory* (New York: Columbia University Press, 2016).

20. For a critical edition of this seminal book, see Jalal al-Din Davani, *Akhlaq-e Jalali* [Jalali's ethics], ed. Abdullah Mas'udi Arani (Tehran: Ettela'at Publications, 1391/2012). The full title of the book is *Lawam' al-Ishraq fi Makarim al-Akhlaq* [Rays of enlightenment on sublime ethics], but the text is known by his own name and referred to as *Akhlaq-e Jalali*.

21. For an excellent essay on the subject, see Maryam Daneshgar, "Ta'sir-e Asar va Afkar-e Jalal al-Din Davani dar Shebh-e Qareh Hend" [The influence of Jalal al-Din Davani's works and thoughts in the Indian subcontinent], *Faslnameh Motale'at-e Shebh Qareh Daneshgah Sistan va Baluchistan* 6, no. 21 (1392/2014): 35–52.

22. Shah Tahmasp ibn Ismaʿil ibn Heidari al-Safavi, *Tazkireh Shah Tahmasp*, ed. Amr Allah Safari (Tehran: Sharq Publications, 1363/1084).

23. Shah Tahmasp ibn Ismaʿil ibn Heidari al-Safavi, *Tazkireh Shah Tahmasp*, 2.

24. Shah Tahmasp ibn Ismaʿil ibn Heidari al-Safavi, *Tazkireh Shah Tahmasp*, 24.

25. For example, in Shah Tahmasp ibn Ismaʿil ibn Heidari al-Safavi, *Tazkireh Shah Tahmasp*, 24 and 35.

26. Shah Tahmasp ibn Ismaʿil ibn Heidari al-Safavi, *Tazkireh Shah Tahmasp*, 67–68.

27. Shah Tahmasp ibn Ismaʿil ibn Heidari al-Safavi, *Tazkireh Shah Tahmasp*, 69.

28. For an excellent study of the art of this period, see the doctoral dissertation of Annu Manuja, "A Critical Study of Mughal Paintings During Akbar's Reign" (PhD diss., Aligarh Muslim University, 1999).

29. See *The Babur-nama in English* [*Memoirs of Babur*], trans. Annette Susannah Beveridge (London: Luzac and Co., 1922), 1.

30. Tannaz Latifian Isfahani, "Meʿmari va Zendegi va Zibaʾi dar Babur-nameh" [Architecture, life, and beauty in *Babur-nameh*] (PhD diss., Shahid Beheshti University, January 2011).

31. Emine Fetvaci, "From Print to Trace: An Ottoman Imperial Portrait Book and Its Western European Models," *The Art Bulletin* 95, no. 2 (2013): 243–68.

32. See Lady Mary Wortley Montagu, *Turkish Embassy Letters* (New York: Little, Brown Book Group, 1994).

33. In "Montagu's Turkish Embassy Letters and Cultural Dislocation," *Studies in English Literature, 1500–1900* 38, no. 3 (1998): 537–51), Mary Jo Kietzman goes a long way in safeguarding Montagu's letters from abusive "Orientalist" reading. But at the same time, her idea of a "migrant moment of dislocation" erases the power dynamics altogether.

34. A bilingual Greek and Latin version of Xenophon's *Cyropaedia* that was published in Europe in 1767 is one of two copies of the text that Thomas Jefferson possessed and that is currently held at the US Library of Congress in Washington, DC.

35. For a biography of Suleiman, see André Clot, *Suleiman the Magnificent*, trans. Matthew J. Reisz (London: Saqi, 1989/2005).

36. For more details, see the excellent book of Supriya Gandhi, *The Emperor Who Never Was: Dara Shukoh in Mughal India* (Cambridge, MA: Harvard University Press, 2020).

37. For more on Abbas Mirza, see *Encyclopedia Iranica*, s.v., "ʿAbbās Mīrzā Qajar," accessed August 24, 2022, https://www.iranicaonline.org/articles/abbas-mirza-qajar.

38. Max Weber, *The Protestant Ethic and the Spirit of Capitalism*, trans. Talcott Parsons (New York: Citadel Press, 1930), 181–82.

39. Jürgen Habermas, *The Structural Transformation of the Public Sphere: An Inquiry into a Category of Bourgeois Society*, trans. Thomas Burger and Frederick Lawrence (Cambridge, MA: MIT Press, 1962/1992), 16.

40. I have developed this idea of the transnational public and parapublic spheres in detail in *Persophilia: Persian Culture on the Global Scene* (Cambridge, MA: Harvard University Press, 2015). Equally insightful is Nancy Fraser's "Transnational Public Sphere: Transnationalizing the Public Sphere: On the Legitimacy and Efficacy of Public Opinion in a Post-Westphalian World," *Theory, Culture & Society* 24, no. 4 (2007): 7–30.

41. I closely study a whole constellation of these travelogues in *Reversing the Colonial Gaze: Persian Travelers Abroad* (Cambridge, UK: Cambridge University Press, 2020).

42. For a comprehensive study of coffeehouses in these regions, see Ralph S. Hattox, *Coffee and Coffeehouses: The Origins of a Social Beverage in the Medieval Near East* (Seattle: University of Washington Press, 1985). For a more recent collection of excellent essays on the subject, see Dana Sajdi, ed., *Ottoman Tulips, Ottoman Coffee: Leisure and Lifestyle in the Eighteenth Century* (London: I. B. Tauris, 2014).

43. The institution of coffeehouses in Iran has been the subject of extensive scholarship—some more serious than others—and the best of them is in fact in Persian and not available in English. A few European Orientalist travelers had casual observations about coffeehouses, like Jean-Baptiste Chardin in his *Journal du voyage du chevalier Chardin en Perse & aux Indes Orientales* (1686), and Jean-Baptiste Tavernier, another French Orientalist traveler before him, in his *Six Voyages de Jean-Baptiste Tavernier* (1676). Mainly on the basis of these impressionistic comments, other more recent Neo-Orientalists have repeated those very same casual tourisms in lieu of serious scholarship; for example, see Kathryn Babayan, *Mystics, Monarchs, and Messiahs* (Cambridge, MA: Center for Middle Eastern Studies of Harvard University, 2002), 439–44. To be fair, coffeehouses are only an afterthought of this study, which is a take on *Ghulat* (extremist Shias), a subject for which we of course have the superior scholarship of Said Amir Arjomand in his pioneering book, *The Shadow of God and the Hidden Imam: Religion, Political Order, and Societal Change in Shi'ite Iran from the Beginning to 1890* (Chicago: University of Chicago Press, 1984), and Matti Moosa, *Extremist Shiites: The Ghulat Sects* (Syracuse, NY: Syracuse University Press, 1988). But even more extensively, we have a more recent study of the Ghulat in Persian by Ne'amatollah Safari Foroushani, *Ghalian: Kavoshi dar Jarayan-ha va Barayand-ha* [Ghulat: A research in movements and consequences] (Mashhad: Astan Quds-e Razavi, Bonyad-e Pazhyuhesh-ha-ye Islami, 1378/1999). These Persian sources (by far the best on the subject) are scarce known to the Neo-Orientalists on North American campuses. As for the study of coffeehouses proper, a pioneering study is Khosrow Khosravi, "Motale'ha-'i dar bareh-ye Ghahveh-Khaneh" [A study of coffeehouses], *Kavosh* (1341/1962): 84–91. This was followed by Nasrollah Falsafi, *Tarikh Qahveh and Qahveh Khaneh dar Iran* [History of coffee and coffeehouses in Iran] (Tehran: 1353/1974). Equally important is Sakineh Khatun Mahmoudi and Marziyeh Qasemi, "Ta'amol Naql-o-Naqsh dar Qahveh Khaneh-ha ye Irani" [The interaction between narrative and painting in Iranian coffeehouses], *Do Fasl Nameh Honar-ha-ye Tajassomi* 2, no. 3 (1391/2012). For an excellent recent study of coffeehouses in the Safavid period, see the exquisite work of Mohammad Karim Yusef Jamali and Mohammad Reza Ishaq Nimuri, "Qahveh Khaneh dar Sakhtar-e Jame'eh-ye Safavi va Tafrihat-e Ra'ij dar Qahveh Khaneh-ha" [Coffeehouses in the structure of Safavid society and customary entertainments in coffeehouses], *Faslnameh-ye Elmi–Pazhuheshi Miskawayh* 6, no. 17 (1390/2011): 123–40. These sources are just too many to cite here, but the pioneering work that mapped out the literary and poetic sources of the period to show how the institution of coffeehouses had appeared in Persian poetry before any European Orientalist fancied passing through Iran is by three young Iranian scholars, Naser Nikobakht, Ebrahim Khodayar, and Mohsen Ahmadi, in their excellent essay "Tabalvor Barkhi Anasor Qahveh Khaneh'i dar She'r Asr-e Safavi" [The consolidation of some

coffeehouse features in the poetry of the Safavid period], *Do Faslnameh Farhang va Adabiyat-e Ammeh* 2, no. 4 (1393/2014): 109–34.

44. See *Encyclopedia Iranica*, s.v., "Coffeehouse," accessed August 25, 2022, https://iranicaonline.org/articles/coffeehouse-qahva-kana.

45. I discuss these public spaces in some detail as the locus classicus of the rise of public reason in the Safavid capital in *Shi'ism: A Religion of Protest* (Cambridge, MA: Harvard University Press, 2012), 166–202.

46. Mohammad Karim Yusef Jamali and Mohammad Reza Ishaq Nimuri, "Qahveh Khaneh dar Sakhtar-e Jame'eh-ye Safavi va Tafrihat-e Ra'ij dar Qahveh Khaneh-ha" [Coffeehouses in the structure of Safavid society and customary entertainments in coffeehouses], *Faslnameh-ye Elmi–Pazhuheshi Miskawayh* 6, no. 17 (1390/2011): 123–40.

47. Yusef Jamali and Ishaq Nimuri, [Coffeehouses], 123–40.

48. Yusef Jamali and Ishaq Nimuri, [Coffeehouses], 123–40.

49. See Mir Seyyed Hamadani, *Zakhirat al-Moluk* [Treasury of the kings], ed. Seyyed Mahmoud Anvari (Tabriz: Tabriz University Press, 1358/1979).

50. Mir Seyyed Hamadani, *Zakhirat al-Moluk*, 266–85.

51. Mir Seyyed Hamadani, *Zakhirat al-Moluk*, 285–87.There is an English translation, along with annotations and an introduction of this text, by Mohammad Umar Farooq as his PhD dissertation. Mohammad Umar Farooq, "Mir Sayyid Ali Hamadani's *Dhakiratul Muluk*: An Annotation and Translation" (PhD diss., University of Kashmir, 2009), https://shodhganga.inflibnet.ac.in/handle/10603/55864. For my references, I have used the Persian original.

52. Nasir al-Din al-Tusi, "Al-Adab al-Wajiz li al-Walad al-Saghir" [The short education for the little child], in *Akhlaq-e Mohtashami ba Seh Resaleh Digar Mansub-e beh Ou* [Mohtashami ethics and three other treatises attributed to him], ed. Mohammad Taqi Daneshpazhuh (Tehran: Tehran University Press, 1330/1960), 495–559.

53. For more details on these sources, see Farnaz Sadeghi, "Mo'arrefi Ketab-ha-yeh Ganjineh Tarikh Adabiyat-e Kudak va No-Javan" [Introducing the books in the treasury of the history of literature for children and young adults] (Tehran: Farhangestan Zaban va Adab-e Farsi, 19 Mordad 1399/August 9, 2020), https://apll.ir/1399/05/19/معرفى-ک-ادبیات-تاریخ-گنجینة-های8C%80%E2%/ کتاب-.

54. In his pioneering work *Studien zur Geschichte der älteren arabischen Fürstenspiegeel*, (Leipzig: Hinrichs, 1932), Gustav Richter used the terms "mirrors" for Arabic sources, as did Stefan Leder later in "Aspekte arabischer und persischer Fürstenspiegel: Legitimation, Fürstenethik, politische Vernunft," in *Specula principum Studien zur europäischen Rechtsgeschichte A cura di Angela De Benedictis con la collaborazione di Annamaria Pisapia Ius Commune Sonderheft* 117 (Frankfurt: Klostermann, 1999), 28.

55. My translation of a few lines of the poem based on the critical edition of Zia' al-Din Sajjadi, *Divan-e Khaqani Shervani* (Tehran: Zavvar, 2003), 358.

56. Jacques Lacan, "The Mirror Stage as Formative of the Function of the I as Revealed in Psychoanalytic Experience," in *Écrits: A Selection*, trans. Alan Sheridan (London: Routledge, 1966/1977), 3.

57. Luce Irigaray, *Speculum de l'autre femme* (*Speculum of the Other Woman*), trans. Gillian Gill (Ithaca, NY: Cornell University Press, 1974/1985), 243.

58. Irigaray, *Speculum*, 243.

59. Irigaray, *Speculum*, 255.

60. Nima Yushij, "Kar-e Shab-pa" [The work of the nightwatch], 520–21.

CHAPTER 7

1. Parviz Natel Khanlari, ed., *Divan-e Hafez* (Tehran: Khwarizmi, 1359/1980), 1:364, ghazal no. 174. My translation from the Persian original. Hafez's allusion is to "Alexander's mirror," which was a legendary tower in Alexandria presumably devised by Aristotle on top of which a reflective device was installed on which distant objects could be seen.

2. Rostam al-Hokama, *Rostam al-Tawarikh* [The Rostam of histories] (Tehran: Amir Kabir, 1969).

3. Jalil Nozari, *Nevisandeh Rostam al-Tawarikh* [Who is the author of Rostam-Tawarikh?] (Tehran: Miras-e Maktub, 1396/2017).

4. See Abbas Milani, "Rostam al-Tawarikh va Masʿaleh-ye Tajaddod" [Rostam al-Tawarikh and the question of modernity], *Iranshenasi* 8, no. 30 (1996): 247–65.

5. See Seyyed Ali Al-e Davood, "Rostam al-Hokama: Movarrekh va Adib No Andish" [Rostam al-Hokama: A progressive historian and literature], *Iranshahr-e Emruz* 1, no. 3, (2016): 59–69.

6. Rostam al-Hokama, *Rostam al-Tawarikh*, 63.

7. Rostam al-Hokama, *Rostam al-Tawarikh*, 61.

8. For the most recent scholarship on *Hajv* (burlesque) and satire in general, see Paul Sprachman, "Hajv and Profane Persian," in *A History of Persian Literature*, ed. Ehsan Yarshater, vol. 2, *Persian Lyric Poetry in the Classical Era, 800–1500: Ghazals, Panegyrics and Quatrains* (London: I. B. Taurus, 2019), 579–602.

9. In an excellent essay, Abu al-Hasan Fayyaz Anush comes close to grasping the chivalrous disposition of the prose of *Rostam al-Tawarikh* but fails to grasp its ironic twist. See Abu al-Hasan Fayyaz Anush, "Padideh ye Rostam al-Tawarikh" [The phenomenon of Rostam al-Tawarikh], *Tahqiqat-e Tarikh-e Ijtimaʿi* 1, no. 1 (2011): 97–122.

10. See David Fishelov, "Parody, Satire and Sympathy in Don Quixote and Gulliver's Travels," *Connotations* 12, nos. 2–3 (2002–2003): 126–38.

11. Fishelov, "Parody, Satire and Sympathy," 127.

12. Fishelov, "Parody, Satire and Sympathy," 130.

13. Fishelov, "Parody, Satire and Sympathy," 135.

14. See Abbas Amanat, "Through the Persian Eye: Anglophilia and Anglophobia in Modern Iranian History," in *Iran Facing Others: Identity Boundaries in a Historical Perspective*, ed. Abbas Amanat and Farzin Vejdani (New York: Palgrave, 2012), 127–53.

15. See Hayden White, *Metahistory: The Historical Imagination in Nineteenth-Century Europe* (Baltimore: Johns Hopkins University Press, 1973). Two leading scholars have paid close attention to the literary dimensions of Persian historiography. Marilyn Waldman in her pioneering work *Toward a Theory of Historical Narrative: A Case Study in Perso-Islamicat Historiography* (Columbus: Ohio State University Press, 1980), and more recently, Julie Scott Meisami in her essay "History as Literature," in *A History of Persian Literature*, ed. Ehsan Yarshater and Charles Melville, vol. 10, *Persian Historiography* (London: I. B. Taurus, 2012), 1–55.

16. For more on the figure of Saoshyant in Zoroastrianism, see *Encyclopedia Iranica*, s.v., "Eschatology I. In Zoroastrianism and Zoroastrian Influence," accessed August 26, 2022, https://iranicaonline.org/articles/eschatology-i.

17. I have dealt extensively with this transformative period of the rise of postcolonial nations in *Iran Without Borders: Towards a Critique of the Postcolonial Nation* (New York: Verso, 2016).

18. I have detailed the historical and theoretical roots of this bifurcation between nations and states in *The Emperor Is Naked: On the Inevitable Demise of the Nation-State* (London: Zed Books, 2020).

19. Michel-Rolph Trouillot's *Silencing the Past: Power and the Production of History* (1995), along with two other similarly powerful texts—Sven Lindqvist's *Exterminate All the Brutes* (1996) and Roxanne Dunbar-Ortiz's *An Indigenous Peoples' History of the United States* (2014)—are now the subject of a bold and brilliant documentary by Raoul Peck, *Exterminate All the Savages* (HBO, 2021).

20. On these historic uprisings, see Syed Ahmed Khan, *The Causes of the Indian Revolt* (Oxford: Oxford University Press, 2001); Abbas Amanat, *Resurrection and Renewal: The Making of the Babi Movement in Iran, 1844–1850* (Ithaca, NY: Cornell University Press, 1989); Aysel Yildiz, *Crisis and Rebellion in the Ottoman Empire: The Downfall of a Sultan in the Age of Revolution* (London: I. B. Tauris, 2017).

21. See Hamid Dabashi, *Shiʿism: A Religion of Protest* (Cambridge, MA: Harvard University Press, 2012), 180–200.

22. One of the earliest accounts of the press in this crucial period is by E. G. Browne (in collaboration with Mirza Mohammad Ali Khan Tarbiat), *The Press and Poetry of Modern Persia* (Cambridge: Cambridge University Press, 1914). For a more recent account, see Hossein Shahidi, *Journalism in Iran: From Mission to Profession* (London: Routledge, 2007).

23. For the full text of Dehkhoda's poem and a discussion of its context, see Yahya Aryanpour's monumental book *Az Saba ta Nima* [From Saba to Nima], vol. 2 (Tehran: Zavvar Publications, 1350/1971), 94–97. My translation of the Persian original.

24. For a comprehensive study of the period, see the exquisite doctoral dissertation of Kelsey Rice, "Forging the Progressive Path: Literary Assemblies and Enlightenment Societies in Azerbaijan, 1850–1928" (PhD diss., University of Pennsylvania, 2018).

25. Hamideh Javanshir later published her memoir, which was translated into Persian. See Hamideh Mohammad Qoli Zadeh, *Munes-e Ruz-ha-ye Zendegi: Khateratam dar bareh Mirza Jalil Mohammad Qoli Zadeh* [*A Lifetime Companion: My Memoir of Mirza Jalil Mohammad Qoli Zadeh*], trans. Delbar Ebrahim Zadeh (Tehran: Pazhuhandeh, 1379).

26. For a comprehensive study of Iranian theater, see Willem Floor, *The History of Theater in Iran* (Washington, DC: Mage, 200), 213–304. Chapter 6 is on modern theater.

27. See Dabashi, *Reversing the Colonial Gaze: Persian Travelers Abroad* (Cambridge: Cambridge University Press, 2020).

28. Antonio Gramsci, *The Modern Prince and Other Writings* (New York: International Publishers, 1957), 137.

29. Nima Yushij, *Majmuʿeh Asar-e Nima Yushij, Dafter-e Avval, Sheʿr* [Collected works of Nima Yushij: Poems], vol. 1, ed. Sirus Tahbaz (Tehran: Nashr-e Nashr, 1364/1985), 534–40.

30. Nima Yushij, *Majmuʿeh Asar-e Nima Yushij*, 534–40.

31. Parviz Natel Khanlari, *Divan-e Hafez*, 1:364, ghazal no. 174 (see note 1). My translation from the Persian original.

CHAPTER 8

1. Ahmad Shamlou, "Oqubat" [Punishment], in *Majmuʿeh Ashʿar* [Collected poems] (Giessen, Germany: Bamdad Publications, 1989), 2:955–59. My translation from the Persian original.

2. Rosi Braidotti, "Writing as a Nomadic Subject," *Comparative Critical Studies* 11.2–3 (2014): 163–84.

3. Mohammad Mehdi ibn Mohammad Reza al-Isfahani, *Nesf-e Jahan fi Taʿrif al-Isfahan* (On Isfahan: The center of the world), ed. Manuchehr Sotoudeh (Tehran: Amir Kabir, 1368/1988). I take this information about al-Isfahani from Manuchehr Sotoudeh's learned introduction. *Nesf* is usually translated as "half," but we could also read it as "center."

4. Mohammad Mehdi ibn Mohammad Reza al-Isfahani, *Nesf-e Jahan fi Taʿrif al-Isfahan*, 139–69.

5. There is a vast and growing body of superb scholarship on Shahrashub. One of the earliest accounts was by the eminent scholar Mohammad Jaʿfar Mahjoub, *Sabk-e Khorasani dar Sheʿr-e Farsi* [Khorasani style in Persian poetry] (Tehran: Ferdowsi Publications, 1345/1966), 677–99. The appendix was published earlier, in 1963, in *Ketab-e Hafteh* periodical. Ahmad Golchin Maʿani followed, with a more extensive study, in *Shahrashub dar Sheʿr-e Farsi* [Shahrashub in Persian poetry] (Tehran: Amir Kabir, 1346/1967). In a subsequent edition, Golchin Maʿani expanded on this work. For the most recent scholarship on the subject, see the excellent work of the literary scholar Sunil Sharma, "Shahrashub," in *A History of Persian Literature*, ed. Ehsan Yarshater, vol. 2, *Persian Lyric Poetry in the Classical Era, 800–1500: Ghazals, Panegyrics and Quatrains* (London: I. B. Taurus, 2019), 569–78. There is also a detailed essay on the genre of Shahrashub in Russian by E. O. Akimushkina, "ЭВОЛЮЦИЯ ЖАНРА ШАХРАШУБ В ПЕРСОЯЗЫЧНОЙ ПОЭЗИИ XI–XII ВВ" [Evolution of the genre Shahrashub in Persian language poetry of XI–XII centuries], *RUDN Bulletin, Literary Criticism series*, no. 3 (2011). But the most extensive body of scholarship remains in Persian, conducted by a stellar generation of Iranian scholars. See, for example, Batul Mahdavi, Mohammad Behnam Far, and Mostafa Shamsuddin, "Anvaʿ-e Shahrashub va Kohantarin Shahrashub-e Senfi" [Varieties of Shahrashub and the oldest professional Shahrashub], *Fonun-e Adabi* 8, no. 1 (2016): 43–54; or Parvin Bekhradi, Sirus Shamisa, and Abdolreza Modarreszadeh, "Sabkshenasi Shahrashub-ha-ye Masʿud Saʿd Salman" [Stylistic Studies of Masʿud Saʿd Salman's Shahrashubs], *Faslnameh Elmi Tafsir va Tahlil-e Motun, Zaban va Adabiyat-e Farsi (Dehkhoda)* 13, no. 49, (2021): 209–327. There are countless other equally crucial studies entirely unknown to the English-speaking world. Compared to this body of literature in Persian, what appears in English is often amateurish and superficial. See, for example, the Neo-Orientalist take on Shahrashub in Kathryn Babayan, *The City as Anthology: Eroticism and Urbanity in Early Modern Isfahan* (Stanford, CA: Stanford University Press, 2021), 108–36. This whole book, entirely tone-deaf to the literary and poetic art

of these works, is a take on the body of manuscripts known as *Muraqqa*, falsely translated here as "anthology," whereas more serious scholars have translated the word as "album." It can also be translated as "potpourri" or "medley." This is a manuscript that contains paintings and calligraphies, consisting of beautiful prose and poetry, popular during the Safavid, Mughal, and Ottoman Empires—on which subject, again, the best scholarship is in fact by younger generations of Turkish, Iranian, Arab, and Indian scholars few have even heard of on US or European university campuses. See, for example, Mehrangiz Moradi, "Barresi Vojuh Efteraq va Tashabohat-e Muraqqaʿat-e Doreh Safaviyeh va Osmani (A Comparison of the Similarities and Differences of Safavid and Ottoman Muraqqas)," *Avvalin Hamayesh Beinolmelali Noavari va Tahqiq dar Honar va Olum-e Ensani* (1394/2015). The examples are far too many to cite here. The point is that, in disregarding these superior works of scholarship in non-European languages, Neo-Orientalists are reinventing the wheel in a clumsy way afforded them only in a neo-colonial context.

6. Mohammad Jaʿfar Mahjoub, *Sabk-e Khorasani dar Sheʿr-e Farsi*, 699.

7. Mohammad Jaʿfar Mahjoub, *Sabk-e Khorasani dar Sheʿr-e Farsi*, 684.

8. Ahmad Golchin Maʿani, *Shahrashub in Persian Poetry*, 15 (see note 5).

9. For the most recent scholarship on this period, see F. De Blois, "Pre-Islamic Iranian and Indian Influences on Persian Literature," in *A History of Persian Literature*, ed. J. T. P. de Bruijn, vol. 1, *General Introduction to Persian Literature* (London: I. B. Tauris, 2009), 333–44.

10. Mehdi Akhavan-e Sales, "Qesseh-ye Shahryar-e Shahr-e Sangestan" [The Ballad of the Prince of Stoneville], in *Az in Avesta* [From this Avesta: Collected works], vol. 1 (Tehran: Zemestan Publishers, 1397/2018), 585–95. I am extremely grateful and honored to have received a set of these two magnificent volumes of Mehdi Akhavan-e Sales's complete work signed posthumously on his behalf by his two sons, Zardosht and Mazdak Ali Akhavan-e Sales.

11. Braidotti, *Nomadic Subjects: Embodiment and Sexual Difference in Contemporary Feminist Theory* (New York: Columbia University Press, 1994), 22.

12. See D. T. Potts, *Nomadism in Iran: From Antiquity to the Modern Era* (Oxford: Oxford University Press, 2016).

13. Potts, *Nomadism in Iran*, xiii–xv.

14. For a pioneering study of Ibn Khaldun's philosophy, see Muhsin Mahdi, *Ibn Khaldun's Philosophy of History* (London: George Allen & Unwin Ltd., 1957).

15. "A. Bamdad" is the nom de plume of Ahmad Shamlou. My translation from the Persian original.

16. Nima Yushij, "Qesseh-ye Rang-e Parideh, Ah-e Sard" [The ballad of pale complexion and cold sigh], in *Majmuʿeh Asar-e Nima Yushij, Dafter-e Avval, Sheʿr* [Collected works of Nima Yushij: Poems], vol. 1, ed. Sirus Tahbaz (Tehran: Negah Publishers, 1368/1989), 26. My translation from the Persian original.

17. Braidotti, *Nomadic Subjects*, 4–5.

18. Braidotti, *Nomadic Subjects*, 5.

19. W. E. B. Du Bois, *Writings: The Suppression of the African Slave-Trade / The Souls of Black Folk / Dusk of Dawn / Essays and Articles* (Washington, DC: Library of America, 1987), 364.

20. Mehdi Akhavan-e Sales, "Chavoshi," in *Zemestan* [Winter]: *Collected Works*, vol. 1 (Tehran: Zemestan Publishers, 1397/2018), 413–19.

21. For a full discussion of both the novella and the film, see my *Masters and Masterpieces of Iranian Cinema* (Washington, DC: Mage Publishers, 2007), 167–92.

22. Antoine de Saint-Exupéry, *The Little Prince* (New York: Bloomsbury Publishing, Alma Classics, 2019), 10–11.

CONCLUSION

1. Mehdi Akhavan-e Sales, "Bagh-e Man" [My garden], in *Zemestan* [Winter]: *Collected Works*, vol. 1 (Tehran: Zemestan Publishers, 1397/2018), 423–24. My translation from the Persian original.

2. For the most recent scholarship exploring this link, see Christopher Tuplin, "Plato, Xenophon and Persia," in *Plato and Xenophon*, ed. Gabriel Danzig et al. (Leiden: Brill, 2018), 576–611. See also Christopher Rowe, "Plato and the Persian Wars," in *Cultural Responses to the Persian Wars: Antiquity to the Third Millennium*, ed. Emma Bridges, Edith Hall, and P. J. Rhodes (Oxford: Oxford University Press, 2007), 85–104.

3. See Johannes Haubold, "Xerxes' Homer," *Cultural Responses to the Persian Wars*, 47–64.

4. For more details on this encounter and the link between Platonic and Persian thought, see Philip Sidney Horky, "Persian Cosmos and Greek Philosophy: Plato's Associates and the Zoroastrian Magoi," *Oxford Studies in Ancient Philosophy* 37 (2009): 47–103.

5. For the most recent state of scholarship on Judeo-Persian literature, see V. B. Morten, "Judeo-Persian Literature," in *A History of Persian Literature*, ed. John Perry, vol. 9, *Persian Literature from Outside Iran: The Indian Subcontinent, Anatolia, and the Judeo-Persian* (London: I. B. Taurus, 2018), 390–410.

6. See Edith Hall, "Aeschylus' *Persians* via the Ottoman Empire to Saddam Hussein," in *Cultural Responses to the Persian Wars*, 167–99 (see note 2).

7. For more on this concept, see Verena Andermatt Conley, "Chaosmopolis," *Theory, Culture, Society* 19, nos. 1–2 (2002): 127–38.

8. Hans Heinrich Schaeder, "Die islamische Lehre vom Vollkommenen Menschen, ihre Herkunft und ihre dichterische Gestaltung" [The Islamic doctrine of the perfect man, its origin and its poetic manifestations], *Zeitschrift der Deutschen Morgenländischen Gesellschaft* 79, nos. 3–4 (1925): 192–268.

9. Schaeder, "Die islamische Lehre," 240.

10. For the most recent translation of Attar's poem, see Farid ud-Din Attar, *The Conference of the Birds*, trans. Afkham Darbandi and Dick Davis (London: Penguin Classics, 1984).

11. Hafez, *Divan*, ed. Parviz Natel Khanlari, vol. 1 (Tehran: Kharazmi Publications, 1995), 260.

12. Paul de Man, "Ludwig Binswanger and the Sublimation of the Self," in *Blindness and Insight: Essays in the Rhetoric of Contemporary Criticism* (Minneapolis: Minnesota University Press, 1971), 41.

13. De Man, "Ludwig Binswanger," 46.

14. For an introduction to Mulla Sadra's ontology, see Christian Jambet, *The Act of Being: The Philosophy of Revelation in Mulla Sadra*, trans. Jeff Fort (New York: Zone Books, 2006).

15. Ahmad Shamlou, *Majmuʿeh Ashʿar* [Collected poems], vol. 2 (Giessen, Germany: Bamdad, 1368/1989), 1001–6.

16. See Desiderius Erasmus, *The Education of a Christian Prince*, trans. Lester K. Born (New York: W. W. Norton & Company, 1968).

17. See Junaid Rana, "The Story of Islamophobia," *Souls: A Critical Journal of Black Politics, Culture, and Society* 9, no. 2 (2007): 148–61. Equally insightful in reading this word through Agamben's hesitations is Jill Jarvis, "Remnants of Muslims: Reading Agamben's Silence," *New Literary History* 45, no. 4 (2014): 707–28.

18. For a review of Boochani's memoir, *No Friend but the Mountains: Writing from Manus Prison*, and the context of its publications, see J. M. Coetzee, "Australia's Shame," *New York Review of Books*, September 26, 2019, https://www.nybooks.com/articles/2019/09/26/australias-shame/.

19. For a pioneering study of Namjoo's music, see Nahid Siamdoust, *Soundtrack of the Revolution: The Politics of Music in Iran* (Stanford, CA: Stanford University Press, 2017), 183–208.

20. See Rosi Braidotti, *The Posthuman* (London: Polity, 2013).

21. See Hamid Dabashi, *Corpus Anarchicum: Political Protest, Suicidal Violence, and the Making of the Posthuman Body* (New York: Palgrave, 2012).

22. I first wrote about this opera in "Performing Puccini in Persian: Can Europeans Sing Right to Left?," *Al Jazeera*, July 7, 2019, https://www.aljazeera.com/opinions/2019/7/7/performing-puccini-in-persian-can-europeans-sing-right-to-left.

23. For a close reading of Puccini's opera in terms of its central themes of love and power, see Valerie Peterson, "Mythic Rhetoric: Love, Power, and Companionate Marriage in Puccini's Turandot," *Ohio Communication Journal* 52 (2014): 20–35.

24. There are marked differences between the character of Turandot in the Persian original of *Haft Peykar* and the way she appears in Puccini's opera. In "Modernism and the Machine Woman in Puccini's 'Turandot,'" *Music and Letters* 86, no. 3 (2005): 432–51, Alexandra Wilson discusses the details of how the eponymous character of Turandot was seen as the symbol of an "emotionally sterile modernism." This is the diametrical opposite of all the seven princesses from the seven climes that appear in Nezami's *Haft Peykar*.

25. The character of Puccini's Turandot has been the subject of extensive feminist scholarship. See, for example, J. M. Balkin, "Turandot's Victory," *Yale Journal of Law & the Humanities* 2, no. 2 (1990): 299–341. These studies are mostly unaware of or indifferent to the Persian originals.

26. For the most recent translation, see Nizami Ganjavi, *The Haft Peykar: A Medieval Persian Romance*, trans. Julie Scott Meisami (Oxford: Oxford University Press, 1995).

27. For varied manifestations of Bahram in Persian literature, see *Encyclopedia Iranica*, s.v., "Bahram V Gōr in Persian Legend and Literature," accessed August 28, 2022, https://iranicaonline.org/articles/bahram-05-lit.

28. Two European scholars who have studied Turandot further are Fritz Meier, "Turandot in Persian," *Zeitschrift der Deutschen Morgenländischen Gesellschaft* 95 (1941): 1–27; and Ettore Rossi, "La leggenda di Turandot," *Studi Orientali Roma* 2 (1956): 457–76.

29. For more on this crucial intermediary text of *One Thousand and One Days*, see Justin Juntly McCarthy, ed., *The Thousand and One Days* (London: Chatto and Windus, 1892).

30. The Chinese reception of Puccini's opera is a whole different story, as evidenced by the occasion when Maestro Zubin Mehta and director Zhan Yimou staged and performed the opera in Beijing in 1998. For more detail, see Scarlet Cheng, "At Home, but Out of Place," *Los Angeles Times*, August 23, 1998, https://www.latimes.com/archives/la-xpm-1998-aug-23-ca-15612-story.html.

31. For more on the significance of *Turandot* in Puccini's lifework, see William Ashbrook and Harold Powers, *Puccini's "Turandot": The End of the Great Tradition* (Princeton, NJ: Princeton University Press, 1991).

32. In a provocative study, the Italian scholar Paola Orsatti has dug deep into the historical origins of the figure of Turandot in Persian history and Islamic sources. See Paola Orsatti, *Materials for a History of the Persian Narrative Tradition, Two Characters: Farhād and Turandot* (Venice: Edizioni Ca' Foscaari, 2019). In this study, Orsatti proposes the following: "a character named 'Būrān-dukht' as the prototype from which Turandot, the heroine of the tale well known in Europe from Puccini's opera (1926), springs. Two historical personages, both called Būrān or Būrān-dukht, are relevant in this line of development: the first is the daughter of the Sasanid king Khusraw II Parvīz (r. 580–628 CE), who was queen of Persia for a short period (630–631 CE); the other is the daughter of Ḥasan b. Sahl, wife of Caliph al-Maʾmūn (813–833)."

33. For a report on the performance of Brecht's *Turandot or the Whitewashers' Congress* in English in London, see Edward Kemp, "Brecht's Last Laugh," *Guardian*, September 8, 2008, https://www.theguardian.com/stage/2008/sep/09/theatre2.

34. See Angelo Michele Piemontese, "The Enigma of Turandot in Nizāmī's Pentad: Azāda and Bahrām Between Esther and Sindbād," in *A Key to the Treasure of the Hakīm: Artistic and Humanistic Aspects of Nizāmī Ganjavī's Khamsa*, ed. Johann-Christoph Bürgel and Christine van Ruymbeke (Leiden: Leiden University Press, 2011), 127–44.

INDEX

Page numbers in *italics* indicate figures.

Abbasid caliphate: Barmecide family and, 73, 85, 86, 302n29; historiography during, 62, 63; imperial administration of, 99; Mongol destruction of, 73, 141; in Persian cosmopolis, 21; Persian language use during, 278; rise and expansion of, 73; Shuʿubiyyah movement and, 39; uprisings against, 97, 133, 162, 277; Zoroastrian influences on, 86. *See also specific rulers*
Abbas Mirza (Qajars), 186, 188–89
"Abraham in the Fire" (Shamlou), 261
Achaemenid Empire: Alexander romances and, 105; charismatic kingship in, 72; geographic scope of, 275; Hebrew Bible references to rulers of, 118; imperial administration of, 118, 303n37; Iranian political thought and, 85. *See also specific rulers*
Adab. *See* Literary humanism
Advice literature: characteristic features of, 82; didactic texts in tradition of, 128; Islamic political thought and, 99; mysticism and, 141; philosopher/vizier figure in, 117; politics of royal patronage as source of, 120–21; pre-Islamic, 115–16; on statesmanship, 123. *See also* Mirrors for princes
Aeschylus, xiii, xiv, 8, 85, 185, 255, 273, 275
Aesthetic imagination, 83
al-Afghani, Jamal al-Din, 42, 86
Afsharid dynasty, 206, 209, 212, 283–84
Agamben, Giorgio, 48, 262
Aghraz al-Siasah (Samarqandi), 101
Ahmad Shah–The Last King of Qajar (Mohassess), 263, 264
Akbar (Mughal Empire), 124, 183, 188
Akhavan-e Sales, Mehdi, 26, 213, 238–39, 248–49, 253, 261, 285
Akhlaq al-Ashraf (Zakani), 98, 105, 106, 208, 209
Akhlaq-e Jalali (Davani), 181
Akhlaq-e Mosavvar (Akkasbashi), 199–200
Akhlaq-e Naseri (al-Tusi), 74–75, 82, 104, 105, 129–30
Akhundzadeh, Fath Ali, 33–35, 224, 294–95n13
Akkasbashi, Ibrahim Khan, 199–200
Alexander romances: as earliest form of novels, 150; hypertextuality of, 114; as mirrors for princes, 76, 119; Ottoman

319

Alexander romances (*continued*)
  Empire ideology and, 187; Persian Prince archetype in, 75–76, 84, 105, 124, 275–76; political Persianism and, 99
Alexander the Great: Aristotle and, 112, 115, 116, 119; conquests of, 149, 275–76; *Cyropaedia* as influence on, 52, 118, 234; mirror devised for, 200, 312n1; Persian Prince archetype and, 8, 105, 119, 126; as philosopher-king, 254; in *Shahnameh*, 126, 276. See also Alexander romances
Alishan, Leonardo P., 294n7
Allegorical imagination, 154
"Amen-Bird" (Yushij), 169
Andarz-nameh. See Advice literature
Anderson, Kevin, 233
Annales school, 36, 52–54
Anticolonialism: nationalism and, 30, 216; of *Rostam al-Tawarikh*, 207, 208; as tragedy, romance, or epic, 174, 176; uprisings and, 173, 192, 198, 212, 217–18, 226
Anti-Oedipus (Deleuze and Guattari), 150
Anushirvan. See Khosrow I Anushirvan the Just
Anvar-e Suhayli (Kashefi), 124, 125
Aq Qoyunlu (White Sheep), 8, 109, 181, 281
Arab Awakening (Nahda), 219, 220
Arash the Archer (Kasra'i), 251
Ardeshir-nameh (Shahin-e Shirazi), 145–46
Aristotle: Alexander the Great and, 112, 115, 116, 119; mirror devised by, 200, 312n1; on philosopher-kings, 89; political philosophy of, 9, 89, 91
Arjomand, Saïd Amir, 18–19, 79, 81
Armeno, Cristoforo, 268, 270
Arsacids. See Parthian dynasty
Aruzi, Nezami, 121
Aryanpour, Yahya, 222–23
Asabiyyah. See Collective consciousness

Ashtiani, Abbas Iqbal, 106–7
Askari, Nasrin, 127–28
Association for the Study of Persianate Societies, 18–19
Astarabadi, Bibi Khanom, 41, 250
Astarabadi, Mohammad Mahdi Khan, 283–84
al-Athir, Ali ibn, 74
Attar, Farid ud-Din, 82, 259
Aurangzeb (Mughal Empire), 76, 187, 188, 283
Authorial voice, 160, 163, 165, 209–12, 260
"Avaz-e Par-e Jibril" (al-Suhrawardi), 159
Awfi, Sadid-al-Din Mohammad, 100–103, 199
Awsaf al-Ashraf (al-Tusi), 141–42
Ayni, Sadriddin, 30, 42
Azzam, Abdelwahab, 42

Baba Taher Oryan, 152–53
Babi movement, 31, 206–7, 213–19
Babur (Mughal Empire), 183–85, 188
Badai' al-Waqai' (Vasefi), 208
Badawi, Abd al-Rahman, 299n54
Bahmani sultanate, 188, 282
Bahram V (Sassanid Empire), 267, 268
Bahrani, Ramin, 263
Bal, Mieke, 122, 126
"The Ballad of the Prince of Stoneville" (Akhavan-e Sales), 238–39, 261
Barbaro, Giosafat, 8
Barmecide family, 73, 85, 86, 302n29
Barthes, Roland, 93, 214
Battle of Karbala (al-Musavi), 194
Bayhaqi, Abu al-Fadl, 120, 279
Bedil, Abdul-Qadir, 42, 200
Behafarid (prophet), 162, 164, 237, 238
Behzad, Kamal al-Din, 75, 76
Belles lettres, 50, 87, 93, 120, 130. See also Mirrors for princes
Benjamin, Walter, 102, 172, 286
Bible. See Hebrew Bible
Bidlisi, Idris, 68

Bidoons ("the Withouts"), 47–48, 241, 256, 257
Binswanger, Ludwig, 260
Black, Antony, 78
Blue Intellect (Parsipur), 250, 261
Boochani, Behrouz, 262
Boroujerdi, Mehrzad, 78, 80, 81
Bosnevi, Ahmed Sudi, 108–9
Bourgeois public sphere, 43, 52, 179, 190, 219, 247
Bowering, Gerhard, 78
Bozorgmehr, 112, 115, 116, 163
Braidotti, Rosi: on nomadic subjectivity, 44, 45, 47, 233, 241, 246, 247; posthuman subjects as theorized by, 263; "Writing as a Nomadic Subject," 26, 229–30
Broadbridge, Anne F., 67
Buck-Morss, Susan, 171, 172
al-Buhturi (poet), 66–67, 69
al-Bundari, Qawam al-Din, 74
Burlesque genre, 209
Bustan (Saʿdi Shirazi): chapter overview, 15–17; excerpts from, 3, 16–17, 55, 92, 95, 128–29, 165; importance of, 14, 75; introduction to, 15–16; as literary abode of Persian Prince, 14–18; as mirror for princes, 16–17, 89, 91; moral aspirations of, 130; synecdoche utilized in, 122, 130
Butterworth, Charles, 79
Buyid dynasty, 73, 85, 99, 103–4, 279
Byzantine Empire, 39, 64, 72, 99

Calvino, Italo, 270
Canepa, Matthew P., 65–66
Cassirer, Ernst, 28–30, 46–47, 51, 255, 283, 285–86
Césaire, Aimé, 29, 43, 45
Chahar Maqaleh (Aruzi), 121
Charismatic authority, 71–73, 85, 99, 160, 296n25
Chatterjee, Partha, 216
"Chavoshi" (Akhavan-e Sales), 248

Chelkowski, Peter J., 200
Children's literature, 198–200
China: as domain of civilizational consciousness, 64; in Islamic historiography, 64; Jewish community in, 145
Christianity, 147–48, 219
CIA-MI6 coup of 1953 (Iran), 4, 286–87
Cicero, 11, 200, 276
Cities: anomie and alienation in, 240; as literary tropes, 231; mythologization of, 230–31; in Shahrashub poetry, 231–32, 245
Coffeehouse paintings, 77, 82, 193–95, 194
Coffeehouses, 150, 192–96, 282, 310–11n43
Cohn, Bernard S., 174
Collective consciousness, 30, 41, 181, 204, 230
Collective imagination, 49
Collective subconscious: creative conflict in, 113; intuition of transcendence and, 102; ironic mode of, 131; mapping out, 122; moral imagination in, 102, 121; Persian Prince in, 102–3, 112–14, 134–36, 245; politics undermined by poetics in, 128; re-gendering of, 250; return of the repressed in, 235–36
Colonialism: collapse of Islamic empires under, 76, 172, 186, 189, 216–17; consolidation of European power during, 11–12; critical discourse regarding, 65; hegemony and, 173–75; Islam as site of resistance to, 86–87, 178; manuscript destruction during, 183–84; nomadic subjectivity and, 45, 47, 248; Persian Prince and, 12–13, 30, 50, 177–89; public and parapublic spheres of, 189–92; *Rostam al-Tawarikh* as critique of, 207, 211–12; as tragedy, romance, or epic, 174–77. *See also* Anticolonialism
Commedia dell'arte, 266, 292n9
Conference of the Birds (Attar), 82, 259
Constitutional Revolution (1906–1911), 215, 220
Corbin, Henry, 155–59, 301n21

Cornwall, Owen, 21
Crone, Patricia, 78–79, 92, 298n46
Cyropaedia (Xenophon), xiv; excerpt from, 3; importance of, 118, 156, 186, 254; mirrors for princes modeled after, 233, 273, 275; Persian Prince archetype and, 8, 85, 124; pre-Islamic Iranian pedigree of, 11, 117; world leaders attracted to, 52, 118, 234
Cyrus the Great (Achaemenid Empire): Achaemenid dynasty founded by, 275; in Hebrew Bible, 118, 137, 143–44, 146–47; Machiavelli on exemplary role of, 95, 299n51; Persian Prince archetype and, 8, 143, 144; syncretic disposition of, 101

Dara Shikoh (Mughal Empire), 76, 82, 111–13, 186–88, 283
Darius III (Achaemenid Empire), 8, 149
Darvishi, Aftab, 265, 266
Davani, Jalal al-Din, 180–82
Davood, Seyyed Ali Al-e, 207
Deccan sultanate, 21, 79, 282
De Clementia (Seneca the Younger), 11
Dehkhoda, Ali Akbar, 222–23
Dehkhoda, Iraj Mirza, 208
Dehlavi, Amir Khosrow, 104–5, 231
Deleuze, Gilles, 43, 44, 48, 150–51, 241, 256
dell'Altissimo, Cristofano, 7–9
de Man, Paul, 260
De Officiis (Cicero), 11, 200, 276
Discourses on Livy (Machiavelli), 95
Divan-e Hafez (Hafez-e Shirazi), 205, 259
Don Quixote (Cervantes), 150, 209–10
Du Bois, W. E. B., 45, 226, 248
Durkheim, Émile, 240
Dussel, Enrique, 174, 175, 233

East India Company, 217, 219, 283
Eaton, Richard M., 20–21, 79
Eco, Umberto, 93, 270
Education of a Christian Prince (Erasmus), 255, 261, 282

Egypt: as domain of civilizational consciousness, 64; Fatimid caliphate in, 73, 85, 99; in Islamic historiography, 64; Nahda (Arab Awakening) in, 220; Napoleonic campaigns in, 12, 220; in Persian cosmopolis, 36
Elamites, 274
Emerson, Ralph Waldo, 130–31
Epics, genre of, 175–77
Epistemic violence, 45, 83, 88, 91, 93, 177, 248
Erasmus, Desiderius, 51, 255, 261, 282
Esther, Book of, 118–19, 143, 145–48, 255, 275
Ethics literature, 102, 120
Ethnic nationalism, 4, 6, 21, 38
Eurocentrism, 12–13, 18, 30, 181, 191–92, 233, 246–47
European historiography, 52, 180–81
Ezra, Book of, 118, 145–47
Ezra-nameh (Shahin-e Shirazi), 146–47

The Family of Darius Before Alexander (Veronese), 149, *149*
Fanon, Frantz, 45, 174
Farr-e Izadi (divine dispensation of authority), 71–73, 90, 151
Farrokhzad, Forough, 30, 247, 251
Fascism, 11–13, 28, 29, 190, 269, 274
Fatimid caliphate, 73, 85, 99
Females. *See* Women
Ferdowsi: Alexander romances and, 105, 150; mythic and historic memories of, 84; revolutionary uprisings as influence on, 162. *See also Shahnameh*
Fishelov, David, 210–11
Flatt, Emma J., 21, 79
Foucault, Michel, 44
Fraser, Nancy, 292n14
Freud, Sigmund, 102, 134–35, 201, 260

Ganjavi, Hakim Nezami, 265–70
Ganjavi, Mahasti, 231, 232
Genette, Gérard, 114

Index

Genghis Khan (Mongol Empire), 70, 94, 99, 281
Ghalib, Asadullah Khan, 42
al-Ghazali, Abu Hamid Muhammad, 74, 83, 91–93, 99, 116, 127, 280
Ghaznavi, Sana'i, 231, 232
Ghaznavid Empire: imperial administration of, 99; nomadism and, 243; Persian language use in, 278–80; Persian Prince archetype in, 50; rise and expansion of, 73
Ghurar Akhbar Muluk al-Furs wa Siyarihim (al-Tha'alibi), 22, 53–54, 101, 143, 278
Golestan (Sa'di Shirazi): as advice literature, 120, 128; in education of children, 199; importance of, 14, 75, 128; in Islamic political thought, 81–82; moral aspirations of, 130; synecdoche utilized in, 122, 130
Golshiri, Houshang, 250–51, 261, 269–70, 285
Gorgani, Fakhruddin As'ad, 73, 84, 276
Gozzi, Carlo, 266, 268, 269
Gramsci, Antonio: on European imperialism, 12; on myth-prince, 10, 13, 169, 179, 192; on organic intellectuals, 13, 27, 46; on political parties, 10, 27, 37, 40, 46, 179, 225; *Prison Notebooks*, 10, 11, 51, 165, 285; retheorization of *The Prince* by, 10, 285. See also "Modern Prince"
Great Seljuqs. See Saljuqid Empire
Greco-Persian Wars (499–449 BCE), 273, 275
Green, Nile, 19
Guattari, Félix, 43, 150–51
Gulliver's Travels (Swift), 209–11
Gutierrez, Gustavo, 233

Habermas, Jürgen, 52, 190–91, 219, 292n14
Hadith: on birth of Muhammad, 16, 70, 235; on charismatic authority of Muhammad, 71; in Islamic political thought, 62, 82–83, 85; mirrors for princes influenced by, 91
Hafez-e Shirazi: *Divan-e Hafez*, 205, 259; irony utilized by, 114, 123, 131; mirror metaphors in work of, 200; modernist readings of, 236; moral imagination of, 107; Persian Prince ideal and, 109, 113; politics in work of, 106–8, 217, 228
Haft Peykar (Ganjavi), 265–70, 317n24
Hall, Edith, 255
Hamadhani, Rashid al-Din Fadlullah, 67, 71, 74, 93–94
Hamadhani, Seyyed Ali, 196–97
Hanaoka, Mimi, 67
Haykel al-Nur (al-Suhrawardi), 181
Hebrew Bible: Cyrus the Great in, 118, 137, 143–44, 146–47; Esther, Book of, 118–19, 143, 145–48, 255, 275; Ezra, Book of, 118, 145–47; mirrors for princes from, 118; Pentateuch and, 145, 281; Persian Prince and, 18, 129
Hedayat, Reza Qoli Khan, 206–7
Hedayat, Sadegh, 42
Hegemony, 173–75
Hekmat-e Khosrawani. See Royal philosophy
Herat School, 281
Hermeneutics, 53, 92–93, 102, 145, 161, 260
Herodotus, 11, 85, 149, 242, 275
Hikmah al-Ishraq (al-Suhrawardi), 154–57
Hikmet, Nazım, 220
Hinduism, 20, 21, 23, 111–12, 188
Historical consciousness, 71, 74, 234, 257, 277–79
Historical imagination, 10–11, 74, 154, 164
Historiography: authorial voice in, 210, 212; European, 52, 180–81; inter-dynastic, 206; Iranian, 21, 60, 74, 162, 181, 274; Jewish, 147; lampoon genre and, 208; *longue durée* approach to, 5, 36, 49–53, 64, 254–55; nationalist, 19–21, 23; Persian, 67, 74–77, 206, 209, 210, 284; Persian as language of, 68, 71, 279–80; tropes utilized in, 94, 122. See also Islamic historiography

Hodgson, Marshall, 19, 20
"Homay and Homayoun" (Kermani), 151–52
Horufiyyah movement, 133
Houshang (Pishdadid king), 65, 104, 279
Humanism: disciplining of carnal soul in, 142; Islamic scholasticism and, 24, 78, 80, 82–83, 87, 102; Orientalist assumptions regarding, 24. *See also* Literary humanism
Hunayn ibn Ishaq, 109, 110, 301n21
Hunsicker, Jacqueline R., 299n51
Hypertextuality, 114

Ibn Khaldun, 41, 53, 240, 243
Ibn Miskawayh, 74, 103–4, 180, 279
Ibn Muqaffaʿ: *Adab al-Kabir* and *Adab al-Saghir*, 91; Arabic translations by, 25, 60–64, 117, 123, 124, 277; on education of children, 199; mythic and historic memories of, 84; Persian heritage of, 62; as Zindiq, 96
Ibn al-Rawandi, 96
Ibn Yamin, 111
Iconography, 75, 77, 147–48
Ilkhanids. *See* Mongol Empire
Illuminationist philosophy, 154–64, 280
Imagination: aesthetic, 83; allegorical, 154; collective, 49; historical, 10–11, 74, 154, 164; imperial, 18, 22, 105, 145, 184, 278; literary, 83, 119, 121–22, 131, 145, 154, 246; political, 39, 76, 85, 88, 154–55, 283. *See also* Moral imagination
Imperial imagination, 18, 22, 105, 145, 184, 278
Imperialism, 12, 36, 65, 76, 80, 189, 196
India: anticolonial uprisings in, 217, 218; British colonialism in, 12, 76, 172–73, 181–82, 219, 285; as domain of civilizational consciousness, 64; in Islamic historiography, 64, 65; nationalist historiography of, 21; partitioning of, 286–87; in Persian cosmopolis, 20; political thought in, 181; wisdom literature from, 70, 90. *See also* Mughal Empire
Indian Rebellion (1857), 217, 218
Intuition of transcendence, 42, 102
Iqbal, Muhammad, 30, 42, 45, 220, 226, 286
Iran: Arab conquest of, 162; CIA-MI6 coup in, 4, 286–87; as domain of civilizational consciousness, 64; in Islamic historiography, 64, 65; Islamic Republic of, 4, 251, 287; Jewish community in, 119, 145, 148; millenarian movement in, 218; nationalist historiography of, 19, 21; nomadic mobility in, 242–43; in Persian cosmopolis, 21, 22, 43; political thought in, 80–81, 85, 115, 140, 180, 235; wisdom literature from, 104
Irani, Ardeshir, 42
Iranian historiography, 21, 60, 74, 162, 181, 274
Iranian mythology: Homay's shadow in, 151, 160; human history within context of, 54; Jamshid's Cup in, 200, 202; pre-Islamic, 64, 157; sacred items in, 238
Iranian Revolution (1977–1979), 4, 287
Iran-shahr, Hossein Kazem Zadeh, 42
Irigaray, Luce, 44, 201–3
Irony, 81, 94, 114, 122–23, 131, 136
Isaiah (prophet), 137, 143–44
Isfahani, Habib, 42
Isfahani, Imad Katib, 74
al-Isfahani, Muhammad Mehdi ibn Mohammad Reza, 230, 231
Isfahani, Tannaz Latifian, 184
Iskandar-nameh. *See* Alexander romances
Islam and Muslims: apostasy in, 96–97, 299n54; early period of, 7, 38, 71; Hinduism and, 20, 111–12, 188; manufactured binary between West and, 11; as site of colonial resistance, 86–87, 178; Sunni Islam, 38, 85, 86, 104, 226. *See also* Hadith; Muhammad (prophet); Qurʾan; Shiʿi Islam
Islamicate, use of term, 19, 20, 293n27

Islamic empires: colonialism and collapse of, 76, 172, 186, 216–17; cultural diversity within, 80; ideological foregrounding of, 39; imperial ethos in making and unmaking of, 50; multicultural disposition of, 24; Persian provenance of, 99, 101, 102; political legitimacy in, 70, 72, 74, 78, 113; rise and expansion of, 64; treatment of non-Muslims in, 197; vizierate in, 73, 99, 100, 115–21, 302n29. *See also specific empires, dynasties, and rulers*

Islamic historiography: grammatical syntax and morphology of, 63; Iranian lineage of, 62–70; *longue durée* approach to, 53; models for, 63, 66; Persian Prince archetype in, 95; *Rostam al-Tawarikh* and, 209; topography of, 65, 67

Islamic law, 24, 50, 81, 88, 96, 129, 251

Islamic political thought: deterritorialization of, 140; Hadith in, 62, 82–83, 85; historic transformation of, 235; institutional discourses on, 88–90; legitimacy in, 70, 72, 74, 78, 113; literature review, 78–80, 132; multicultural components of, 51; Orientalist views of, 78–79, 81, 86; patrimonialism in, 277; Persian literary humanism in, 101, 120; Persian Prince in, 70–77, 132–33, 154; pre-Islamic influences on, 60–62, 82, 84–85, 99; Qur'an in, 62, 82–83, 85; racialized and ethnicized readings of, 81; syncretic nature of, 39; units of analysis in, 28

Islamic Republic of Iran, 4, 251, 287

Islamic scholasticism: humanism and, 24, 78, 80, 82–83, 87, 102; legalistic control of, 50; in moral and political imagination, 88; Orientalist assumptions regarding, 24; Shi'i Islam and, 31, 42, 297n37

Islamophobia, 21, 23, 262, 298n46

Isma'ili uprisings, 111, 133

Ismail I (Safavid Empire), 7–8, 182

Ismailzadeh, Hassan, *194*

Issus, Battle of (333 BCE), 149

Ja'farian, Rasul, 206

Jalal al-Din Mirza (Qajars), 32–33, 35, 284

James, C. L. R., 174–75

Jameson, Fredric, 102

Jami, Abd al-Rahman, 42, 75–76, 91, 105, 109–11

Jame' al-Tawarikh (Hamadani), 71, 93–94

Jamshid's Cup, 200, 202–3

Javanshir, Hamideh, 224

Jawame' al-Hekayat (Awfi), 100–103, 199

Jews and Judaism: Chinese, 145; Iranian, 119, 145, 148; Judeo-Persian literature, 143–48, 255; Midrash and, 143–47; Talmud and, 143, 145–47. *See also* Hebrew Bible

Jones, Jonathan, 172

al-Jovayni, Abd al-Malik, 100

al-Jovayni, Ata Malik, 67, 68, 71, 74, 100, 280–81

Judaism. *See* Jews and Judaism

Judeo-Persian literature, 143–48, 255

Jung, Carl Gustav, 102, 151

Kagemusha (Kurosawa), 205, 217

Kalantari, Parviz, 244, 244–45

Kamola, Stefan T., 94

Kar-Namag-e Ardeshir-e Pabagan (Sassanid text), 117, 276

Kashefi, Husain ibn Ali Va'ez, 124, 125

Kasra'i, Seyavash, 251

Kavad I (Sassanid Empire), 133–34

Kavir (Kalantari), 244, 244–45

Kaykavus (Ziyarids), 91, 92, 127, 278–79

Kelilah and Dimnah (Indian text): as advice literature, 123; in education of children, 199; in Islamic political thought, 81–82; in metaphoric register, 122–25; translations of, 25, 61, 63–64, 123–24, 277; as wisdom literature, 70

Kermani, Agha Khan, 42, 237, 238

Kermani, Reza, 215–16

Keyumars, 46, 53, 54, 63, 157–60, 241, 258

Khalidi, Tarif, 68
Khalili, Khalilullah, 30
Khan, Jahangir, 222, 223
Khan, Malkam, 42
Khaqani (poet), 69
Khatchadourian, Lori, 65
Khayyam, Omar, 236
Kherad-Nameh-ye Iskandari (Jami), 91
Khoi, Esmail, 263
Khomeini, Ayatollah, 236, 247, 251
Khorramdin, Babak, 31, 97, 162, 164, 237, 277
Khosrow I Anushirvan the Just (Sassanid Empire): Bozorgmehr and, 112, 115, 116, 163; *Bustan* on, 3, 16, 92; charismatic authority of, 72; in Islamic historiography, 69–70; Mazdakite uprisings and, 133–36; as patron of wisdom and good judgment, 75; in Persian historiography, 77; as philosopher-king, 254; study of previous rulers by, 276–77
Khwaday-Namag (Sassanid text), 60, 63–64, 70, 101, 277
Khwarazmshahids, 33, 280
Kiarostami, Abbas, 271, 271, 287, 287
Kietzman, Mary Jo, 309n33
King of the Benighted (Golshiri), 269–70
Kitab al-Hikmah al-Khalidah (Ibn Miskawayh), 104, 279
Kurosawa, Akira, 205, 217

Lacan, Jacques, 102, 201, 202
Lahuti, Abolqasem, 30, 42
Lakerveld, Miranda, 265, 266
Lambton, A. K. S., 7, 87–89, 92, 115, 120, 130
Lampoon genre, 208, 263
Lefebvre, Henri, 24
Legalism, 24, 50, 86, 87, 108
Leibniz, Gottfried Wilhelm, 43, 241
Lerner, Ralph, 79
The Letter of Tansar (Sassanid text), 117, 234–35

Literary consciousness, 236, 246–47
Literary humanism: Islamic scholasticism and, 24, 87; in moral and political imagination, 88; vizierate and, 100. *See also* Persian literary humanism
Literary imagination, 83, 119, 121–22, 131, 145, 154, 246
The Little Prince (Saint-Exupéry), xiii, 252
Longue durée approach, 5, 36, 49–53, 64, 254–55
Lukács, György, 260

Macaulay, Thomas Babington, 173, 177
Machiavelli, Niccolò: *Cyropaedia* as influence on, 118; on Cyrus the Great, 95, 299n51; *Discourses on Livy*, 95; political philosophy of, 8, 9, 28–29. *See also The Prince*
Mahdi, Muhsin, 79
Mahdi movement, 217–18
Mahjoub, Mohammad Jaʿfar, 232
Mahmoud (Ghaznavid Empire), 54, 73
Majmaʿ al-Bahrain (Dara Shikoh), 76, 82, 111–12, 283
Majus, 96, 97, 197
Makdisi, George, 19, 78, 297n37
Maktubat (Akhundzadeh), 33–35, 294–95n13
Maʿmari, Abu Mansur, 59–63
al-Maʾmun (Abbasid caliph), 61, 63
Mani and Manichaeism: characteristics of, 276; in early Islamic period, 71; Persian Prince archetype and, 30, 49; Zindiqs and, 96–97
Maraghehʾi, Zeyn al Abedin, 42
Markiewicz, Christopher, 68
Martí, José, 45, 174
Martyrs, 76, 77, 125, 193, 283
Marx, Karl and Marxism, 12, 135, 189, 191, 233, 286
al-Mashariʿ wa al-Mutarihat (al-Suhrawardi), 157, 158
Masnavi (Rumi), 89, 145, 199, 269

Masnavi al-Atfal (Mazandarani), 199
Massad, Joseph, 293n27
Mass media, 221–26
al-Masʿudi (historian), 64, 65
Mayakovsky, Vladimir, 25, 43
Mazandarani, Mahmoud ibn Yusef, 199
Mazdak and Mazdakism: cosmology in, 144; in early Islamic period, 71; Illuminationist philosophy and, 156; metaphors in, 223; Persian Prince archetype and, 30, 49; on reincarnation, 162; socialism and, 133, 277; uprisings by, 97, 133–36, 163, 241
Mbembe, Achille, 233
Medes, 274–75
Metaphors: historiography and, 94, 122; for homelessness of postcolonial subject, 43; of "Islam and the West," 83; for justice in Islamic empires, 54; in *Kelilah and Dimnah*, 122–25; Mazdaian, 223; of mirrors, 200–201; in Platonic cave allegory, 202; for shadow archetype, 151; in "Shatranjiyeh," 132; women as metaphoric tropes, 126; Zoroastrian, 223
Metonymy, 94, 122, 126–28, 217, 283
Midrash, 143–47
Mignolo, Walter D., 175, 233
Millenarianism, 208, 218
Mirrors for princes: Alexander romances as, 76, 119; children's literature and, 198, 200; *Cyropaedia* as model for, 233, 273, 275; epistemic violence and, 88, 91; from Hebrew Bible, 118; Islamic historiography as variation on, 66; kaleidoscopic, 103–14, 121; *Kitab al-Taj* genre of, 91–92; literary dimensions of, 87–92; Maʿmari on writing style for, 63; Ottoman Empire and, 112; Persian provenance of, 92; political dimensions of, 87–92; pre-Islamic influences on, 89–92, 115–16; Sassanid Empire and, 60–62, 90–92, 127, 276; textual mimicry of, 196–98; al-Thaʿalibi's formulation of, 53; transhistorical, 91, 113, 114; Zakani's dismantling of, 105. *See also specific texts*
Mirror stage of identity formation, 201
Misogyny, 4, 17, 125–26, 198
"Modern Prince" (Gramsci): excerpt from, 169, 225; on political parties, 10, 27, 37, 225; on retheorization of *The Prince*, 10, 285
Mohassess, Ardeshir, 263, 264
Mongol Empire: Abbasid caliphate destroyed by, 73, 141; dynastic traditions of, 94; imperial administration of, 99; Islamization of Anatolia during, 68; nomadism and, 243; in Persian cosmopolis, 21; in Persian historiography, 67, 74–75; Persian language use in, 71, 75, 280; Persian Prince archetype in, 50, 71; women's role in, 67. *See also specific rulers*
Montagu, Mary Wortley, 185, 309n33
Moral demand system, 133–35
Moral imagination: Alexander romances and, 105; archetypes in, 39, 76, 140–41, 283; in collective subconscious, 102, 121; of colonized nations, 177; in Islamic historiography, 63; literary and poetic culture in, 52, 55, 88, 102, 107, 129–30; metaphysics of, 113; multicultural sources in, 155; in Persianate world, 23, 75; in prison writings, 165; in public and parapublic spheres, 220; ruler and rebel in identical frame of, 133; of al-Suhrawardi, 306n33; syncretic nature of, 41; of transcendentalists, 130; of al-Tusi, 142
Moral philosophy, 104, 120, 141–42, 159, 192, 275
Moretti, Franco, 176
Morss, Susan Buck, 286
Muʿavedin ("the Returnees"), 47–48, 241, 256, 257
Mudimbe, V. Y., 45, 174, 175, 233

Mughal Empire: coffeehouses in, 192, 282; colonialism and collapse of, 76, 172, 182, 186, 216; imperial administration of, 99; manuscript production in, 188; Persian Prince archetype in, 50, 76, 187–88; *Rostam al-Tawarikh* on, 212–13. *See also specific rulers*
Muhammad (prophet): birth of, 16, 70, 116, 235; charismatic authority of, 71–73; divine mission of, 71, 129; in Iranian mythology, 54
Mukhtar, Omar, 217–18
Munshi, Nasrullah, 123–24
Muqaddimah (Ibn Khaldun), 41, 53, 243
al-Muqannaʿ (prophet), 31, 97, 162, 237, 238, 277
Musa-nameh (Shahin-e Shirazi), 145, 281
al-Musavi, Abbas, 194
Mush-o-Gorbeh (Zakani), 106
Muslims. *See* Islam and Muslims
"My Garden" (Akhavan-e Sales), 253
Mysticism: advice literature and, 141; comparative, 111; hermeneutics and, 145; homocentrism of, 83; in *Majmaʿ al-Bahrain*, 76; mirrors for princes and, 89–91; perfect human being in, 258; in Persian cosmopolis, 22; in political thought, 87, 88. *See also* Sufism
The Myth of the State (Cassirer), 28–29, 255
Mythology. *See* Iranian mythology; Persian mythology

Naderi, Amir, 261, 263
Nahda (Arab Awakening), 219, 220
Nameh-ye Khosrovan (Jalal al-Din), 32–33, 35
Namjoo, Mohsen, 262–63
Naser al-Din (Qajars), 215, 238
Nasihat al-Muluk (Ghazali), 91–93, 116, 127
Nationalism: anticolonial, 30, 216; ethnic, 4, 6, 21, 38; in historiography, 19–21, 23; political, 216
National sovereignty, 46, 213–16, 247

Nativism, 4–5, 216
Nazism, 13, 28, 29
Neo-Orientalism, 298n46, 310n43, 314–15n5
Neruda, Pablo, 25, 43
Neshat, Shirin, 263
Netzer, Amnon, 143–44
Nezami (poet), 69, 105, 150
Nietzsche, Friedrich, 95, 115, 134–35
The Nightwatch (Rembrandt), 169–71, 170, 204
Nisab al-Subyan (al-Sijistani), 199
Nizam al-Mulk: political thought of, 74, 81, 83, 99, 280; *Siyasat-nameh*, 6, 101, 116, 125–27, 130, 253
"Nocturne" (Shamlou), 243
Nodjoumi, Nicky, 263
Nomadic subjectivity: Braidotti on, 44, 45, 47, 233, 241, 246, 247; colonialism and, 45, 47, 248; deterritorialization and, 43–45, 48; epistemic roots of, 260; in Persian chaosmopolis, 256–57; philosophical articulation of, 48; in postcolonial context, 233, 256; renegade texts and, 44, 45; repressed memories and, 245
Nozari, Jalil, 206–7

On Isfahan: The Center of the World (al-Isfahani), 230, 231
Organic intellectuals, 13, 27, 46
Orientalism: Arabist, 160, 161; in colonial era, 173, 177; on Islamic political thought, 78–79, 81, 86; literary blindness and, 92–93; militant, 298n46; Neo-Orientalism, 298n46, 310n43, 314–15n5; in popular culture, 4; power dynamics involving, 185; of Puccini, 268–69; on racial divide in scholasticism and humanism, 24; Shuʿubiyya movement and, 38
Orsatti, Paola, 318n32
Ottoman Empire: art and architecture of, 184–85, 187; coffeehouses in, 192, 282; colonialism and collapse of, 76,

172, 186, 217; European knowledge of, 8; foundational premises of the rise of, 69; imperial administration of, 99; mirrors for princes and, 112; in Persian cosmopolis, 21; Persian language use in, 283; Persian Prince archetype in, 50, 187; *Rostam al-Tawarikh* on, 213; Tanzimat reforms in, 219, 220; uprisings in, 217, 218; women in, 185. *See also specific rulers*

"Padeshah Fath" (Yushij), 226–28
Pahlavi regime, 4, 237, 251, 285, 291n4
Panchatantra (Sharma), 11, 25, 123, 124, 277
Parapublic sphere. *See* Public and parapublic spheres
Parody, 208–12, 286
Parsipur, Shahrnush, 250, 261
Parthian dynasty, 63, 67, 69, 73, 84, 276
Partov-nameh (al-Suhrawardi), 159–60
Patrimonial tribalism, 38, 39, 115, 277
Peacock, A. C. S., 68–69
Pentateuch, 145, 281
Peripatetic philosophy, 155
Persianate world: colonial conquest of, 286; historical longevity of, 249; Iranian provenance of domain of, 69; legacy of Islamic intellectual history for, 286; map of Persian Empire, *xvii*; mass media within, 223; moral imagination in, 23, 75; non-Muslim perspective on literary heritage of, 234; political culture of, 127, 196, 226, 278–80, 282; posthuman subjects in, 262; public sphere of, 27, 183; third space within, 24; trajectory of imperial archetype in, 255; use of term, 18–19, 21–23. *See also specific empires, dynasties, and rulers*
Persian chaosmopolis, 256–58
Persian cosmopolis: collective imagination of, 49; conceptualizations of, 20–22; dynastic empires within, 46; in global context, 234; historic provenance of, 35–36, 142; in Islamic frame of reference, 40; Judeo-Persian literature in expansion of, 145, 146; Muslim and non-Muslim relations in, 235; nomadic disposition of, 41–43, 48; Persian Prince in, 18–25, 137–40, 142
Persian historiography, 67, 74–77, 206, 209, 210, 284
Persian literary humanism: of Akhundzadeh, 33; ambulatory spacing of, 42; canonical sources of, 235; cosmopolitan worldliness of, 19; didactic texts in tradition of, 128; internal dynamics of, 256; in Islamic political thought, 101, 120; kaleidoscopic mirroring of Persian Prince and, 109; legacy of, 14
Persian mythology, 53, 113, 218, 251, 280
Persian Prince, xiii–xv; in Alexander romances, 75–76, 84, 105, 124, 275–76; in Christian context, 147–48; in coffeehouse paintings, 77, 195; in collective subconscious, 102–3, 112–14, 134–36, 245; in colonial context, 12–13, 30, 50, 177–89; consolidated conceptions of, 126, 127, 275, 278; deracialization of, 27, 38, 50, 273–74, 281; figurative nature of, 10, 110–11, 129, 219, 235–36, 246; as floating signifier, 41, 50, 52, 102–3, 246, 279; in Greco-Roman domain, 117, 142, 144, 186, 275, 281; in Hebrew habitat, 143–48; heteroglossia of, 34–36, 41, 101, 256; historical transformation of, 48–49, 260–61; at intersection of race, gender, and ethnicity, 36–41; in Islamic political thought, 70–77, 132–33, 154; kaleidoscopic mirrors for, 103–14, 121; literary habitat of, 14–18, 103, 105; literary provenance of, 60, 101, 120, 124; martyred, 76, 77, 125, 283; metamorphosis of, 181–82, 191, 213, 216–22, 237; in musical compositions, 148, 265–70; nonbinary disposition of, 218, 232, 284; as paradoxical figure, 14, 95–97, 114–15, 133, 142, 217, 240; in Persian cosmopolis, 18–25, 137–40, 142;

Persian Prince (*continued*)
  as philosopher-king, 154, 157, 159–63; political domain of, 22, 46, 142; for postclassical agency, 249–52; prophetic poets and, 12–14, 27–32, 36, 40, 48, 91, 192; resubjection of, 198–203; self-portrayals of, 182–85; syncretic ideal of, 70, 71, 84, 101; vizier/chief philosopher by side of, 115–21. *See also* Rebel-poets

The Persians (Aeschylus), xiii, xiv, 8, 85, 185, 255, 273

Philosopher-kings: Aristotelian, 89; Babur as example of, 183; charismatic authority of, 160; Iranian, 157, 158; Persian Prince and, 154, 157, 159–63; Platonic, 89, 105, 162, 180, 254, 255; prophetic, 157; wisdom of, 88

Piemontese, Angelo Michele, 270

Plato: cave allegory of, 202; on philosopher-kings, 89, 105, 162, 180, 254, 255; political philosophy of, 9, 89, 91; *The Republic*, 118, 156

Poets and poetry: Constitutional Period, 226; modernist, 223, 226, 236; philosophical force of, 103; poetic dramaturgy, 224, 226; political thought in, 88–90; prison writings by, 164–65; Shahrashub, 231–32, 245, 314–15n5; spheres of influence for, 42; talismanic power of, 46, 226; as voice of emancipatory causes, 111. *See also* Prophetic poets; Rebel-poets; *specific authors and works*

Political consciousness, 91, 212, 220, 245

Political imagination, 39, 76, 85, 88, 154–55, 283

Political nationalism, 216

Political parties: Cassirer on state control by, 29; Gramsci on, 10, 27, 37, 40, 46, 179, 225; as hindrance to expansion of public and parapublic spheres, 192; in postcolonial nation-states, 214

Pollock, Sheldon, 19, 21, 22

Postcolonial nation-states: Bidoons within, 47–48, 241, 256, 257; collective consciousness of, 30; dyadic domain of, 36; emergence of, 173, 215; gendered disposition of, 41; Muʿavedin within, 47–48, 241, 256, 257; public and parapublic spheres of, 23, 38, 177–79; rebel-poets in, 178–79, 213–14; sovereignty of, 46, 213–16, 247

Posthuman subjects, 45, 47–48, 256, 262–64

Potts, Daniel T., 242

The Prince (Machiavelli): archetypal princes in, 8; Cassirer on amorality of, 28–29, 283; imperial cases utilized in, 6; influences on composition of, 282; political philosophy in, 9–10; retheorizations of, 10, 51, 285

Prince Ehtejab (Golshiri), 250–51, 261, 285

Prince of Persia: The Sands of Time (film), 4

Prison Notebooks (Gramsci), 10, 11, 51, 165, 285. *See also* "Modern Prince"

Prison writings, 164–65

Prophetic poets, 12–14, 27–32, 36, 40, 48, 91, 192

Public and parapublic spheres: bourgeois, 43, 52, 179, 190, 219, 247; coffeehouses as epicenter of, 192–94; of colonial modernity, 189–92; formative forces of, 10, 192; gendered, 13, 31, 36, 40, 219, 250; Habermas on, 52, 190–91, 292n14; moral imagination in, 220; of Persianate world, 27, 183; postcolonial, 23, 38, 177–79. *See also* Transnational public and parapublic spheres

Puccini, Giacomo, 265, 266, 268–70

"Punishment" (Shamlou), 229

Qabus-nameh (Kaykavus), 91, 92, 101, 115, 127, 278–79

Qajar dynasty: Babi uprising against, 31, 215, 217; coffeehouse painting during, 77; colonialism and collapse of, 76,

186, 189, 217; consolidation of power by, 284; imperial administration of, 99; lampooning of, 263; reform efforts by, 219, 220; *Rostam al-Tawarikh* on, 212–13. *See also specific rulers*
Qara Qoyunlu (Black Sheep), 181, 282
Qazvini, Aref, 220
Qazvini, Mohammad, 59–61
Qazvini, Taher Vahid, 231–32
Qesseh Ghorbat Gharbiyyeh (al-Suhrawardi), 245
Qolizadeh, Jalil Mohammad, 224
Qorrat al-Ayn, Tahereh, 30–33, 40–42, 218–21, 250, 284
Qubadiani, Naser Khosrow, 111, 120, 132, 245
Quijano, Anibal, 175
Quint, David, 176
Qur'an: on charismatic authority of Muhammad, 71; in Islamic political thought, 62, 82–83, 85; mirrors for princes influenced by, 91, 92

Racism, 5, 32, 38, 173, 177, 237
Rahat al-Sudur (al-Rawandi), 153
Rana, Junaid, 262
al-Rawandi, Muhammad bin Ali, 153
al-Razi, Muhammad ibn Zakariya, 96
Rebel-poets: in Babi movement, 31–32; as messengers of truth, 238; metamorphosis of, 10, 32, 222–23; nomadic subjectivity and, 45; origins of term, 294n7; in Persian chaosmopolis, 257; postcolonial, 178–79, 213–14; prophetic voices of, 12–14, 27, 30–32, 36, 192; Sarbedaran uprisings and, 111; self-subversive nature of, 286; in transnational public sphere, 13, 35, 36, 179; as unacknowledged legislators of history, 46
Red Intellect (al-Suhrawardi), 160–61, 250
Rembrandt, 169–72, 170, 204
Renegade texts, 44, 45
The Republic (Plato), 118, 156

Rieff, Philip, 113–14, 133–35
Rightly Guided Caliphs, 72, 73
Rijksmuseum (Amsterdam), 170–72
Roads and Rain (Kiarostami), 271, 271, 287
Ro-Hozi theater, 292n9
Rosenthal, Erwin I. J., 79
Rostam al-Hokama, 206–9, 211
Rostam al-Tawarikh (Rostam al-Hokama), 206–13
Royal philosophy, 154, 157, 159, 162
Rudaki (poet), 61, 89, 124
Rumi (poet), 69, 89, 199, 236, 269
Ryan, Mary, 292n14
Rypka, Jan, 19

Sachedina, Abdulaziz, 79
Sacred Order (Rieff), 135
Saʿdi Shirazi: abusive readings of, 81; Emerson's eulogy for, 130–31; lampoon genre and, 208; Persian Prince represented by, 94, 280; travelogues of, 245. *See also Bustan; Golestan*
Sadra, Mulla, 260
Safarnameh (Qubadiani), 132
Safavid Empire: art and architecture of, 76, 182; coffeehouses and coffeehouse paintings in, 77, 150, 192–93, 282; colonialism and collapse of, 76, 172, 186; European knowledge of, 8, 9; imperial administration of, 99; Persian Prince archetype in, 50. *See also specific rulers*
Saffarid dynasty, 73, 278
Safineh Talebi (Tabrizi), 199
Said, Edward, 4, 22, 45, 51, 174, 185
Saint-Exupéry, Antoine de, xiii, 252
Salaman and Absal (Jami), 109–11
Saljuqid Empire: historical imagination in, 74; imperial administration of, 99, 127; nomadism and, 243; in Persian cosmopolis, 21; Persian language use in, 278, 280; Persian Prince archetype in, 50; territorial expansion of, 74. *See also specific rulers*
Salman, Masʿud Saʿd, 231, 232

Samanid Empire, 50, 61, 73, 99, 126, 278–79
Samarqandi, Suzani, 208, 209
Samarqandi, Zahiri, 101, 125
Sanskrit cosmopolis, 19, 20, 22
Sarbedaran uprisings, 111, 133
Sariyannis, Marinos, 112
Sassanid Empire: Arab conquest of, 5, 32–33, 60, 64, 72, 237; aristocratic elitism in, 39; geographic scope of, 276; imperial administration of, 118; in Islamic historiography, 67; mirrors for princes and, 60–62, 90–92, 127, 276; political culture of, 85, 116; theories of kingship in, 72; uprisings against, 241. *See also specific rulers*
Satire, 105–6, 113–14, 120, 208–12, 224, 232, 269
Savant, Sarah Bowen, 66–67
Schaeder, Hans Heinrich, 258–59
Schama, Simon, 171
Schiller, Friedrich von, 266, 268, 269
Scholasticism. *See* Islamic scholasticism
Schwartz, Kevin L., 19
Scott, David, 174–75, 215
Seleucid Empire, 25, 276
Seljuqs. *See* Saljuqid Empire
Semnani, Ala' al-Dowleh, 131–32
Shadow archetype, 151
Shahin-e Shirazi, 145–47, 281
Shahnameh (Ferdowsi): Alexander the Great in, 126, 276; Arabic translation of, 74; coffeehouse paintings of scenes from, 193, 195; excerpt from, 177–78; Ghaznavid sponsorship of, 73; on Houshang, 65; influences on writing of, 61, 63, 66; Iranian mythology and, 234; literary and poetic provenance of, 127; on Mazdakite uprisings, 133–34; as mirror for princes, 89, 91, 127–28; paradoxical tension in, 133; Persian Prince archetype in, 122, 126, 274, 279; political Persianism and, 99; temporal epochs of, 176; tragic heroes of, 77, 126
Shahnameh (Ma'mari), 59–63

Shahnameh (Tahmasp I), 138–39, 182, 184
Shahrashub poetry, 231–32, 245, 314–15n5
Shami, Nizam al-Din, 75
Shamlou, Ahmad, 223, 229, 243, 247, 251, 261
Shari'ah. *See* Islamic law
Sharma, Vishnu, 11
"Shatranjiyeh" (Semnani), 131–32
Shervani, Khaqani-e, 200
Shi'i Islam: in *Akhlaq-e Naseri*, 104; charismatic authority in, 73, 85, 99; clerical ulema in, 86; infallibility of Imams in, 73, 258; martyrology in, 77, 125, 193; on *Rostam al-Tawarikh*, 206–8; Sarbedaran uprisings and, 111; scholasticism and, 31, 42, 297n37; Sunni divide with, 226
Shu'ubiyyah movement, 38–39
al-Sijistani, Abu Nasr Firahi, 199
Sindbad-nameh (Samarqandi), 125
Siyasat-nameh (Nizam al-Mulk), 6, 101, 116, 125–27, 130, 253
Slavery and slave trade, 171–72
Smeulders, Valika, 171–72
Socialism, 133, 277
Sohrab (Is Being) Killed by Rostam (Ismailzadeh), 194
Soja, Edward, 24
Sovereignty, national, 46, 213–16, 247
Speculum of the Other Woman (Irigaray), 201–3
Sufism, 8, 68, 82, 87, 111, 141, 193
al-Suhrawardi, Shihab al-Din Yahya: "Avaz-e Par-e Jibril," 159; *Haykel al-Nur*, 181; *Hikmah al-Ishraq*, 154–57; Illuminationist philosophy of, 154–64, 280; *al-Mashari' wa al-Mutarihat*, 157, 158; moral imagination of, 306n33; *Partov-nameh*, 159–60; pre-Islamic Iranian themes in discourse of, 90; *Qesseh Ghorbat Gharbiyyeh*, 245; *Red Intellect*, 160–61, 250; revolutionary uprisings as influence on, 162; royal philosophy of, 154, 157, 159, 162; *al-Talwihat*, 157

Suleiman I the Magnificent (Ottoman Empire), 186–87
Sunni Islam, 38, 85, 86, 104, 226
Sunpadh (prophet), 31, 97, 162, 237, 238, 277
Synecdoche, 94, 122, 130

al-Tabari (historian), 63–69, 72, 74, 276–77
Tabataba'i, Seyyed Javad, 80, 180–81
Tabrizi, Agha, 224
Ta'dib al-Atfal (Mazandarani), 199
Taghizadeh, Seyyed Hasan, 237
Tahirids, 33, 278
Tahmasp I (Safavid Empire), 8, 138–39, 182–85
Tahzib al-Akhlaq wa al-Tathir al-A'raq (Ibn Miskawayh), 104
Taj al-Saltaneh (Qajars), 41, 250
Talmud, 143, 145–47
al-Talwihat (al-Suhrawardi), 157
Tangsir (film), 261
Tanzimat reforms, 219, 220
Tao Te Ching (Laozi), 11
Taqizadeh, Hassan, 42
Textual mimicry, 196–98
al-Tha'alibi, Abu Mansur, 22, 53–54, 101, 143, 162, 278
Third space, defined, 24
The Three Princes of Serendip (Armeno), 268, 270
Timurid Empire, 75–76, 106, 188, 208, 281, 282
Tobacco Revolt (1890), 226
Transcendentalists, 130
Transnational public and parapublic spheres: circulatory disposition of, 43; democratic aspirations in, 220; emergence of, 30, 34, 180, 183, 189, 191, 196, 219; gendered, 40; global topography of, 30; literary consciousness in, 236, 246–47; mass media in, 221–26; postcolonial, 23, 44, 213–15; rebel-poets in, 13, 35, 36, 179
Transubstantial motion, 260

Travelogues, 8, 191, 213, 218, 224–25, 245
Tribal patrimonialism, 38, 39, 115, 277
Trouillot, Michel-Rolph, 214
Tughril Beg (Saljuqid Empire), 152, 153
Turan Dokht (Darvishi and Lakerveld), 265, 266
Turandot (Puccini), 265–70, 317n24, 318n30, 318n32
Turkish Embassy Letters (Montagu), 185, 309n33
al-Tusi, Nasir al-Din: *Akhlaq-e Naseri*, 74–75, 82, 104, 105, 129–30; *Awsaf al-Ashraf*, 141–42; political thought of, 83, 99

Umayyad caliphate: Persian language use during, 278; Persian Prince archetype in, 70–71; rise and expansion of, 72; tribal patrimonialism of, 39, 115, 277; uprisings against, 97, 162
Urbanity. *See* Cities
Ustadhsis (prophet), 97, 162, 237, 238
Uzun Hasan (Aq Qoyunlu), 8, 109, 281

Vacca, Alison, 66–67
Veronese, Paolo, 149, *149*
Vico, Giambattista, 243
Vis-o-Ramin (Gorgani), 73, 82, 84, 276
Viswanathan, Gauri, 172–73
Vizierate, 73, 99, 100, 115–21, 302n29

Walsh, Catherine E., 175
Watts, William Montgomery, 79
Weber, Max, 53, 72, 98–99, 134–35, 189–92, 286
White, Hayden, 94, 122, 174–75, 212
Wisdom literature, 70, 90, 104, 128
Women: advocacy for rights of, 41, 224; education of, 17; misogyny and, 4, 17, 125–26, 198; in Mongol Empire, 67; in Ottoman Empire, 185; political power of, 40; resubjection of, 202
"The Work of the Nightwatch" (Yushij), 203–4

"Writing as a Nomadic Subject" (Braidotti), 26, 229–30

Xenophon. *See Cyropaedia*
Xerxes I (Achaemenid Empire), 118–19, 148, 275

"Yad Ar, Zeh Shamʿ-e Mordeh Yad Ar!" (Dehkhoda), 222–23
Yazdi, Sharaf al-Din Ali, 75
Yilmaz, Hüseyin, 79
Yushij, Nima, 30, 169, 179, 203–4, 226–28, 236, 244

Zafarnameh (Shami), 75
Zafarnameh (Yazdi), 75
Zakani, Ubayd: *Akhlaq al-Ashraf*, 98, 105, 106, 208, 209; irony utilized by, 114, 123, 131; *Mush-o-Gorbeh*, 106; Persian Prince ideal in work of, 109, 113; satire of, 105–6, 113–14, 120, 208
Zakhirat al-Moluk (Hamadani), 196–98
Zand dynasty, 33, 206, 209, 212, 284
Zindiqs, 96–97
Ziryab (Abu al-Hasan Ali ibn Nafi), 70–71
Ziyarid dynasty, 127, 278–79. *See also specific rulers*
Zoroaster and Zoroastrianism: Abbasid caliphate and, 86; in early Islamic period, 71; Illuminationist philosophy and, 156; Majus and, 96, 97, 197; messianic figures in, 213, 239; metaphors in, 223; in musical compositions, 148; Persian Prince archetype and, 30, 49; prophetic imagination of, 274; theories of kingship in, 72, 116

The authorized representative in the EU for product safety and compliance is:
Mare Nostrum Group
B.V Doelen 72
4831 GR Breda
The Netherlands

www.ingramcontent.com/pod-product-compliance
Lightning Source LLC
Chambersburg PA
CBHW031847220426
43663CB00006B/531